36325 COO 3 wks

£44.99

Blackstone's
Senior Investigating Officers'
Handbook

D1422233

City and Islington College

CAS1180

CAS 1180

Blackstone's

Senior Investigating Officers' Handbook

Fifth Edition

Tony Cook

With contributions from

Andy Tattersall

OXFORD
UNIVERSITY PRESS

OXFORD
UNIVERSITY PRESS

Great Clarendon Street, Oxford, OX2 6DP,
United Kingdom

Oxford University Press is a department of the University of Oxford.
It furthers the University's objective of excellence in research, scholarship,
and education by publishing worldwide. Oxford is a registered trade mark of
Oxford University Press in the UK and in certain other countries

© Oxford University Press 2019

The moral rights of the authors have been asserted

First Edition published in 2008
Fourth Edition published in 2016
Fifth Edition published in 2019

Impression: 5

All rights reserved. No part of this publication may be reproduced, stored in
a retrieval system, or transmitted, in any form or by any means, without the
prior permission in writing of Oxford University Press, or as expressly permitted
by law, by licence or under terms agreed with the appropriate reprographics
rights organization. Enquiries concerning reproduction outside the scope of the
above should be sent to the Rights Department, Oxford University Press, at the
address above

You must not circulate this work in any other form
and you must impose this same condition on any acquirer

Crown copyright material is reproduced under Class Licence
Number C01P0000148 with the permission of OPSI
and the Queen's Printer for Scotland

Published in the United States of America by Oxford University Press
198 Madison Avenue, New York, NY 10016, United States of America

British Library Cataloguing in Publication Data

Data available

Library of Congress Control Number: 2019937062

ISBN 978–0–19–883167–9

Printed and bound by
CPI Group (UK) Ltd, Croydon, CR0 4YY

Links to third party websites are provided by Oxford in good faith and
for information only. Oxford disclaims any responsibility for the materials
contained in any third party website referenced in this work.

CITY AND ISLINGTON COLLEGE
CAS LIBRARY
311 - 321 GOSWELL ROAD
LONDON EC1V 7DD
TEL 020 7520 7471

Contents

Preface

The new edition has undergone some essential changes, amendments, and inclusions since the last. Despite being similar in terms of layout and headings, there is some significant content addition and upgrading. As with previous editions, the aim is to try and distil a vast amount of procedural and practical information into one volume.

Understandably, I play to my strengths in terms of contents selection and topics. It has always been an aspiration to cover and include many more specialist areas of serious and complex crime investigation, but owing to word count restrictions it has not been possible. The OUP has nonetheless been very generous once more in allowing a slight increase for which I am truly grateful.

The requirement for this practical guide is proven from its popularity and success. I could not have predicted it would still be in production some eleven years after the first edition was released. It has, however, been an immensely rewarding project and one for which I have been able to reap rewards and satisfaction from having seen it in use on training courses, in classrooms, lying open on officer's desks and best of all on live operations.

Maintaining continuous professional development is an absolute must in the field of criminal investigation. Being able to receive, absorb, and exchange important knowledge and good practice forms an essential part of building a portfolio and developing the necessary skills and knowledge. It is hoped these contents make a significant contribution towards meeting those requirements.

Whether an academic studying-related subjects, a chief officer filling knowledge gaps, a next generation trainee investigator, or appropriately a new or seasoned Senior Investigating Officer, it is for you this book has been written.

If you have acquired this as an officer who investigates serious and major crime, I recommend you keep it somewhere handy and within reach. Quick and easy reference is what it was always intended for. Keep it with you as the next big case is only just around the corner.

It is an amazing privilege to be the one in overall charge of a fascinating and challenging criminal investigation. For those who are, I wish you all the very best of luck and good fortune. You have my wholehearted support, huge respect, and total admiration.

Tony Cook
June 2019.

Acknowledgements

A fifth edition would have been impossible without the foundations of the previous four. Therefore those acknowledged previously deserve my continued appreciation. I wish to express my sincere gratitude to those colleagues and friends from whom advice, assistance, and wisdom has been obtained to produce or review the contents of this book. Organisations as well as individuals have provided practical assistance and access to information, in particular the College of Policing, International Homicide Investigators Association (IHIA), UK Homicide Working Group, National Police Chief's Council (NPCC), my former force Greater Manchester Police, and my colleagues at the National Crime Agency.

My gratitude must go once more to Oxford University Press, whose staff have once again been extremely patient, forgiving, and supportive.

Most importantly, my immense gratitude goes to some particular trusted and reliable individuals and subject matter experts whom I have called upon to contribute their wisdom, knowledge, expertise, and advice. I want to give special thanks to the following people who have made significant contributions. In alphabetical order:

Sonya Baylis (Head of NCA National Injuries Database)
Dr Ivar A. Fahsing (Detective Chief Superintendent, Norwegian Police University College, Oslo, Norway)
Murray Haynes (NCA National Search Advisor)
Dr Zoe Hilton (former Head of Safeguarding NCA CEOP)
Mike Hyde (National Digital Media Adviser NCA)
Dave Marshall QPM (retired DCI from MPS and author of Blackstone's *Effective Investigation of Child Homicide and Suspicious Deaths*)
Roy Sinclair (NCA AKEU Specialist Adviser)
Gary Shaw MBE (Former National Investigative Interviewing Adviser NCA)
Dr Kevin Smith (Witness Intermediary Adviser NCA)
Andy Tattersall (retired SIO GMP)

Glossary of Terms, Abbreviations, and Acronyms

1D	one dimensional
3D	three dimensional
3 × Ps Principle	Positive, Positive, Positive
3 × Rs Rule	Retain, Record and Reveal (CPIA rule)
4G	fourth generation (phones)
4P	Pursue, Protect, Prevent & Prepare
5WH	Who?, What?, Where?, When?, Why? and How?
A	Action
A&E	Accident and emergency
ABC	Assume nothing, Believe nothing, Challenge/check everything
ABE	Achieving Best Evidence
ABP	Applicable Bail Period
ACC	Assistant Chief Constable
ACPO	Association of Chief Police Officers (now named NPCC)
ADM	Appropriate Decision Maker
AFI	Accredited Financial Investigator
AFO	Authorised Firearms Officer
AFR	Automatic Facial Recognition
AKA	also known as
AKEU	Anti-kidnap and Extortion Unit
AM	Action Manager
ANPR	Automatic Number Plate Recognition
AO	Authorising Officer (RIPA)
APP	Authorised Professional Practice
AQVF	alibi questionnaire verification form
ARV	armed response vehicle
ATM	Automatic telling machine
ASAP	as soon as possible
ASB	anti-social behaviour
AYR	Are You Ready?
BASE	Barnardos Against Sexual Exploitation
BCU	Basic Command Unit
BF	UK Border Force
BIA	Behavioural Investigative Adviser
BWV	Body worn video (camera)

BST	British Standard Time
BTP	British Transport Police
BWV	body-worn video cameras
CAID	Child Abuse Image Database
CAIU	Child Abuse Investigation Unit
CAM	Child abuse material
CAP	common approach path
CASWEB	casualty bureau weblink
CATCHEM	Centralised Analytical Team Collating Homicide Expertise and Management
CAU	Crime Analysis Unit
CBA	Crime Business Area
CCD	Corporate Communications Department
CCRC	Criminal Cases Review Commission
CCTV	closed circuit television
CD	communications data
CDI	Communications Data Investigator
CDOP	Child Death Overview Panel
CDR	child death reviews
CEOP	Child Exploitation and Online Protection Centre (NCA)
CGI	Computer generated imagery
CHIS	covert human intelligence source (informant)
CI	critical incident
CIM	critical incident management
CIA	Community Impact Assessment
CICA	Criminal Injuries Compensation Authority
CICS	Criminal Injuries Compensation Scheme
CII	Covert Internet Investigator
CIM	critical incident management
CISO	Crime Investigative Support Officer
CJA	Coroners and Justice Act 2009
CJS	Criminal Justice System
CLO	Communications Liaison Officer
CMB	Case Management Book
CMS	Case Management System
COBRA	Cabinet Office Briefing Room A
COD	cause of death
COLRAF	Case Overseas Liaison Risk Assessment Form
CoP	Codes of Practice
COS	Crime Operational Support (NCA)
CPA	Child Protection Advisor
CPA	crime pattern analysis
CPD	continued professional development
CPIA	Criminal Procedure and Investigations Act 1996

CPR	Child Practice Review
CPS	Crown Prosecution Service
CRA	child rescue alert
CSAE	Child Sexual Abuse & Exploitation
CSAM	child sexual abuse material (see also CAM)
CSC	Crime Scene Coordinator
CSI	Crime Scene Investigator
CSM	Crime Scene Manager
CSO	child sex offender
CSP	Community Safety Partnership
CSR	current situation report
CTAIL	NSPCC Child Trafficking Advice and Information Line
CT scan	Computed Tomography scan
DBS	Disclosure & Barring Service
DC	Detective Constable
DCI	Detective Chief Inspector
DCSF	Department for Children, Schools and Families
DDOS	Distributed Denial of Service
DF	Digital Forensics
DHR	Domestic Homicide Review
DI	Detective Inspector
DIDP	Detective Inspectors Development Programme
DMD	Disclosure Management Document
DMI	Digital Media Investigator
DNA	deoxyribonucleic acid
DO	Disclosure Officer
DOA	dead on arrival
DPP	Director of Public Prosecutions
DR	Document Reader
DS	Detective Sergeant
DSA	directed surveillance authorities
DSIO	Deputy Senior Investigating Officer
DSTL	Defence Science and Technology Lab
DSU	Dedicated Source Unit
DSupt	Detective Superintendent
DV	domestic violence
DVCV	Domestic Violence, Crime and Victims Act 2004
DVCVA	Domestic Violence Crime and Victim's (Amendment) Act 2012
DVDD	Drowned Victim Detection Dogs
DVI	disaster victim identification
DVLA	Driver & Vehicle Licensing Agency
DWP	Department Work and Pensions
EA	Equality Act 2010
EAD	Expert Advisers Database

EAW	European Arrest Warrant
ECHR	European Convention for the Protection of Human Rights
EEK	early evidence kit
ENQS	make enquiries
EO	Exhibits Officer
EPO	Emergency Protection Order
EU	European Union
FCP	forward command post
FCP	Forensic Clinical Psychologist
FCT	Full Code Test
fDNA	Familial DNA
FI	Financial Investigator
FIB/U	Force Intelligence Bureau/Unit
FIIP	Fighting International Internet Paedophilia Project
FLA	Family Liaison Advisor
FLC	Family Liaison Coordinator
FLO	Family Liaison Officer(s)
FMG	Forensic Management Group
FOD	fact of death
FOI	Freedom of Information Act 2000
FPO	File Preparation Officer
FPSG	Forensic Pathology Specialist Group
FSS	Forensic Science Service
FSR	Forensic Science Regulator
FTE	Full Time Employee
FTO	Foreign Travel Order
FVEY	Five Eyes (intelligence alliance comprising Australia, Canada, New Zealand, United Kingdom, and the United States)
GDPR	General Data Protection Regulations
GG	Gold Group
GLAA	Gangmasters and Labour Abuse Authority
GMP	Greater Manchester Police
GP	General practitioner (Local Doctor)
GPRS	General Packet Radio Service
GPS	Global Positioning System
GPMS	Government Protective Marking Scheme
GSB	Gold, Silver, Bronze
GSR	Gunshot residue
H&S	Health and Safety
H2H	house-to-house (enquiries)
H2HC	House-to-House Co-ordinator
HEHR	High-end of high-risk
HEML	High end money laundering
HMC	Her Majesty's Coroner

HMG	Her Majesty's Government
HMICFRS	Her Majesty's Inspectorate of Constabulary and Fire and Rescue Services
HMO	Houses of Multiple Occupancy
HMRC	Her Majesty's Revenue and Customs
HO	Home Office
HOLMES	Home Office Large Major Enquiry System
HORP	Home Office Registered Pathologist
HOSDB	Home Office Scientific Development Branch
HP	high priority
HR	human rights
HRA	Human Rights Act 1998
HSE	Health and Safety Executive
HT	Human Trafficking
HTA	Human Tissue Act 2004
HTC	Human Trafficking Centre
HUMINT	human intelligence (eg informants)
HVM	high volume messaging
HWG	Homicide Working Group
I	Indexer
IAG	independent advisory group
IC	identifying characteristic
ICIDP	Initial Crime Investigators Development Program
ICR	Internet connection records
ICSE	International Child Sexual Exploitation (Interpol CAM image database)
ICT	Information Communications Technology
IDENT1	UK central national database for holding, searching, and comparing biometric information (fingerprints, palm prints, and crime scene marks)
IED	improvised explosive device
IIMARCH	information, intention, method, administration, risk assessment, communications, human rights
ILO	International Liaison Officer
ILOR	International Letter of Request
IMSC	Initial Management of Serious Crime
INI	Impact Nominal Index
IO	Investigating Officer
IIOC	indecent images of children
IOCB	Investigating Officer's Casebook
IOPC	Independent Office for Police Conduct (formerly IPCC)
IP	Internet Protocol
IPA	Investigatory Powers Act 2016
IPA	Independent Public Advocate (UK victims)

IPCC	Independent Police Complaints Commission (now IOPC)
IPCO	Investigatory Powers Commissioner's Office
IPL	Investigation Policy Log
IPLDP	Initial Police Learning and Development Programme
IPSO	Independent Press Standards Organisation
IR	Intelligence Requirement
IRG	independent reference group
ISA	Information Sharing Agreement
ISP	internet service provider
ISP	identify, secure, protect
ISVA	Independent Sexual Violence Advisers
IT	information technology
IVC	initial visual check
JAR	Joint Agency Response
JDLR	just doesn't look right
JIT	Joint Investigation Team
JP	Justice of the Peace
KDL	Key Decision Log
K&E	Kidnap & Extrotion
KIRAT	Kent Internet Risk Assessment Tool
LADO	Local Authority Designated Officer
LCN	low copy number
LCU	Logistics Coordination Unit
LEA	law enforcement agency
LKP	last known position
LOE	lines of enquiry
LP	low priority
LPP	Legal Professional Privilege
LSCB	Local Safeguarding Children Board
M	message form
MACP	Military Aid to Civil Power
MAST	mobile armed search teams
MAPPA	Multi-Agency Public Protection Arrangements
MBWA	management by walkabout
MCIS	Major Crime Investigative Support (NCA)
ME	medical examiner
MHR	Mental Health Review
MI	major incident
MIM	Murder Investigation Manual
MIR	Major Incident Room
MIRSAP	Major Incident Room Standardised Administrative Procedures
MIRWeb	major incident room weblink
Misper	missing person
MIT	Major Investigation Team

MLAT	Mutual Legal Assistance Treaty
MLO	Media Liaison Officer
MLOE	main lines of enquiry
MLSC	Management Linked Serious Crime
MO	modus operandi
MOD	manner of death
MODP	Ministry of Defence Police
MOSOVO	Management of Sex offenders and Violent offenders
MOU	Memorandum of Understanding
MP	medium priority
MPU	Missing Persons Unit (NCA)
MPS	Metropolitan Police Service (UK)
MRI scan	Magnetic Resonance Imaging scan
MSA	Modern Slavery Act (2015)
MSHT	Modern Slavery and Human Trafficking
MSM	Mainstream Media
mtDNA	mitochondrial DNA
N	Nominal
N/A	Not applicable
NABIS	National Ballistics Intelligence Service
NCA	National Crime Agency
NCPE	National Centre for Policing Excellence
NCTT	National Community Tension Team
NDMM	National Decision Making Model
NDNAD	UK National DNA Database
NFA	No further action
NFLMS	National Firearms Licensing Management System
NGO	Non-Governmental Organisation
NHS	UK National Health Service
NID	National Injuries Database (NCA)
NIIS	National Investigative Interviewing Strategy
NIM	National Intelligence Model
NMAT	National Mutual Aid Telephony
NOK	next of kin
NOS	National Occupational Standards/ National Office for Statistics
NPCC	National Police Chiefs' Council
NPIA	National Policing Improvement Agency
NPT	neighbourhood policing team
NRM	National Referral Mechanism
NRPSI	National Register of Public Service Interpreters
NSA	National Search Adviser (NCA)
NSIOA	National SIO Adviser
NSPCC	National Society for the Prevention of Cruelty to Children

NSTCG	National Strategic Tasking and Coordinating group
NWG	National Working Group for Sexually Exploited Children and Young People
OBT	obtain
OCG	organised crime group/gang
OCGM	Organised Crime Group Mapping
OCSAE	online child sexual abuse and exploitation
OCU	Operational Command Unit
OFFSEN	Official Sensitive (protective marking)
OIC	Officer In Charge
OIC	Organised Immigration Crime
OIOC	Officer in Overall Command
OOH	out of hours
OM	Office Manager
OP(s)	Operation(s)
OPSY	Operational Security (officer)
OSC	Office Surveillance Commissioners
OSINT	open source intelligence
OSM	Open Source Material
P2P	peer-to-peer (sharing of IIOC)
PACE	Police and Criminal Evidence Act 1984
PACE	Parents Against Child Sexual Exploitation
PAS	Prison Advisers Section
PAT	Problem Analysis Triangle
PCA	Protection of Children Act 1978
PCC	Press Complaints Commission
PCC	Police and Crime Commissioner
PCSO	Police Community Support Officer
PDF	personal descriptive form
PEACE	
P	—Preparation and planning
E	—Engage and explain
A	—Account clarification and challenge
C	—Closure
E	—Evaluation
PEO	Principle Exhibits Officer
PII	public interest immunity
PIO	Prison Intelligence Officer
PIP	Professionalising Investigation Programme
PL	Policy Log
PLE	pronouncing life extinct
PLS	place last seen
PM	post-mortem
POI	person of interest

PPP	persons of public prominence
PMA	positive mental attitude
PNC	Police National Computer
PND	Police National Database
PNLD	Police National Legal Database
POCA	Proceeds of Crime Act 2002
PoFA	Protection of Freedoms Act 2012
POI	person of interest
POL	proof of life
POLKA	Police Online Knowledge Area
PolSA	Police Search Adviser
PolSC	Police Search Coordinator
PoT	position of trust
PPE	personal protective equipment
PPP	Person of Public Prominence
PPU	Public Protection Unit
PSNI	Police Service of Northern Ireland
PSoS	Police Service of Scotland
PST	Police Search Team
PTB	person to blame
Q & A	Question and Answer
R	Receiver
RADI	Rotation, Acceleration, Deceleration, Impact
RARA	Remove, Avoid, Reduce, Accept
RAT	Routine Activity Theory
RCT	Rational Choice Theory
Re	Regarding
RF	Radio frequency (propagation surveys)
RFI	request for intelligence
RG	reasonable grounds
RI	re-interview
RIPA	Regulation of Investigatory Powers Act 2000
ROCU	Regional Organised Crime Units
RRAA	Race Relations Amendment Act 2000
RSO	registered sex offender
RUI	Released Under Investigation
RVP	rendezvous point
SA	situational awareness
SAFCOM	situation, aim, factors, choices, option, monitoring
SAG	Specialist Advisory Group
SAM	scent article method (police dogs)
SAR	Suspicious Activity Report
SCAS	Serious Crime Analysis Section (NCA)
SCAIDP	Specialist Child Abuse Investigator Development Programme

SCC	Surveillance Camera Commissioner
SCCRC	Scottish Criminal Cases Review Commission
SCD	Serious Crime Division
SCG	Strategic Coordination Group
SCR	Serious Case Review
SCT	standards, competencies, and training
SEOC	sexual exploitation of children
SFC	Strategic Firearms Commander
SGII	self-generated indecent imagery
SIAG	Strategic Independent Advisory Group
SHPO	Sexual Harm Prevention Order
SIDS	sudden infant death syndrome
SigWIT	significant witness
SIM	Senior Identification Manager
SIO	Senior Investigating Officer
SIODP	Senior Investigating Officer Development Programme
SIRENE	Supplementary Information Request at National Entry (Bureau)
SISII	Schengen Information System II (2nd generation pan-European database)
SMARTER	(Actions/tasks) Specific, Meaningful, Achievable, Realistic, Time-Specific, Ethical, Recorded
SME	Subject matter expert
SMT	Senior Management Team
SOA	Sexual Offences Act 2003
SOC	Specialist Operations Centre (NCA)
SOCA	Serious Organised Crime Agency
SOCMINT	social media intelligence
SOCO	Scenes of Crime Officer
SOCPA	Serious Organised Crime and Police Act 2005
SOE	sequence of events
SOI	subject of interest
SOLO	Sexual Offence Liaison Officers
SOP	Standard Operating Procedure
SOPO	Sexual Offences Prevention Order
SOS	Specialist Operational Support (NCA)
SPAG	Spelling and Grammar
SPoC	single point of contact
SPoE	single point of entry
SPR	Strategic Policing Requirement
SRO	Sexual Risk Order
STI	sexually transmitted infection
SUDC	sudden unexpected death in children
SUDI	sudden unexpected death in infancy
SUDICA	sudden unexpected death in infants, children, and adolescents

SWOT	strengths, weaknesses, opportunities, and threats
SYP	South Yorkshire Police
TACT	Terrorism Act 2000
TB	tuberculosis
TCSO	transnational child sex offender
TDI	Time death interval
TEI	Targeted Equipment Interference
TFC	Tactical Firearms Commander
TFST	take further statement
THR	Threat, harm, and risk
TI	trace/interview (or trace/investigate)
TI	Targeted Intercept
TIE	trace/interview/eliminate (or trace/investigate/evaluate)
TLO	Telecommunications Liaison Officer
TOD	time of death
ToR	Terms of Reference
ToR	The Onion Ring (dark web application)
TRIAD	triad of injuries
TS	Top Secret
TSD	Time since death
TST	take statement
TT	Threshold Test
TTL	Threats To Life
UCOL	Undercover online (covert officer)
UF	unidentified female
UK	United Kingdom
UKBA	United Kingdom Border Agency
UM	unidentified male
UU	unidentified unknown
UV	unidentified vehicle
UAV	Unmanned Aerial Vehicle
UWO	Unexplained Wealth Order
VCO	Victim Care Officer
VCS	Victim Contact Scheme
VCOP	Victims Code of Practice
VID	Victim Identification
ViSOR	Violent and Sex Offender Register
VODS	vehicle online descriptive search
VOIP	voice over Internet protocol
VOWI	voice over Wi-Fi
VPN	Virtual Private Network
VPS	Virtual Private Servers
VPS	Victim Personal Statement
VPT	Vulnerable Persons Team

VTC	Video teleconferencing Capability
WCU	Witness Care Unit
WOFD	warrant of further detention
W/T	'Working Together' report 2018
YJCE	Youth Justice and Criminal Evidence Act 1999
YT	Youth Offending

Medical Glossary: Useful Medical Terminology

Abrasion An injury caused by blunt force rubbing off the epidermis, which is the most superficial layer of the skin. In everyday language, an abrasion would be called a graze.

Acute Appearing rapidly (eg acute inflammation), but not necessarily severe as in common usage (contrast with chronic).

Aetiology Cause of a disease.

Agonal Terminal event, immediately prior to death.

Allele A viable DNA coding that occupies a given *locus* or position on a chromosome.

Allele Frequency A measure of the relative frequency of an allele showing the genetic diversity of a population or the richness of its gene pool.

Amnesia Loss of memory.

Anaemia Abnormally low blood haemoglobin concentration.

Angina Spasmodic pain.

Ante-Mortem Before death.

Anterior The front.

Anoxia Lack of oxygen.

Ascites Abnormal accumulation of fluid in the peritoneal cavity.

Asphyxia Consequence of suffocation or mechanically impaired respiration.

Atheroma Furring up of the arteries by fatty deposits.

Atherosclerosis Atheroma causing hardening of the arteries.

Atrophy Pathological or physiological cellular or organ shrinkage.

Autoeroticism Arousal and satisfaction of sexual emotion within or by oneself through fantasy and/or genital stimulation (and partial asphyxiation).

Autopsy Synonymous with necropsy or post-mortem examination (autopsy = 'to see for oneself' rather than relying on signs and symptoms).

Bacteraemia Presence of bacteria in the blood.

Biopsy The process of removing tissue for diagnosis, or a piece of tissue removed during life for diagnostic purposes.

Bruises An injury caused by blood leaking out of damaged blood vessels beneath the skin. Fresh bruises are usually red, blue, purple, or black, depending on their depth beneath the skin. Although they may enlarge or become more prominent at a variable rate after infliction, this does not help to age a bruise. Later, the bruise may turn brown, yellow, green, or orange due to release of pigments from the breakdown of red blood cells. The earliest change is said to be yellow discolouration, which does not usually occur until approximately eighteen hours after the bruising began. However, such changes are quite variable, and may be subjected to observer variation. The rate of healing in a bruise is very variable, but it is not unusual for a bruise to be visible several weeks after it was inflicted. Consequently, it may not be possible to be accurate about the ageing of bruises.

Cancer A general term, in the public domain, implying any malignant tumour.

Carbon Monoxide A colourless, odourless, very toxic gas, formed by burning carbon or organic fuels.

Carcinoma A malignant tumour.

Cardio Denoting relationship to the heart.

Cardiovascular Pertaining to the heart and blood vessels.

Carotid Arteries of the neck.

Cellulitis Diffuse acute inflammation of the skin caused by bacterial infection.

Cerebral Pertaining to the cerebrum which is the main portion of the brain occupying the upper part of the cranium.

Cervical Pertaining to the neck, or cervix—neck of womb.

Chronic Persisting for a long time (eg chronic inflammation) (contrast with acute).

Cirrhosis (liver) Irreversible architectural disturbance characterised by nodules of liver cells with intervening scarring, a consequence of many forms of chronic liver injury, especially alcohol abuse.

Clot (blood) Coagulated blood outside the cardiovascular system (contrast with thrombus).

Coagulate Become clotted.

Comatose Unconscious and unresponsive to stimuli (note that a comatose person is not dead).

Comminuted (fracture) Bone broken into fragments at fracture site.

Complications Events secondary to the primary disorder (eg complicated fracture involves adjacent nerves and/or vessels; cerebral haemorrhage is a complication of hypertension).

Congenital Condition attributable to events prior to birth, not necessarily genetic or inherited.

Congestion Engorgement with blood.

Consolidation Solidification of lung tissue, usually by an inflammatory exudation; a feature of pneumonia.

Contusion Bruise that results from rupture of the blood vessels.

Coronary Pertaining to the heart.

Cranium The skull or brainpan.

Cyanosis Blueness of the skin, often due to cardiac malformation resulting in insufficient oxygenation to the blood.

Degeneration Disorder characterised by loss of structural and functional integrity of an organ or tissue.

Diffuse Affecting the tissue in a continuous or widespread distribution.

Disease Abnormal state causing or capable of causing ill health.

Dorsal Pertaining to the back.

Duodenum First portion of the small intestine.

Ecchymoses Any bruise or haemorrhagic spot, larger than petechiae, on the skin (may be spontaneous in the elderly, usually due more to vascular fragility than to coagulation defects).

Ectopic Tissue or substance in or from an inappropriate site (but not by metastasis).

Effusion Abnormal collection of fluid in a body cavity (eg pleura, peritoneum, synovial joint).

Embolus Fluid (eg gas, fat) or solid (eg thrombus) mass mobile within a blood vessel and capable of blocking its lumen.

Emphysema Characterised by the formation of abnormal thin-walled gas-filled cavities; pulmonary emphysema—in lungs; 'surgical' emphysema—in connective tissues.

Erosion Loss of superficial layer (not full thickness) of a surface (eg gastric erosion).

Erythema Abnormal redness of skin due to increased blood flow.

Fibrillation Fluttering of the heart not controlled by motor nerves.

Focal Localised abnormality (contrast with diffuse).

Gangrene Bulk necrosis of tissues; 'dry' gangrene—sterile; 'wet' gangrene—with bacterial putrefaction.

Haematoma Local swelling filled with effused blood, generally the result of a haemorrhage or internal bleeding.

Haemorrhage Heavy bleeding.

Histology The study of the form of structures seen under the microscope. Also called microscopic anatomy, as opposed to gross anatomy, which involves structures that can be observed with the naked eye.

Hyoid Bone Small U-shaped bone at base of tongue.

Hypertension High blood pressure.

Hypostasis The settling of blood in the lower half of an organ or the body as a result of decreased blood flow, or poor or stagnant circulation in a dependent part of the body or an organ.

Hypoxia Reduction in available oxygen.

Iatrogenic Caused by medical intervention (eg adverse effect of a prescribed drug).

Idiopathic Unknown cause; synonymous with primary, essential, and cryptogenic.

Incision A wound inflicted by an instrument with a sharp cutting edge.

Infarction Death of tissue (an infarct) due to insufficient blood supply.

Intestine The membranous tube that extends from the stomach to the anus.

Intra Prefix meaning within.

Ischaemia An inadequate supply of blood to an organ or part of it.

Lacerations An injury caused by blunt force splitting and/or tearing the full thickness of the skin.

Lesion Any abnormality associated with injury or disease.

Lividity Post-mortem discoloration due to the gravitation of blood.

Malformation Congenital structural abnormality of the body.

Malignant Condition characterised by relatively high risk of morbidity and mortality (eg malignant hypertension—high blood pressure leading to severe tissue damage; malignant neoplasm—invasive neoplasm with risk of metastasis) (contrast with benign—relatively harmless).

Membrane A thin layer of tissue which covers a surface or divides a space or organ.

Meninges Thin membranous covering of the brain.

Mitochondrial DNA Mitochondrial DNA is inherited from the mother and offers reduced discriminating factors.

Myocardium The heart muscle.

Parallel intradermal bruising A specific pattern of injury caused when a linear object strikes the body, leaving parallel tracks of bruising in the skin either side of the impacting surface.

Petechial haemorrhages Minute (pin-like) haemorrhages that occur at points beneath the skin. Classic signs of asphyxia usually found in skin and eyes, the conjunctivae, sclera, face, lips, and behind the ears—due to raised venous pressure.

Phalanx Any bone of a finger or toe.

Posterior The rear, behind.

Post-mortem After death.

Prognosis Probable length of survival of injury or disease.

Pulmonary Pertaining to the lungs.

Putrefaction Decomposition of soft tissues by bacteria and enzymes.

Rancid Having a musty, rank taste or smell.

Rigor mortis A rigidity or stiffening of the muscular tissue and joints of the body after death.

Sclerosis Induration or hardening.

Septic Infected.

Septicaemia Chronic blood disease characterised by blood poisoning.

Sharp force injury Sharp force injuries are traditionally divided into incised wounds and stab wounds. In an incised wound, the length of the wound on the skin surface is longer than the depth of the wound, which implies that the wound was inflicted with a slashing or cutting motion. Incised wounds may be made by a variety of weapons, including broken glass and sharp plastic, as well as the more obvious bladed weapons.

In a stab wound, the length of the wound on the skin surface is shorter than the depth of the wound, which implies that the wound was inflicted with a stabbing or thrusting motion.

Shock State of cardiovascular collapse characterised by low blood pressure (eg due to severe haemorrhage).

Signs Observable manifestations of disease (eg swelling, fever, abnormal heart sounds).

Steatosis Fatty change, especially in the liver.

Stroke Sudden or severe attack, with rupture of the blood vessel.

Suppuration Formation of pus; a feature of acute inflammation.

Tamponade (cardiac) Compression of the heart, and therefore restriction of its movement, by excess pericardial fluid (eg haemorrhage, effusion).

Thorax Chest.

Thrombo Denoting relationship to a clot.

Thrombophlebitis Venous inflammation associated with a thrombus.

Thrombus Solid mass of coagulated blood within cardiovascular system.

Toxaemia Presence of a toxin in the blood.

Toxicologist An expert in the knowledge and detection of poisons.

Toxin Substance having harmful effects, usually of bacterial origin by common usage.

Trachea The windpipe.

Trauma Wound or injury.

Vascular Pertaining to or full of blood vessels.

Vein A vessel which conveys the blood to or towards the heart.

Venereal Transmitted by sexual intercourse or intimate foreplay.

Ventricle One of the two lower cavities of the heart.

Viraemia Presence of a virus in the blood.

Vulva The external genital organs in the woman.

Role of the SIO

1.1 **Introduction**

'Senior Investigating Officer' (SIO) is the title usually given to the person in charge of a serious or complex criminal investigation. This is when they are placed in command of a specially chosen team of trained and accredited investigators comprising a unit sometimes called a Major Incident Team (MIT) or similar. Some UK police forces might utilise collaborative agreements between areas and units to pool resources in order to ensure there are sufficient resources available.

Homicide cases have been the standard type of serious crime allocated to MITs. This is unsurprising as statistics show that by August 2018, there had been 100 murders in London alone. It had been the worst year in the capital for murders since 2009. Widespread media coverage quoted Office for National Statistics (ONS) statics showing an upward trend of violent crime across the whole of the United Kingdom; stabbings and violent crime being the norm, with a mixture of shootings, assaults, and other such incidents.[1] Recorded crime in general in England and Wales rose by 32 per cent between 2015 and 2018.[2]

Most SIOs today, however, are expected to carry out their duties while investigating a much wider selection of serious and complex criminality. The criminal, global exploitation of technology through the Internet and digital communication, for example, has made a massive difference in the way crime is committed. New threat types have been created, causing a rise in offences against children and vulnerable persons, such as human trafficking and modern slavery, and a surge in cybercrime, online fraud, and computer hacking. Organised crime has shown a significant increase too. The landscape has changed and there are fresh challenges for an SIO.

Leading a complex crime investigation places a high personal and professional responsibility and accountability upon anyone occupying the hot-seat. It remains one of the most challenging roles in law enforcement. SIOs are accountable to a long list of people, processes, oversight bodies, and agencies. The list includes the judiciary, Police and Crime Commissioners (PCC), internal and external review mechanisms, the media, Independent Office for Police Conduct (IOPC, formerly IPCC), Her Majesty's Inspectorate of Constabulary and Fire and Rescue Services (HMICFRS), the (Scottish) Criminal Cases Review Commission (S/CCRC), HM coroner, Serious Case and Domestic Homicide Review panels. Last but not least are members of the general public, particularly victims, their families, and communities.

When things go wrong, the SIO can be an easy target as a person to blame (PTB). More often than not, though, things don't go wrong and there is enormous personal and professional satisfaction and pride in achieving successful outcomes. The vast majority of cases result in the apprehension and conviction

---

[1] As reported by R Watts and J Simpson, 'A grim milestone in the rise of violence' *The Times* 24 August 2018.
[2] R Ford, 'Irrelevant' police forces struggle with rising crime' *The Times* 25 October 2018.

of extremely dangerous individuals (the bad guys), from which immense job satisfaction is derived.

Clearly, those who attain the highly valued status of an accredited PIP3 SIO need to know what they are doing. A significant increase in the number of those who are thus qualified has been largely due to the highly successful Professionalising Investigative Programme (PIP). Cumulative learning from studies of investigative successes and failures, standardised national occupational standards and training, and good ethical practices have been embedded in the United Kingdom alongside a supporting programme of continuous professional development (CPD).

In truth, being an SIO is a craft and art form (appropriately described one of the world's most famous law court, see box below) that is not the easiest to learn and master. It most certainly carries with it a sizeable amount of reputational risk and personal accountability. It is, however, by far the most enjoyable, satisfying, and personally gratifying role in law enforcement. This first chapter outlines some of the key challenges, requirements, skills, and attributes required to perform the role,

> Inside the dome of the lobby in the Grand Hall at London's Central Criminal Court, aka the Old Bailey, are intricate murals painted by the artist Gerald Moira. They depict figures representing Art, Labour, Learning, and Truth.

1.2 **Crime Types and Challenges**

Today, there is a much wider range and variety of crime types than were ever originally intended to fall under law enforcement jurisdiction. The following is a non-exhaustive list of high-end crime types an SIO may have to investigate:

- Local, regional, national, and international serious and organised crime.[3]
- High end of high-risk (HEHR) criminality.
- Homicide (including serial/mass/spree killings and suspicious deaths).
- Major historical crime investigations (eg Operation Stovewood).[4]
- Article 2 deaths and corporate manslaughter.
- Deaths or serious injury caused in healthcare/medical treatment settings.

---

[3] Serious crime, as defined in s 93(4) of the Police Act 1997, is: (a) conduct which involves the use of violence, results in financial gain or is conducted by a large number of persons in pursuit of a common purpose; or (b) an offence for which a person who has attained the age of twenty-one years and has no previous convictions could reasonably be expected to be sentenced to imprisonment for a term of three years or more.

[4] Operation Stovewood. This is the National Crime Agency (NCA) investigation into non-familial child sexual exploitation and abuse in Rotherham, South Yorkshire between 1997 and 2013. It is the largest ever investigation into non-recent CSEA undertaken by law enforcement and the complexity of the investigation is unparalleled, with 1,500+ victims.

- Linked series serious crimes.
- Crimes in action (eg kidnap and extortion, abduction, blackmail, gun/knife attacks, terrorism, and threats to life).
- Suspicious and high-risk missing person enquiries, including 'no body' murders.
- Rape and other serious and series sexual offences.
- Drugs and firearms importations and offending.
- Armed robberies and high-value thefts.
- SUDC/SUDI deaths.
- Child sexual abuse and exploitation (CSAE).
- Modern slavery and human trafficking (MSHT).
- Organised Immigration Crime (OIC).
- Cybercrime/cyber attacks on public and private infrastructures.
- Economic crime, eg fraud, corruption, and high-end money laundering (HEML).
- Corruption and professional standards investigations.
- Prison- or custody-related deaths.
- Mass fatality incidents/fires/aviation/civil disasters and emergencies.[5]
- Mass public disorder incidents.
- Foreign and transnational offending and offenders.

Crimes that cannot be quickly or easily solved pose more of a challenge, particularly if the case becomes high profile. A long-running, undetected case, such as homicide or serial stranger rapes, soon attracts attention, internally and externally. Further challenges might arise from losing resources that have been borrowed or shared under collaborative agreements, despite there being numerous important outstanding lines of enquiry. This is when an SIO benefits most from having good support and advice networks to provide reassurance they are getting the best out of their resources and that their enquiry is heading in the right direction.

1.2.1 **Consequences of unsolved crimes**

Aside from reputational risks (personal/organisational) and cost implications,[6] unresolved cases can hinder the healing process for victims, families, and local communities and allow offenders to commit further crimes and target other victims.

---

[5] Eg the Grenfell Tower disaster in North Kensington, London. On 14 June 2017, a fire started in a fridge freezer in the kitchen of a fourth floor flat and rapidly spread throughout the entire twenty-four storey residential block resulting in the tragic loss of seventy-two lives. Operation Northleigh, led by an SIO, resulted in one of the largest ever Metropolitan Police Service (MPS) criminal investigations outside counter terrorism. A public enquiry was also launched.

[6] Each murder in England and Wales costs society more than £3 million, a report published by the Home Office has estimated (R Ford, 'Every murder costs £3m amid emotional and physical fallout' *The Times* 25 July 2018.

Increased fear and loss of public faith and confidence can lead to a reluctance of the public to come forward, report crimes, or assist investigations. This is heightened in communities under threat from fear and intimidation (caused, for example, by organised crime gangs and drugs, guns, and 'turf war' or county lines criminality).

Nonetheless, every case begins with a level of solvability and a probability of success. Fortunately, most homicide cases for example, are relatively straight-forward, with the majority (up to 70 per cent) being 'self-solvers' rather than 'whodunits'.[7] Others can be more difficult, complex, and seemingly impossible to solve, such as those where there are no witnesses, no intelligence nor forensic evidence, and no suspects or form part of a linked series and consequently provide greater challenges.

1.2.2 Serious, complex, and high-profile cases

Some cases, although in the minority, are by their very nature not merely serious and complex but also highly capable of attaining high-profile status. Solved or unsolved, these are cases that are thrust into or (if non-recent) reappear in the public spotlight. This occurs for a variety of reasons, such as public and media interest and scrutiny, complexity, or simple high-profile notoriety.

Some examples include the Stephen Lawrence case (1993);[8] the Moors murderers (Ian Brady and Myra Hindley, 1965); the Yorkshire Ripper (Peter Sutcliffe, 1981); Madeleine McCann, missing child investigation in Portugal (2007); Jamie Bulger (abducted, tortured, and murdered by two ten-year-old boys on 12 February 1993); and the disappearance of Suzy Lamplugh in 1986, who was presumed dead and murdered in 1994. Such cases might be the supreme test of a law enforcement agency, not only the SIO, as the decisions made and outcomes are discussed, reviewed, queried, and periodically analysed and re-appear in the media.

1.2.3 Joint and linked series crimes

Linked series homicides and other serious crimes pose specific challenges, particularly if they involve joint command-and-control structures with both separate and linked investigations. For example, information sharing, communication flows, and shared intelligence management functions between forces, regions, or agencies (that might have different powers or jurisdictions) require a sophisticated approach, in addition to linking up data and managing joint investigative strategies such as family liaison and TIE (trace/investigate/evaluate) enquiries (see Chapter 8).

---

[7] M Innes, 'The process structures of police homicide investigations' (2002) 42 *British Journal of Criminology* 669–88.

[8] The murdered victim, Stephen Lawrence, now has a dedicated memorial day on 22 April each year.

In determining whether to link offences, one early consideration might be the accurate evaluation of the correlation between offences and offenders. Similarities between victims, crime scenes, and modus operandi require careful examination, together with the linking up of data and good communication flows.

It is always advisable to seek help and advice from trusted experts such as a PIP4 or the National Crime Agency (NCA) Major Crime Investigative Support (MCIS) team as soon as a link between crimes is suspected. A number of services, such as comparative case analysis and Behavioural Investigative Advisors (BIAs), can help guide judgements on the identification of commonalities and linkage.

KEY POINT

Any incident that is deemed to be a serious and complex criminal investigation or 'crime in action' requires a PIP3-accredited and experienced SIO to take the lead who may wish to consider support from an accredited PIP4 and/or the NCA.

1.3 **SIO Role and Key Skills**

The *Murder Investigation Manual* ('MIM') states:

> An SIO is the lead investigator in cases of homicide, stranger rape, kidnap, or other investigations. This requires the SIO to:
> - Perform the role of officer in charge of an investigation as described in the Code of Practice under Part II of the Criminal Procedure and Investigations Act 1996.
> - Develop and implement the investigative strategy.
> - Develop the information management and decision-making systems for the investigation.
> - Manage the resources allocated to the investigation.
> - Be accountable to chief officers for the conduct of the investigation.
>
> The role of the SIO in a homicide investigation is potentially one of the most complex and challenging positions within the police service. It combines two elements—the role of investigator and the role of manager, each of which must be performed to the highest standards.[9]

The Criminal Procedure and Investigations Act 1996 (CPIA) also sets out duties for the SIO (and all investigators involved in the case), not simply in relation to disclosure but also in respect of the investigation itself. Section 23 refers to the treatment and retention of material and information generated during such an investigation, and subsection 23(1)(a) contains a requirement for the police to carry out an investigation. It states that

---

[9] ACPO, *Murder Investigation Manual* (NCPE, 2006), 25–6.

where a criminal investigation is conducted, all reasonable steps must be taken for the purposes of the investigation and in particular, all reasonable lines of enquiry are pursued.

Part II of the CPIA Code of Practice defines the 'officer in charge of an investigation' and what their role is within the Act:

> The *officer in charge of an investigation* is the officer responsible for directing a criminal investigation. S/he is also responsible for ensuring that proper procedures are in place for recording information, and retaining records of information and other material in the investigation.

1.3.1 Core qualities and skills

According to a police research paper,[10] the SIO role requires a combination of three different types of skills categorised as:

1. Investigative ability
2. Professional knowledge
3. Management skills

1.3.1.1 Investigative ability

This comprises a multitude of abilities such as:

- Investigative competence (eg formulating lines of enquiry, hypotheses building, good problem/puzzle solving with a good mix of effective fast/slow decision making and recording skills, and the ability to apply the National Decision Model (NDM) consistently).
- Ability to assess, prioritise, and manage any threats, harms, and risks.
- Strategic and tactical savviness.
- Razor-sharp observation.
- Ability to appraise, analyse, retain, and recall salient facts and information (including interpreting and assimilating information).
- Ability to apply professional curiosity and scepticism.
- Drive, determination, adaptability, flexibility, and resilience.
- Innovation and creativity.
- Exceptional communication skills—verbal and written.
- Confidence, professional courage, nerve, and self-belief.
- Calmness and composure under pressure and in time-critical situations.
- Ability to work at pace and deal with high volumes of information.
- Multi-tasking dexterity, diligence, and prioritising effectiveness.
- Time management skills.
- Dogged determination, commitment, and passion for the role.

---

[10] N Smith and C Flanagan, The effective detective: Identifying the skills of an effective SIO (2000), Home Office Police Research Series, Paper 122.

1.3.1.2 Professional knowledge

- Knowledge of legal frameworks, powers, mandatory requirements (eg CPIA, s 11 Children Act 2004) and procedures, case law, rules of evidence, definitions (eg the terms 'reasonable suspicion' and 'reasonable grounds to believe', see section 12.6), Codes of Practice (eg Code of Practice for Victims of Crime, 2015—see section 11.3).
- Adequate training and continuous professional development by improving/ expanding knowledge and skills, using numerous sources such as open-source material (OSM), circulars, statistics, bulletins, national policies and reviews, legal databases, eg Police National Legal Database (PNLD), relevant case law and legislation, journals, reports (eg the Byford report), manuals, media articles, blogs etc, requisite courses, conferences and seminars, and the National Police Library at College of Policing.
- Knowledge of national guidelines and policy, best practice guidance, and learning points (eg via POLKA[11] communities and College of Policing Authorised Professional Practice[12]), strategic debrief reports, National Police Chiefs' Council (NPCC) position statements, IOPC, HMICFRS, Home Office/Her Majesty's Government (HMG), Office of Surveillance Commissioners (OSC), and Investigatory Powers Commissioner's Office (IPCO) reports, recommendations, and nationally disseminated good practice.
- Knowledge of forensic procedures, techniques, and opportunities (traditional, new, and digital/cyber based), investigative and technological advances, crime scene search/examination tactics, evidence recovery/processing, medical/pathology principles, financial and fraud investigation, specialisms, experts and (inter)national assets (eg NCA, Europol, Interpol, Non-Government Organisations (NGOs)).
- Understanding of terminology, eg in the medico-legal or agency, unit, or cyber/digital sense for when communicating with professionals, experts, pathologists, doctors, scientists, and colleagues, and understanding terms and language, particularly frequently used organisational terminology and acronyms.
- Operational knowledge, such as Major Incident Room (MIR) procedures and case management systems, eg HOLMES, producing TIE policies, Achieving Best Evidence (ABE) guidelines, covert (eg 'red side') and overt ('white side') proactive tactics, managing intelligence, producing investigative strategies,

---

[11] POLKA is the Police Online Knowledge Area provided by the College of Policing. One of its communities is aimed at supporting SIOs entitled 'Major Crime Investigation' (see <https://polka.pnn.police.uk/communities/home>).

[12] Authorised Professional Practice (APP), <http://www.app.college.police.uk/>.

be treated as a weakness. It should be actively encouraged and usually is nowadays. Arranging peer reviews for unsolved or difficult cases and critical friends for seeking advice who might have experience of dealing with similar cases is a good way of learning. Reflecting on personal performance is an important process plus engaging in honest and open non-threatening feedback opportunities is something that can prove highly beneficial. The golden rule is not to 'check your own homework' but to get others to cast an independent eye over your work, and get the best support when its needed.

KEY POINTS

1. Processes such as PIP or 'licence to practice' usually require maintenance of an assessed CPD portfolio. Failure to produce one may lead to loss of accreditation.
2. Having a trusted mentor and using peer reviews allows ideas to flow and facilitates learning opportunities and self-reflection.
3. A senior investigator never stops learning and always remains a student in the art of investigation.

1.6 **Preparing for the Role**

Calls or requests for an SIO may come when least expected. This might be at unusual or inconvenient times, or during unsociable hours, particularly when performing 'on-call' duties. These are times when an SIO needs to be extremely well prepared, ready to spring into action and hit the ground running. Effective SIOs are always ready and prepared for the day they get a major case or, 'the big one'. An acronym to remember is AYR:

> **A** Are
>
> **Y** You
>
> **R** Ready?

SIOs might have to remain on duty for a considerable time, particularly in the early stages of a new enquiry. Working long hours without sufficient rest or sustenance, together with pressure and time constraints, is unhelpful when busy making critical decisions. Therefore, there is a need to be well prepared and ready for any challenge that lies ahead and to be able to manage oneself effectively in order to perform the role. Having good basic kit and accessories at the ready in a grab bag/case or similar is a habit worth adopting.

Checklist—SIO's basic tool kit

- Reliable and accurate watch/timepiece/calendar.

- 'Casebook' or work/note/day book (and spare) with reliable writing implements to record information, sketches, notes, details, and decisions (or digital equivalent).

- Fresh policy log (and spare).

- Laminated card (or similar) outlining the NDM.

- Official identification and personal business cards.

- Weatherproof and secure bag/file/case in which to carry important documents and papers.

- Useful forms/documents (eg start-up case management system, list of actions raised, blank actions, officer debriefing sheets, major incident (MI) write-up sheets, message and H2H forms, aide-memoires, and checklists).

- Reliable communication devices (eg mobile phone plus charger, radio, tablet, laptop).

- Useful contact numbers (eg supervisory staff, team leaders, specialists).

- Foul weather gear (eg waterproof/warm protective clothing and suitable footwear, hat/gloves).

- Personal protection equipment (PPE).

- Standby refreshments (food and drink).

- Local maps (eg digital mapping or satellite navigation system).

- Flashlight and batteries.

- Crime-scene barrier tape, scene logbooks, exhibit bags/labels, permanent markers for use on tamper-proof bags.

- Digital camera (with charged batteries plus secure memory card).

- Forensic suit/mask/gloves/overshoes.

- Suitable transportation (eg vehicle topped up with fuel and window notice that signifies to whom it belongs).

- Money/loose change/credit/debit cards for emergencies.

- Personal comfort and welfare necessities and supplies (eg spectacles, medicines).

- Addresses and postcodes of, directions to, and access codes for buildings, details of parking facilities, and locations of rendezvous points for crime scenes.

- Details of local Wi-Fi codes.

- Overnight bag plus details for booking short-notice overnight accommodation.

- *Blackstone's Senior Investigating Officers' Handbook.*

1.7 **Performing the Role**

SIOs are expected to take command of an investigation and review activities undertaken by others and the initial response to any reported circumstances. They must demonstrate solid leadership and management skills from the outset, taking control and providing adequate direction by making key decisions, initiating early investigation plans and identifying main lines of enquiry, ensuring immediate and fast-track activities (or 'Actions') are allocated and completed in a timely manner.

If applicable, a visit to a crime scene(s) is essential to make an early assessment, agree parameters and ensure adequate policies are in place for identifying, securing, and protecting (ISP) evidential material. Identifying resourcing requirements for the initial and subsequent stages of the investigation will be necessary so that teams are assembled with adequate equipment and facilities in order to commence a professional investigation.

The SIO is responsible for maximising all evidential opportunities, gathering information, and formulating hypotheses, making high-level decisions with accompanying rationale to explain thought processes, and justifying and explaining how the decisions were made. Everything should be meticulously checked, recorded, and logged, details of which will be picked over for accuracy and relevance.

The SIO must also ensure that vulnerable victims and their families are safeguarded and/or supported and witnesses are encouraged to offer any evidential information. Good lines of communication should be maintained with high-quality staff meetings and briefings, and media interviews may need to be orchestrated, tight deadlines met, and staff and superiors briefed, simultaneously managing other competing demands in what might be the chaos and confusion experienced in the Golden Hour(s).

These few paragraphs provide a brief snapshot of what performing the SIO role entails. During these moments, the SIO must remain totally unflustered, calm, and composed. They are to lead and manage an enquiry and hold themselves accountable to those who possess the right to scrutinise their performance.

This sounds a lot to take in and fortunately help is at hand. All is about to be explained in the remaining chapters of this *Handbook*.

Bibliography

ACPO, *Equality, Diversity and Human Rights Strategy for the Police Service* (Home Office, January 2010)

ACPO, *Murder Investigation Manual* (NCPE, 2006)

ACPO, *MIRSAP Manual* (NCPE, 2005)

College of Policing, 'Code of Ethics: Principles and Standards of Professional Behaviour for the Policing Profession of England and Wales' (April 2014) <http://www.college.police.uk/what-we-do/Ethics/Documents/Code_of_Ethics.pdf>

Home Office, *Multi-Agency Statutory Guidance for the Conduct of Domestic Homicide Reviews* (Home Office, 2013)

Maslow, AH, 'A theory of human motivation' (1943) *Psychological Review* 55, 370–97

Pascale, R, *Managing on the Edge* (Penguin Books, 1990)

Rogers, C, *Leadership Skills in Policing* (Oxford University Press, 2008)

Smith, N and Flanagan, C, 'The effective detective: Identifying the skills of an effective SIO' (2000), Home Office Police Research Series, Paper 122

Leadership and Management

2.1 **Introduction**

Performing a senior leadership and management role in a major or serious crime investigation is unique in comparison to other areas of law enforcement. This is because SIOs are expected to lead investigations in addition to performing general management duties and responsibilities. The role involves building and maintaining extensive knowledge of key facts, making investigative decisions, and retaining an overarching responsibility for all aspects of a complex case while effectively directing, controlling, and managing finance and resources.

Regardless of how absorbing, and challenging a case might be, the SIO carries additional responsibility for staff management under their command. Those assigned to their enquiry teams, temporary or otherwise, are entitled to be supervised and managed properly as well as having an effective investigation lead. SIOs carry a legal duty of care for the staff under their control, not only for performance and welfare but also standard setting, policy implementation, motivation, learning, professional development, and conflict resolution.

Style and approach to both leadership and management are a matter of professional judgement and personal choice. Some degree of flexibility is perfectly normal. When required, firm authoritative direction may be necessary to ensure urgent decisions are made (not avoided), high priority tasks are completed, and risks managed, whereas at other times (ie in less critical scenarios), a more engaging and consultative style is appropriate.

Leaders can still be effective at engaging with their staff while retaining that all-important steel streak to step in and take charge when necessary. They are expected to maximise outputs and manage their staff while simultaneously bringing an added dimension of effective leadership by inspiring and motivating.

Personal resilience plays a role in all this in order to manage the pressures of investigating at the highest level. This chapter cannot address every issue as there is too much ground to cover, however it offers food for thought and a reminder about key related areas such as managing diversity and applying high ethical standards in the workplace.

KEY POINT

The SIO role involves dual leadership and management responsibilities: (i) maximising output and managing staff; and (ii) effective leadership in a serious and challenging major investigation.

'Managers do things right while leaders do the right thing.'[1]

---

[1] P Drucker, cited in R Pascale, *Managing on the Edge* (Penguin Books, 1990), 65.

2.2 **Leadership and Management Styles**

Leadership and management styles are defined by individuals and accordingly, they vary somewhat. What works for one person does not always work for another. Some believe good leaders give off a certain 'presence', 'gravitas', 'aura', or 'authority', while others believe it is more about being charismatic and popular. It depends on what is suitable and appropriate for the individual and circumstances. Gaining open and honest 360-degree feedback may help determine what works best for any given person.

In time-critical and urgent situations, such as crimes in action and threats to life (TTL), kidnaps, suspects at large, and high-risk ongoing incidents, leadership and decision making needs to be more authoritative, dynamic, and direct, plain and simple. Such situations demand prompt and decisive leadership in order to manage investigations and staff effectively in order to protect the public, prevent offending, and pursue offenders. That is why the police service, for example, has a disciplined, military-style rank structure. In other less urgent circumstances, a well-managed and self-sufficient team can more or less function adequately on a less direct but more inclusive and democratic approach.

There are a number of different styles of leadership. Kurt Lewin, a management theorist, suggested the following three:[2]

1. **Autocratic**: Direct orders and directives being issued through one-way communication with little or no involvement from subordinates. Advantages include speed of response by enabling a quick decision-making process through greater control and immediate direction. Drawbacks are that staff may become frustrated by the autocratic manner of decision making which allows for little or no involvement from those who have good or better ideas than the leader.
2. **Democratic**: Involvement of subordinates in the decision-making process through consultation. Advantages are that staff are more involved and can contribute towards strengthening the outcome of a decision and they feel more motivated. Drawbacks are that this style can become too slow and cumbersome, which means it is difficult to make time-critical decisions and an SIO cannot make the decision they feel is best. It also allows those who are risk-averse to avoid making tough decisions.
3. **Laissez-faire**: Involves minimal involvement in decision making, allowing subordinates to decide for themselves. This may be feasible when staff are fully competent to make their own decisions. Advantages are similar to the democratic style, with motivational levels high because power and control is devolved, which may enrich team and individual roles and jobs. Drawbacks are that this leadership style may mean that subordinates have little or no

---

[2] K Lewin, *Resolving Social Conflicts* (Souvenir Press, 1973).

17

leadership, direction, or coordination, and that their work is largely unstructured and inconsistent.

Individuals are free to choose which style suits them or the given circumstances best. Sometimes an autocratic style is entirely justifiable and necessary (eg in urgent operational or time-critical situations), and at others a more democratic style, or even a hybrid of different styles is more appropriate, ie somewhere in between ('auto/democrat').

Great leaders have the ability to adapt, adopt, and improve styles by calling upon a wide spectrum of behaviours and personal qualities. Personal style may depend, however, on character and personal preference for the situation as opposed to keeping to one preferred style. An SIO must decide which style to select, remembering that effective leadership needs to be moving, fluid, and dynamic.

There is no standard set of qualities that make the perfect leader, yet 'influencing' and 'inspiring' characteristics seem particularly well suited. This includes being able to influence the team to 'up their game' and work hard to solve the case. It also means being able to influence not just downwards but also across and upwards in any hierarchical organisation. Confidence in decision making and problem solving is also central to leadership (see Chapter 3) because it enables tasks to be communicated and completed properly. Leaders often have to do the right thing even though it may be unpopular, rather than taking the easier or softer option.

Good leaders remain calm and considered and control their emotions when under pressure. They provide a strong sense of direction, reassurance, clarity, and purpose while giving off a high degree of energy and enthusiasm. Panic or an inability to make decisions or freezing under pressure are absolute no-nos. At some incidents and crime scenes where there is pandemonium or chaos, with an initial response being somewhat disorganised, a good leader takes control by managing and directing operational resources effectively. The attending SIO must not allow themselves to become paralysed, and needs to remain cool, calm, composed, and in control. Displaying confidence, inner calm, and self-assurance in high-pressure situations (being unflappable) are key attributes as they reassure those around them that an effective leader has taken charge.

KEY POINT

How an SIO presents and behaves is crucial. This involves looking unruffled, positive, confident, using convincing verbal and non-verbal communication, having good posture, being calm, using a steady tone of voice and projecting it with a steady pace and volume, using clear, open gestures and facial expressions. In other words, looking, sounding, and acting the part of a leader in complete control.

2.3 **Team Building**

Management and leadership involve building a team into an efficient and cohesive unit. The modern approach to crime investigation recognises that there is no place for the lone entrepreneur in the team (including the SIO). The role is to be the leader of a team, to provide investigative focus, to coordinate, motivate, and be accountable for every aspect of the enquiry whilst managing a host of resources.

> **KEY POINT**
>
> Strong leadership is about carrying colleagues with you and being collegiate.

Professor John Adair, internationally renowned in the field of management and leadership development, describes how team building consists of three complementary and overlapping requirements:

1. Task
2. Team
3. Individual

He says tasks that need completing create frustration and low morale if those who own them are prevented from completing them or are unable to do so. Team maintenance needs are equally important as group cohesiveness is essential under the 'united we stand, divided we fall' principle. Individual needs are also key and include psychological and physical needs such as reward and recognition, a sense of doing something worthwhile, job satisfaction and status. The three overlapping elements are represented in this diagram:

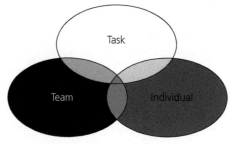

The overlapping circles indicate how all three elements are mutually inter-dependent. In theory, if team maintenance fails, performance of tasks becomes impaired, and individual satisfaction reduced. If individual needs are not met, the team will lack cohesiveness and performance of tasks will be affected. Effective managers tend to try and satisfy all three elements. In other words, too much emphasis on one can be detrimental to the other two.[3]

2.3.1 Partnership building

Teamwork often involves working with other agencies and partners, some of which could be principle contributors to the investigation and may even have mandatory responsibilities for certain functions (eg Local Authorities for safe-guarding and protecting vulnerable people, or the fire and rescue service for investigating arson attacks, the Health and Safety Executive (HSE), etc). The SIO must seek to gain the willing cooperation of key stakeholders from the outset and involve them in decision-making processes. Consultation arrangements and protocols should be agreed or adhered to (if local agreements are already in existence). A Memorandum of Understanding (MoU) may be necessary (with legal advice being advisory) to outline exactly who has responsibility for what and how a joint working agreement will operate.

Some operations and investigations can benefit from the formation of a key stakeholders' liaison group. These groups are particularly useful if the SIO needs to gain assistance from key agencies and partners as well as keeping them in-formed and updated. These groups can help build good external team relations and assist those organisations that might have other responsibilities to consider beyond the criminal investigation.

2.4 Supervision and Support

The ability to supervise indirectly can be an asset, provided swift interven-tion is made when things aren't going well. This sends out the right message regarding (non-) acceptable professional standards. Being able to pick up, read, and interpret signals is important—eg quickly noticing and acting when morale is dipping or complacency and lethargy are beginning to creep in to the team. This includes managing and dealing with any tensions and inappro-priate behaviour.

The SIO must know or find out what, if any, problems their team are fa-cing and must never assume they can completely empathise with their staff. Teams respect a leader who is visible and willing to leave their own comfort zone, talk to them, and find out for themselves what working environments are

---

[3] J Adair, *The Best of Adair on Leadership and Management* (Thorogood, 2008).

like first-hand (often referred to as 'management by walkabout' or through the acronym 'MBWA').

2.5 **Maintaining Morale**

Motivated people are bound to be more productive due to their sheer enthusiasm, commitment, and energy. In long-running, sensitive, or complex investigations, particular attention should be paid to the morale of enquiry staff. This is especially important where there are perceptions that the investigation is not making progress, or if the enquiry is attracting some degree of internal and/or external scrutiny or criticism.

When engaged on hard-to-solve cases or those within environments where there may be a distrust of the police and authorities, teams need regular motivation, reassurance, and strong leadership. They could be coming up against barriers from individuals on whose help they may rely on due to a number of potential reasons (eg fear of assisting or being labelled informants), and these can be very challenging enquiries to work on.

The SIO and their management team will need to monitor and carefully risk assess any potential causes to try to come up with solutions to improve morale if it drops. Ideas include gaining feedback, improving the work environment, showing appreciation, and giving praise, acknowledging core milestones, task rotation, bringing in senior commanders or key stakeholders to speak with the staff, holding 'away days' to give staff a break from the usual work environment, improving well-being and discussing key areas of the enquiry, etc.

2.5.1 **Positive psychology**

Positive attitudes and attributes are infectious; they rub off on others. Very little can be achieved without them. Negative attitudes, on the other hand, drain energy and motivation. Negative and pessimistic traits are unhelpful, self-fulfilling, and become culturally the norm. Optimistic, positive mental attitudes (PMA), however, allow tasks to be approached with greater vigour, energy, and vitality, focusing on what can be achieved and not what cannot. Those who constantly raise problems instead of proposing solutions, play the 'devil's advocate', and are destructive rather than constructive need to be challenged by balancing their negative views with positive ones.

SIOs should regularly remind themselves and their staff to remember the 3P principle, which can be summed up in three very important words:

POSITIVE
POSITIVE
POSITIVE

KEY POINTS

1. Negative attitudes can become enthusiasm and energy drainers. They suck the life out of people and gradually infect everyone with a similar low level of energy. This *must be prevented* as it impacts on performance and general job satisfaction.
2. 'A pessimist sees the difficulty in every opportunity; while an optimist sees the possibility in every difficulty' (Sir Winston Churchill).

2.6 Maximising Potential

It is good to have a rich mix and spread of skills and attributes amongst team members. Some, for example, may have a relaxed, easy communication style, readily adaptable to fit most circumstances, and they like to be seen and heard. Quieter, more introverted types may just get on with allocated tasks in a less obvious fashion and may prefer to be left alone. Some thought must go into understanding individuals and how best to get the most out of each of them. A skilful manager analyses the strengths and weaknesses of their team and allocates tasks according to attributes. For example, trying to encourage and support potential witnesses to provide testimony or information may be a task better suited to some people than to others. Watching hours and hours of closed circuit television (CCTV) footage or searching the open web for intelligence gathering purposes, although arguably both core investigator skills, may be better suited to some types of individuals and not others.

SIOs need to be aware of their own strengths and weaknesses too in order to build a team around them. This helps to identify gaps where their needs are greatest. Taking responsibility for continuous self-development, setting high personal and moral standards, and leading by example plus being able to accept liability for when things go wrong are useful attributes. Giving credit, praise, and recognition for any effort, struggle, and determination can also be enormously beneficial to building good team spirit.

Introducing a healthy amount of command and control should not seek to stifle any investigator's natural desire to use their skills, flair, and expertise. Staff should be empowered to apply their skills and knowledge to their investigative activities within the framework of action management of a major incident room (MIR) or case management system. This will allow teams to realise their full potential and not only maintain a high level of morale but also perform at the highest level.

2.7 Personal Management, Resilience, and Support

Management has to include an element of managing oneself in order to cope with the pressures and demands of the role. There are both physical and mental demands placed on an SIO, particularly in the early stages of a fast-moving enquiry when it is often necessary to be on duty long before others arrive and long after they leave. It is essential, no matter how experienced, enthusiastic, or professional an individual is, to be able to cope under pressure, manage fatigue, and heavy workloads, operate at a fast pace, and juggle the demands of a work/ personal life balance.

Stress has psychological and physiological elements that are quite normal human reactions. Some cope better than others and may even perform better when their adrenalin is flowing and in a high-intensity environment. Managing stress, responsibility, and pressure is a unique and personal attribute. The consequences of being unable to cope can manifest themselves in many different forms, eg loss of patience, being argumentative, showing anger, unusual or irrational behaviour. These symptoms must be recognised in order to manage the causes.

KEY POINT

Under the right circumstances, stress and pressure can actually raise performance, which is why world records are not generally broken during training sessions.

Sometimes an SIO's office/work area may resemble a surgery, with people queuing up waiting to speak urgently on a one-to-one basis. An 'open-door policy' is admirable, but sometimes 'the door' needs closing in order to get on with important work, to read and study material, to concentrate and focus clearly, or hold meetings in private. There must be some control over who makes personal or unplanned demands of an SIO's time, and other supervisors down the chain of command should not be circumvented.

Having a reliable and trustworthy deputy increases resilience, and having a trusty assistant (aka 'staff officer') who can also monitor the SIO's welfare is to be highly recommended. The SIO cannot and should not try to do everything themselves (which will demoralise and undermine their staff) because the appropriate delegation of key tasks will relieve workloads and make staff feel more valued. Suitable 'deputies' can be tasked with arranging and managing important themed tasks, conducting cascade briefings, and managing administrative and supervisory/quality assurance tasks, provided whoever has those delegated responsibilities reports back to the SIO at regular intervals. This can be at stipulated times, such as during formal or informal briefings, team discussions, and one-to-one meetings.

Time management is essential to avoid becoming overburdened. Being ruthlessly efficient at getting the most out of available and valuable time is key. Some matters and certain individuals (including seniors and chief officers) can conspire to commandeer time if allowed, and this can be managed by being respectful but firm and courteous, pointing out that other matters may be more pressing and urgent (managing upwards).

Meetings and briefings need careful management to ensure pre-prepared agendas and allocated times are adhered to rigidly (see Chapter 9). Planning and managing daily priorities is equally extremely important while appreciating there can be sudden changes in circumstances at a moment's notice. Being unable to manage and complete all necessary and urgent tasks will raise stress levels unnecessarily and cause staff to become counterproductive.

An SIO need not and should not be alone in managing complex enquiries. Every opportunity should be taken to gain support and advice from trusted and reliable peers, colleagues, and specialists. Having someone available to bounce ideas off and chat through complex theories and areas of an investigation, bringing in a wider field of experience, is not only reassuring but recognised as good practice. The role of a PIP4 (SIO/Gold Strategic and Tactical Advisor) can fulfil this role in large-scale enquiries. The National Crime Agency (NCA) also has experienced accredited PIP4 National SIO Advisers (NSIOAs) who can offer their nationwide experience, knowledge, and specialist services to act as a critical friend to the SIO or provide reassurance and advice at any stage during an enquiry.

KEY POINT

Don't mark your own homework. Have a critical friend review your thoughts and decision making.

Mentally switching off and disengaging from workload challenges can help relieve stress and aid relaxation, while for some people it might be helpful to discuss issues with a trusted and patient listener. Whatever suits the individual works. It can, however, be very tempting to concentrate on little else than a stimulating and absorbing enquiry, yet creating some time to unwind, relax, and relieve tension at a suitable point is usually beneficial in reducing mental anxiety and stress and bringing clarity to the mind.

It is unprofessional and unhealthy to work continuous prolonged hours (which might be identified by an inspection/review team, should things go wrong) or go without proper rest and food; energy and adrenalin levels will eventually crash, which is when it becomes far more difficult to focus and function correctly. Hunger can be an unnecessary distraction. Sleep deprivation affects the ability to make good judgements, to perform under pressure, and with sufficient energy, notwithstanding the longstanding effects on health and physical condition. Being stressed, tired, and overworked should not be seen as some kind of 'badge of honour' or sign of commitment. Everyone has physiological and psychological needs and SIOs are no different.

KEY POINTS

- Personal management is as important as management of the team.
- Nominating a personal assistant or 'staff officer' is a wise choice.
- Personal health management and welfare is fundamentally important, with a need to match energy and stamina levels with workloads.
- Having a trusted mentor or advisers to bounce ideas off and seek advice from can help relieve some of the pressure and assist in making good choices.

2.7.1 **Resilience**

A research study[4] concluded that 'resilience' comprised a number of recurrent themes. Resilient people, they found, tended to use similar coping strategies when confronted with high levels of stress. The study identified nine coping mechanisms that proved to be effective which are referred to as 'resilience factors'. These amounted to maintaining a realistic outlook, seeking and accepting social and moral support, and imitating sturdy role models. Many attended to their health and well-being and kept themselves physically fit and mentally sharp. Most were active problem solvers who looked for meaning and opportunity in the midst of opportunity and used humour when appropriate.

Checklist—Nine Resilience Factors

1. Trusted individuals are used for the role of support officer.

2. Some responsibilities are delegated to enable necessary time off and rest.

3. Not becoming too emotionally involved in a case as it limits objectivity.

4. Personal management is important.

5. Maintaining good levels of physical and psychological fitness.

6. High personal standards help ensure a good moral compass.

7. Not being afraid to ask for help, advice, and support.

8. Having a sturdy and reliable mentor, a critical friend, and a role model.

9. Remaining positive and optimistic.

---

[4] M Southwick and D Charney *Resilience: The Science of Mastering Life's Greatest Challenges* (Cambridge University Press, 2012).

2.8 **Managing Diversity**

Investigations need to take full account of any matters appertaining to race, gender, ethnic origin, religion, culture, age, disability, sexual orientation, nationality, or place of abode. There is no place for personal prejudices, discriminatory behaviour, or stereotyping of any sort and it is particularly important that assumptions are not influenced by any prejudice or bias. Full account must be taken of vulnerable persons, whatever that vulnerability may be.

Communication and relationships can easily break down if there are perceptions of alienation, distrust, or negativity resulting in loss of confidence in the investigation. This, in turn, leads to potential loss of public assistance and non-receptiveness. The SIO must remain cognisant of this potential and manage the requirement in a Community Impact Assessment document (CIA) and policy decision.

The Equality Act 2010 (EA) consolidated discrimination legislation and contained new measures to strengthen protection against discrimination, stipulating protected characteristics in relation to age, disability, gender reassignment, race, religion or belief, sex and sexual orientation. Section 149 of the Equality Act 2010 places a duty on public authorities to consider equality in all decision-making processes. This is further reinforced by Article 14 of the Human Rights Act 1998 which outlines a prohibition of discrimination.

The SIO in their leadership role must be committed to managing diversity, internally and externally, by ensuring it is demonstrably part of an enquiry team's culture and philosophy. Positive action must be taken against any inappropriate and illegal language or behaviour at all times, with adequate mechanisms to monitor compliance with the legislation.

2.9 **Ethical Leadership**

Most law enforcement officers start their careers by swearing on oath to act with fairness and impartiality. This is a code that must never be forgotten. No-one benefits if a person is wrongly accused or convicted, and it is the job of the SIO and an ultimate responsibility to ensure that a criminal investigation is conducted to the highest degree of professional, moral, and ethical standards. The emphasis must be on a 'search for the truth' not a 'search for the proof'.[5]

Just like victims and witnesses, some suspects may also be vulnerable and therefore likely to be open to suggestion, coercion, or may just be an easy target to accuse. Suspect management is discussed in Chapter 12 with the declaration of suspect status being classed as a defining moment in any investigation. It is one that needs to be given carefully thought. It is often advisable to 'play devil's

---

[5] P Taylor and R Chaplain (eds), *Crimes Detected in England and Wales 2010/11*, Home Office Statistical Bulletin 11/11, Home Office.

advocate' or to apply the 'what if' scenario to try to test a theory about the **non**-involvement of a potential suspect (see Chapter 3 on decision making).

It must be remembered that the UK criminal justice system is founded on two basic principles:

1. Presumption of innocence ('innocent until proven guilty' rule).
2. Due process and belief that any allegations of criminality must be proven beyond all reasonable doubt, by fair process.

'Beyond all reasonable doubt' means just that: irrefutable evidence of guilt. This is the standard used in any criminal case and it is a lot higher than that used by the civil code, which sets a much lower threshold based on the balance of probabilities.

Just as there might be evidence on behalf of the prosecution, there may also be evidence on behalf of the suspect that raises doubt as to their guilt. In either case, those accused are always entitled to the benefit of the doubt. In the majority of UK criminal law, there is no burden placed on any person to prove their innocence, and investigators must be satisfied there is sufficient evidence to provide a realistic prospect of conviction. Any case that fails the stringent evidential threshold test must not proceed, no matter how serious, emotive, or sensitive it might be. For this reason, all investigators are required to pursue *all* reasonable lines of enquiry, that is their task, whether those enquiries point towards or away from anyone who is under suspicion.

KEY POINTS

- When conducting criminal investigations, investigators should pursue all reasonable lines of enquiry, whether they point *towards* or *away* from a suspect.
- The 'Towards or Away' Rule—Codes of Practice to CPIA 1996 section 3.5.
- Investigators must be governed by the highest of professional standards and must not be allowed to become unduly influenced by personal views regarding ethnicity, origin, gender, disability, age, religion or belief, sexual orientation, or gender identity.

Lack of professional behaviour and standards adversely affect reputations as well as possibly lead to potential miscarriages of justice. Public trust and confidence depend on honesty, transparency, and integrity. Statutory regulations such as the Human Rights Act 1998 (HRA) and the Police and Criminal Evidence Act 1984 (PACE), and oversight bodies (eg Independent Office for Police Conduct (IOPC)) provide the pathways for challenging inappropriate investigative activities and actions, and the CPIA places a legal requirement on ensuring that evidence is captured that points away from as well as towards any possible suspect.

In order to build and maintain public confidence, SIOs must lead their teams in a manner that ensures investigations are carried out professionally, ethically, and to an agreed and expected high ethical standard. This is the golden thread that must run throughout all investigations and is the aim of all PIP training and accreditation.

KEY POINTS

1. Most investigators begin their careers swearing on oath to act with fairness and impartiality—this code must never be forgotten.
2. Professional investigators learn to control their emotions and follow irrefutable facts and evidence, always.

The framework offered by the law (eg PACE, HRA, Regulation of Investigatory Powers Act 2000 (RIPA), CPIA 1996, the Equality Act 2010 (EA) and Freedom of Information Act 2000 (FOI)) creates rigid boundaries for ethical practice. Compliance with the legislation provides SIOs and their investigators with a degree of protection from ill-founded allegations of dishonesty, unfairness, or discrimination. This is illustrated in what is known as the 'integrity paradigm'.

INTEGRITY PARADIGM

Right method Right result ✓	Right method Wrong result
Wrong method Right result	Wrong method Wrong result

During major and serious crime investigations, investigators are usually under close supervision via regular briefings, quality assurance mechanisms and rigorously managed administration or case management systems. All activity should be properly tasked, allocated, monitored, reviewed, and supervised with a high degree of scrutiny because the stakes are high. In turn, this should produce a robust, and inquisitorial management system. These integrated administrative controls must be in place to ensure compliance with legislation, correct guidelines/procedures, manage risk effectively, and to ensure the investigation is thorough, entirely professional, transparent, and there is enquiry team accountability..

Section 78(1) PACE

In any judicial proceedings, a court may refuse to allow evidence on which the prosecution proposes to rely if it appears, having regard to all the

---

circumstances in which the evidence was obtained, the admission of the evidence would have such an adverse effect on the fairness of the proceedings that the court ought not admit it.

2.9.1 Code of Ethics

In 2014, the College of Policing issued a Code of Ethics[6] as a code of practice under section 39A of the Police Act 1996 (as amended by section 124 of the Anti-Social Behaviour, Crime and Policing Act 2014). It outlines principles and standards of professional behaviour for police in England and Wales. These principles are intended to inform every decision and action across the police service and apply to everyone in the profession. They also state that 'those with leadership roles have additional expectations placed upon them to lead by example'.

The Code of Ethics promotes the use of the National Decision Model (NDM) to embed its principles at the centre of decision making (see Chapter 3 and Appendix A). It is the golden thread that runs through all decision making.

The code outlines ten standards of professional behaviour under the following headings:

1. Honesty and integrity.
2. Authority, respect, and courtesy.
3. Equality and diversity.
4. Use of force.
5. Orders and instructions.
6. Duties and responsibilities.
7. Confidentiality.
8. Fitness for work.
9. Conduct.
10. Challenging and reporting improper behaviour.

Bibliography

Adair, J, *The Best of Adair on Leadership and Management* (Thorogood, 2008)
Adhami, E and Browne, DP, 'Major crime enquiries: Improving expert support for detectives' Police Research Group Special Interest Series, Paper 9 (Home Office, 1996)
Adam, EC, 'Fighter cockpits of the future' (1993) Proceedings of 12th IEEE/AIAA Digital Avionics Systems Conference (DASC), 318–23

---

[6] College of Policing, 'Code of Ethics: Principles and Standards of Professional Behaviour for the Policing Profession of England and Wales' (April 2014, College of Policing).

College of Policing, 'Code of Ethics: Principles and Standards of Professional Behaviour for the Policing Profession of England and Wales' (College of Policing, April 2014)

Innes, M, 'The process structures of police homicide investigations' (2002) 42 *British Journal of Criminology*, 669–88

Kelley, H, 'The warm–cold variable in first impressions of persons' (1950) 18 *Journal of Personality*, 431–9

Moray, N, *Robotics, Control and Society* (CRC Press, 2005)

Peters, S, *The Chimp Paradox* (Vermillon, 2012)

Southwick, M and Charney, D, *Resilience: The Science of Mastering Life's Greatest Challenges* (Cambridge University Press, 2012)

3

Decision Making

3.1 **Introduction**

This chapter examines fundamental methods and processes that can assist Senior Investigating Officers in making sound decisions. This is a core skill and directly linked to requirements of the role highlighted in Chapter 1. It is also a key requirement for the accreditation process and one tested extensively in full-scale exercises at so-called Hydra[1] simulation suites. Having an appreciation and knowledge of the best processes, theories, and logic (some academically acclaimed) will enable an SIO to become more confident and competent in their decision making and problem solving.

This chapter seeks to provide guidance and a deeper understanding of concepts and methods of decision making. Learning, applying, and improving them will greatly help develop a more rounded capability for making consistent and methodical, sound decisions, and produce clearer audit trails explaining how they were derived. This protects the SIO and their organisations by providing a means to explain what, when, why, how, and by whom a decision was made. What counts is not only the decision but also what methods and thought processes were applied and how these were recorded.

Understandably, a high level of skill is required in decision making; after all, the SIO is the key decision maker in major investigations. There is an expectation of transparency and compliance with the general principles outlined in the following sections of this chapter. SIOs must anticipate some if not all their decisions to come under close scrutiny and be tested on not just what they were and how they turned out but also how they were made and why. Understanding strengths and weaknesses associated with human decision making and an awareness of the principles mentioned and described in this chapter will make an invaluable contribution to an SIO's toolkit and daily practice. Decision making is at the heart of everything an SIO does, hence the importance of what follows.

3.2 **'Fast' and 'Slow' Decision Making**

Daniel Kahneman's popular book, *Thinking, Fast and Slow*, describes two different systems of thinking involved when making decisions:

1. operates automatically and quickly with little or no effort and little sense of voluntary control.
2. allocates attention to the effortful mental activities that demand it, including complex computations. The operations of system 2 are often associated with the subjective experience of agency, choice and concentration ... only the slower system 2 can construct thoughts in an orderly series of steps. When

---

[1] Hydra is an interactive immersive simulation training system designed to facilitate the development of operational decision-making skills (cited in Ask and Fahsing, 2016).

system 1 runs into difficulty, it calls upon system 2 to support more detailed and specific processing that may solve the problem of the moment. System 1 has biases, however, systematic errors that it is prone to make in specified circumstances and can sometimes try and answer easier questions than the one it is asked and has little understanding of logic and statistics.[2]

These two alternatives are now examined in more detail.

3.2.1 **Fast-time decision making**

Fast-time decisions are required in almost every aspect of daily life, much as they are in major crime investigations. The challenge is to recognise when there is or isn't the time or need for further analysis or deliberation. The risk of making a decision swiftly versus not making one at all must be determined, with considerations and actions decided duly recorded and explained in a policy log accompanied by supporting reasons. This is where accurate recording in the context of what was happening and what information was known and available at the time becomes highly significant (see also Chapter 4).

Clearly, investigative decision making should avoid any so-called *paralysis by analysis* that creates indecisiveness and can prove catastrophic during the early stages of time critical or even life-threatening incidents where every second counts. In some situations, there simply isn't the luxury of discretional delay as the pace and requirements of the circumstances dictate that every second is critical. During live operations and crimes in action such as suspect hunts, kidnaps, threats to life (TTL) situations, firearms, or terrorism incidents, indeed whenever there are collapsing time frames, high-pressure decision making needs to be swift, dynamic, fluid, and readily adaptable to fast-moving and developing circumstances (see also Chapter 12 on suspect management).

3.2.1.1 **Using instinct**

Fast-time decisions are often influenced by intuitive (instinctive) thoughts and experiences. Even though this involves risk, such instincts are hard to ignore and will, in many situations, be both important and reliable. One such instinctive principle, known as *Just Doesn't Look Right* (aka JDLR), relies heavily upon such intuition. It means that when something usually looks wrong it *is* wrong, but we don't always immediately know or understand why. Initial responders can and do draw upon this gut feeling when making important, instinctive spontaneous decisions, and judgements.

> In certain types of investigations such as those where there is a lack of information available, detectives will rely more heavily upon their experience and knowledge, thereby engaging in more intuitive decision making

---

[2] D Kahneman, *Thinking Fast and Slow* (Penguin, 2012).

processes ... the ability to draw inferences and make decisions from basic information during the crucial 'golden hour' is an extremely important skill for detectives to develop.[3]

Reliable instincts usually originate from good training, knowledge, and experience. Such intuition is generally important and is not to be ignored *under the right circumstances*. However, such intuitions or gut feelings should first of all help investigators stop, think, and develop new questions and *not* make them jump to conclusions based on limited or uncertain information. This is sometimes harder than it sounds. Moreover, investigators need to be mindful that previous experience and reliance upon instincts can sometimes unconsciously introduce an unwanted and unhelpful element of bias or prejudice, leading to an incorrect comparison or interpretation.

Jumping to the wrong conclusions and instantly trusting instinct is illustrated in the famous Müller-Lyer illusion. These horizontal lines are identical in length, but intuitively most people would say line (a) is longer than line (b).

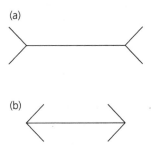

3.2.2 Selective attention

A psychological concept termed 'selective attention' is central to human reasoning because we neither have the mental capacity nor need to take in every small detail. It refers to a mental process whereby a single feature or message is selected and focused on to the detriment of other information available simultaneously. This has been academically proven and referred to in many scientific tests and theories (one of the most famous being 'The invisible gorilla')[4] and is a distraction method use by illusionists and magicians. In short, if you focus too much on one feature you will inevitably lose sight of another.

It is a concept worth considering when making or reviewing early assessments of decisions made on an 'interpretation' of what was thought to have been presented, eg at crime scenes or incidents. The golden rule for astute investigators (when not time critical) is to remain professionally sceptical and

---

[3] M Wright, *Detective Intuition: The Role of Homicide Schemas* (University of Liverpool, 2008).

[4] Selective attention is defined in <http://www.dictionary.reference.com> and 'The invisible gorilla' test can be retrieved from a number of internet sources such as <http://www.theinvisiblegorilla.com/gorilla_experiment.html>.

curious, always looking for the bigger, broader, or richer picture by considering if any potential central feature might have gone unnoticed in the first interpretation.

3.2.3 Heuristics and biases

The theory of 'heuristics' refers to the use of experience-based knowledge (or 'working rules') for problem solving, particularly in automated, fast-time, and initial-response situations. This happens when previous knowledge or experience is used to compare scenarios and draw similar conclusions from perceived commonalities (ie 'it looks like something I've dealt with or seen before, therefore that is what it must be' or 'it looks like a duck therefore it is a duck').

This is crucial and will, in the majority of cases, help establish the right hypotheses early on and identify crucial evidence. In-depth knowledge of typical crimes, motives and their indicators is a core competence for any SIO, but experience-based intuition is never 100 per cent reliable. It can be unduly influenced by unconscious personal biases or prejudice, such as preconceptions about people, situations, locations, or stereotypes (eg what a duck *should* look like), or become affected by lack of information or incorrect recall of the knowledge or experience being relied upon. Unconsciously, the human mind can take shortcuts unless greater control of thoughts is consciously applied. One example of a heuristic bias is in a sexual abuse investigation, where an officer who has previously dealt with a false allegation assigns a greater probability to the next allegation he/she deals with as also being fabricated.

Such failings have a knock-on effect and can adversely impact other important lines of enquiry. For example, when a preferred hypothesis based on intuition becomes a fixation at the expense of other theories and leads to selective evidence gathering and unconscious biased interpretation of material supportive of the preferred choice at the expense of exploring alternatives. This is commonly known as 'verification' or 'confirmation' bias, the most dangerous and deceiving cognitive bias identified through widespread research on underlying causes for errors of justice.[5]

> Instinct can be either your best friend or worst enemy. This is the 'gut instinct' paradox and needs to be managed carefully and kept under control. Instinctiveness will probably come before rational thought processes kick in. The skill is in getting them to work together. Your instinct is offering up a suggestion not a command and you have a choice to accept or reject it.[6]

---

[5] K Ask and IA Fahsing Investigative decision-making. In A Griffiths and R Milne (eds) *The Psychology of Criminal Investigation—From Theory to Practice* (Routledge, 2018).
[6] S Peters *The Chimp Paradox* (Vermillon, 2012).

> **KEY POINT**
>
> Instinct, confirmation bias, and selective attention are forces that need to be kept under control. Good decision making is evidence based and relies upon a professional, methodological, sceptical, and curious approach to every circumstance.

3.2.4 Slow-time decision making

Some respected SIOs are renowned for their style of applying a slower, more deliberate, and controlled approach to decision making. This allows for greater depth, structure, and order by calming things down and creating an element of what is often described as 'slow time', or 'putting a foot on the ball'.

This technique provides a distinct advantage when making tough decisions as it enables sufficient information to be gathered and an opportunity to think things through methodically and consider a greater number of plausible alternatives. Taking a step back facilitates greater awareness to gain a wider perspective and reduce negative effects from unconscious selective attention (mentioned earlier). Even in high-pressure situations it can be more advantageous to remain cool, calm, and detached. Frantic rushing around creates tunnel vision and an impression of being under stress or in panic.

3.2.5 Situational awareness

Situational awareness is knowing what is going on all around a given scene and is a term often used by the emergency services (eg fire and rescue) and the military and aviation, not just in law enforcement.

The concept is linked to perceptions of time and environments (temporal and spatial elements) in contexts that are critical and influential in complex and dynamic decision making. In investigations, situational awareness (SA) refers to being aware of what is or was happening in and around the vicinity of an event or incident in order to make sense of relevant details about specific times, locations, events, and activities.

Having a sense of situational awareness and using good observational skills provides an innate feel for situations and environments. Noticing what's happening and picking up valuable available information from all around you helps prevent errors in decision making and reduces closed-mind syndrome. This is particularly important when there is a high level of information flow, and decisions rely heavily upon the recognition of SA factors.

There are a number of definitions available for SA, including:

- 'The perception of elements in the environment within a volume of time and space, the comprehension of their meaning, and the projection of their status in the near future.'[7]

---

[7] MR Ensley, 'Toward a theory of situation awareness in dynamic systems' (1995) 37(1) *Human Factors*, 32–64.

- 'Knowing what is going on so you can work out what to do.'[8]
- 'Accessibility of a comprehensive and coherent situation representation which is continuously being updated in accordance with the results of recurrent situation assessments.'[9]
- 'Keeping track of what is going on around you in a complex, dynamic environment.'[10]

SA indicates how decision making and problem solving are more than one dimensional activities; one needs to observe and appreciate what is happening in three dimensions (3D), not just two. Key decisions often have to take into account information and situational factors within complex circumstances that might have to be quickly assimilated, interpreted, and factored into deliberations. Being dynamically aware of and managing other events that are occurring and changing information (aka multitasking) is the best option.

KEY POINT

SIOs can gain much richer information to aid decision making if they take a few steps back before making any decisions in order to build a more comprehensive picture about a given situation. This is referred to as taking a 3D or 'helicopter view' in order to obtain a much wider and more advantageous perspective.

3.3 **Investigative Mindset**

The 'investigative mindset'[11] is the theory of keeping an open mind and remaining receptive to alternative suggestions, looking for other plausible

---

[8] EC Adam, 'Fighter cockpits of the future' (1993) Proceedings of 12th IEEE/AIAA Digital Avionics Systems Conference (DASC), 318–23.

[9] NB Sarter and DD Woods 'Situation awareness: A critical but ill-defined phenomenon' (1991) 1 *International Journal of Aviation Psychology*, 45–57.

[10] N Moray, *Robotics, Control and Society* (CRC Press, 2005), 4.

[11] ACPO, *Practice Advice on Core Investigative Doctrine*, 2nd edn (NPIA, 2012).

alternatives and explanations to a given set of circumstances. It promotes thoroughness and greater judgement in order to avoid jumping to premature conclusions. An investigative mindset is achieved by acknowledging the risks associated with intuitive judgements and applying a more conscious, balanced, objective, and methodical approach to decision making. It has become an important doctrine to be applied and is championed by more calculated investigators.

For this rule to be applied properly, careful use of language and terminology need to be followed. Terms such as 'this could be' or 'possibly' will show that the SIO is being truly open minded to different theories and is not shackled to what might turn out to be the wrong conclusion or bad choices. With this in mind, an SIO is right to change their minds when faced with better and more compelling information. This rule neatly segues into the next: the ABC.

KEY POINTS

1. To comply with the rule of the investigative mindset, the terms 'possibly' and 'could' are watchwords for use in every investigation and at every crime scene.
2. There is no harm in changing your mind when faced with a more compelling and sounder alternative (and to note the rationale).

3.4 'ABC' Rule

Decision making relies upon accurate detail therefore all information must be carefully scrutinised, reviewed, and assessed. This necessitates remaining initially sceptical and testing the accuracy, reliability, and relevance of any material relied upon. A simple rule to be applied is the 'ABC' principle:[12]

A—Assume nothing
B—Believe nothing
C—Challenge/check everything

Nothing should be taken for granted nor accepted at 'face value'. It can prove fatal to assume things are what they seem. SIOs must remain objective and try to seek corroboration, and should re-check, review, and confirm facts and information. Applying professional scepticism (not cynicism, something entirely different and extremely unprofessional) is the right approach to take and helps avoid placing too much initial reliance on anything presented. This supports an investigative mindset approach via impartial fact finding.

---

[12] Cited in ACPO, *Practice Advice on Core Investigative Doctrine*, 2nd edn (NPIA, 2012), 88.

3.5 **Problem Solving**

All decisions involve an element of problem solving and applying sequential logical processes to individual circumstances. Certain techniques can simplify these processes by incorporating a methodical collection and analysis of information to produce alternative solutions and better outcomes.

There are several varieties of problem-solving models and most contain similar structures. These comprise simple step-by-step processes[13] involving identifying the problem, gathering information, weighing up the pros and cons of alternative options, and selecting the most compelling.

Decision-making processes can be embedded within the framework of policy log entries. This is like explaining how an arithmetic problem has been solved, showing the 'working out' to illustrate how the answer was calculated. A similar audit trail of the various components of decision making will indicate how and why the chosen option was selected and is used as a means of explaining to others, such as at handover or review, or to other interested third parties (and act as a personal aide memoire).

3.5.1 **SWOT analysis**

Problem solving involves producing, considering, and choosing from various options, with a final decision relating to a plan in the short, medium, or long term. Alternative options can be graded as part of a contingency, eg plan A or plan B (used if plan A fails).

A method of analysing the pros and cons (advantages and disadvantages) of options is to examine their strengths, weaknesses, opportunities, and threats (SWOT analysis). For example, looking at what threats there are (such as time, resources, and cost implications) weighed against what opportunities the option can provide (eg maximise evidence-gathering opportunities).

3.5.2 **'Do nothing', 'defer', or 'monitor'**

Decisions sometimes must determine whether any action is necessary. For example, if disadvantages may outweigh the advantages. There may be an option to record the decision as one of 'do nothing' (ie take no further action), 'defer' (put off until later), or 'monitor' (eg wait and see). In an arrest situation, for example, it may be operationally beneficial to delay an arrest while further evidence is gathered (covertly or otherwise). This may provide an option to 'defer' an arrest until such time as it becomes feasible or more operationally beneficial—a decision that must be monitored and kept under review.

Such a decision is a decision itself and should be recorded, with reasons about why it has been made. In critical circumstances where other offences may be committed and are preventable, an inaction (do nothing) decision has to be defensible. The SIO will need to ensure any risk of further danger to victims or the public can

---

[13] Also cited in J Adair, *The Best of Adair on Leadership and Management* (Thorogood, 2008).

be adequately controlled and managed. An example of this is where there is known information about a likely suspect that is not acted upon, then there would have to be valid reasons recorded as to why the 'do nothing' or 'defer' option was chosen.

KEY POINT

A decision to 'do nothing' or 'defer' must be justifiable. Not making a decision is a decision itself which should be made for the right reasons, properly recorded, and communicated clearly where necessary to enquiry teams in some cases, victims, their families, the media, public enquiries, etc.

3.6 Risk Management

Managing risk has to remain dynamic and the following saying is worth bearing in mind: *'if it is predictable it is preventable'*. Key decisions are rarely made where risks don't form part of the considerations, particularly if there is uncertainty about the likelihood and impact of any outcomes. Some organisations have gone to the trouble of employing specially trained individuals to assist with identifying and managing security risks, often referred to as Operational Security Officers (or OPSY).

Operational and investigation work is a risk-oriented business. This is catered for in the National Decision Model (NDM) when weighing up the pros and cons (benefits and harms) of each option. The terms 'threat, harm, and risk' (**THR**) have become part of law enforcement agency (LEA) discourse and they feature at stage 2 of the NDM: *'assess threat and risk and develop a working strategy'* (see Appendix A).

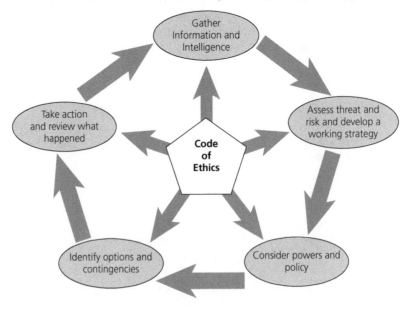

National Decision Model
© College of Policing 2019

For the THR principle, decisions are assessed based upon the degree of **Threat (T)** multiplied by the amount of likely **Harm (H)** to produce an assessment of **Risk (R)**. This process is not intended to be bureaucratic 'back covering' nor aid the creation of a total 'risk-free' or 'risk-averse' working environment. It does, however, help in the identification and calculation of a sensible and reasonable management grading to produce important risk values in order to minimise, monitor, and control (ie manage) the probability and impact of unwanted outcomes. Simultaneously, it can also supply benefits to the investigation. The formula is very simple:

$$\text{Threat} \times \text{Harm} = \text{Risk} \dots (T \times H = R)$$

3.6.1 Threat and harm identification

As an example, a threat could mean a communicated or perceived intent or potential to cause harm, loss, or damage to someone, or something whereas harm could mean the likely outcome of doing, causing, or inflicting the threat, eg injury or damage whether it be physical, psychological or financial. The risk would then refer to the likelihood of the event occurring. This process depends on an accurate defining of the risk and threat associated to the activity. It requires accurate information or advice on which to base a decision, and it is advisable to reference any source information or material relied upon for any later review or scrutiny of the final decision that is made (ensuring an accurate copy is kept).

Assistance in identifying threat and harm values can come from a range of sources:

- Evidence from witnesses and victims.
- Advice from specialists, analysts, experts, and advisors.
- Accurate and comprehensive source information or intelligence.
- Information from third party organisations and environmental or open source scanning.
- Monitoring and review processes (internal and external).
- Individual awareness, knowledge, and training.
- Organisational learning and policy.
- Legal and ethical frameworks.
- Published doctrines, policy, and guidance.
- Public enquiries and case studies (eg IOPC findings).
- Historical information and published knowledge/lessons learnt.
- Assessment of impact on those individuals or organisations who or that might be affected by likely harm, eg if they are vulnerable due to their situation or circumstances and/or unable to adequately protect themselves

Examples:

- Identifying threats to safety and reducing risk of harm to Family Liaison Officers (FLOs) in deploying amongst a hostile family/community or where the suspect is believed residing.

- Determining the circumstances of child victims to assess risk of vulnerability.
- Assessing the circumstantial information in a high-risk missing person report to identify scale of risk from threats and harms to which they might succumb or be exposed.
- Timing the arrest of a suspect by assessing possible risk of threats and likely harms by delaying to other potential victims, the public or officers.
- Reviewing bulk digital data and applying prioritisation methods to assist in identifying threat from high-risk offenders and reducing harm to vulnerable victims.

3.6.2 Risk assessment scoring matrix

The matrix in Table 3.1 shows how the top row (harm/impact) is multiplied by the left-hand column (threat/probability) to produce a risk score. This draws on the principle that the greatest risk is assessed when the harm-versus-threat score is high. Risks that score as being low are less worthy of concern.

For example, if there is a high threat level/probability of harm when planning to arrest a suspect because it is assessed strong resistance and physical violence might be used (5), and if this occurs then the harm/impact to arresting officers could be very serious (4), the risk assessment score can be calculated as being 20 (ie T × H or 5 × 4 = R 20). This figure can be reduced

Table 3.1 Risk-scoring matrix

IMPACT → PROBABILITY ↓	CATASTROPHIC (5)	VERY SERIOUS (4)	SERIOUS (3)	MODERATE (2)	MINIMAL (1)
HIGHLY PROBABLE (5)	High (25)	High (20)	High (15)	Moderate (10)	Low (5)
PROBABLE (4)	High (20)	High (16)	High (12)	Moderate (8)	Low (4)
POSSIBLE (3)	High (15)	High (12)	Moderate (9)	Moderate (6)	Low (3)
UNLIKELY (2)	Moderate (10)	Moderate (8)	Moderate (6)	Low (4)	Low (2)
VERY UNLIKELY (1)	Low (5)	Low (4)	Low (3)	Low (2)	Negligible (1)

and mitigated however by introducing effective control measures, such as deploying a team of specially trained and equipped officers to conduct the arrest using protective equipment and staging the operation in the early hours of the morning to introduce an element of surprise. The score can then be recalculated because it is now less likely (2) the arrest will be successfully physically resisted or that officers will be injured in the process, producing a more acceptable risk score of 8 (ie 2 × 4).

The SIO needs to be assured that operational risk assessments are not only being properly completed by suitably trained and experienced officers but also that assessments are accurate, adequate, and sufficient. There must be recognition of individual awareness amongst teams of the importance of risk management and effective control measures. Adherence to correct policies, sufficient training and resources, and monitoring compliance with risk mitigation plans by intrusive checking or dip sampling are key to effective risk management.

3.6.3 Management options

Once a risk is identified and scored, a control strategy can be considered. In one model there are four options to choose from represented by the acronym RARA:

R—Remove
A—Avoid
R—Reduce
A—Accept

Changing tactics while achieving the same objectives will afford a means of removing, avoiding, or reducing risks. Alternatively, the risks may be deemed so negligible they can be accepted.

Organisational risk factors must also be taken into account when deciding how to manage risk such as the availability of finance and resources, competing demands, legal requirements, internal policies and processes, reputational damage plus any undue influence or directives from senior management. Other influences can include time constraints or external factors such as official reviews or public expectations, other agency involvement, or high levels of likely threat or reputational harm.

A carefully scripted record of risk management decisions with accompanying rationale is recommended for whenever they may have to be explained or defended. This is one reason why an SIO must maintain a comprehensive policy log of all their key decisions (covered in Chapter 4).

Risk Management = Checklist

- Use the T × H = R and RARA models to identify and manage risk.

- Risk management forms part of the NDM cycle (see below) and should be recorded in a policy log.

- Risks are usually fluid and require dynamic monitoring and review.

- Trained individuals such as OPSYs can assist in identifying and managing security risks.

- Risk assessments depend on a number of factors including accurate source information. This should be kept as reference material for later scrutiny.

- The rule to remember is: If it is predictable, it is preventable.

3.7 National Decision Model

The National Decision Model (NDM) was introduced to aid, structure, and record consistent decision making. It offers the gift of a standard template that can be used in most areas of law enforcement and comes with the full backing of the UK College of Policing and the National Police Chiefs' Council (NPCC). It would almost certainly be referenced when testing compliance by review processes and mechanisms should an important decision come under close scrutiny.

It is highly recommended that this model is used day in and day out in order to structure decision making and policy log entries. The model needs to be committed to memory and/or placed in a prominent position in amongst the SIO's casebook/policy log and as part of their toolkit (see section 1.6). Having the model available on a laminated card is one suggestion, and it are also printed within most hardcopy policy logs.

The College of Policing (via Authorised Professional Practice (APP))[14] decrees that the NDM is suitable for:

- spontaneous incidents or planned operations.
- individuals or teams of people.
- operational and non-operational situations.
- structuring a rationale to support a decision maker.
- reviewing decisions and actions and promoting learning.

Understanding the rudiments of the NDM helps develop an appreciation of the right components that make up effective decision making. The NDM's six key elements including the central Code of Ethics (see section 2.9.1) are shown below and for ease of reference at Appendix A.

---

[14] See <https://www.app.college.police.uk/app-content/national-decision-model/>.

KEY POINT

The NDM pentagon diagram in Appendix A is a visual aid that should be kept alongside or near to the SIO's Policy Log and as part of the SIO's toolkit (see section 1.6).

National Decision Model

Stage 1: INFORMATION: Gather Information and Intelligence

During this stage, the decision maker defines the situation (ie defines what is happening or has happened) and clarifies matters relating to any initial information and intelligence.

• What is happening/has happened?
• What do I know/not know?
• What further information do I need to know?

Stage 2: ASSESSMENT: Assess Threat and Risk and Develop a Working Strategy (THR—Threat/Harm and Risk; see section 3.6)

This stage involves assessing the situation, including any specific threat, the risk of harm, and the potential for risk or benefits.

• Do I need to act immediately?
• Do I need more information?
• What could go wrong/go well?
• What is causing the situation?
• How probable is the risk of harm?
• How serious would it be?
• Is the level of risk acceptable?
• Is this a situation for an LEA to deal with alone?
• Am I the appropriate person to deal with it?
• What am I trying to achieve?
• Will my action resolve the situation?

Stage 3: POWERS AND POLICY: Consider Policy and Powers

This stage involves considering what powers, policies, and legislation might be applicable in this particular situation.

• Legal powers required.
• National guidance covering the type of situation.
• Local/organisational policies or guidelines.
• Applicable legislation.
• Research available.

Note: As long as there is a good rationale for doing so, it may be reasonable to act outside policy.

Stage 4: OPTIONS: Identify Options and Contingencies

This stage involves considering the different ways to make a particular decision (or resolve a situation) with the least risk of harm.

Decision maker should consider:

- Options available.
- Immediacy of the threat.
- Limits of information.
- Time available.
- Available resources and support.
- Knowledge, experience, and skills.
- Impact of potential action on situation and the public.

Contingencies

- What to do if things do not happen as anticipated.

Stage 5: ACTION and REVIEW: Take Action and Review What Happened

This stage requires decision makers to make and implement appropriate decisions. It also requires decision makers, once an incident is over, to review what happened.

Action
Respond

- Implement the option selected.
- Decide who else needs informing.

Record

- Record actions taken and rationale in a policy log.

Monitor

- What happened as a result of the decision?
- Was it what was wanted or expected?

  If the incident is continuing, repeat the process again if necessary.

Review

If the incident is over, review decisions using the NDM.

- What lessons can be taken from how things turned out?
- What might be done differently next time?

3.8 The '5WH' Principle

Effective problem solving and decision making rely heavily upon accurate information and material. A decision is only a decision if there are choices, and good information generates the right choices. Comprehensive questions help generate the necessary information and provide alternatives that naturally fall out of the process.

The 5WH (5 × W + H) principle is a highly effective tool for gathering information. It helps stimulate thought processes and meets the requirements of stage 1 of the NDM. The 5WH method stands for six strong, leading, interrogative pronouns and critical questions (that can be used in any order):

Six critical questions

Who   Who is/are/was the target (eg victim/(s)offender(s)/witnesses)?

What   What has happened/what do we know so far?

Where Where did it happen?

When   When did it happen?

Why   Why did it happen?

How   How did it happen?

The primary 'Wh' usually prompts supplementary questions to produce a quick, simple, easy-to-apply model that can be adapted to fit most circumstances. The following table provides an example (Table 3.2).

The list of 5WH information can be developed into a useful table/matrix to help identify information gaps by setting out all the relevant details in a logical sequence and will be easier to visually display and understand. The table can

Table 3.2 Primary and supplementary 5WH questions

Primary question	Supplementary questions
Who is the victim?	What are their personal details?
	How many victims are there?
	What status have they been given (victim or complainant)?
	How is their support/welfare being managed?
	What are they saying happened?
	Why were they targeted?
	Why were they vulnerable?
	How were they selected?
	Were they a repeat victim?
	What risks are there of repeat victimisation?
	What 'victimology' information is available?
	Who and where are their family, relatives, and close friends?
	What did the victim do post offence?
	Who else has the victim spoken to post offence?
	What protection measures are required?
What happened?	What crime has been committed/not committed?
	What is currently known?
	What are the information gaps?
	What are the likely hypotheses?
	What type/category of crime has occurred?
	What has been done to verify information?
	What other incidents may be linked?
	What are risks other similar incidents might occur
	What action has been taken at the crime scene?

(continued)

Table 3.2 Continued

Primary question	Supplementary questions
Where did the crime take place?	What is being done to identify, secure, and protect (ISP)?
	Where is the crime scene and how many scenes are there?
	How have the crime scenes been sequentially numbered?
	Who is at the scene?
	What is at the scene?
	Who has control of the scene?
	What has been done to avoid cross-contamination?
	Who is managing the crime scene log?
	What is known about the surrounding location?
	Why was the location chosen?
	Was it a repeat location?
	What does geography tell us?
	How was the location chosen?
	Why was the victim or offender at the scene?
	How did offenders get to/from the crime scene?
	What type of property has been targeted?
	What is the link between location, victim, and offender?
	What/who else is in the locality that could be linked to the scene, victim or offender?
What searches have taken place?	What type of searches and where?
	Who by and how?
	Who was/is in charge of them?
	How long did they take?
	What equipment or resources were used?
	What has been found? Where is/are it/they now?
	What records of searches have been made?
	What H2H enquiries have been conducted?
	What CCTV has been recovered or is available?
	What evidential material has been recovered? What has been done with it?
When did the offence take place?	What is significant about the time and date?
	Why has the crime been committed at this time?
	Was this a core operating time?
	How have the time and date been confirmed?
	What else was taking place simultaneously?
	What are the frequency and intervals between linked offences?
	Has there been an increase in these types of offences?
When was the crime discovered?	Who discovered it, why, and how?
	Who reported it, why, when, where, how, and to whom?
	What do we know about the person reporting the crime?
	What actions did the person reporting the crime take?

Table 3.2 Continued

Primary question	Supplementary questions
How was the crime reported?	When was the crime reported?
	Where was the crime reported?
	Why was the crime reported?
	What was said by those reporting?
What is the modus operandi?	What weapon, tools, equipment, or methods were used?
	What trace or forensic evidence might have been left?
	What transport might have been required/used?
	What is unique about the crime method?
	What are the associated traits and methods?
	What knowledge/skills were required by the offender?
	What specific methods have been used to evade capture?
Who are the witnesses?	How many witnesses are there?
	What are there details?
	Where are they now?
	What has been done with them?
	Who is managing them?
	Who has interviewed them; if so how?
	What is the witness' reliability, credibility, or vulnerability?
	Why and how did they witness the crime?
	What is the relationship between victim, offender, and witness?
	What is their status (significant, vulnerable, or intimidated)?
	Who else have they spoken to about what they know?
	What is their relationship to the location?
Who is (are) the offender(s)?	How many offenders were involved?
	Who are the key suspects?
	Why have they been deemed suspects?
	What efforts have been made to trace/arrest them?
	For what have they been arrested?
	How have they been managed?
	What is known about the offender(s)?
	What does their behaviour tell us about them?
	What is the description of the offender(s)?
	How were/can the offenders be identified?
	What intelligence is suggesting possible offenders?
	Who has previously carried out this type of offence?
	Where could the offender(s) be now?
What are the main lines of enquiry?	What fast-track actions are required?
	What other actions have been allocated?
	What is the outcome of any enquiries completed?
	Who has conducted them?
	Where and how have the results been recorded?
	What are the supporting investigative strategies?
	What are the likely solvability factors?

(continued)

Table 3.2 Continued

Primary question	Supplementary questions
Why was the crime committed?	What was the motive? How was it committed—spontaneous or pre-planned? Was there any involvement of alcohol/drugs/OCG? Was it due to jealousy, revenge, financial gain? Was it part of a series? Was it sexually or racially motivated?
What specialist resources are required?	What/who are they? What and whose authority are required? How can they be obtained? How much will they cost? Who will brief and manage them? What is required of them? Where and whom should they report to?
What forensic, CCTV, or digital evidence is available?	What type of evidence is available? What types of forensic examination are required? How has any forensic material been preserved? What arrangements have been made to examine it? Who has been asked to examine it? Who is the Crime Scene Investigator /Manager? What initial trawl for CCTV has been conducted? What type of digital forensic examination might required?
What exhibits are there?	What exhibits have been recovered? What has been done with them? Where are they stored? How have they been processed (eg labelled and packaged)? Who is in charge of all exhibits? What needs to be fast-tracked?

be populated as the enquiry progresses and used as a source of reference for the basis of applying the problem-solving model and any associated decision making. The matrix can be cross-referenced to decisions as and when they are made and can serve to illustrate just what is/was known or not known at the time any particular decision is/was made—an important point for justifying why a particular course of action was taken (or not taken).

The matrix can be populated by adding extra columns, for example to cover what is known, unknown, and possible sources of where it can be found (see Table 3.3). This is not just for an SIO or analyst to complete but is a shared responsibility amongst the team during a continuous process of raising and answering questions and filling the gaps with answers, particularly at meetings and (de)briefings.

Once created, the matrix should be treated as a 'living document' that can be amended or extended as the enquiry progresses. An analyst can assist in helping to

Table 3.3 Homicide example—displaying information and identifying gaps

5WH	KNOWN	UNKNOWN	POSSIBLE SOURCE
Who was killed?	31-year-old lone white female (named victim) Single with child from previous relationship. Well known/liked in locality. Resided with parents. Possibly had/having affairs with married men. Carried two smartphones. Worked at local convenience store.	Detailed victimology. Any previous attacks? Was she intended victim? Other attacks likely? Details of previous relationships.	Family/friends, colleagues, local community, intelligence, open source data, social media/lifestyle analysis, financial status, house/work search. Crime recording. Comparative case analysis (SCAS database) and crime pattern analysis. Intelligence checks. Risk analysis for further victims.
Who is/are the likely suspect(s)?	Victim in stormy relationship with boyfriend—possible suspect? Recent dispute at work with two unknown menacing-looking male customers.	Having other affairs? Full details of incident, persons involved, and action taken. CCTV? Witnesses? Descriptions/identities? Linked incidents/motive?	Identify and declare suspect(s) and set TIE categories/ parameters Victimology. Subject profile(s). T/I work colleagues. Comms data/social media analysis. Intelligence assessment.
Who witnessed?	Male walking dog found victim's body at 6.30 a.m.	Identify other significant witnesses. Confirm time of alleged finding.	Media appeals and H2H enquiries. Priority T/I actions.
What happened?	Battered and strangled semi-naked body found in woodland area near to home address. Trousers and underwear pulled down around ankles. Contents of handbag emptied onto ground. Bra wrapped around neck as improvised ligature.	Anything stolen? Defensive marks on body? Does manner of death give indication as to age, sex, physical capability of offender? Other weapons present/missing? Brought to scene by the offender, victim, or improvised?	Conduct inventory of personal belongings. Re-examine body for further marks/bruises. Check clothing for damage, rips, and tears. Consult NCA National Injuries Database. Check origin of ligature and method of strangulation. Knot expertise?

(continued)

Table 3.3 Continued

5WH	KNOWN	UNKNOWN	POSSIBLE SOURCE
What occurred prior to murder?	Victim in public house with friends. Then spent time alone with boyfriend. Walked home alone, having left boyfriend's flat after argument.	Sequence of events and timeline for movements of victim and boyfriend. Est. any forensic evidence in boyfriend's flat (treat as possible crime scene) Did victim have any significant arguments, contacts, messages or other activities in time prior to last confirmed sighting? Was she being stalked?	Crime scene examination of flat. Comms. Data/social media analysis. TIE all persons in vicinity of scene and at public house (time parameters?). Search for CCTV in area. Check boyfriend's account and produce timeline of movements
		Did she arrange to meet someone by prior arrangement?	Analysis of witness statements. Mobile phone/social media analysis H2H enquiries, CCTV
What other significant events took place?	Raised voices heard—couple possibly arguing at approx. 1.15 a.m.	Establish if linked to murder incident.	HP action—TI/TST witness(es). Consider media appeal and conduct H2H enquiries in vicinity. Check if any other relevant linked incidents or reports
When did it happen?	Bet. 12.30 a.m. and 6.30 a.m. Sat. (date).	More precise time of death.	Witnesses, 'back record conversion' of alcohol/blood levels, pathologist, entomologist. Gastroenterology (stomach contents exam), CCTV, assessment of physical evidence in conjunction with other events—eg weather—victim's clothing on ground and clothing wet after the rainfall. Is ground under clothing wet—yes/no? What time did rain start/end?

Where did it happen?	(named location)	Attack occurred there or elsewhere or is it a deposition site? Risk analysis for further attacks. How did victim/offender get to location? Prior local knowledge required? Could they have been there for some other purpose? Does victim use location to meet boyfriends for liaisons?	Full scene interpretation. Forensic analysis of body plus palynological survey. Crime pattern analysis. Social and demographic information. Geographic profiling. Local intelligence re regular users/visitors. Victimology. Covert obs. at site.
Why did it happen?		Motive. Victim knew offender? Stranger/sexual attack? Robbery/theft? Anger/jealousy? Stalker?	Check mobile traffic and social media from/to victim. Forensic and pathological interpretation of scene. Use of behavioural profiler. Interpretation of injuries. Scene assessment.
Cause and manner of death.	Post-mortem cause of death—asphyxiation by ligature placed around neck. Blunt trauma to face and head, possible footwear mark on side of face. No trace of recent sexual activity or assault	Re-examine to see bruising/marks visible? Full medical history of victim and antecedents. Toxicology results for alcohol levels and drug traces.	Forensic pathologist. Victim's GP and hospital records. Forensic results. Second post-mortem, National Injuries Database (NID) expertise. Footwear analysis of any suspect and TIEs.
Why that location?		On or near victim's route home? Was victim forced to go there or went voluntarily? Scene interpretation. Has victim/offender visited previously? Location linked to suspect or any other TIE subject?	Victim- and suspectology. Crime pattern analysis (CPA). Subject profile analysis. Full forensic exam of scene. Possible media appeal with reconstruction. High-profile enquiries in location. Check precursor incidents.
How offender arrived at/left scene?		Is there easy escape route? On foot, vehicle, local transport, bus, train, taxi? Any footwear, vehicle, or unattributed marks found at the scene?	Scene examination. Enquiries with local transport companies. Media appeals. CCTV and passive data trawl (automatic number plate recognition (ANPR)?). Intelligence checks on suspect/TIEs. Stolen and abandoned vehicles check. Footwear checks included in TIE process.

analyse, identify, and fill gaps using standard analytical techniques. This process will generate key information and be an aid to decision making during the investigation.

Checklist—source material

Source material relied upon must remain under review with frequent checks to confirm validity, accuracy, and relevance. Investigative decision-making processes, strategies, and main lines of enquiry (MLOE) that rely upon this process need to be constantly scrutinised and evaluated to determine:

1. Accuracy of information and detail.

2. Conflicting or contradicting material.

3. Emerging patterns or (in)consistencies.

4. Significance of material, eg if it supports a particular hypothesis.

5. If sufficient material/evidence to review the status of any subject.

6. Whether any evidence would be admissible in judicial proceedings.

7. Whether 'relevant' under the Criminal Proceedings and Investigations Act 1996 (CPIA) requirements.

It is worth noting that the 5WH method can be used when (de)briefing or being briefed about any incident or circumstances. This will provide a better structure for delivering and receiving information rather than at random or in disjointed fashion. Additional detail can be captured by adding further questions on topics that have not been covered.

3.8.1 'Who?'

Identifying and managing victims, suspects, and witnesses is dealt with in other chapters.

3.8.2 'What?'

A primary 5WH question is 'what happened?' or 'what are we dealing with?' One objective of the initial response and assessment is to determine accurately what happened and ascertain the precise nature and type of incident. Initial responders (including Investigating Officers (IO)/SIOs) *must* exercise extreme caution, remain sceptical, and keep an open mind by making good use of the investigative mindset (mentioned earlier in section 3.3), by obtaining as much information from the scene and any witnesses/sources of intelligence as possible (using the 5WH model). Care should be taken to question and clarify all facts presented (applying ABC principle), and record and note everything. Asking 'what if?' is a useful means of stretching the imagination to consider alternative explanations.

3.8.2.1 Using hypotheses

The *Oxford Dictionary of English*[15] defines a hypothesis as 'a supposition or proposed explanation made on the basis of limited evidence as a starting point for further investigation'. In simple terms, this means 'playing the percentages' by coming up with plausible explanations or theories about what happened that are eliminated one by one until the most likely remains.

The process of generating and building hypotheses is a well renowned technique and means of populating stage 4 of the NDM (identifying options). Well-developed hypotheses are useful for speculating when there isn't much information to go on; and good hypotheses need to make full use of all available information and material.

Dr Ivar Fahsing (2016) described a useful six-stage hypothesis testing process that can be repeated in all investigations from the first call until the closing of the case. Based on the work of Dean (2000), Fahsing named it the 'Investigative Cycle', and its six stages in the wheel are known as 'The 6 × Cs'.

The 6 × Cs of the Investigative Cycle

1. *Collect*—all relevant available information.
2. *Check*—if the information is relevant, accurate, and reliable.
3. *Connect*—does information from other or different sources match, or not?
4. *Construct*—what possible testable criminal or non-criminal explanations (hypotheses) does this information allow for?
5. *Consider*—which information needs to be prioritised that will most effectively test the competing hypotheses?
6. *Consult*—someone who might help in seeing things differently.

The cycle can be repeated to narrow down the scope of any options and play 'devil's advocate'. The effect of using the so-called devil's-advocate approach has proven to be an important strategy to reduce bias in complex decision making.

A number of studies show that the most difficult mental challenge in investigative processes with a high degree of uncertainty is not finding or testing information but asking the right questions; that is, the difficulty in setting up the correct hypothesis. Therefore, there must a continuous process of seeking consultation (C6: Consult) with consideration of any hypotheses that should be tested and maybe downgraded or replaced by more compelling ones (C4: Consider). However, it is important to start with the most obvious theories about *what* might have happened (What). All the 5WH questions in the inner

---

[15] *Oxford English Dictionary*, 3rd edn revised (OUP, 2009).

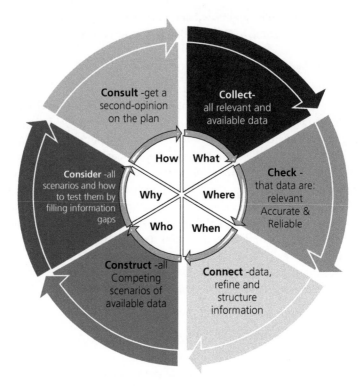

Figure 3.1 The 6×Cs investigative cycle and the 5WH questions

wheel can be spun around to feed into each one of Fahsing's 6 × Cs outer segments as illustrated in Figure 3.1.

Any information relied upon for an hypothesis must be subject to the ABC principle. As an investigation ebbs and flows, more information becomes available and developing facts emerge: therefore, *hypotheses should always remain provisional*. This in turn means that they can be amended at any time and can and should remain under regular and dynamic review. Wherever possible, it is worthwhile making a record of the information that was available at the precise time at which the hypothesis/hypotheses was/were made, which, as stated in the next chapter, is an important part in any recording process linked to decision making.

3.8.3 Billy Occam's Razor

William of Occam (also spelt Ockham) was a fourteenth-century medieval logician, philosopher, and Franciscan friar. Ockham was the village in the English county of Surrey where he was born. The rule of Billy Occam's Razor (sometimes expressed in Latin as *lex parsimoniae*, meaning the law of parsimony, economy, or succinctness) is a principle recommending that, from among competing hypotheses, the theory that makes the fewest complex assumptions is usually the right one. In other words, when there are multiple competing theories, the simplest explanation is usually correct.

Often crime investigations are characterised by missing or ambiguous information, and decision making becomes more complex, which in turn encourages complicated theories and hypotheses. Investigators can get easily drawn into listening to or considering *overly* complex theories and hypotheses, causing errors in decision making and judgement. Applying the principle of Occam's Razor helps mitigate this risk. This rule connects with a principle known as *'abductive reasoning'*, ie the problem-solving process of seeking competing explanations and always first choosing the simplest and most likely.

Checklist—Hypotheses generation

- Hypotheses are useful when there is limited information.
- The investigative mindset principle must be applied —'keeping an open mind'.
- There are usually other/alternative hypotheses to consider.
- Check thoroughly for relevance and reliability of any material relied upon (i.e. wrong information = wrong conclusion).
- Identifying information gaps to any potential hypothesis is part of the process.
- Hypotheses remain provisional and must remain under review.
- Involve the investigation team in hypotheses generation.
- Playing 'devil's advocate' helps prevent bias or prejudice.
- Billy Occam's Razor: states the simplest explanation is usually right.

3.8.4 'Where?'

The location where an offender commits a crime (ie crime scene) and surrounding geography, community, and environment can reveal clues. Questions to ask are: What choices have been made in selecting the location? How have key persons got there (including victims) and exited? What is the proximity of significant features such as residence, housing estates, premises of note, transport hubs, etc? What evidence is there of association between offenders and victims to the location? All these are useful factors to consider. This is why geographical profiling is a handy tool for use in criminal investigation.

Such profiling can assist in determining the most probable location of an offender's anchor point (eg their place of residence or other base, such as their place of work). This is a proven method and forms part of the guidelines in the *Murder Investigation Manual* (MIM).[16] Academic theories can assist in assessing the relevance of geography and its effect on typical human behaviour.

KEY POINT

A location of importance to an investigation might also include a digital location such as an Internet website, forum, in the cloud, or on the dark web.

3.8.4.1 Routine Activity Theory

Routine Activity Theory (RAT), developed by Lawrence Cohen and Marcus Felson,[17] is based on the premise that offenders tend to commit crimes in areas with which they are familiar (ie in their normal routine), and in which they have had the opportunity to commit a crime without someone or something preventing them.

Examining the spatial and geographic characteristics of the surrounding crime scene environment, eg local neighbourhood, usually provides a good 'feel' for the crime under investigation. This is one reason why visiting and assessing a crime scene in person is vitally important (and forms part of 3D situational awareness mentioned earlier). It provides an opportunity to assess the location and determine how and why an offender chose it in consideration of the RAT (and some other similar theories that follow).

It is recommended that a crime scene visit (which may be supplementary to an initial one) is conducted at/on a similar time and day at which the offence occurred. This makes it more relevant and informative. For example, entering a crime scene that would have been dark at the relevant time should be conducted under the same conditions to gain an appreciation of what an offender, victim, or witness might have experienced.

3.8.4.2 Rational Choice Theory

Rational Choice Theory (RCT) suggests that most offenders make a conscious decision to commit crime by weighing up the pros and cons of the rewards against the chances of being caught. This means that a decision to commit a crime is a rational and predictable one.[18] This is relevant because it relates to the geographic differences in opportunities for committing crime, ie some locations providing better opportunities than others, and this may be the reason why a particular location and victim have been chosen over others.

---

[16] ACPO, *Murder Investigation Manual* (NCPE, 2006).

[17] LE Cohen and M Felson, 'Social change and crime rate trends: a routine activity approach' (1979) 44 *American Sociological Review*, 588–608.

[18] See D Cornish and R Clarke, *Understanding Crime Displacement—An Application of Rational Choice Theory*, cited in ACPO, *Practice Advice on Analysis* (NPIA, 2008), 12.

3.8.4.3 Least effort principle

George Zipf (1949) claimed that most human beings seek to minimise the effort required to achieve their aims. Put simply, offenders choose offence locations which are closer to them. This can be affected by barriers, physical (natural and built environment), and mental (individual's subjective perception; see Rossmo, 1999). Routes taken are usually those perceived as the most direct. (ie route one) This principle can be important in understanding the choice of crime location and offender's pre- and post-offence movement and is helpful in identifying the location of an unknown offender's anchor point.

3.8.4.4 Distance decay

Most offender journeys (criminal and non-criminal) are short and close to their anchor point. As distance from an anchor point or awareness space increases, according to this principle their activity decreases. The aforementioned 'least effort principle' can also be a key determinant, together with the RAT (Brantingham and Brantingham, 1981).

3.8.4.5 Problem Analysis Triangle

One further theoretical dimension to the importance of geographic information at crime scenes is the Problem Analysis Triangle (PAT), aka 'Coincidental Elements of a Crime' (see Figure 3.2). This proposes a theory that for a crime to occur, an offender and suitable target must come together in a specific location without an effective deterrent.[19] This association can be considered when making decisions as to who an offender might be in the context of their links to the victim and location.

Figure 3.2 Problem Analysis Triangle

---

[19] Cited in ACPO, *Practice Advice on Analysis* (NPIA, 2008).

> **KEY POINT**
>
> Many benefits can be gained from visiting a crime scene, no matter how much later after the crime was committed, to gain a 3D perspective of the location, social environment, and local community (and situational awareness) and to consider relevant academic theories, eg PAT, least effort principle, etc.

3.8.5 'When?'

The timing (temporal) aspect of an offence links with parameter setting for sightings and movements of victims and potential suspects, elimination procedures and alibis, and viewing times for passive data and CCTV. It also informs how and when reactive and proactive operational tactics might be best mounted (eg observations for an offender returning to commit further crime) and ensuring resources are deployed at the most effective times and locations.

An offender may have calculated the best time to commit a crime, based on the risk or most beneficial opportunity to achieve their objective and evade capture. The time of the offence may also have been chosen deliberately because it is of significance or personal link to the offender, eg it coincides with a particular anniversary or event that is meaningful to them.

It should be determined, based on reliable evidence and sound logic, what is considered to be the most accurate time and date (aka 'relevant time') for when a relevant event (eg the primary offence under investigation) occurred. This is because it influences many aspects of an enquiry from alibi times to parameters for witness, CCTV, and TIE enquiries and trawls etc.

It follows that when recording times and dates, eg from victims, witnesses, or passive date, they must be carefully checked for accuracy. Prosecutions can fail if defendants are able to prove they were elsewhere when the offence is alleged or believed to have been committed Wherever possible, corroboration should be sought using an accurate time source (eg via the UK BT speaking clock '123' service or when a call is made or an internet service is accessed) and any relevant calendar dates reliably confirmed. Prompts can prove useful for those unable to recall times and dates. Popular and reliable times of events can be used, such as TV programmes, sporting or national fixtures, or (inter)national events of note. These may have to be evidentially verified if timing becomes critical in judicial proceedings.

SIOs and their investigators must also ensure their own record of times and dates are accurate. For example, the time and date a decision was made, or when they arrived at a crime scene, or when they were informed of something. The possession and use of an accurate timepiece and calendar are vital accessories to have readily available (see section 1.6).

In some cases, producing a 'timeline' is a valuable technique for piecing together movements, activities, or significant events. This helps identify sequential gaps in time and/or highlight moments and timings that can overlap and become significant to the investigation. One may also be required to establish for how long some types of information has been known or available (eg if questions are asked about the length of time taken to act upon information received). Analysts can be tasked with producing handy charts, using computer software, as visual aids and for use during briefings/presentations or for court purposes.

KEY POINTS

1. Care should be taken when stipulating the relevant time an offence or incident is believed to have occurred. Errors can prove highly detrimental to confidence in the investigation, particularly if they have to be corrected subsequently. These will also confuse the investigation itself.
2. Using a timeline is a useful technique for piecing together movements, activities, or events. It helps identify sequential gaps in time and/or highlight moments and timings that can overlap and become significant.

3.8.6 'Why?'

Establishing what cause, reason, or motive was behind an offender committing a crime is a line of enquiry that may help identify who the offender(s) is(are). It can also assist in linking incidents by matching the modus operandi.

On the other hand, if a motive is wrongly diagnosed and publicly stated, it may unfairly demonise a victim and/or the community with which they are associated. Examples include wrongly identifying the motive as a hate crime or as a result of criminal revenge or associating a victim with a particular activity (eg sex worker) or crime or gang. This could alienate the investigation from important sources of information they need and discourage people from assisting.

Checklist—Types of Whys (motives)

- Gain or greed.
- Revenge.
- Personal cause.
- Jealousy.
- Gang/OCG related (drugs, territory, power, control, criminal enterprise).
- Hate crime (eg racism, homophobia, misogyny).
- Anger or loss of control (rejection, disagreement, argument).

- Self-aggrandisement or hubris (power, importance, vanity).

- Drug/alcohol related.

- Crime concealment or witness/evidential elimination.

- Sexual/violence gratification.

- Thrill/excitement.

- Mental illness/personality disorders (eg psychopath, delusions, narcissism, paranoid, schizoid).

- Political/religious/ritualistic/ideological causes.

- Terrorism.

- Cover-up or in the process of another crime (eg arson, burglary).

- 'Noble' cause (eg mercy killing).

Motives can also link in with contributory causes of crime, such as narcotics or alcohol-induced behaviour. There is evidence to suggest that some violent offenders have taken/consumed either of these prior to committing a violent act and this may feature as part of their mitigation. It is possible for victims to have taken the same substance too, which may provide an indication as to what sort of activity they were involved in prior to a crime being committed. This is useful information when building up an accurate picture on which to base a motive and understand the personality and habits of a victim or the profile of an offender. Violent offences such as a serious assault may also involve an element of victim precipitation, whereby the victim is the first to initiate violence towards the offender and this can be considered as part of an investigative mindset approach.

Bibliography

Alison, L and Rainbow, L (eds), *Professionalising Offender Profiling: Forensic and Investigative Psychology in Practice* (Routledge, 2011)

Asch, S, 'Forming impressions on personality' (1946) 41 *Journal of Abnormal and Social Psychology*, 258–90

Ask, K and Granhag, P, 'Hot cognition in investigative judgements: The differential influence of anger and sadness' (2007) 31 *Law and Human Behavior*, 537–51

Ask, K and Granhag, P, 'Motivational sources of confirmation bias in criminal investigations: The need for cognitive closure' (2005) 2 *Journal of Investigative Psychology and Offender Profiling*, 43–63

Bar-Hillel, M, 'The base rate fallacy in probability judgements' (1980) 44 *Acta Psychologica*, 211–33

Bernoulli, D, 'Specimen theoriae novae de mensura sortis [exposition of a new theory of the measurement of risk' (1738) 5 *Commentari Academiae Scientrum Imperialis Petropolitanae*, 175–92

Brantingham, P and Brantingham, P, *Environmental Criminology* (1981)

Chabris, C, and Simons, D, 'The Invisible Gorilla' (1999). Available at <http://theinvisiblegorilla.com/gorilla_experiment.html>

Chapman, LJ, 'Illusory correlation in observational report' (1967) 5 *Journal of Verbal Learning and Verbal Behavior*, 151–5

Cohen, LE and Felson, M, 'Social change and crime rate trends: A routine activity approach' (1979) 44 *American Sociological Review*, 588–608

College of Policing, *Authorised Professional Practice*. Available at: http://www.app.college.police.uk/risk; <https://www.app.college.police.uk/app-content/national-decision-model/>

Cornish, D and Clarke, R, *Understanding Crime Displacement—An Application of Rational Choice Theory* (cited in ACPO, *Practice Advice on Analysis* (NPIA, 2008)), 12

Davies, M, 'Belief persistence after evidential discrediting: The impact of generated versus proved explanations on the likelihood of discredited outcomes' (1997) 33 *Journal of Experimental Social Psychology*, 561–78

Dean, G (2000). *The Experience of Investigation for Detectives*. (Doctoral Dissertation), Queensland University of Technology, Brisbane, Australia.

Endsley, MR, 'Situational Awareness Global Assessment Technique (SAGAT)' Proceedings of the National Aerospace and Electronics Conference (NAECON) (IEEE, 1988), 789–95

Endsley, MR, 'Toward a theory of situation awareness in dynamic systems' (1995) 37(1) *Human Factors*

Evans, J, *Bias in Human Reasoning: Causes and Consequences* (Erlbaum, 1989)

Fahsing, IA (2016). *The Making of an Expert Detective: Thinking and Deciding in Criminal Investigations*. (Doctoral thesis). Gothenburg: University of Gothenburg, Department of Psychology. Retrieved on 20 May 2018 from <http://hdl.handle.net/2077/47515>

Gilovich, T, Vallone, R, and Tversky, A, 'The hot hand in basketball: On the misperception of random sequences' (1985) 17 *Cognitive Psychology*, 295–314

Jacowitz, K and Kahneman, D, 'Measures of anchoring in estimation tasks' (1995) 21 *Personality and Social Psychology Bulletin*, 1161–7

Kahneman, D, *Thinking, Fast and Slow* (Penguin, 2012)

Kahneman, D and Tversky, A, 'On the psychology of prediction' (1973) 80 *Psychological Review*, 237–51

Katz, S and Mazur, MA, *Understanding the Rape Victim: Synthesis of Research Findings* (John Wiley, 1979)

Keren, G and Tiegen, K, Yet another look at the heuristics and biases approach., In D Koehler and N Harvey (eds), *Blackwell Handbook of Judgement and Decision Making* (Blackwell Publishing, 2004)

Klein, GA, Orasanu, J, Calderwood, R, and Zsambok, C E (eds), *Decision Making in Action: Models and Methods* (Ablex, 1993)

Koriat, A, Lichtenstein, S, and Fischoff, B, 'Reasons for confidence' (1980) 6 *Journal of Experimental Psychology: Human Learning and Memory*, 107–18

Marshall, B and Alison, L, 'Stereotyping, congruence and presentation order: Interpretative biases in utilising offender profiles' (in press) *Psychology, Crime and Law*

Moray, N, 'Where are the snows of yesteryear?', in DA Vincenzi, M Mouloua, and PA Hancock (eds), *Human Performance, Situational Awareness and Automation: Current Research and Trends* (LEA, 2004), 1–31

Nickerson, R, 'Confirmation bias: A ubiquitous phenomenon in many guises' (1998) 2 *Review of General Psychology*, 175–220

Nisbett, R, Borgida, E, Crandall, R, and Reed, H, Popular induction: Information is not necessarily informative. In D Kahneman, P Slovic, and A Tversky (eds), *Judgement under Uncertainty: Heuristics and Biases* (Cambridge University Press, 1976)

Ormerod, TC, Barrett, EC, and Taylor, PJ, *Investigative sense-making in criminal contexts*. Proceedings of the seventh international NDM conference, Amsterdam, The Netherlands, ed J M C Schraagen (June 2005)

Oxford English Dictionary, 2nd edn revised (Oxford University Press, 2005)

Payne, J, Bettman, J, and Luce, M, Behavioral decision research: An overview. In M Birnbaum (ed), *Measurement, Judgment and Decision Making* (Academic Press, 1998)

Petty, R and Cacioppo, J, *Communication and Persuasion: Central and Peripheral Routes to Attitude Change* (Springer-Verlag, 1986)

Rossmo, DK, *Geographic Profiling* (1999)

Ross, L and Anderson, C, Shortcomings in the attribution process: On the origins and maintenance of erroneous social assessments. In A Tversky, D Kahneman, and P Slovic (eds), *Judgement under Uncertainty: Heuristics and Biases* (Cambridge University Press, 1982)

Ross, L, Lepper, M, and Hubbard, M, 'perseverance in self-perception and social perception: Biased attributional process in the debriefing paradigm' (1975) 32 *Journal of Personality and Social Psychology*, 880–92

Sarter, NB and Woods, DD, 'Situation Awareness: A Critical but Ill-defined Phenomenon' (1991) 1 *International Journal of Aviation Psychology*, 45–57

Schwartz, N, Strack, F, Hilton, D, and Naderer, G, 'Base rates, representativeness and the logic of conversation: The contextual relevance of "irrelevant" information' (1991) 9 *Social Cognition*, 67–84

Synder, M and Swann, W, 'Hypothesis-testing processes in social interaction' (1978) 36 *Journal of Personality and Social Psychology*, 1202–12

Tversky, A and Kahneman, D, 'Judgement under uncertainty: Heuristics and biases' (1974) 185 *Science*, 1124–31

Tversky, A and Kahneman, D, Judgements of and by representativeness. In D Kahneman, P Slovic, and A Tversky (eds), *Judgement under Uncertainty: Heuristics and Biases* (Cambridge University Press, 1982)

Watson, P, 'On the failure to eliminate hypotheses in a conceptual task' (1960) 12 *Quarterly Journal of Experimental Psychology*, 129–40

Zipf, G, *Human Behaviour and the Principle of Least Effort* (1949)

4

Policy Logs and Casebooks

4.1 **Introduction**

Investigation Policy Logs (IPL/PL—also known as Policy Logs/Files and Key Decision Logs, 'KDLs') are a vital element of the decision-making process. They are a formal record of all key decisions and the supporting rationale as to why these decisions were made, or in some cases not made, at a particular time in an investigation or operation. There is a well-known saying: *'if it isn't written down, it didn't happen'*.

Policy Logs are an important decision-making support tool to help understand and explain thoughts and considerations. They are used in most if not all major incidents, operations, and serious and organised crime investigations where strategic and tactical decision making is deemed critical.

Some say the professionalism of an investigation can be measured not only against the quality of decisions made but also by the way in which they were recorded. How decisions are judged when under close scrutiny might depend on the meticulousness of wording in entries. It is not uncommon for SIOs and lead investigators to be formally called to account to explain a policy decision, at which time their PL becomes a huge asset.

The primary objective of a PL is to provide and record decision making, investigative direction, policy, parameters, and priorities whilst complying with the requirements of the Criminal Procedure and Investigation Act 1996 (CPIA). As outlined in Chapter 3, operational decision making involves an element of risk management involving competing demands, finite resources, and sometimes limited information. SIOs are accountable for their decisions and will be required to produce a record of not only the decisions made but the rational that underpins them. All this adds to the importance of accurate record keeping.

Note keeping and the use of investigation casebooks is also covered in this chapter as investigators could and should be keeping accurate notes as they carry out their day-to-day operational duties. Like every other record, the contents and security of any record keeping are always potentially disclosable and open to scrutiny.

4.2 **5WH of Policy Logs**

4.2.1 **Who**

The SIO (or lead investigator) is the person who makes key decisions and is the one who should make entries in a PL. If they don't enter the decision themselves, they should check and review any entries made on their behalf. If an entry is made by a third party, eg a deputy or senior officer, then the SIO should check and countersign to state they agree with and consent to the decision and contents.

4.2.2 **What**

Maintaining an IPL in a meticulous manner provides a transparent and accountable record of the decision-making process adopted during the course of an investigation. It is a matter for the decision maker to decide what decisions are important enough to warrant an entry. As a general rule, all significant or key decisions *should* be recorded. Any other matters deemed to be less significant can be recorded within a casebook. This is purely a matter of personal choice and judgement.

The purpose of an IPL is not to capture each and every (micro) decision made during an investigation, but almost certainly the key/macro ones. Key decisions are those that materially affect the course of an investigation. Routine decisions and ones that merely reflect the implementation of investigative procedure need not always be recorded. According to Sir Ronnie Flanagan (Review of Policing—Interim Report (2007), p 8): '*A distinction must be made between necessary and unnecessary bureaucracy and there must be greater discretion allowed for the exercise of professional judgement in making this decision.*'

As a general rule, the importance and seriousness of the decision and circumstances are factors to consider, together with the extent of risk and likelihood of harm occurring. It must be remembered, however, that recording a decision has enormous benefits and serves as an everlasting record that will protect the decision maker and their organisation. The basic rule repeated, however, is that discretion can be applied together with the exercise of professional judgement in determining <u>what</u> decisions are recorded.

What to include in a policy decision log is based on some fundamental elements. These are:

1. Consecutive and chronological numbering.
2. Identity of decision maker (who).
3. Time (precise time) and date of decision (when).
4. Decision details (what).
5. Reason or rationale for the decision (why).
6. Information and resources known and available at the time (what).

Point 6 is one that can easily get forgotten or omitted. It is an important requirement that recorded decisions are put into context and combined with essential detail outlining what was *known* and *available* at the *precise time* the decision was made. This is why recording an accurate time a decision is made becomes so important, because information known later might not have been available when the decision was made. Linking decisions to associated and relevant documents or material on which a decision was based can prove extremely beneficial, for example, an intelligence log.

To confirm this point, the IOPC (formerly IPCC) stated the following:

Police officers and staff are accountable for the decisions and actions they take and are expected to provide a rationale for those decisions when questioned … we recognize that police operational decisions involve taking risks and in assessing decision-making we will focus on whether the decision was reasonable and proportionate in all circumstances *(including the information and intelligence available and the operational policing context)* as they existed *at the time* … in considering the decisions and actions of individual officers we recognise that police operational decisions often need to take into account competing objectives, timescales and limited resources.[1]

What needs to be included in the contents can be split into headings or topics. The following are some examples:

4.2.2.1 Enquiry management

- Appointment of SIO/DSIO.
- Key areas of risk management.
- Gold Group involvement and nominated roles, eg use of a PIP4 and primacy if other forces or agencies involved (eg Fire Service, Health and Safety Executive or Local Authority).[2]
- Appointment of other key roles such as Crime Scene Manager (CSM), Family Liaison Officer (FLO), House to House (H2H) coordinator, analysts, researchers, intelligence cell, Victim Care Officer, Exhibits and Disclosure Officers, etc.
- Role of any designated/linked Silver Commanders (including their terms of reference).
- Details of incident/enquiry room location and case management system (CMS).
- Management structure and enquiry teams.
- Identification of key posts in a major incident room (MIR) (eg Receiver, Disclosure and Exhibits Officers).
- Details of any parallel investigation such as a Serious Case Review, Domestic Homicide Review, or independent body oversight referral.
- Key partners and agencies involved (eg Crown Prosecution Service (CPS)).
- Disclosure policy (under CPIA 1996).
- Review or oversight mechanisms and timescales.
- CPS liaison.
- Case disposal and closure details.

4.2.2.2 General administration

- Acknowledgement of any appointed finance/administration officer.
- Increase/reduction/refusal for increase in staff numbers.

---

[1] IPCC, 'Learning the lessons, risk in police decision making and accountability in operational policing' (2011) Bulletin 14. Available at <http://www.learningthelessons.org.uk/>.

[2] Gold Commanders, PIP 4s, and other agency senior managers will also probably complete their own PLs and record their own decisions and strategies.

- Human Resources strategy (staffing, welfare, training/experience, role descriptions).
- Resources required, obtained, refused, or withdrawn (eg collaborative agreements, covert assets, part-time agency staff, contingent labour, specialists).
- Budget and financial agreements and arrangements, eg for travel and subsistence, monitoring of working hours, overtime, annual leave, and temporary secondments.
- Use of vehicles, mileage allowances, pool or hire cars.
- Booking on and off arrangements for staff, tours of duty, leave, and public-holiday working arrangements.
- Management of welfare issues/health and safety.
- Management (eg timing) of briefings/debriefings and management meetings.
- Additional equipment or resources required.

4.2.2.3 Investigation management

- Objectives of the investigation.
- Key critical and tactical decisions.
- HP Actions.
- Debrief of initial responders.
- Identification of victim(s) and key witnesses.
- Designating suspect status.
- Investigative strategies (eg victims, witnesses, suspects, search, intelligence, passive data, communications data, H2H, CCTV, TIE, (digital) forensic, media/communications, financial).
- Identification, definition, and parameters of any scene(s) and policy for security and eventual release, relevant time.
- Decisions relating to witness statements (ie when required), personal description forms (PDFs), TIE categories and investigation criteria, alibi times and verification.
- Action management policy (eg how many per team, timescales for submission).
- Deployment of mobile and specialist incident vehicles resources.
- Criteria for intelligence research on nominals, eg TIEs.
- Important events or changes to the direction of the investigation.
- Details of any linked incidents under consideration.
- Disclosure strategy.

4.2.2.4 Main Lines of Enquiry (MLOE)

- Outline of MLOE (indicating high priority/fast track - see section 7.7).
- Suspect hunt strategies/crimes in action management details.
- Variations on discontinued lines of enquiry (with reasons).
- Details of declared suspects.
- Use of specialists, tactical advisers, or subject matter experts.

KEY POINTS

1. PL entries should, where appropriate, incorporate or reflect elements and principles of the NDM (see Appendix A).
2. It is equally important to record a decision and reason for *not* doing something as for doing something, and to record any changes or retractions of any previous decisions.

4.2.3 **Where**

Policy decisions have traditionally been entered into an A4-sized bound log book. Such pre-printed versions are usually law enforcement agency (LEA) badged, serial numbered, and labelled with details of the investigation or operation including the SIO, their deputy, and dates the enquiry commenced and concluded. Inside pages are sequentially numbered with self-carbonating tear-out duplicates with various instructions and guidance notes or prompts contained within the inside covers.

An electronic version of a PL may be incorporated into a CMS in which decisions can be digitally recorded in the same way as a bound book using stylesheets, templates, or macros. In some LEAs this may be the default position. Benefits of using an electronic version are that entries are automatically date and time stamped and can sometimes be accessed via a portable device that serves as a secure means of access and usually security (password) protected. However, the necessary means (eg digital device/computer) of access and retrieval must be practical and readily available. If this method of policy recording is adopted, entries must be easily made, accessible and retrievable (eg remotely) and ultimately stored on a central and secure master server.

For practical reasons, some decisions may have to be initially recorded in a 'casebook' or 'notebook'. If so, these can be later transferred into a more official PL at a convenient time, but there should be no undue delay in doing so. Every effort must be made to avoid an unwieldy backlog of decision details that inevitably require transferring, especially if there is to be a handover and transition from one SIO to another (who needs to be aware of key decisions already made and recorded).

4.2.4 **Why**

Completing an IPL in a consistent and meticulous way provides a transparent and accountable record of the decision-making processes adopted by the SIO during the course of operational activity. Decisions formally recorded and constructed in the right way are better able to withstand independent scrutiny and can also form the basis of any handover to a new SIO. IPLs demonstrate, long after a decision is made or case closed, the various factors and options that were rigorously considered, placing the SIO in a much stronger position to explain key decisions.

Decisions recorded in PLs are important because they are often scrutinised in many different settings, such as at court, in public enquiries, during internal reviews or investigations by independent oversight bodies (eg the Independent Office for Police Conduct (IOPC)). Moreover, the logs serve as an important audit trail and safety net for both decision maker and their organisation. They are an official and definitive record to be relied upon when having to recall and account for important decisions. This is why they are used in major and serious crime investigations, complex operations, and incidents.

4.2.5 **When**

PLs are commonly used where an investigation or operation is of a major, serious, critical, or complex nature. The decision to use may be at the discretion of the SIO or dependent on agency policy regarding in what types of cases they should be used (eg on all cases that have been allocated through a formal tasking process). However, every opportunity should be taken to practise recording decisions in this way in order to develop an essential skill that needs to be honed and adopted as routine procedure.

When a decision needs to be physically recorded (ie entering into a log) might depend on certain practicalities. Contemporaneous recording is best practice but is clearly not always possible. If it is not, then any decisions should be formally recorded as soon as is reasonably practicable afterwards. What needs to be avoided is a large backlog of entries as this is when mistakes will happen (and memories fade).

Most entries are usually recorded soon after they are made, taking into account the fact that the longer the gap between a decision and the time of entry may render it harder to remember what the precise decision was and why. In reactive investigations it is acceptable for there to be a tolerable gap between the time a decision is made and the time an IPL entry is made. It is unrealistic to expect all entries to be recorded the precise moment they are made unless done so via dictation, which in any event may appear contrived.

However, in fast-moving proactive-style operations (such as suspect hunts and 'crimes in action' where life is at risk) there will be a requirement to record all decisions and reasons as they happen to keep pace with events. The dynamic nature of circumstances may mean there is too much occurring in real time to have the luxury of being able to play catch-up and therefore all decisions will need to be recorded immediately. Technology embedded within some case management and intelligence systems may allow for decisions to be recorded instantaneously and linked in to other information and material that is being received at the same time. Some SIO training courses utilise a simulated system such as the 'Hydra Minerva'[3] suite to use and develop these skills.

---

[3] Mentioned in section 3.1.

If an IT-based version of a PL is not being utilised then the more traditional bound book can be used and at times can prove more practical. There may be occasions when an SIO does not have access to a networked system but still needs to record key decisions.

KEY POINT

The precise time and date a key decision is made is vitally significant and must be totally accurate to be considered in the context of simultaneous events. This is why it is essential to have access to a reliable timepiece (and calendar) to ensure the time/date a decision is made is recorded correctly (see SIO's basic kit, section 1.6)

4.2.6 **How**

A suggested structure for a PL is outlined in the MIRSAP manual.[2] It states that entries should be written in a 'decision/reason' divided format with only one entry per page and to run alongside a log of events. This has never changed. However, depending on preference, another option is to use a single policy file that combines a log of events and decisions in a free-text narrative 'storybook' style. This can sometimes make progress of the enquiry easier to follow and keeps decisions in chronological order, flowing alongside events as they occur in sequence. More importantly, decisions can be made alongside developments as and when they happen, which helps indicate information that was available at the time a given decision was made (see Figure 4.1 for a sample PL).

In a standard PL, chronological entries are entered sequentially on numbered pages with no spaces left between entries. If using a hardcopy version, the pages are usually carbonated so a copy of each entry can be easily removed for entering onto a CMS.

The exact wording of each individual decision is, of course, vital. Care should be taken to record entries so they convey the intended meaning and are clear, understandable, and unambiguous. Details and facts cited need to be accurate, including the spelling of names and places, grammar (spelling and grammar—SPAG) and any referenced numerical data to show that there is a keen eye for detail and meticulousness (and to avoid unnecessary errors in entries on a CMS and to mitigate the risk of making a wrong assertion).

Each and every decision is recorded in a legible and durable format. Entries can be made at dictation by a nominated entry/log maker, staff officer, or trusted assistant working to the SIO. All entries are timed and dated (ie both when the decision was made and when the entry was made, if different), and signed by both the person making the entry and the person making the decision (if not the SIO, the SIO should countersign to say they agree the decision and have noted the entry).

No. 4	Officer making decision: Tony Cook (SIO) Signature: *Tony Cook*
Date/Time	xxxx/xxxx
Decision:	(Title) Objectives of the investigation 1. Conduct thorough, professional and ethical investigation 2. Establish full facts and if/what criminal offences have been committed 3. Provide support to victim's close family 4. Seek and identify witnesses 5. Identify, trace and pursue offenders 6. Secure and gather all available information, material and evidence and adhere to CPIA disclosure rules 7. Pursue all reasonable lines of enquiry 8. Produce case file and relevant evidence to the CPS
Reason:	It is important to give the investigation and the team clear direction and focus. These objectives shall remain under review throughout the course of the enquiry.
Officer Making Entry (if different)	Name/Grade: N/A Signature: Date/Time:

No. 8	Officer making decision: Tony Cook (SIO) Signature: *Tony Cook*
Date/Time	xxxx/xxxx
Decision:	(Title) Victim's Family Liaison Strategy 1. Ensure immediate support being provided to victim's family 2. Appoint FLOs and brief re case circumstances and SIOs objectives 3. SIO & DSIO to meet victim's family at earliest opportunity 4. Maintain constructive relationship with victim's family and conduct relationship assessment at regular intervals 5. Ensure full compliance with Code of Practice for Victims of Crime

Figure 4.1 Random sample PL entries (see stabbing incident, section 7.9.4)

	6. Provide highest standards of service and support to the victim's close family throughout the investigation and prosecution process
	7. Build and maintain confidence in the investigation and prosecution team
	8. Ensure the victim's family receives all their entitlements in accordance with organisational policy, practice, and procedure
	9. Utilise any external support organisations through referral mechanisms as deemed necessary and proportionate
Reason:	Supporting, protecting, and safeguarding the victim's family is of utmost importance, both from ethical and duty of care perspectives and also in order to retain the trust and confidence of them and the wider community and media. It is also aimed at meeting the requirements of the Victim's Code.
Officer Making Entry (if different)	Name/Grade: N/A Signature: Date/Time:

No. 11	Officer making decision: Tony Cook (SIO) Signature: *Tony Cook*
Date/Time	xxxx/xxxx
Decision:	(Title) TIE Strategy N4 Siobhan Taylor, N5 U/M I/C3, and N6 Alice Keegan will be made TIE subjects and HP actions raised and allocated immediately.
Reason:	All three persons fit one or other of the TIE categories for being either in scene (1) at the relevant time or as known associates of the victim. They are either key witnesses or connected to an incident that may have caused his death. The circumstances of their potential involvement need to be fully investigated and evaluated. N6 Keegan has been included as she is the current girlfriend of the victim and resides at 8 Gould Street which is adjacent to where the victim was found injured; N4 Taylor is his ex-girlfriend and was standing crying outside 8 Gould Street at the relevant time; and U/M N5 (identity currently u/k) was attending the victim when paramedics arrived at the scene. The action requirements will comply with the TIE policy set by the SIO (see D.8)

Figure 4.1 Continued

Officer Making Entry (if different)	Name/Grade: James Dolan D/C (Loggist)
	Signature: *Jim Dolan*
	Date/Time: xxxx/xxxx

No. 14	Officer making decision: Tony Cook (SIO)
	Signature: *Tony Cook*
Date/Time	xxxx/xxxx
Decision:	(Title) Search Strategy
	An application for a search warrant under S.8 PACE will be made for the address of 10 Gould Street and if granted executed without delay. An operational order has been prepared (D.14) for the search.
Reason:	Reliable intelligence has been received (contained within intelligence log D.13) stating an item that may be of evidential significance (ie a blood-stained knife) has been hidden in the rear garden of the address and believed to be linked to the death of N1 Brownlow. Research indicates this is neighbouring property of the home address of his current girlfriend, N.6 Alice Keegan, who is subject of a TIE action. Failing to act swiftly will pose a risk of missing an opportunity to seize important evidential material and recover a lethal weapon. An s.8 warrant is the correct legal power to search the premises and will permit entry if consent is refused and the operational order will give clarity to the tactical plan for execution and be useful for briefing the staff and maintaining a record of the action taken.
Officer Making Entry (if different)	Name/Grade: James Dolan D/C (Loggist)
	Signature: *Jim Dolan*
	Date/Time: xxxx/xxxx

Decision No. 16	Officer making decision: Tony Cook (SIO)
	Signature: *Tony Cook*
Date/Time	xxxx/xxxx
Decision:	(Title) Media Strategy
	An initial holding statement to be released by the MLO is as follows:
	1. It will be confirmed that (on time/date) an incident has taken place in the locality of the Gould Street area which the police are investigating

Figure 4.1 Continued

75

	2. A male died at the scene and his death is being treated as suspicious 3. A post-mortem examination is due to take place and the male victim has yet to be formally identified 4. An incident room has been opened at (location) and anyone with any information is asked to contact the investigation team on (tel. number)
Reason:	It is highly likely there will be media interest in the incident, and until there is more information available a holding statement will buy some time. There is limited knowledge at the moment and incorrect facts or assumptions are best avoided so as to avoid making corrections. The victim has yet to be formally identified by his NOK so his details cannot be released until such time. This is also a useful opportunity to make an early appeal for information by announcing the contact details of the MIR.
Officer Making Entry (if different)	Name/Grade: James Dolan D/C (Loggist) Signature: *Jim Dolan* Date/Time: xxxx/xxxx

Figure 4.1 Continued

4.3 Cross-referencing and Indexing

Policy file entries may need cross-referencing against any 'stand-alone' documents in existence, eg if there is a separate arrest strategy, or CCTV recovery and viewing strategy, or forensic strategy, which may be lengthy separate entities/ policy documents in their own right. It is sometimes more practical to make reference to their existence (and which version is referred to) rather than try to cram all the details into one single entry/page (and most pre-printed policy books only allow for single-page entries).

Stand-alone policies can themselves be completed in a format similar to a normal PL entry, with the decision and accompanying reasons included, signed, and dated by the SIO, then registered and uploaded onto a CMS. The recording of such cross-referencing provides reassurance that any 'stand-alone' strategy and policy has been commented upon and noted in the main PL.

If there are multiple entries focusing on the same topic or subject area, it may be useful to cross-reference between them for consistency and ease of reference. Some PLs allow for the subject matter to be categorised using headings in a grid format or index which is contained on a separate page (eg at the rear). This is to assist others not familiar with the contents to locate decisions that relate to the same topic when necessary, eg during reviews or when the course of the investigation changes or decisions made earlier are changed. It can also be used to group topics under headings to locate all the decisions that may, for example, relate to media, victims, witnesses, CCTV, forensic, etc.

An index of decisions may be a useful addition in a PL and will aid the retrieval of decisions that are attributable to certain themes or topics. It simply makes them easier to find when grouped under headings. These can be used in a table format that might include subjects such as MLOE, witnesses, suspects, media, disclosure, forensic, TIEs, search, resources, and so forth.

4.4 'Sensitive' Logs and Disclosure

As a general rule, everyone in an enquiry team should have access to the SIO's key policies and decisions and allowed unfettered access to the contents of a PL. The contents should be shared with all members of the investigation, so everyone understands the direction of the enquiry and what and why certain decisions have been made (or not made). This is made much simpler if the entries are entered onto a CMS normally under the document reference of 'D1', making digital access so much easier. The log belongs to the investigation and should be available to the investigation team, but care should be taken regarding access where sensitive and confidential material is concerned.

An additional 'sensitive' PL might be required if there are confidential matters and/or material that needs to be protected due to its sensitive nature (eg outlining covert tactics or sensitive source information). If this kind of PL is created, the level of access must be determined as a security measure. The first entry of a sensitive policy file should stipulate who is allowed access, for example the SIO, Deputy SIO, and Office Manager. If using a CMS such as HOLMES, restrictive access levels can be agreed and arranged through the account manager. The requisite Government Protective Marking Scheme (GPMS) should be applied where appropriate.

It is worth noting that some sensitive material may have to be preserved for a long period of time, well after an investigation has finished. Sensitive documents, important as they are, can end up stored in 'libraries' (ie storage of archived case material), for which long-term access can be difficult to control. Once protected with restrictive markings on a CMS, access is much easier to control and protect and less susceptible to getting interfered with or mislaid, there will also be a digital audit trail of those who have accessed it.

It should be noted, however, the existence of any sensitive PL must be brought to the attention of the Disclosure Officer and the CPS and prosecuting counsel in accordance with the rules of CPIA for consideration of (non) disclosure under the principles of public interest immunity (PII). PLs are, of course, included on the disclosure schedule submitted to the prosecuting lawyer.

In most cases, in agreement with the CPS, contents of PLs are not usually disclosed to third parties unless a legal instruction stipulates otherwise. As a general rule, defence legal teams are not allowed access, nor are victims or their representatives, etc. However, independent oversight bodies such as the IOPC usually have full access in order to conduct their own investigation.

Checklist—Policy Logs

- Used for recording key strategic/tactical decisions in complex investigations.

- Should include or reflect principles of the NDM where possible (Appendix A)

- An accurate timepiece is essential for recording precise times decision are made.

- Only one PL is used per enquiry (plus a 'sensitive' one if used)

- Stand-alone or 'other' documents may be referred to in entries, with their sequential index number.

- Entries should clearly identify the decision maker. If someone other than the SIO makes a decision, the entry should be countersigned by the SIO to confirm it has been made on their behalf and with their knowledge, consent, and agreement.

- A PL is to be maintained on a regular basis throughout the life of the investigation, including up to the trial and beyond, if an appeal or case review is likely.

- PLs are usually entered onto a CMS and allocated a reference (eg Document 1, or D1). Care must be taken to ensure the contents are accurately entered (eg if typed) and proof read by cross-checking against original entries.

- Entries made on behalf of the SIO should be reviewed and countersigned as a quality assurance measure.

- Spelling and grammar (SPAG) checks will avoid incorrect details being entered onto a CMS and creation of incorrect records and to avoid mistakes/misinterpretation.

- Contents are not usually disclosed to third parties (eg defence teams) unless directed by the CPS or court order.
- Arrangements should be made for safe and long-term storage plus any separate sensitive file.

4.5 Investigators' Casebooks

Most investigators, including SIOs, need to record and keep copious notes during their time on an investigation. These are usually entered into what is often referred to as an investigating officer's casebook (aka 'notebook' or 'day-book'). A daily routine is adopted of recording details of operational activities, briefings, observations, useful information, notes, and facts, etc in one of these books, and it would be highly unusual or even unprofessional for anyone involved in complex investigations not to do so.

The traditional UK police officer's pocket notebook has stood the test of time, but these days has been generally superseded by more contemporary means of note keeping. Nonetheless, the traditional art of routinely recording information into a case/notebook in some form or other will always play a significant part in practical law enforcement and day-to-day operational business.

Correct procedures for keeping and storing notes during the course of an enquiry may be a matter that requires clarification in order to meet the disclosure rules of the CPIA 1996 and to ensure there is a satisfactory degree of professionalism (ie rather than officers using scrap paper or random books/separate sheets). Some notes can and often do become important items of evidence, and therefore the integrity of record-keeping processes and policy may come under scrutiny.

The security of information being recorded is significant, particularly if the loss of any notes made would be likely to cause embarrassment or create unnecessary risk if they were to fall into the wrong hands (eg third parties such as the media, or those under suspicion, or to an organised crime group (OCG)). This requirement is unmanageable if officers are using a variety of different note-keeping methods involving loose-leaf paper or books that can be misplaced or have their pages easily removed.

Like PLs, most LEAs distribute branded 'investigators' casebooks' for use by officers. For practical reasons, these are usually printed and bound A4 writing books and contain similar detail on the front to those on PLs, with margins on each page for date and time recording of individual entries. There may be in existence some organisational or departmental policy outlining the correct procedures on their issue, use, security, and storage.

Officers should be reminded of the need to maintain the integrity of their notes and entries, and to record accurate information. This is particularly important if entries are at odds with material entered into the evidential chain, eg the description of a suspect given by a witness, or on an action write-up for instance. Any alterations, crossings out, blank pages, etc may have to be accounted for at a later stage. Any material recorded that is deemed at the time, or at any later stage to be sensitive should be highlighted and brought to the attention of the disclosure officer.

4.5.1 **Audit and security**

When case management books/investigator notebooks are in use it may be necessary to nominate someone to manage their allocation, submission, retention, and security within the operational team. Their task is to keep accurate records of serial-numbered allocated casebooks and arrange the issue of them against officers' signatures. This will ensure all the books allocated can be accounted for at the end of the enquiry and collected for submission to the case management team/disclosure officer. There may of course, be a good reason for an officer to keep their book post termination of the enquiry (eg for an operational requirements). An important point is that all usage, movement, and accountability for all casebooks is managed properly to mitigate risk of them being lost and to show that good procedures are in place.

Any book, notes, or recording and digital storage devices that contain operational information, especially sensitive or confidential information, must have a policy and risk management plan to prevent them getting into the hands of third parties.

Officers should be reminded that any loss of official documents, material, or equipment is a breach of security. It is their personal responsibility to thoroughly check there has been no loss or mishap. Shoddy procedures can allow this to happen and if it does will most probably cause the SIO and their organisation untold distraction, embarrassment, and unnecessary risk through compromise by sensitive material falling into the wrong hands (particularly if it contains confidential personal details, eg of sexual abuse victims/accusers, key witnesses, previous convictions, intelligence, family status, and contact details, etc).

Note: Powerful photography equipment can get close-up shots of items carried by officers. A senior Scotland Yard Commander lost his job after being snapped by the media walking into a COBRA briefing outside the Prime Minister's offices at 10 Downing Street in London, carrying documents that had confidential details on the front sheet that compromised a major police counter-terrorism operation.[4]

Checklist—Casebook management

1. SIOs should determine and establish what type of record keeping method, ie casebooks, are being used by their enquiry teams, with an appropriate security and audit policy to mitigate risk of them being lost or falling into possession of third parties.

2. Investigator's casebooks should be allocated against signature and a record made (usually in a register) of all those issued and used.

3. Dates and times of when completed books are returned, or their location (if not with the case management team), are to be recorded.

4. An audit trail should be maintained of subsequent movements of casebooks.

5. Staff must report any lost casebooks and if lost, proper records are kept (and a thorough investigation made).

---

[4] On 8 April 2009, an Assistant Commissioner from the Metropolitan Police Service arrived at the briefing inadvertently carrying a document marked 'Secret', with suspect address details, that was photographed by the media, forcing officers to strike earlier than planned on their terrorist suspects for Op Pathway.

6. Casebooks that contain protectively marked, sensitive, or classified material should not be carried in places away from a secure place of duty, especially in areas of heightened risk or when having to leave them in vehicles, unless by approved secure means.

7. Certain planned operational activity (eg executing searches of premises) should cater for the prevention of losing casebooks and any other operational material, eg by making a final sweep of the premises searched to check for any casebooks or material that otherwise may inadvertently get left behind).

5

First Response

5.1 **Introduction**

The key to a successful reactive investigation usually lies in an effective pro-active first response. This involves efficient resource deployment, gathering, and recording of accurate and detailed information, making the right decisions, taking the right action, and securing the best evidence. This process starts the very first moment an initial call or report is received by a call taker about a crime or incident and continues with subsequent attendance and management of the crime scene(s) and investigation.

The first response to a serious incident can become the focus of media and public attention (and public enquiries) if things go wrong. This is where a law enforcement agency risks its reputation if mistakes are made, which in turn can have an adverse effect on any relationship with the public, the very source from which assistance is often required. More importantly, as far as the SIO is concerned, it is fundamental that all those involved in an initial response adopt a professional approach as there is often only one chance to get it right. Initial assessments and decisions made by or fed back to call handlers/resource despatchers and supervisors (ie key decision makers at the time) determine how an incident is graded, treated, prioritised, and responded to. This is a period often referred to as the 'Golden Hour(s)'.

Any assumptions made during this crucial stage need to be reviewed, as there can be a tendency to 'buy into' the simplest option of treating something to be of less importance than it actually is. For example, treating a missing person report as a low or medium risk when it is indicative of homicide, abduction, child trafficking, or sexual exploitation, ie very high risk. Linked precursor incidents also require assessing and responding to correctly.

Something that may not be so obvious when dealing with an initial response to any incident, and of prime importance, is the training and development of personnel. No opportunity should be lost in applying a methodical and professional approach. This affords officers the opportunity of becoming familiar with using correct procedures, checklists, and rehearsing a professional approach for creating greater preparedness.

Two main points this chapter highlights are first, that an investigation can be given a significant boost if things are done properly by first responders. Second, as the SIO is rarely a first responder themselves, they must check and review any important decisions that have been/have not been made, actions (not) taken, and information (not) gathered. This emphasises the importance of debriefing those who have been part of the response phase, a topic that is picked up in Chapter 9.

KEY POINTS

- Checklists are useful for ensuring nothing is forgotten or missed. Surgeons and commercial pilots use them, and the trick is to treat them as guidelines, not tramlines. They will greatly assist in organising initial thoughts and considerations.
- *'The first 24 hours, the first clue, the first line of enquiry, the first breakthrough'*—in reactive crime investigation, the first of anything can mean everything to the chances of success.

5.2 **Teamwork**

An SIO assumes responsibility for investigations into crimes that are of utmost gravity and likely to contain many complex and connected decisions, actions, challenges, and procedures. A number of constituent parts need to come together in the initial stages, during which an essential ingredient is *teamwork*.

Each role and stage of the process needs to connect in a chain that is only as strong as its weakest link. The SIO is unlikely to be involved from the start, but as soon as they are they must set the right tone for a teamwork approach by leading, managing, and coordinating activity. Momentum and progress need to be consolidated and maintained to provide the right foundations for a coordinated investigation. This requires a shared sense of purpose, a positive professional attitude, and the pooling of skills and expertise.

Effective teams acknowledge individuals around them who have complementary skills. Effective cooperation and communication with the sharing of information and knowledge helps bring everyone together to achieve a common goal. This becomes even more relevant if a response involves multiple agencies, and effective coordination and leadership will help to provide a more coherent and integrated joint effort.

5.3 **'Golden Hour(s)' Principle**

The 'Golden Hour(s)' principle derives from the medical profession. Healthcare professionals have a basic rule in trauma cases that patients who are treated quickly are more likely to make a full recovery. However, contrary to what the description suggests, the Golden Hour is not restricted to a rigid 60-minute period and can extend much longer, depending on the circumstances. Also, if the first five or ten minutes are what count the most, then this timespan could potentially be called the 'Platinum' period.

There are clear benefits for effective criminal investigations offered by a speedy and effective response, as prompt actions and decision making have far-reaching advantages. This is what the Golden Hour(s) principle comprises.

It is a period when evidence is fresh and easier to detect (eg body fluids, such as blood, are still wet, or a washing machine is still in the process of cleaning evidence from clothing), memories are still sharp, witnesses are more likely to be at their most cooperative, and offenders are nervous or unguarded, with any untruths or false alibis most vulnerable to detection. It is well acknowledged that a witness testimony provided spontaneously and soon after an event is going to be far more compelling and less at risk of contamination or loss of memory. This is why it is so important to capitalise on all the available investigative high-priority actions and evidence-gathering opportunities during the Golden Hour(s).

Correct incident categorisation, call handling (be it crime or not), and decision making during this period falls under this rule. Many crimes are quickly resolved through prompt and decisive resource dispatch: locating offenders, witnesses, seizing CCTV footage that might get recorded over, seizing a digital device that is switched on and open at an important website or page, or finding and preserving forensic evidence while still available. This principle is what helps generate the most advantageous bank of fast-track actions in the early stages of an investigation.

5.4 **Five Building Blocks**

Both the *Core Investigative Doctrine*[1] and *Murder Investigation Manual*[2] (MIM) describe the Five Building Blocks principle that underpins most reactive phases and initial stages of an investigation. Visually, these principles have been made quite simple to remember (see diagram below). Headings contained within the 'blocks' are self-explanatory and are all covered within this *Handbook* (particularly when considering the initial actions of first responders).

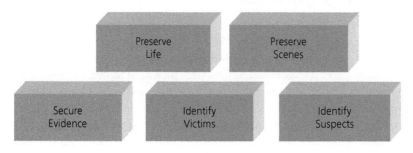

---

[1] ACPO, *Core Investigative Doctrine* (NCPE, 2005).
[2] ACPO, *Murder Investigation Manual* (NCPE, 2006).

5.5 **Report Receiving and Call Handling**

Those who are the first receivers of information about an alleged crime, otherwise known as 'call takers', are by default important participants in the investigative chain. This is primarily because they can immediately and positively influence the outcome by what they record and actions they take. Their role in professionally receiving and recording vital information, and judging what the response needs to be, sometimes at the point of first delivery, is absolutely critical.

When a call or report is handled skilfully, important information is obtained and relayed to the right resources to launch and direct the initial lines of enquiry in the Golden Hour period. Therefore, an SIO at some point should review any record or log that has been made to scrutinise initial decision making and check any actions taken so that any vital information and opportunities are not missed. For example, if a witness makes contact, any notes made by the receiver are likely to contain a first account of what they have seen or heard, detail that should be examined carefully. This includes interim logs or recordings of calls to other emergency services and third-party service providers before being relayed to the correct agency to handle.

Incident logs recorded by call handlers sometimes become live running commentaries about crime incidents or crimes in action and contain useful information about the report and reporter, as well as being a contemporaneous record of actions taken and decisions made. This includes prioritising (something that might be influenced by local policy), resources dispatched, agencies informed—their names, contact details, and times. These records are a useful source from which to begin raising initial actions and help commence an investigation.

5.5.1 **Role of call takers/handlers**

Call takers are initially in the position of key decision maker, handling and extracting useful information, and recording contemporaneous details of enormous value to an investigation. They are entrusted with the task of identifying, linking, and grading important facts and information, such as precursor incidents, that can help solve a case and prevent further incidents. Many serial and dangerous offenders, for example, have been proved to have spent time researching their victims, tracking and stalking them, and spending time in targeted locations looking for suitable opportunities to commit their crimes. These are matters that might be reported and so therefore must be evaluated, graded accurately and dealt with correctly.

Victims, too, make emergency calls sometimes asking for help and warning they are under threat, particularly if they know their abuser/attacker. When these matters are reported there is a danger of over-reliance on downgrading the incident and the importance of the report going unrecognised, sometimes leading to grave outcomes.[3]

Call takers are expected to (re)classify reported information into categories and determine the level of response. When the initial report has a title or category quickly allocated to it (eg reported 'suicide'), there is a danger the incident will automatically default to that category and be treated as such by first responders. This would undermine the fundamental ABC principle (see section 3.4). It could create a preconceived notion that this is precisely what they are dealing with when it might actually be something completely different (eg suspicious death or homicide). This emphasises the importance of the role of the call taker and the ABC rule.

Like all good investigators, call takers are expected to adopt an investigative mindset approach, using open questions to elicit information and apply the 5WH principles (Who? What? Where? When? Why? How?). A telephone call might be the only opportunity to extract urgent information from a caller, who may also be a victim, witness, or offender. Most callers have a wealth of information to offer that can benefit the investigation and they simply need to be asked the right questions to draw it out of them.

Some callers might have to listen to harrowing accounts and first-hand details of horrific attacks and grisly crimes. In extreme cases, the call might include the last words spoken by those who are about to die. They might be trapped in crime scenes or in the midst of ongoing major disasters, such as the 9/11 terrorist attacks when victims rang the emergency services (and their loved ones) in the full knowledge that their deaths were imminent. More recent examples include the calls received from victims who never survived the Grenfell Tower fire in London in 2017. A welfare issue arises for those who may have to receive or listen to these distressing calls; this will also have to be considered and includes investigators who may have to listen to these conversations at a later stage.

The capture and review of an emergency call is a vital piece of evidence. The transcription (word by word) of the call narrative must be meticulously checked for accuracy and correct translation or interpretation, and compared against any subsequent written accounts or statements in order to ensure accuracy and identify inconsistencies. A first account is usually the most accurate and truthful of all accounts given. At times, background noise or activity may also provide useful clues, and sometimes comments from offenders or victims can get captured on record. For offenders or those who make false reports to the emergency services, the next best thing to a confession or admission is a

---

[3] A victim named Raneem Oudeh (twenty-two years old) allegedly called the police three times in the hours before she and her mother, Khaola Saleem (forty-nine years), were murdered in Solihull, having been stabbed by Janbaz Tarin (twenty-one years), a shopkeeper originally from Afghanistan who was quickly named as the prime suspect (29 August 2018, 'Murder victim warned police of threat', BBC News <http://www.bbc.co.uk/news>).

provable lie (eg a killer who makes a 999 call to try and cover their tracks, appear genuine, and make them look innocent but who then makes provable factual errors).

KEY POINTS

1. Initial responders and call handlers need to decide what, where, how, and when resources should be put to best use, eg if suspects are making good their escape, covering possible exit routes instead of going directly to the scene.
2. Call handlers may have the best chance of obtaining vital detailed information from callers who may be victims, witnesses, or even offenders. What they record and log must be accurately captured and carefully scrutinised.

A further point to note is the provision of advice on basic scene preservation and evidence recovery where and when possible. It may prove challenging to protect a crime scene in the early stages, but advice from a call taker can, through the provision of the right advice, reduce the risk of contamination and assist in preserving evidence. The person calling may be at the crime scene themselves (particularly if they are victims of sex offences). For this reason, it is hoped the call handler is skilled in forensic awareness and witness care as part of their training.

5.5.2 Reports to officers/public enquiry counters

Similar principles apply as those for call handlers with an added advantage that the person reporting is likely to be physically present, even though some may refuse to provide their personal details. In this case, the recipient should record all details possible: full description, clothing worn, who was with them at the time of the crime, vehicles used, direction of travel, etc. This may assist in later establishing their full identity and conducting follow-up enquiries (CCTV may also assist).

The reportee could also be a victim, witness, or perpetrator. If there are reasonable grounds to suspect involvement as an offender, then consideration should be given to having them arrested (ie under s 24 PACE). An early assessment of what they are saying will dictate what action needs to be taken. Early involvement of a PIP2 accredited investigator might be useful for providing advice on the right decisions to be made.

One further point is that it is not uncommon for offenders to speak to officers and make reports at or near a scene of crime, in order to appear helpful or normal, provide themselves with an alibi, return to find out what the police response is or even offer themselves up as 'witnesses'. Some may find it irresistible to court the media.[4]

---

[4] Eg During the Soham double murder investigation, Ian Huntley voluntarily spoke to both the police and media, providing misleading information before he was arrested for the murder of two children,

> **KEY POINTS**
>
> 1. Public enquiry counters and reception areas are invariably covered by CCTV/ audio recording equipment. Early recovery and examination is essential.[5]
> 2. Those who report details of crime may themselves be victims, witnesses, or offenders, and the decisive action and dispatch of an accredited investigator might improve early evidential gathering opportunities.

5.6 **First Responders**

A major crime scene, eg a homicide/suspicious death or serious violent or sexual assault, is probably one of the most important an officer will ever attend and may only occur once or twice during their career. Nonetheless, they must be prepared as they are the initial investigating officer(s) responsible for making key decisions until more experienced and specialist resources arrive. A whole range of critical decisions and procedures depend upon the effectiveness and professionalism of these officers. Note: the term 'first responders' might include other persons or agencies.

They are expected to challenge assumptions, control their instincts, and not jump to any conclusions by applying the all-important ABC principle to their thoughts and actions (see Chapter 3):

> **A**—Assume nothing
>
> **B**—Believe nothing
>
> **C**—Challenge/check everything

Attending officers need to draw on their practical and investigative skills and good situational awareness (see section 3.2.5) to gain, interpret, and note/remember/record as much information as possible, and, of course, take the right action. Aspects that may seem irrelevant can gain much more significance later, so all actions and information recorded if relevant are always potentially 'disclosable' under CPIA rules.

SIOs may find it useful to recover the actual recording made of any radio transmissions sent and/or received to confirm exact wording and detail of the information obtained and passed on by first responders, and to view any body-worn video (BWV) recording devices.

Holly Wells and Jessica Chapman, in August 2002. His initial statement helped to implicate him in the crime for which he was eventually convicted. This is why it vital to record as much detail as accurately as possible at all times (the next best thing to an admission or confession is a provable lie).

[5] See the case of Tony McCluskie who, in 2012, murdered and dismembered the body of his sister, Gemma McCluskie, and lied when he tried to report her as a missing person to a police enquiry counter.

Rarely is the first responder a witness to the actual incident (although they might become a significant witness post-attendance), so they must rely upon and manage with what they see and hear. Whatever the circumstances, response officers will begin the preliminary investigation. All their senses need to be applied to note what they see, hear, touch/feel, and smell (odours, eg exhaust fumes, gas, perfume/aftershave, bleach, alcohol, drugs, tobacco/vaping smells) that may prove useful to the subsequent investigation. They are the first on the scene and unquestionably in the best possible position to gather information at a time when it is most likely to be available; aka the 'Golden Hour'.

Initial responders (including crime investigators) need to remain alert and use their 'sixth' sense to notice things that seem significant and unusual using the JDLR principle ('Just Doesn't Look Right'). They should try and *identify* useful investigative material before it gets lost or spoilt, and *secure* and *protect* it (ISP). Examples might include weapons, forensic traces, discarded items, open doors or windows, signs of a struggle, forced entry/exit points, lights switched on or off, curtains drawn, dry shapes of a missing vehicle set against an otherwise wet road or driveway, or hand, footwear, and tyre marks.

Observing and noting what is said, what is happening, and what is available at the time of arrival—such as persons present (eg victims, by noting their condition and anything they might say before being taken away for treatment, or offenders who make significant statements) and the atmosphere and mood of those around (watching the watchers), descriptions, things being talked about or said and who by, persons or vehicles leaving suddenly—is all part of the big picture available to first responders. It is this type of information that often diminishes quickly and for which there is usually only one opportunity to capture, some of which may need immediate action (eg deploying scent dogs or directing other resources to follow trails or direction of travel). This is why it is so important to debrief initial responders and call takers (see Chapter 9).

First responders might also be the ones who deal with potential victims and have an opportunity to provide them with vital initial support as well as taking details from them. Initial victim engagement is dealt with in section 11.4 which outlines how they should be engaged with in a respectful and supportive manner for the benefit of not just them but the investigation. This might apply to witnesses too.

KEY POINTS

1. First responders have the best opportunity to observe important detail that may diminish quickly. They should be debriefed to ensure all they have noted and recorded is captured and made available to the investigation team.
2. Initial professional engagement with and supporting of victims and witnesses is of major importance and will aid not just them but also the investigation.

5.6.1 **Preservation of life**

One of the five building blocks is the preservation of life (see section 5.4). The rule applies to anyone: victims, vulnerable people (eg children), witnesses, the public, officers, and even suspects (usually in that order). The first response to any crime scene carries an overriding responsibility of searching for and attending to any persons who might have immediate medical and welfare needs. If there is any doubt as to death or possible signs of life, first aid and resuscitation (if required) should be administered and medical assistance summoned. Due to significant advances in medical science and emergency techniques, casualties who have suffered serious trauma can often be treated (if done promptly) to make full recovery.

With fatalities, only qualified medical personnel can certify a person to be deceased (or life extinct). Once a person has been certified dead, the avoidance of evidential contamination becomes highly relevant (see the following checklist).

Checklist—Dealing with a deceased person

- Only when absolutely necessary should an exploratory examination be made for marks or injuries (eg wounds, burn or ligature marks, incisions, abrasions, injuries, or any signs of recent trauma).

- Any checks should be minor and limited to exposed parts of the body (ie head, face, neck, and forearms).

- Assistance of a Crime Scene Investigator (CSI) and Medical Examiner (ME) should be sought as soon as practicable.

- Photography/video capture before and after any disturbance and/or making a sketch of the deceased at the scene is recommended.

- Protective equipment such as gloves should be worn, and substantial disturbance of any forensic evidence avoided (and the SIO notified if occurred).

- Checking clothing or possessions for identification may be important, eg for mobile phones, but such action must be disclosed (eg to consider contamination and not give a false impression of an attack, theft, or robbery).

5.7 **Health and Safety**

Crime scenes can pose a range of hazards to responders that, owing to the attending spontaneity, may require dynamic risk assessments. Risk examples include:

- Dangerous offenders and/or hostile crowds, difficult onlookers (rubber-neckers), violent groups or individuals.
- Decomposing bodies or body parts.
- Liquid blood and body fluids.

- Dangerous animals, infestations, and parasites.
- Fire, water, electricity, or gas hazards.
- Drugs and drug paraphernalia, eg syringes, drug production equipment.
- Hazardous or noxious substances and chemicals.
- Explosives, improvised explosive devices (IEDs), biological, radiological, and nuclear agents including toxic substances.[6]
- Unsafe buildings, machinery, or materials.
- Firearms and other dangerous weapons.
- Sharp items.
- Difficult terrain or dangerous environments and inclement weather.
- Infection and diseases
- Abusive images and material such as IIOC or other distressing content (eg torture and beheadings) or data.

Generic organisational risk assessments usually cater for attendance at crime scenes. However, wherever possible advice should be sought, and personal protective equipment worn if required. At a major crime scene, once cordons are in place, standard protection within an inner cordon as a minimum usually comprises a full protective scene suit with hood up, face mask, overshoes, and protective gloves (and these requirements need to be recorded in a risk assessment/scene management policy).

5.8 Preserving Crime Scenes

Another of the five building blocks is preserving crime scenes. This can be separated into three key elements known as the 'ISP' principle:

> **I**—IDENTIFY
>
> **S**—SECURE
>
> **P**—PROTECT

This is a straightforward rule and it means what it says: all areas relating to a crime scene(s), once identified, are to be secured and protected. A key task of initial responders is to prevent disturbance and unauthorised persons entering and/or disturbing and contaminating crime scenes. This includes supervisory staff, unless there is an urgent operational need. The three procedures are outlined below and also explained in Chapter 6.

1. **Identify**. There may be more than one crime scene and the initial response may identify and deal with just one of a number of scenes. The identification

---

[6] The Salisbury and Amesbury Novichok poisoning incidents in 2018 led to one police officer undergoing tests for possible exposure, having attended the scene where the victims, Sergei and Yulia Skripal, were found unconscious.

of all other potential crime scenes can originate from information, witnesses, observations, or CCTV, etc. If there is more than one scene, each should be sequentially numbered, eg Scene 1 (S1), Scene 2 (S2), and so on. A list of what may constitute a crime scene (such as a location, victim, escape route, vehicle(s) used, attack sites, suspects) is outlined in Chapter 6.

2. **Secure**. There are a number of ways to secure a crime scene and much depends on the circumstances and environment. In serious and major cases, cordons are used with high-visibility tape to mark out the sterile area, with staff appointed to restrict and control access. Indoor scenes are generally easier to secure than outdoor locations, which require more resources to maintain security.

3. **Protect**. In addition to safety issues, scenes need to be protected from any disturbance and interference from the public, media, weather, animals, etc. A common approach path (CAP) should be established for a single access and exit route, which needs to be the route least likely to have been used by the offender(s).

Any item at a scene can be of evidential value and usually the golden rule is that *nothing should be touched or moved*. If, however, something of a physical nature is in immediate danger of being lost, destroyed, or contaminated, steps should be taken to protect or recover the item in order to preserve it. Removal should be conducted with minimum disturbance, carefully recording the exact position and location of the exhibit. If possible, it should be photographed in position (in situ) first. This includes fragile material such as footprints, blood marks, and footwear or tyre impressions in mud/soil that may be destroyed by weather. Improvisation may be necessary to cover and protect items using available 'make-do' objects until the right equipment arrives.

It is sometimes difficult to determine exact boundaries for scene cordons and preservation. If indoors, the task is much easier. Outdoors, however, there are added complications such as the weather, general public, vehicular traffic, terrain, and location. As a general rule, it is better to make cordons as wide as possible, using natural boundaries, as they can always be reduced later. It is not always possible the other way around.

Note: In serious sexual assaults there are specific guidelines for dealing with victims, such as the use of early evidence kits (EEK). This enables first response officers to quickly and effectively recover forensic material from victims before a medical examination takes place that could otherwise be lost.

5.8.1 **Basic crime scene kits**

Basic scene kits equip staff to meet the ISP requirement and minimise the chances of contamination. These should be routinely carried by all operational personnel and as a minimum contain:

- cordon/barrier tape
- 2 × pairs of disposable overshoes

- 2 × pairs of disposable gloves
- scene log and cordon documentation
- exhibit bags and boxes plus labels
- tape for sealing bags and scissors
- EEK for sexual offence
- first-aid kit
- *aide-memoire* of actions

5.9 Emergency Responders

Emergency responders such as paramedics (medical teams) and fire crews may also attend crime scenes and initially their actions take precedent where lives are at risk. They perform their duties and have a habit of quickly redeploying elsewhere so they will need hot-debriefing.

They usually keep their own records of attendance and involvement, including the circumstances of what they found and what they are told upon arrival. Often, they obtain or hear and record information from victims, witnesses (including bystanders), or even offenders. In some instances, consideration may need to be given to treating them as significant witnesses depending on the extent of what they have seen or heard.

Emergency services personnel are not trained investigators. Debriefing questions might have to include how they gained entry to the scene (indoors or outdoors), where they have been and what they may have touched or moved. They should be asked questions such as who was present? What did they see? What did any victims or witnesses say? What medical intervention was made and what items were left behind at the scene? Why did they remove something? (ie 5WH principles).

Medical teams can unavoidably disturb and/or contaminate potential evidence. This should be considered when interpreting a crime scene. Resuscitation devices such as defibrillator pads cause injuries or marks which, together with any discarded medical equipment, need accounting for, including establishing what they have touched (eg leaving blood traces on a light switch they have accessed to try and improve visibility).

If considering responders themselves or their equipment as potential evidential items (or even a crime scene), sensible and pragmatic judgement needs to be applied. For example, when seeking to recover trace evidence from emergency services' personnel, clothing, footwear, or vehicles, eg ambulances, local agreements usually provide guidance on what should/should not be retained or impounded for forensic examination. Usually samples can be taken without disrupting the ability of the emergency resources to return to providing an operational emergency service. If ambulances and/or rapid response vehicles are located within a cordon, a path can be cleared for their release and tyre impressions or photographs taken prior to their removal or at some later stage for elimination purposes. Normally if victims are placed within ambulances, the only items that should be considered seizing are blankets; it is inappropriate to seize equipment needed for other patients, such as defibrillators.

Emergency services providers may take their own images and create their own records, which could contain valuable information about who was around the scene (eg the fire service may take photographs to assist their own assessment and investigation into a fire, which could contain details of an arsonist, an associate, or a significant witness). Some fire and ambulance service vehicles and personnel carry their own CCTV/dashcams/BWV. These should be made subject of an HP action to obtain and examine, usually facilitated by the respective Trust that employs them at the earliest opportunity.

KEY POINTS

- Emergency services responders have primacy at crime scenes until their role of saving lives, administering medical treatment or making the area safe is concluded They can then hand over to the investigation team.
- They may obtain useful evidence or information during their attendance and will require hot-debriefing before redeploying. An HP action may be needed to recover any evidential material they might have gathered during the course of their duties.

Bibliography

ACPO, *Emergency Procedures Manual* (NCPE, 2002)

ACPO, *Murder Investigation Manual* (NCPE, 2006)

Cook, T, Hibbitt, S, and Hill, M, *Blackstone's Crime Investigator's Handbook*, 2nd edn (Oxford University Press, 2016)

Crime Scenes, Searches, and Exhibits

6.1 Introduction

The nineteenth-century French medico-legal pioneer, Edmond Locard, conceived the principle known as 'every contact leaves a trace'. It means that everyone who enters a crime scene takes something in with them or leaves something behind. This is known as Locard's Principle of Exchange,[1] and is one reason why the professional management of crime scenes, searches, and exhibits is so important.

One advantage of forensic or physical evidence is that it cannot be affected by faulty memory, prejudice, bad eyesight, or an individual deciding 'not to get involved'. However, in order to use it evidentially, it must be proved beyond all reasonable doubt that the correct and necessary procedures have been applied and managed rigorously. This is to maintain the 'integrity' of those processes and avoid accusations of interference or cross-contamination. The chain of custody of scenes, exhibits, and forensic samples must receive meticulous care and attention and all relevant legislative authorities' procedures and powers strictly complied with to ensure important evidential discoveries cannot be discredited.

There is much to be gained from applying procedures covered in this chapter. Managed correctly, they will reap dividends for the benefit of the investigation. The success of serious and major crime investigations often relies heavily on essential processes of scene, search, and exhibit management.

KEY POINT

A murder victim is killed once; a murder scene can be killed many times.

6.2 Identify, Secure, and Protect (ISP)

The ISP principle is one of the five building block principles referred to in section 5.8. Dealing with identification first, any one or a combination from the list below could be identified and designated as a crime scene. It is worth remembering that crime scenes come in a wide variety of forms and the following list seems to grow.

Checklist—Crime scenes

- Indoor or outdoor locations, public or private.
- Place where offence believed committed.

---

[1] E Locard, *Traité de Criminalistique* 7 vols (Lyons Police Authority, 1914).

- Premises searched.

- Means of transport (eg motor vehicles, vessels, trains, buses, or bicycles).

- Place where significant object is suspected to be or is located.

- Victims (their body if deceased, or body part).

- Where a victim was last seen (eg if missing).

- Locations where a victim has been deposited (deposition site) or moved from.

- Witnesses who have come into contact with victims, offenders, or related crime scenes.

- Suspects.

- Attack sites.

- Anywhere there is trace or physical evidence, eg footprints, fingerprints, or blood.

- Articles connected to victims, witnesses, or offenders, eg clothing or weapons.

- Cyber (virtual) scenes including digital items and communication devices, Wi-Fi routers, tablets, mobile phones, gaming devices, cloud storage, digital images, social media sites and entries, and web forums and chatlogs.

- Premises or places connected with suspects or offences (including industrial and business premises).

- Access and escape routes.

- Location(s) where a crime has been planned or to which it has a significant connection.

Whether what could be 'identified' as a crime scene actually constitutes a crime scene is really up to the SIO to decide, and in doing so they would be very wise to consult with appropriate experts and specialists for advice. If the initial responders have already made decisions as to what is/is not a crime scene, then these decisions will need to be reviewed.

Some crime scenes are not always what you'd expect; for example, in a train disaster a signal/junction box may be deemed a crime scene; in corporate manslaughter or a death in healthcare setting cases, offices, filing cabinets, ledgers, treatment areas, or surgical instruments may become crime scenes; or in a suicide/mass murder by an airline pilot, his home address and parents' addresses might need to be treated as crime scenes.[2]

---

[2] As in the case of Andreas Lubitz, who deliberately crashed his Germanwings A320 airbus into the French Alps, killing himself and 149 others on board in March 2015.

KEY POINT

Once identified, crime scenes are allocated a distinguishable sequential number (Scene 1, Scene 2, etc). Using numbers rather than the notation 'primary' or 'secondary' crime scenes is preferable in order to avoid perceptions that one scene has been treated more preferentially than another. The term 'multiple crime scenes' is safer.

Crime scenes may not be uncovered if they are not immediately obvious until a physical or forensic search has taken place. The sooner this search happens, the more chance there is of successful evidential capture. Once identified, crime scenes should be *secured* and *protected* from unauthorised interference (including family, friends, and relatives of victims, non-essential police/medical personnel, animals, onlookers, and journalists). This is to avoid any evidence being altered, moved, destroyed, lost, or contaminated. No unauthorised persons should ever be allowed to enter a crime scene except in an emergency, such as to give medical aid or save life, until the arrival of a senior investigator and/or the SIO and Crime Scene Manager or Investigator (CSM/CSI).

Any persons who do not have a *specific or valid reason* for being inside a crime scene cordon should be regarded as *unauthorised*. Only an SIO or CSI (with agreement of the SIO) may grant authority to access a crime scene, and this directive has to be clearly communicated to all those in and around the crime scene location.

KEY POINTS

- Medical personnel may have to disturb a crime scene to administer treatment and it is important to debrief them to ascertain what evidence they may have disturbed when securing access for their vehicles and equipment and providing treatment. Any medical 'consumables' left at the scene must be accounted for.
- When police (or journalistic) helicopters hover close to outside scenes (including air ambulances), their downdraught can disrupt and prove detrimental to crime scene preservation.

6.2.1 Security of crime scenes

Security cordons are useful for guarding crime scenes and protecting officers and staff working inside them. Also, for controlling the public, sightseers, and the media, preventing unauthorised interference and access (eg by offenders), preventing sensitive activities, conversations, and comments being observed or overheard, and for preserving evidence and avoiding contamination. They will also prevent entry into areas that are contaminated or considered to pose a risk of danger.

Initial responders need to arrange scene security at the earliest opportunity by setting up cordons quickly. This can prove challenging and can be resource-intensive, particularly if there is a large area to protect, ie out of doors. At some later stage, it may have to be proved beyond all reasonable doubt that there was zero possibility of interference with or contamination of a crime scene, particularly if vital trace evidence links an offender to it.

Cordons can be resource and time consuming and usually rely upon uniformed officers to provide the most suitable, recognisable, and visible resources to be effective. These officers effectively become the 'visible' element of the investigation and what the public see when they are near the scene or watching news reports. Apart from the essential security and scene sterility function, cordon control officers can influence community confidence about how the enquiry is being managed. Therefore cordon duty officers must at all times behave properly and appear totally professional and remain alert and look interested while on duty at a scene cordon.

KEY POINTS

1. Those engaged in cordon duties should make themselves clearly visible to the public. They are on show and indicative of the level of police professionalism. Unacceptable behaviour from officers looking disinterested or being undisciplined (eg sitting in vehicles eating food or playing with their phones) sends out the wrong message and can adversely affect public confidence.
2. Cordon officers should be encouraged to communicate with people visiting, loitering around, or passing by as they may hold vital information. They should be reminded, however, not to give out too much detail about the incident or investigation without prior briefing or sanction from the SIO, especially to journalists or members of a victim's family or community.

Early review and assessment of cordon security arrangements, parameters, position, and adequacy of cordons is advisable. This should take cognisance of the circumstances of the case and available information, such as entry and egress routes by offenders. Precise scene cordon parameters, when determined, should be recorded and indicated clearly and accurately on a drawing, sketch, plan, and/or map. If any alterations are made to these parameters, then these need accurately recording, together with the reasons why.

Indoor scenes are usually comparatively easier to secure by the closing of doors and access points restricting entry into premises, initially by the presence of officers at entrance and exit points. They are usually relatively self-contained. However, most outdoor scenes provide additional complications, such as adverse weather conditions, large areas, and difficult terrain, challenging environments, crowds, animals, traffic, security, media intrusion, or elevated observation points nearby. Outdoor cordons should be made as large as possible as they can be reduced.

Restricting access to outdoor scenes can be achieved by the use of metal barriers or cordon tape, vehicles to block entrances, the use of uniform or Community Support Officers. Some LEAs may opt to use private security staff to control outer perimeters and entry/exit points. Dog handlers and mounted officers, if available (if a large rural area, for instance), can also be utilised to ensure boundary lines are not crossed.

Natural boundaries such as hedges, fences, and walls can be used to form part of a cordon, bearing in mind the potential for offenders to have discarded evidential items such as weapons, blood-stained clothing, mobile phones, keys, or stolen items over or into them. Road blocks may also be necessary, dependent on the location. Basically, scene cordons *must* be adequately guarded along their entire perimeter to ensure there is no unauthorised access.

Responsibility for managing/supervising cordons should be given to a supervisor who is sometimes referred to as a designated 'Scene Bronze Commander'. Their task is to ensure adequate resources and arrangements are in place for safeguarding the integrity and security of a scene and eliminating unauthorised access. The role includes briefing and continuously supervising all those on cordon security duties. It includes ensuring that scene logs are completed correctly. Their effectiveness in performing this role may play an important part in proving the sterility and integrity of key exhibits in a prosecution case or review of the investigation.

KEY POINT

SIOs and supervisors need to be intrusive when assuring the effectiveness of cordon management and scene security. This can be achieved by arriving unannounced at cordons and querying officers about their duties, asking if they have been briefed properly, who is supervising them and checking the content, accuracy, and quality of their scene log(s).

There are usually two types of cordons—inner and outer. In some circumstances it may be necessary to set up an additional (third) outer cordon. This would be much wider, covering both inner and outer cordons, and might be needed if there is more than one significant scene within close proximity. On Operation Sumac, for example (a linked series of five female homicides in December 2006 near Ipswich in Suffolk), two of the five victims' bodies (Annette Nicholls and Paula Clennel) were located close together and adjacent to a busy country road. At these scenes, both inner and outer cordons were created, with an additional (third) outer cordon used to keep the media and public out of both perimeters.[3]

---

[3] See NPIA (2008) 4(2) *Journal of Homicide and Major Incident Investigation*, 94–7.

OP SUMAC—CORDONS/SCENE SEARCH

Where bodies were recovered from land, there were obviously more forensic opportunities. In these cases, the Police Search Adviser, Police Search Coordinator (PolSC) and CSI attended each scene to formulate a joint approach to scene examination and search in agreement with the relevant SIO. This worked well and enabled the PolSC to start planning for the search when the scene was released by the CSI ... cordons at all scenes were made as large as possible. It was recognised that this increased the cost of policing, but it was crucial for preserving the integrity of the scenes. Once the scenes were released to PolSA, the areas within the cordon were subject to detailed or fingertip search. The force dog unit was used to search areas outside the cordon. This worked well and provided reassurance that nothing was missed ... A clear audit trail was maintained by the search team office regarding which teams had been used on which search, what measures had been put in place to minimise cross contamination and the location, usage and cleaning of equipment. At the end of each day statements were submitted from all staff involved in searching even if nothing was recovered. This provided an audit trail of the whole search strategy.

NPIA Professional Practice, *Strategic Debrief—Operation Sumac*
(NPIA, 2008), p 29.

Note: Terms such as 'hot zone', 'warm zone', and 'cold zone' are sometimes used when referring to crime scenes that involve contaminated areas (eg in terrorism cases). These are areas that are graded depending on how likely they are to pose a threat to the health and safety of anyone located within their boundaries.

6.2.2 **Protection—inner and outer cordons**

1. *Inner cordon*—designated area closest to where the main examination takes place. It may be where a body lies or the main offence site (eg at an illicit drug laboratory/storage place). It usually has quite narrow parameters and provides a boundary for detailed forensic examinations and must be very tightly controlled. This is where there may be consideration of a large tent or other similar screening equipment to safeguard privacy from onlookers or long-range media cameras or observation and listening equipment (and the use of airborne drones that carry very high-spec lenses and directional microphones). Without effective cordons, briefings for examiners and searchers and their actions/reactions can be seen, heard, or recorded.

2. *Outer cordon*—broader containment area covering peripheral parts of the inner scene. Provides a secure area not only for examination, but also preparatory work to be undertaken and adequate distancing of the public and media. This area may also be subject to forensic examination and physical searching but this is unlikely to be as detailed as the inner cordon.

Each cordon must have effective 'access control' to ensure only authorised people gain entry. Adequate policies and clear instructions are needed for cordon officers to clearly tell them who is/is not to be allowed entry; which may differ between inner and outer cordons. These decisions are best made in consultation with the CSM/CSI and there may need to be separate and distinct policies for both areas. For these reasons, both cordons require a separate scene log to be completed for each one (scene logs are covered later).

6.2.3 Rendezvous point (RVP)

An RVP is usually the best place to site the person completing the outer cordon scene log as it constitutes precisely what the name implies. A suitable location should be found where all required scene resources can congregate to plan and prepare examination and search tactics. A signed vehicle that is easily identifiable may be used in the first instance, and if there are good communication systems on board, they can be put to good use while there.

There may be practical and logistical difficulties to consider (such as parking or briefing facilities) out of the sheer volume and type of resources required. It may be easier to manage resources, however if they are directed to an RVP located at a cordon. If specialist services or agencies that bring large vehicles and equipment (eg an underwater or specialist search unit) are involved, then a large enough area needs to be identified where these resources can safely assemble, park up, gain access to facilities, brief, change clothing, take refreshments, rest and recuperate, etc, where they will not be impeded by the public or media. In such a case, someone should be nominated to take control of managing these resources. This may include traffic management officers if there are vehicle and public route diversions. These roles are usually designated as Bronze roles (see section 7.2).

Suitability of RVPs, and secondary RVPs such as a forward command post (FCP), can be utilised for mobile command facilities and locating Silver and Bronze Commanders (as used in major incident response contingency plans). Risks and any health and safety concerns have to be considered when locations are chosen, particularly in terrorism cases, where suspected secondary devices may have been deliberately placed. In cases such as these, any potential RVP will have to be searched before it is deemed safe beforehand.

6.2.4 Common approach paths (CAPs)

A CAP should be determined and marked out at the earliest opportunity. This is used as the sole route into and out of a crime scene for all those subsequently attending (eg for examination purposes or treatment/removal of victims). It is most likely the direct route to any victims or premises that will already have been taken by initial response teams including emergency and first responders. Wherever possible, this same route should be used to leave the area, unless it becomes clear that the offenders have also used that route (eg if eye witnesses or CCTV indicate or there are footwear marks or other tell-tale signs). Protective stepping plates are frequently used to protect the surface underneath and particularly in premises, where trace evidence on flooring and carpets may need preserving.

It is vital that details of all those initially attending are recorded so that their route taken can be clarified before the CAP is determined. A sketch plan may be helpful, which can be exhibited and registered on a case management system (CMS). The golden rule is that a CAP should be along the *least likely route taken by the offender(s) or victim(s)*.

KEY POINTS

1. At outdoor scenes, hard-standing, or compact, gravel-type path areas are ideal for a CAP as they are more practical to use; they are also easier and quicker to search in order to render them clear than other surfaces, such as foliage or grassland.
2. A CAP may have to be suitable for transporting equipment or removing casualties.
3. A CAP needs to be the *least likely route taken by the offender(s) or victim(s)*.
4. In terrorism cases, RVPs may need to be checked for secondary devices.

Checklist—Scene security and protection

- Both inner and outer cordons are required (ie two × cordons).

- The largest possible area should be cleared; parameters can be narrowed later.

- Two separate scene logs are completed (one for inner, one for outer).

- For parameters, a quick and objective evaluation can be based upon:

  o location of offence, incident (or victim),

  o likely presence of physical evidence,

  o eyewitness accounts and/or information/intelligence/CCTV.

- Outdoor scenes—use can be made of natural boundaries (eg trees, streams, gates, walls, fences, lamp-posts, building lines) as cordon boundaries.

- Consider the possibility of other linked crime scenes (eg abandoned vehicles or an attack site) that may also need to be preserved.

- Cordon areas should be clearly marked (ie with identifiable crime scene tape).

- Cordons allow access only to authorised persons—this must be clearly communicated.

- Outdoor scenes may need early consideration of protective covers or high screens (regardless of weather forecast) eg to protect dignity of victims from public/media).

- Inner cordons can be map grid-referenced to show exactly where items are located.

- Nominated Bronze commanders can be tasked with managing and supervising cordons.

6.2.5 Displaced residents and vehicles

Some scenes are located in areas that are difficult to contain, such as places where local residents have their homes, possessions, or vehicles that are inside a cordon. This may include homes or business premises where the placing and security of secure cordons means third parties become victims of collateral interference and are effectively displaced by restricted access.

Sensible solutions (in consultation with a CSI/CSM), such as having vehicles examined by a CSI and recording or photographing of their type and exact position to allow them to be released, should be enacted. When satisfied there is no link to the crime, supervised removal can be arranged. Residents can be permitted to use their rear doors rather than front, for instance, and, if necessary, they can wear protective suits or overshoes to allow access in and out of the cordon. A protectively suited officer can visit each address to explain the reasons for the restrictions and arrangements for safe movements. An explanatory note from the SIO and/or local policing team, apologising for the inconvenience, might reduce potential frustrations directed against the enquiry team. This policy can be included as part of a 'community impact' control strategy (see section 11.8).

6.2.6 Legal issues—entering and securing crime scenes

The majority of the law-abiding public are willing to cooperate and allow access to and examination of crime scenes on their properties. They believe it is sensible to follow police advice, which may be supported by other agencies such as the fire and rescue service, health professionals, or local authority representatives. There are also legal powers conferred in sections 8, 17, 18, and 32 of the Police and Criminal Evidence Act 1984 (PACE) and other legislation to enter premises (using reasonable force if necessary) for the purpose of conducting a search.

In the case of *DPP v Morrison*,[4] a decision confirmed that under common law the police have the power to erect a cordon in order to preserve the scene of a crime. The Divisional Court upheld this rule in this case, given the importance of this function in investigating serious crime.

---

[4] *DPP v Morrison* QBD, 4 April 2003; *Daily Telegraph*, 17 April 2003; *The Times*, 21 April 2003.

105

The case of *Rice v Connolly*[5] previously reaffirmed long-established principles that have not been challenged. It was confirmed that the police are entitled to take all reasonable steps to keep the peace, prevent and detect crime, and bring offenders to justice. It is according to these principles that the police are entitled to secure scenes of crime for examination by specialists, forensic scientists, etc. If anyone were to frustrate, hinder, or obstruct the securing of a crime scene, they would potentially commit the offence of obstructing a police officer in the execution of their duty. This includes non-warranted staff, such as scene investigators, who are regarded as formal investigators under the Criminal Procedure and Investigations Act 1996 (CPIA).

Murder Investigation Manual (MIM) states:

> Where a scene is on private property, SIOs will need to negotiate access with those in control of the premises. Considerable tact and diplomacy will often be necessary for this, particularly where the scene is occupied or controlled by a suspect's family or associates or where the scene requires to be searched for objects suspected of being buried or concealed. If necessary, alternative arrangements should be made for their accommodation until the scene is released. Where a crime scene is likely to have a significant impact on commerce, SIOs should consult their force legal department for advice about the length of time it can be held.[6]

Care must be taken if a crime scene is released and then, for whatever reason, it becomes necessary to reapply the cordons and perform searches. Under these circumstances, it may be legally safer to apply for a court warrant (eg under section 8 of PACE) or utilise other legislation to guarantee there is a firm legal basis for further activity at the particular location.

6.3 Crime Scene Assessments

The SIO and CSM/CSI and other specialists and experts (eg the PolSC/PolSA) need to work together as a team to establish and agree what constitutes a scene, the parameters, preservation measures, and physical/forensic searches, tactics, examination, and evidence recovery plans. This includes any separate and additional policy that may be required to recover special items, such as human remains. Once agreed, the strategy and tactics are usually recorded and signed-off by all contributory parties.

A crime scene assessment is the precursor to a tactical meeting and is the first stage in the process. It provides an opportunity to review and check that adequate preservation procedures are in place and for the SIO to get a first-hand 'feel' for the scene and surroundings. It may be some time before images are available for viewing and an experienced investigator such as an SIO can still apply *their own* skills and knowledge to the crime scene assessment. This

---

[5] *Rice v Connolly* (1966) QB P414.
[6] ACPO, *Murder Investigation Manual* (NCPE, 2006), 136.

will avoid becoming overly influenced by experts either who may not have the same level of training in the law, points to prove, investigative mindset, or the same awareness and knowledge of the wider investigation.

The SIO may also require those who have already been involved at the scene (such as the investigator who responded and initially took charge) and the CSM to accompany them during a 'walk and talk' (aka 'walkthrough) session through the crime scene. In doing so, great care should be taken to prevent any risk of (cross) contamination and protective clothing should be worn.

Scene assessments also allow for a review of cordons and screening arrangements. In the case of a fatality at the scene, the assessment would also usually include a Forensic Pathologist. Assessments can be aided by CCTV footage or video recording of the crime scene, and any first-hand accounts from witnesses, paramedics, or initial responders.

Assessments can also provide an opportunity to identify any physical evidence that may need recovering quickly, not just forensic items such as bloodstained clothing or weapons but also other items and material such as passive data (eg from CCTV or automatic number plate recognition (ANPR) cameras). Dangerous items, such as loaded firearms, knives, toxic chemicals, combustible, or biological materials, or explosive devices would also fall under this category and would need close guarding and risk management until rendered safe.

6.3.1 Scene contaminators

Scene assessments can cover the identification of potential contaminators or destroyers.

Checklist—Potential crime scene contaminators

- Weather—particularly if outdoors, blood, prints, body fluids, DNA, etc can be ruined by inclement weather such as rain, frost, snow, wind, direct sunlight, and heat.

- Suspects or associates—attempting to destroy or remove any incriminating evidence, or legitimately putting themselves at the crime scene.

- Spectators, onlookers, curious members of the public (eg rubber-neckers), or displaced persons.

- Officials, experts, or supervisors—those who think they have a right to enter.

- Scavenging animals and insects.

- Media (covered in section 9.6).

- Geological disturbances (eg flooding, landslides, seeps, springs, subsidence, gas emissions, landfill and waste, areas of ground contamination, pollution, weathering, and erosion).

6.3.2 **Maps, plans, sketches, and digital images**

Detailed maps, plans, and digital images of crime scenes and surrounding areas are always extremely useful for assessment purposes and setting parameters. The exact position, scale, proximity, and dimensions of locations and objects in the context of their location are invaluable. Scene photographs or digital images are good at recording 'close-ups' etc, but a detailed plan or map can show precise locations and context, particularly at complex or large crime scenes. These can also be used for effective communication of detail about crime scene information that is helpful when teams and specialists need briefing.

Maps can also be used to delineate search areas. These shouldn't prevent the SIO from producing their own rough sketches or plans of scenes when they undertake assessments to use as an aide-memoire, and for marking out cordon and search parameters, aid early hypotheses evaluation, as a prop when conducting briefings, etc. There may be a significant time delay before official maps, plans, or images become available, which is when a rough sketch will prove useful.

Aerial and drone photography can assist in finding and recording the exact location of scenes and can help make other significant discoveries. Reachback images will provide a valuable tool for assessments, briefings and decision-making processes. The SIO may also wish to take advantage of some of the satellite imagery available on the Internet, although the time and date the imagery was produced must be borne in mind.

KEY POINT

A detailed crime scene plan or map should have a relevant title, date, time, and orientation, usually given by the inclusion of a north- (N) pointing arrow.

6.3.3 **Digital scene reproduction**

There may be opportunities to produce a computerised digital reproduction and/or a reconstruction of a crime scene to help gain a better understanding of what took place, in what sequence, and how events happened. This can help in:

- putting the crime scene and its surroundings into context
- formation of hypotheses
- testing individual hypotheses by additional analysis
- producing the most probable reconstruction theory

Sophisticated computer enhancements, animated reconstructions, robotic panoramic crime scene cameras, 3D models, and 360-degree camera angles can recreate a crime scene and check witness timings, distance, exhibit locations etc. These can be used in court to show a jury the most likely sequence of events and positions, and the importance of exhibits and forensic samples, or how the evidence combines, to present a clearer picture of fragmented or complex evidence.

6.4 **Crime Scene Coordinators and Managers**

Most large and complex crime investigations have an appointed CSM and/or Coordinator (CSC) if more than one major scene is involved. The status or seniority of these roles may vary according to the nature of the investigation. For some investigations, including most homicide cases, the roles should go to accredited CSMs, although for less serious cases an experienced CSI may be utilised.

Their role involves assessing, deploying, and managing experts both from the crime scene examination perspective and also from other relevant agencies. They can act as advisers on examination strategies, evidential types, values, and prioritisation of exhibits, and they should maintain comprehensive records of scene strategies and contribute to forensic strategies. They are effectively the focal point for all forensic-related enquiries during the examination of the scene and during the subsequent forensic submissions and analysis processes.

The sooner a CSM/CSC is involved, the better managed and more coordinated the forensic investigation will be. For pre-planned crime investigations, involving a CSM at the preparation stage can enable appropriate tactical options to be implemented prior to the execution of searches and for forensic recovery potential to be maximised.

The CSC appointed to an investigation should be the SIO's first point of contact for any deployment of CSI staff. The CSC is also the most appropriately qualified person to deploy additional CSI staff, as they hold an overview of all other aspects of the investigation, and are also able to develop and offer appropriate strategies and advice on the most suitable sampling techniques and best practice, and to brief forensic staff and other specialists on behalf of the SIO. A CSM, on the other hand, will direct staff at one particular scene, and usually there is a CSM at each scene of 'multiples', whereas a CSC can oversee such deployments across all the crime scenes.

KEY POINT

CSCs/CSMs have a major influence on decisions made at crime scenes, forensic strategies, and examination priorities and policies. The final decision, however, always rests with the SIO as the crime scene 'belongs' to them as the person in overall charge. If in doubt, there is always the option of commissioning a peer review (second opinion) by an independent crime scene expert and/or forensic adviser.

6.5 **Physical Searches**

Most investigations require some sort of physical search to be conducted. There have been countless examples when a thorough search operation has had a direct and positive bearing on the quality and quantity of evidence recovered. The opportunity to maximise an evidential harvest through effective search and recovery processes is an integral part of most investigations. For this reason, wherever possible, trained, licensed, and experienced search experts and teams should be deployed.

A decision will be required as to what, if any, type of physical search is required and how it will link in with a forensic (ie more detailed and scientific) strategy, which usually takes precedence. This will be guided by the circumstances of the case. Searching first may inhibit forensic recovery, but a forensic examination is not a search, and therefore items can be missed. The interface between search and crime scene examination must be properly managed, with a clear understanding of which takes precedence and who is responsible for each phase.

Unless the person who is conducting the scene examination has received accredited search training (this is highly unlikely), the forensic scene examination phase cannot be considered a 'physical search' and the use of search-trained personnel will be required. Similarly, search teams do not usually have the same level of forensic awareness and ability as CSIs. Therefore, if a search takes place after a forensic scene examination, it is possible that new evidence and articles may be found, and a strategy will be required for dealing with them.[7]

A physical search may be required as an investigative tool for locating:

- victims or suspects
- human remains/body parts
- crime scenes
- investigative material (eg weapons, vehicles, stolen property, discarded items, digital data storage devices, CCTV, drugs)
- storage and/or deposition sites
- access/exit routes from a scene
- missing persons
- intelligence

An initial visual check (IVC) is a preliminary and quick overview for anything obvious (eg a victim or suspect) and is conducted in order to make rapid and early identification of anything likely to assist the investigation. This is likely to be a fast-track (Golden Hour) activity. It must be remembered that the preservation of life is always an overriding objective (one of the five building blocks; see section 5.4). These checks (searches), however, should wherever possible be

---

[7] See also ACPO, *Practice Advice on Search Management and Procedures* (NCPE, 2006), 164–6.

systematic, thorough, and recorded in detail so they can assist any subsequent more substantial (fully managed) searches.

With an initial search there is a potential for compromising any necessary forensic examination due to contamination and disruption, but this may have to be a calculated and managed risk. Dependent on available timescales, cautious tactics can be adopted and close consultation with a CSI/CSM and/or forensic scientists can help manage the risk.

Physical searching should, wherever possible, be led by intelligence. Those conducting these searches require briefing (and later debriefing) fully on the details of the investigation and what the objectives and tactics are for the search, eg what to look for and how to preserve/recover items. Listing items required is important but there must also be some latitude to allow searchers to use their own initiative to recover anything they consider might be relevant. This is why it is useful for search teams to have a good understanding of the case.

KEY POINT

When conducting initial searches, it is essential to look up as well as look down to see, for example, if anything of significance is located above ground level, eg in trees, on flat rooftops (aerial photography can sometimes assist).

Anything required for forensic examination when found should, as a general rule, be left in its original position to await a decision on how best to recover it. For general items, this is normally by a CSI (in consultation with the CSM or forensic scientist). The examination of large or fragile items may need careful planning. These are decisions made through a teamwork approach between the SIO, CSM/CSI/PolSC/PolSA, and specialists with everyone working together.

A crime scene assessment (as noted in the previous section) and planning process provides an opportunity to discuss and plan any search sequence and the recovery of specific items, eg cadavers. The crime scene team, CSM, CSI, forensic scientists, forensic pathologist, and any other required scientific advisers and experts, such as fingerprint experts, biologists, environmental profilers, digital forensic advisers, anthropologists, and ballistics experts, led by the SIO, must adopt a joined-up approach working towards specific objectives—NOT just for the benefit of individual specialisms. There are a number of considerations that will influence the way in which a search is managed and in what sequence, such as:

- search objectives
- identification of whether it is a search *for* a scene or *of* a scene
- most appropriate resources
- areas to be designated as crime scenes
- parameters of each search
- measures to control the risk of contamination
- appropriate reviews ('plan it—do it—review it')

KEY POINTS

- Cross-contamination is a hugely important consideration. Ensure those conducting searches have not been in contact with other crime scenes (eg suspects).
- In some circumstances it may be necessary to conduct an IVC and recover evidence immediately, balancing risk against opportunity and necessity.
- Outdoor searches provide added benefits of visible reassurance and often become popular images for use in media reporting (eg fingertip searches). These can be incorporated into community impact control strategies.
- Media and sightseers need controlling, including the witnessing, recording, or broadcasting of any recoveries.
- The term 'search' should always be prefixed with an adjective that qualifies it, eg 'flash', 'PolSA led', 'forensic', 'initial visual', 'hasty' or 'underwater', search.

6.5.1 Roles of the Police Search Adviser (PolSA), Police Search Coordinator (PolSC), and Police Search Team (PST)

Fully managed searches are far more intrusive and detailed than initial (or hasty) searches and usually conducted by those who are trained and accredited.[8] These types of searches are managed under the control and supervision of a Police Search Adviser (PolSA).

A PolSA can:

- advise on all aspects of physical search techniques and specialist assets.
- plan, direct, manage, and implement searches.
- manage Police Search Teams (PST).
- obtain technical resources.
- advise on search plans.
- maintain comprehensive records of the search.

A PolSA and their PST are invaluable assets who have their own briefing requirements in order to perform their roles. Accordingly, they should not be left to work in isolation and must be provided with the necessary information and briefings on developing intelligence with regard to the crime scene, the investigation and their objectives. Any search team is an operational arm of the enquiry and must be fully integrated into the investigation. Wherever practicable, the PolSC/PolSA should be invited to partake in enquiry team briefings and cascade information to their search teams; a strong communications link MUST exist between the enquiry team and the PolSC/PolSA/PST.

---

[8] College of Policing accredit PolSA and PolSC.

112

The SIO retains full responsibility for deciding which persons, premises, or areas are to be searched, the prioritisation of searches, and for agreeing the parameters in accordance with their investigative objectives. A PolSA can advise on the best parameters, methodology and techniques, search assets, health and safety aspects, logistical and technical constraints, and which other agencies and specialists are required, eg blood/victim recovery dogs, underwater search, air support, height access, marine experts, confined space teams, and use of volunteers.

6.5.2 **Role of the PolSC**

If there is more than one PolSA involved in search activity, then a Police Search Coordinator (PolSC) may be required to manage and supervise all the various search operations and act as primary link between the SIO and major incident team.

A PolSC is responsible for:

- overseeing all operational search responsibilities.
- coordinating multi-venue search operations.
- maintaining search role standards and competencies.
- supporting resource acquisition.
- quality assuring searches and associated documentation.

6.5.3 **Role of the PST**

A PST (Police Search team) works under the supervision of a PolSA and comprises officers who are trained by the College of Policing in specific search techniques for searching persons, vehicles, buildings, areas, and routes. Their role is to:

- provide a consistent approach to search tasks.
- be properly equipped and resourced to provide an effective search response.
- produce appropriate records and an audit trail relevant to their search.
- provide high levels of assurance and raise the probability of success.
- provide heightened awareness of health and safety measures and dangerous materials.

The enquiry team should liaise with the PolSC/PolSA and CSM/CSI in order to discuss and agree the search plan and parameters. The SIO should insist on agreeing a properly recorded formal tactical search plan (sometimes referred to as a 'search strategy document') which should be signed, timed, and dated by all parties. The PolSC/PolSA will develop a tactical plan, the aim of which is to deliver the search in accordance with the SIO's search and investigative objectives.

Checklist—Tactical search plan—suggested content

- When and where the search is being conducted and by whom

- What information is relevant to the search.

- What the search objectives are (including specific items sought).

- What the search parameters are—clearly marked out on maps/plans of the search area (with title, scale, north arrow, legend, date, and initials/name).

- Why the area is being searched (or not) and relevant lawful authority.

- How the search will be conducted, methodology, instrumentation, resources/assets, and anticipated timescales.

- What risks are involved and how they will be managed.

- What area, building, and/or subsurface or utility plans are needed or referred to, including historical and current Ordnance Survey maps, geological maps, local archives, and photographs.

- What other useful knowledge, information, or contacts is relied upon (eg local water authority or bailiff when searching canals, rivers, or streams).

- What specialist resources are being used and order of (phased) deployment.

- What site reconnaissance has been conducted to identify logistical or technical constraints (such as points of access, locations overhead, or underground utilities which may exclude the use of certain geophysical instruments).

- What the standard Operating Procedures (SOP) are for the search. This helps to provide a high level of consistency and allows independent peer review.

- How any media or community impact considerations will be managed.

- How evidence is to be preserved and recovered and who it will be handed to (eg Exhibits Officer).

- How any important results will be fed back to the SIO.

- When and how a review and reassessment will be performed eg in light of search progress or new intelligence.

6.5.4 Searching premises

During the course of an investigation it is highly probable there will be a requirement to conduct searches of premises that may or may not constitute crime scenes. This could include places where an offence has occurred, where there might be evidential or intelligence material, to locate a suspect, victims, missing persons, or vulnerable people. It could also include premises that are to be searched under the power of a warrant.

Adequate planning and preparation must be completed prior to any premises search with identified and communicated aims and objectives. For a thorough physical search of premises, a PolSA-led PST should be considered. This will ensure a high-assurance search is conducted. The SIO should also consider including one of their own investigators to be on hand to advise and assist the search team with their in-depth knowledge of the case and investigative skills. A trained EO (Exhibits Officer) will most definitely be required. A CSI should, whenever possible, be on hand to record the evidence accurately and advise on the appropriate recording/photographing, forensic recovery, packaging, transportation, and safe storage of seized items.

The type of premises/incident under investigation and the stage the investigation is at will determine what the search tactics should entail. For example, the minimum standard required when searching for a person such as an offender or missing person on premises is an 'open door' search. This means that all rooms, outbuildings, lofts, cupboards, wardrobes, etc will be accessed and checked.

When recovering clothing and items against set criteria, there must be a clear policy that stipulates what should/should not be seized as evidence and how they should be seized. For example, if checking footwear, taking photographs, or making drawings to compare tread patterns and markings may avoid having to seize and store too many exhibits.

Search officers need to work to a clear examination and retrieval strategy. For instance, when recovering clothing that is to be forensically packaged and sealed, best practice is to have it photographed prior to recovery, and then take front and back photographs prior to packaging. Although time consuming, this negates the need to submit numerous items for assessment to a forensic service provider, and allows the prioritising of certain items as they are more difficult to see or describe once sealed in bags that can only be opened under laboratory conditions. Photographs of items should aim to show not just the item itself but its context in relation to other items and layout, such as blood spray on a wall in the context of its position in a room.

When reviewing a search, the total time taken and the amount and types of resources utilised should be checked to give an indication of standard and thoroughness. Official documentation should note what, if any, damage was caused during the search and may help plan for or mitigate future compensation claims. If this is a foreseen possibility, then a plan to have a photographic record before and after the entry and search might prove useful.

Cordons erected around search premises will provide protection, enable the search to take place undisturbed, and provide safety for those conducting the search. This may be a control tactic for any identified risks where prolonged search operations are required and where the premises are in areas that are hostile to law enforcement agencies (LEAs), or are connected to hostile and dangerous families and individuals (eg connections with an OCG).

Checklist—Premises searches considerations

- Use a scene log and cordons (if necessary).
- Check for any health and safety risks (eg dangerous premises, persons, or animals).
- Legal powers (if by warrant see section 6.5.5)
- Signs of entry and exit, plus route to and from the premises by offenders.
- Use of specialist search dogs, such as blood, cadavers, attack sites, body parts, drugs, firearms, weapons, explosives, accelerants, and hi-tech devices.
- CAP for into/out of premises and cordons to protect procedure and staff.
- Personal protective equipment (PPE) policy, ie face mask, oversuit, gloves, overshoes.
- Scene protection eg stepping plates (being aware of slippery surfaces underneath).
- Exhibit recovery policy (eg photographing and/or forensic examination).
- Utilities, gas, water, electricity—include in safety check.
- Additional lighting requirements.
- Visual/still/aerial/360-degree photography or plan drawing of premises.
- Forensic strategy and resources (eg CSI, experts, and specialists on standby).
- At time of entering, check whether lights on or off, heating on or off, curtains/blinds open/closed when found, door, window, and curtain positions.
- Clothing and footwear checks (potential impressions on flooring and mats).
- Checking for stolen or missing property.
- Specific items related to the case (eg incapacitants or cleaning materials).
- Plan for dealing with associated vehicles/pedal cycles.
- Communication devices,[9] landlines, mobile phones, SIM cards, computers/laptops (specialist recovery advice), tablets, gaming consoles, digital storage devices, DVDs, broadband and Wi-Fi routers, cameras, cloud accounts, digital wristbands, passwords, and PIN numbers.

---

[9] Sections 50 and 51 of the Criminal Justice and Police Act 2001 (CJPA) grant power when carrying out a lawful search on premises or persons to seize anything for which there are reasonable grounds to believe may be or may contain something for which it is authorised to search and it is not reasonably practicable to conduct the examination at the time of seizure from the premises or person.

- Satellite navigation, maps, plans, directions, postcodes, travel cards, public transport tickets, taxi numbers, flight and airline travel details, hire car companies, and luggage tags.

- Mail, newspapers, diaries, letters, photographs, newspapers, diaries, address lists, notes, phone numbers, letters, drawings, and doodles.

- Financial information, receipts, bank details and statements, credit/debit, cards, utility bills and final demands, loan details, business or appointment cards.

- Signs of any struggle, disturbance, broken items or clean-up activity.

- Obvious traces of blood, body fluids, mud etc, or other unusual deposits.

- Items of interest or that appear out of place (unusual clothing or well-cleaned areas in an otherwise untidy house, missing knives) and the Just Doesn't Look Right (JDLR) principle.

- Intelligence search (eg lifestyle information, associates and contacts, drug/alcohol abuse, fetishes, associates, places visited, routines, habits, hobbies, reading material, photographs/DVDs, ornaments, medicines, appointment cards, bin contents, social habits, and preferred websites).

- Linked premises, gardens, sheds, outbuildings, vehicles, or keys that may belong to associated premises/vehicles/lock-ups (search/recovery plan for vehicles).

- Washing machines, dryers, and laundry baskets (eg for clothing, blood traces, or soiling).

- Baths, sinks, showers, water traps, towels, soap, and shampoo containers, and toilets, if used by offender (when removed gloves). Bathrooms and kitchens are popular places to wash away forensic traces, dirt, body fluids, gunshot residue etc, and even to dismember bodies/body parts.

- Door handles, mats, curtains, and carpets for trace evidence.

- Beds and bedding for sexual activity and sexual partners (DNA samples).

- Checking cups, cutlery, glasses, and discarded items for trace evidence.

- Searching under floorboards, in loft, behind bath panels, inside water cisterns, and in other likely concealed areas.

- Searching nearby rubbish, bins, drains, and communal chutes.

- Checking what, where, and whose possessions are in the premises (may need inventory of all items in premises or certain areas or rooms to account for and prove attribution/ownership of items).

- Checking for obvious missing items (eg if missing person, shower curtain may have been used to wrap up the body; damaged or missing furniture may be indicative of fight or attack; severed communication cables may be significant).

- CCTV covering the premises or nearby.

- House-to-house (H2H) enquiries around the address for information.

- Contingency for non-case-related finds and offences.

- Plan for innocent displaced third parties or any vulnerable persons, eg children who may require safeguarding or adults who have been trafficked/modern slavery and human trafficking (MSHT) victims.

- Resilience and welfare for prolonged searches and handover periods.

- Arrangements for fast-tracking important finds.

- Checking records are completed afterwards, including total time taken to complete, items recovered, and any damage caused.

- Using someone who is familiar with the premises (mindful of contamination) to help identify anything that is out of place, missing, unusual, or suspicious, or any factors (in)consistent with the lifestyle of the victim.

- Specialists or equipment needed to search certain areas (eg below floors or behind walls).

- Surrounding community impact and potential media attention.

As well as looking for specific items, searchers should be shrewd enough to notice things that are of interest, eg no mobile phone but a charging lead plugged in to a wall socket or empty delivery box; laptop case or manual and software but no actual laptop; or indentations in carpet where a piece of furniture was once positioned. Searching officers have to be afforded some latitude to use their skills and detective instincts to spot things that might eventually be of interest to the enquiry (or 'just don't look right'—JDLR principle).

KEY POINT

A Behavioural Investigative Adviser (BIA) or Forensic Clinical Psychologist (FCP) can be requested to assist with producing a crime scene assessment and/or briefing officers conducting searches on what to look for. (These specialist assets are available from the National Crime Agency (NCA)).

6.5.5 **Search warrants**

Due to the intrusive nature of searches, the invasion of privacy, and the potential threat to individuals' human rights, a decision to search a person's home or premises should never be taken lightly. The granting of search warrants is an area where the process and procedure can easily be challenged by legal teams and care should be taken not to allow any errors to creep into the application and execution processes. They are frequently inspected (eg by Her Majesty's Inspectorate of Constabulary and Fire and Rescue Services (HMICFRS)).

There are risks in relying upon evidence gained from search warrants where the application process for and execution procedures of them are flawed or defective. This is why it is important to check to ensure no errors have been made, otherwise there could be a risk of a legal challenge to the admissibility of a key piece of evidence due to poor processes and procedures.

Checklist—Search warrants

- The applicant of a search warrant needs to be fully briefed on the investigation before the application is made.

- All necessary information to justify the application should be covered.

- Likelihood of in-depth questioning by the magistrate/judge should be anticipated.

- The information *form* can be used as an aide-memoire for the application.

- It is important to consider in advance anything that might mitigate against the application being granted.

- Ensure any questions and answers during the application stage are recorded (see *R v Sheffield Justices* (2003)).

- Keep a record of additional material for the application.

- If sensitive source information is relied on, decide how any sensitive source will be protected if revealed during the application process.

- Seek advice from the Crown Prosecution Service (CPS) on sensitive information that may be required for the application process to see if the material can be protected.

- Record reasons for justification if search not done at reasonable hour.

- Ensure the Officer in Charge (OIC) of a search under a warrant briefs their staff properly (so everyone knows their role, the objectives and extent of the search, powers, and documentation, risk assessment, etc).

- If occupier not present when warrant executed, a copy of the warrant should be left in a prominent position and consideration given to photographing in situ as evidence it was clearly visible to the returning occupants/owners.

- If there is any possibility material being searched for may contain or include special procedure material (ie LPP),[10] legal advice MUST be sought.

- Maintain good oversight and supervision of search warrant procedures to ensure there is good adherence to standards and consistency.

---

[10] LPP—Legal Professional Privilege.

Magistrates are given guidance on the process and the questions to ask during a warrant application process (as per District Judges (Magistrates Court) Benchbook 2000). Extracts from the Benchbook include the following questions (Table 6.1):

Table 6.1 Warrant applications—court queries examples

Has application been checked by a clerk?	Is application template signed?
Who has authorised the application?	What preliminary enquiries have been made?
Who will conduct the search?	When will search be conducted?
What is search for? (material, docs, articles)	What offences are being investigated?
How is material sought relevant?	Why can't consent be obtained?
Legislation under which application is made?	How many times will premises be searched?
Details of premises to be searched?	Are details provided specific enough?
Have premises been searched previously?	Have any previous applications been refused?
If from human intelligence (HUMINT)—source reliability?	Is source information corroborated?
Antecedent details of suspects?	How soon will warrant be executed?

6.5.6 Searching open areas

Open area searches can encompass a wide range of environments and settings, ranging from parkland, rural areas, open fields and spaces, farmland, woodland, remote moorland, and mountains to urban streets and estates, town centres, and precincts. By their very nature, these searches tend to be more complex and larger in scale and can therefore sometimes pose difficulties when defining boundaries and parameters. It is usual for the SIO, CSM, and PolSA (plus any other specialists called in) to visit the proposed search site as part of a reconnaissance (scene assessment).

A sensible decision about cordoning should be made when ensuring vital evidence is not left outside the search parameters. For example, in the case of a public outdoor recreation area, an entire park does not necessarily need to be cordoned off as doing so could result in extensive time, resource, and cost implications. The focus should be on what is being sought and a predicting where those items may be best located, ie the search is intelligence led. It may be considered proportionate only to search the park's paths and tracks to locate and recover any evidential items discarded by an offender during their escape.

Search fatigue and morale are relevant considerations. These will have to be managed carefully if prolonged searches are conducted over large swathes of open land. Weather conditions and reduced winter daylight hours may also influence the search type and duration.

> **KEY POINT**
>
> Searching large outdoor areas should, wherever possible, be 'intelligence led' and based on facts and information currently available, such as direction of travel, last sighting, noises heard, forensic traces, witness evidence, CCTV, etc.

When conducting searches for concealed and buried items, the use of specialist geological and archaeological advice and equipment can be engaged. A forensic geologist can advise on ground conditions (ie soils, rock, groundwater, and any artificial deposits) and what could be the most appropriate, cost-effective geophysical detecting equipment for the environment. Once the choice of equipment has been identified, the most effective method for its deployment can then be decided.

Specialist search equipment and resources can be sourced from the National Experts Database and/or NCA National Search Adviser and also via the Defence Science and Technology Lab (DSTL)), and sometimes the military.

6.5.7 Searches in and around water

Where a search in or around water is required, the PolSA will usually seek advice from underwater search specialists who have equipment and resources such as robotic submersible cameras and sonar devices. There are a variety of geophysical and other instruments available for searching in lakes, ponds, rivers, streams, reservoirs, canals, and other water bodies.

Further advice and guidance can be sought from experts such as geologists, geomorphologists, or marine scientists with regard to water types and quality (eg saline or fresh), flow, discharge and recharge rates, tidal movements, current paths, bathymetry, sedimentation rates, and flood plains. Inland and off-shore waters are covered by regulatory bodies such as the Waterways Authority and Environment Agency. Water bailiffs and any other persons or organisations who use waterways, such as water utility companies, local boat owners and users, and river and canal cleaners, are often good sources of information and expertise for providing local advice useful to search teams. They often know where debris and discarded items get washed up, become entangled, snagged or come to rest. Other services such as the fire and rescue service also have specialist capabilities for water searches.

Drowned Victim Detection Dogs (DVDD) can prove useful when searching for victims of drowning, missing persons, and victims of a criminal act. Drowned Victim search is an additional skill for National Police Chiefs' Council-approved Victim Detection Dogs and involves searching for the scent emanating from a submerged cadaver. Gas molecules and particles of human skin or tissue are released into water as a result of normal bacterial activity during decomposition. The process may also result in a cadaver floating to the surface. These events result in a scent trace being present in and over the water, which a specially trained scent dog detect and can be used to assist in prioritising a search area.

Consideration should be given to how items (particularly corpses and body parts) are to be recovered and removed from water *in advance* of being found and what forensic evidence recovery (and/or identification) requirements may be required. Once located, dealing with onlookers and the media is something to consider. This may need attention if and when, for example, a high-profile, vulnerable, missing person's body is suddenly found when lots of reporters are already in place waiting around the curtilage of the search area. Some degree of subterfuge may be necessary so as not to tip the media and public off in order to give the body recovery plan time to get underway and to ensure a minimum of intrusion.[11]

6.5.8 Searching vehicles and vessels

Vehicles or vessels can be involved either as crime scenes themselves or for transporting offenders or victims to and from crime scenes. UK PolSA and PSTs are trained in and employ methods to search vehicles and vessels systematically, methods which are over and above what would be conventionally conducted by crime scene or forensic examiners. Vehicles and vessels contain many voids that can be used to conceal evidential material. The search strategy can be aimed at moving proportionally from a non-invasive search (eg using specialist instruments such as X-ray equipment or scent dogs) to a more invasive search of voided areas.

6.5.9 NCA National Search Adviser

The National Search Adviser (NSA) is a resource provided by the NCA who provides strategic and tactical guidance and support to police forces, SIOs, and the police search community engaged in serious and complex crime investigations and 'suspicious' missing person enquiries. Their advice can include the development of search strategies, tactical plans, and the provision of advice including the use of specialist assets. These include:

- complex searches on homicides, no-body murders, missing persons, abductions, and mass fatality disasters.
- locating human remains, concealed or otherwise.
- reviewing previous search activity or strategies on critical or cold cases.
- preparing and recording search plans and strategies for SIOs and PolSAs.

---

[11] Alice Gross was a fourteen-year-old English girl who went missing in London on 28 August 2014. After a month of intensive searching, her body was found on 30 September 2014, wrapped in a bag, weighted down, and submerged in the River Brent. The search had been the largest deployment of Metropolitan Police Service officers since the 7 July 2005 London bombings. Her body had been weighted down and submerged and was found by London Fire Brigade divers. She had been murdered by a Latvian male, Arnis Zalkalns, who later committed suicide by hanging in a wooded area less than a mile away from where his murder victim had been found.

The NSA has access to experts in all scientific disciplines that are relevant to search, including archaeology, anthropology, biology, geology, and the use of geophysics. Additional assets from the UK military and private and commercial enterprise may also be available.

6.6 **Scene Administration**

Types of scene administration and documentation vary depending on the force or agency but will generally include the following:

- scene logs.
- examination and search strategies/tactics and plans.
- search records.
- lists and details of exhibits identified and seized.
- exhibit recovery processing, ie packaging, labelling, transportation, and storage.
- exhibit recording 'books' (forms or computerised systems).
- sketches, maps, and plans indicating scene parameters and cordons, location of victims, and exhibits etc.
- CSM/CSI/other experts' notes and their own exhibit lists.
- other lists and details of exhibits recovered.
- photographs and digital imagery (including aerial and satellite imagery).
- images taken independently by attending officers, searchers, experts etc.
- crime scene reconstruction materials.
- legislative authorities utilised, correct and accurate formal documentation, and copies of executed/non-executed search warrants and application details.
- witness statements made by those making recoveries and seizing exhibits.

6.6.1 **Crime scene logs**

Scene logs provide an official audit trail and record of everyone who enters and exits a crime scene (see example in Figure 6.1). They prevent unauthorised access and help preserve the sterility of a crime scene. Specifically, designed forms can be used which, when completed, include all details of those completing the log, details of all persons who enter or leave the scene against signature, the

Date	Person details and signature	Reason for entry	Protective clothing worn	Time entered	Time left

Figure 6.1 Crime scene log

exact date and time in and out, the reason for entry, and whether protective clothing was worn. There are usually clear instructions printed inside the front cover of scene logs to provide guidance.

One (and only one) scene log is maintained for each crime scene and cordon, which means there is a separate log for both inner and outer cordons (and another for a third cordon if used). All logs, once completed, become registered documents on a CMS and should be submitted to an incident room for examination and processing.

The officer maintaining a scene log is usually positioned at the designated RVP. They should not enter the scene themselves except for emergencies, eg to save life or arrest offenders. Their duties include recording details of all those who physically enter or leave the crime scene (ie the 'sterile' area) including the reasons why and how they entered (ie wearing appropriate protective clothing). Where entry to the scene is authorised and necessary, the cordon officer should ensure that the CAP is identified to them and then properly used.

A sensible approach to log keeping can be taken. For example, if CSIs are returning to and from vehicles or equipment that are located just outside the outer cordon on a regular basis, there may be no need for them to be constantly logged in and out as they are effectively still 'in the scene', provided the SIO and CSM are satisfied there is no risk of contamination.

All entries need to be detailed, accurate, and complete. If for any reason the correct log forms are not immediately available, then a pocket notebook or other note-taking format should be utilised, and the same amount of care must be taken even if recording details in this ad hoc way.

Those maintaining the log must be reminded that they are not to allow any person, including officers of high rank, to enter the cordoned area unless authorised by the SIO, and they have a specific reason for doing so and a specific task to perform (eg CSI). Any persons already at the scene when the log is begun should be added to it and marked as being 'already at the scene' in the 'reason for entry' column. Where a log has been started in a pocket notebook or elsewhere prior to the commencement of the formal log, details should be transferred into the correct scene log form and cross-referenced.

Most scene logs look similar amongst forces and agencies, like the one illustrated here. Further columns can be added for details of who authorised entry, what protective clothing was worn, and details of anyone refused entry and why.

Checklist—Scene logs—common errors

- Incorrect forms or none used. Makeshift pieces of paper or a pocket notebook suffice but do not look very professional, whereas if official forms are used then usually the requisite detail is recorded.

- Precise details not recorded. Each and every box and question on the form is there for a specific purpose. There should be no gaps; eg if protective clothing has not been worn, the log should state as such and not be left blank. If it is a requirement to note the weather conditions at regular intervals, this should be duly completed.

- Incorrect detail. Attention to detail is vital. Scene logs may be entered onto a CMS with names of those entering the scene. Any names spelt incorrectly will lead to dual registration, fouling up the nominal indices.

- Entries not signed. Some officers feel awkward about asking people who are wearing protective suits to keep signing themselves in and out of scenes. All entries should be made against signature—no excuses.

- Briefing and supervision. It can be a tedious and thankless task to maintain a scene log and perform security duties. Those tasked need to be fully briefed on the importance of the role, and their log keeping checked at regular intervals by a supervisor to ensure they are completed correctly.

- Handover periods. These need to be recorded as to date, time, and persons involved, and professionally managed to ensure consistency and professionalism in approach.

6.6.2 **CSM and CSI notes and exhibit lists**

Whenever a crime scene exhibit list is compiled by a CSM or CSI during their scene examination, the list (and their notes) should be copied and handed to the EO for checking and processing by the incident room. This is because they may contain details of important items that the SIO needs to be aware of so that important decisions can be made and actions raised. The lists should not be left, for example, until a forensic strategy meeting is held, which may be too late to instigate fast-track actions. This rule also applies to any other experts who attend and examine aspects of the scene and may prepare their own exhibit lists, such as forensic providers.

6.7 **Releasing Crime Scenes**

A crime scene should always be retained as long as is necessary to allow for all potential searches and forensic examinations to conclude. Any decision to release a scene *must* be very carefully considered, depending on practical and resource implications and public disruption, eg if situated in a residential or urban area. The SIO and CSC work closely together to make this decision, taking all relevant circumstances into account. A review of the scene examination strategy should take place initially in order to ensure sufficient time has been allowed and nothing is missed, both from a prosecution and defence perspective (ie in compliance with CPIA rules).

A significant crime scene must not be released until high-priority main lines of enquiry have been completed, such as interviewing significant witnesses, viewing vital CCTV footage, or interviewing suspects. Fresh information may emerge that requires putting into context or physically checking at the crime scene. New witnesses might come forward or suspects may disclose information that requires clarification, or forensic experts may want to revisit the scene. Once a scene is released, its sterility and integrity are lost forever. Scene examination needs to be conducted painstakingly and thoroughly so the rule needs repeating: *never release a crime scene too early*.

KEY POINTS

1. Crime scenes may present health and safety hazards not just for the police but for the public. If so, they cannot be released until thoroughly cleansed and deemed fit for use.
2. Before release, the SIO and CSM/CSI should conduct a final 'walk through'.
3. Some crime scenes, eg empty premises, can become a magnet for thieves and vandals once security has been removed. Owners must be encouraged to acknowledge responsibility for security and given appropriate crime prevention advice.
4. Never release a crime scene too early.

6.8 Exhibit Management

There are correct and proper procedures and processes for the handling, packaging, transportation, continuity, and integrity of exhibits, compliance of which must be provable beyond all reasonable doubt to a court of law. Lawyers like to search for mistakes and omissions to get a ruling in their favour when vital evidence relies upon proving the integrity of an exhibit or process.

6.8.1 'Continuity' and 'integrity'

These are key terms within the context of crime scene, exhibit management, and evidence recovery. These are:

Continuity—A continuous, complete, and accurate record of all the movements of any evidential material from identification at a crime scene, subsequent recovery, transportation, examination, storage, and any other investigative processes until the material reaches the ultimate destination—production at court.

Integrity—The handling, packaging, and storage of evidential material that can demonstrate beyond all reasonable doubt that there has been no interference, contamination, cross-transfer, tampering, destruction, or loss that could have occurred to the item, either intentionally or accidentally.

Contamination—When something is added to an evidential sample from another sample, either accidentally or intentionally.

Cross-transfer—Process in which material from one location, person, or item is transferred to another.

6.8.2 **Power to seize evidence**

When not under the power of a magistrate's search warrant (eg section 8 of PACE which allows anything to be seized and retained for which the search is authorised), then section 19 of PACE is often relied on for a power to seize evidential items which are *on premises*. This power applies to a constable or civilian designated an Investigating Officer (under section 38 of the Police Reform Act 2002, Sch 4, Pt 2, para 19(a)) provided:

1. they are *on premises* lawfully; and
2. there are reasonable grounds for believing:
   (a) the item seized is either (1) an item which has been obtained in consequence of the commission of an offence (s 19(2)): eg stolen items or the proceeds of crime); or (2) that it is evidence in relation to an offence under investigation or *any other offence* (s 19(3)); and
   (b) it is necessary to seize it in order to prevent it being concealed, lost, damaged, altered, or destroyed (s 19(2)(b) and (3)(b)); and
3. the item is not one for which there are reasonable grounds for believing it to be subject to legal privilege (as defined in s 10 (s 19(6)).

The term 'on premises', for the purposes of this power under PACE, is one that is extensive and includes vehicles, vessels, aircraft, and hovercraft, and any tent or movable structure (PACE 1984, App 1). However, the case of *Ghani v Jones*[12] provides a ruling on the justification for taking articles where no-one has been arrested or charged and is not restricted to being 'on premises'. This power should also extend to civilian investigating officers under Schedule 4 to the Police Reform Act 2002. The ruling states there must be reasonable grounds for believing:

1. serious crime has been committed;
2. article was either the fruit of the crime or the instrument by which it was committed or was material evidence to prove its commission;
3. person in possession of the article had committed the crime or was implicated in it;

---

[12] *Ghani v Jones* Court of Appeal 1969 No 2947 [1970] 1 QB 693.

4. police must not keep the article or prevent its removal for any longer than is reasonably necessary to complete the investigation or preserve it for evidence; and

5. lawfulness of the conduct of the police must be judged at the time and not by what happens afterwards.

There may be occasions when this case ruling is useful, for example when dealing with persons who are potential 'crime scenes' but not under arrest or on premises and items are required from them for examination, such as clothing or personal effects or communication devices.

6.8.3 Forensic management and exhibit reviews

A forensic strategy determines what items are prioritised for examination. This will require a regular meeting to discuss each and every item and exhibit methodically that may be considered suitable for examination. A Forensic Management Group (FMG) can be formed to perform this function and ensure that every available evidence recovery opportunity is used to full potential. This group might comprise the SIO/DSIO, CSM, forensic providers and specialists, fingerprint experts, EO, the Major Incident Room Office Manager, and any internal forensic budget holder. The group can be brought together and tasked with managing all the forensic issues in the enquiry. The meetings should be recorded and actions raised and prioritised from decisions made.

The FMG responsibilities include keeping all seized exhibits under continuous review. This can be achieved by adopting a screening process at regular review meetings whereby each exhibit is rated for both forensic potential and priority. The EO may distribute a list of all exhibits and score each one as per the following grid example:

F—shows whether the exhibit has forensic potential, then graded with a score of '1–3'; 1 being high, 2 medium, and 3 low priority.

FP—fingerprint examination required.

FD—DNA examination required

O/D—other document or exhibit for disclosure only.

O/R—other document or exhibit for research.

O/C—other document or exhibit required for court.

All exhibits graded 'F1' should be discussed at a forensic strategy meeting in order to ensure the appropriate examination is considered. In view of the high costs of forensic examination, it is essential that care is taken to prioritise only those items that may provide a result of significant evidential value.

Further review meetings can be held throughout the investigation to ensure all priority exhibits are fully debated for forensic examination. Minutes of all meetings should be recorded and registered onto a CMS. Reasons why items were sent for examination or why they were not should be noted, along with an explanation of decisions made. Meetings and decisions on minutes taken can be cross-referenced in the SIO's policy file.

During the early stages of an investigation, the FMG can seek to identify *fast-track* forensic submissions that may result in the early identification of a suspect and lead to a speedy arrest or elimination. These should be a standard feature and agenda item for discussion at any forensic exhibit meetings.

6.9 Exhibits Officers (EOs)

A trained and experienced EO has a pivotal role in a major and serious crime investigation and is usually an experienced and accredited (PIP2) investigator. They should be trained in all aspects of exhibit management, including packaging, storage, documentation, and computerised management system together with an up-to-date knowledge of forensic techniques and their applications. They should also be conversant with relevant parts of health and safety legislation, CPIA, and PACE.

The EO(s),[13] once appointed, usually remain(s) dedicated to the role for the duration of the investigation through to completion of trial and case disposal. They attend briefings and establish a close working relationship with the CSM, CSIs, first officers responding, and indeed all the investigating team to ensure that all recovered exhibits are properly handled and packaged, together with the necessary signed labels. They must guard against any risk of contamination or cross-contamination throughout the entire exhibit-handling process. The importance of *preserving the integrity of any exhibit* cannot be overstated.

The EO should be allocated suitable facilities and accommodation with appropriate secure storage, freezer and drying facilities, and IT equipment. This is to ensure all exhibits are kept under close review, particularly those sent for specialist forensic or fingerprint treatment or examination.

Tracing physical evidence and potential exhibits is important to investigations so the EO may be allocated tasks/actions to check relevant found property records and stores for any items that may be of interest to the investigation, such as knives, blood-stained clothing, footwear, bicycles, or mobile phones.

6.10 Health and Safety Considerations

Crime scenes and some types of exhibits present a range of hazards that require risk assessments and control strategies to avoid breaching health and safety requirements. Examples of such hazards include:

- Blood and other such body fluids.
- Infestations and parasites.

---

[13] A case may be of such a size and complexity that more than one EO may be required. In which case a Principle EO (PEO) will be required to take the lead.

- Drugs and drugs paraphernalia (eg syringes).
- Hazardous chemicals, poisonous gases, and biological agents.
- Fire, heat, and hot environments.
- Explosives and improvised explosive devices (IEDs).
- Decomposing human remains.
- Unsafe and collapsing buildings or structures.
- Firearms and ammunition.
- Dangerous weapons and sharp items.
- Some animals and pets.
- Difficult terrain or environments (eg high-voltage electricity, traffic, and weather conditions).
- Difficult or dangerous individuals and offenders.
- Hostile crowds.

Determining scene and exhibit safety for investigative personnel is essential to limit the risk of physical injury. Generic risk assessments may exist for attendance at crime scenes. However, wherever possible appropriate advice should be sought and personal protective clothing and equipment used when required. In addition to protecting individuals, this minimises the possibility of cross-contamination. At a major or serious crime scene, standard protection usually consists of a full scene suit with hood up, face mask, overshoes, and protective gloves.

When dealing with scenes containing blood staining or known infectious diseases, extra care must be taken to avoid hazards and risk from any blood-borne infections, eg HIV or hepatitis B. Gloves should always be worn when handling items or persons covered in blood or other bodily fluids. Dried blood is also a hazard as it can enter the body through mucus membranes. Wearing a disposable mask reduces the risk of inhaling or exhaling particles. Footwear or other items of officer's clothing may also need to be decontaminated to avoid the risk of cross-transfer.

Staff deployed at crime scenes must remain vigilant to spot dangers, think quickly, adapt, and take a dynamic approach to managing risk. In extreme cases, they may have to abandon crime scenes using only their instincts, pick up exhibits, or leave a deceased in place because of the severity of the danger or risk involved. Potential threats to members of the public and/or officers in some circumstances may present no alternative. Some priorities (eg Five building blocks principles: 'preservation of life', see Chapter 3) override the needs of the investigation and it may not always be possible to keep a crime scene sterile.

Safety of the public and those engaged at a scene is at all times of paramount importance and non-negotiable. If there is a conflict of interest between personal safety and the investigation, the former always takes precedence, although it should always be the aim to try to minimise the destruction or loss of evidential material. Reasons why any emergency actions were taken should be recorded and made known to the SIO and CSM/CSI as soon as practicable. Actions that have limited the potential for forensic recovery must be justified at a later stage. This demonstrates good standards of integrity and honesty of purpose.

KEY POINTS

1. Adequate safeguards are required for the safety and well-being of all those engaged at crime scenes. Search and examination teams may need to spend a lot of time in what might be wet, cold, or unpleasant or dangerous working conditions, and provisions should be made for their welfare and safety. Providing warm and dry rest, changing, cleaning, toiletries, and refreshment facilities within easy access can make a huge difference when working in a difficult environment and can help maintain high levels of morale.

2. Appropriate personal protective equipment (PPE) must be incorporated into scene and exhibit risk-management strategies.

Bibliography

ACPO, *National Crime Scene Investigation Manual*, Issue 1 (NPIA, 2007), 46–7

ACPO, *Practice Advice on Search Management and Procedures* (NCPE, 2006), 164–6

<http://www.nationalcrimeagency.gov.uk/publications/687-nca-warrant-review-closing-report/file> ('Warrant Review Closing Report', NCA, 12 April 2016)

7

Investigation Management

7.1 **Introduction**

Professional management of an investigation is paramount to success. Courts and juries can be positively influenced by the efficient management of an investigation evident during a court case. There are examples of historical cases that have proved less successful and which became catalysts for change. Lord Byford, for example, commented in the famous Yorkshire Ripper (Peter Sutcliffe) case that 'the incident room had become overwhelmed by a welter of information'.[1] Soon afterwards came the introduction of a case management system (CMS) named HOLMES (Home Office Large Major Enquiry System), because some enquiries simply struggled to cope with managing a vast amount of information in high-volume cases.

In Operation Fincham, the tragic case in Soham (2002) of the murders of Holly Wells and Jessica Chapman, Her Majesty's Inspectorate of Constabulary's (HMIC) report commented:

> the delay in putting into place appropriate mechanisms had an impact on the extent to which the force was able to manage the sheer volume of information which was to descend upon it in connection with what rapidly became one of the largest enquiries of its kind in the UK for many years.[2]

This chapter outlines some of the core roles, responsibilities, and standard procedures which can be used to manage a full-scale proactive or reactive investigation. There is an outline not only of roles and processes but also of responsibilities that need to cohere to support an effective investigation. There are necessary and essential administrative tasks to launch and manage an investigation proficiently. They enable greater professionalism and accountability to meet formal requirements enshrined in law, eg the disclosure principles under the Criminal Procedure and Investigations Act 1996 (CPIA), and serve as a solid foundation for any investigation.

The chapter includes sections on formulating main lines of enquiry and how to deal with information, and action management, including fast-track actions and statement policies. The chapter concludes with the very topical subject of 'disclosure'. These are all *'must dos'* for the SIO.

Get the basics right ... deal with the extraordinary in an ordinary way.'[3]

---

[1] Sir L Byford, *The Byford Report* (1981) HMIC, London.

[2] Sir R Flanagan, *'A Report on the Investigation by Cambridgeshire Constabulary into the Murders of Jessica Chapman and Holly Wells at Soham on 4 August 2002'* (June 2004), HMIC, London. Note: the triage process that Cambridgeshire Police did eventually introduce became the precursor to developing the modern-day MIRWeb that now deals with a high volume of incoming information in a flexible way against criteria set by the SIO (eg Op Sumac in Suffolk.

[3] The SIO's comment while presenting to HWG National SIO's Conference, 4–6 November 2013, during the presentation of Op Tempest, one of the largest missing person searches in UK history in Machynlleth, Wales, in October 2012 for April Jones, aged five. It was a child homicide committed by local man Mark Bridger who was subsequently arrested, charged, and convicted of her abduction and murder.

7.2 **Command Roles**

Dependent on their nature and severity, some cases require a management structure that contains clearly outlined command roles and responsibilities. The United Kingdom uses a nationally recognised tiered system known as Gold, Silver, and Bronze (aka GSB). These are:

GOLD[4]—Strategic

SILVER—Tactical

BRONZE—Operational

These roles do not have to be rank specific, although clearly there is a practical advantage if they are. They are relevant to levels of responsibility, decision making, and to the skills, training, and expertise of the role holders.

This model of command is sometimes utilised by other emergency services and public bodies in the United Kingdom which enables individuals in different agencies to become interoperable. This is a useful advantage if the investigation involves a critical or major incident and multi-agency response.

Each of the role holders needs to determine, outline, and understand fully their roles and responsibilities. Knowing who has responsibility for what, when, where, why, and how is critical and helps lay the foundations for an unambiguous command and control structure. The 'how' is important because each role holder should record their own strategy. This book covers what the SIO's strategies look like, and equal clarification should be sought from others in the command chain as to what their strategies are.

Most incidents and operations deemed 'critical' (see section 11.8) necessitate the implementation of a GSB structure. Gold Group (GG) meetings then follow to discuss all strategic related matters affecting not only the incident under investigation but also wider issues such as organisational impact, reputation, public and political trust and confidence, media reporting, multi-agency response, resourcing, finance, etc. The SIO (who usually has a Silver or Bronze role as they are more tactical and operational than more junior staff) is usually required to provide updates to the GG on the progress of the investigation. They should be expected to be probed on matters that might affect any of the aforementioned areas of concern. As a Silver Commander, they will also be expected to manage the effectiveness of any Bronze operational resources for whom they are responsible.

In circumstances where there are likely to be consequential management issues (such as community or media reaction) arising from a complex

---

[4] In some serious and complex cases, there is one more role above Gold known as 'Platinum'. This would probably be at Chief Officer level to focus on preserving the interests of the organisation and managing wider strategic issues such as reputational risk.

investigative or operational activity, or even parts thereof (eg arrests or high-profile searches), consideration should be given to forming a Gold group. This has advantages for the SIO as it provides some overarching 'top cover' if there is likely to be any adverse reaction to the way the enquiry is being conducted.

In a complex series of cases or a historical child sexual abuse case, the membership of a CG might comprise of co-opted members such as:

- (Gold) Senior Commander/(Asst.) Chief Officer level from investigating agency (usually chairs).
- Senior officers or representatives from other forces or agencies involved.
- Local Authority (Chief Executive level).
- Local area policing commander.
- Internal community partnerships or strategic representative.
- Senior Child Protection Adviser/local social services and social care/Local Safeguarding Children Board (LSCB)/Local Authority Designated Officer (LADO).
- Local Health, Education, and Probation Authorities (or other relevant agencies).
- Crown Prosecution Service.
- Non-Governmental Organisations (NGOs) (eg Lucy Faithful Foundation, National Society for the Prevention of Cruelty to Children (NSPCC).
- Legal team representative (eg law enforcement agency (LEA) or Local Authority solicitors).
- Communications Officer (media and public relations).
- Local community leaders or independent advisory group (IAG) member(s).
- PIP4 Adviser.
- PIP3SIO.
- Foreign and Commonwealth Office (if the case involves overseas offending).
- Operation Hydrant representative (if the case meets their criteria; see section 11.5.2).

Even when such a governance structure is put in place, the SIO is the person who has ultimate responsibility for managing the investigation. This is a continuous and lasting responsibility covering all aspects appertaining to tactical decision making. It is non-negotiable and is contained within the SIO's job description (if it isn't, it should be). Any interference by a higher grade officer, such as a Gold Commander, in operational tactical decisions must be strongly resisted as it is not within their job description. Whatever rank or grade of other officers involved, they must not be allowed to interfere or effectively take over the running of the investigation. If this happens, one option is to make a policy entry in the log and ask the more senior person concerned to sign their name against the decision they have made to prove that they own it. This relationship between the various command (GSB) roles needs to be managed by the SIO with a strong and confident style[5] that will help resist unhelpful interference, no matter how well meaning.

7.3 Major Incident Rooms

A Major Incident Room (MIR) is the 'beating heart' of an investigation. Establishing one quickly is key, particularly when a 'crime in action' (eg kidnapping, threat to life, or suspect hunt) is in progress. The sooner one is up and running, the sooner the enquiry can be properly managed and operational and administrative functions stabilised.

When determining the location for an MIR, a number of factors should be considered. The geographic siting near to the area the focus of the investigation and the provision of suitable accommodation are always beneficial, although it is common to have centralised incident room facilities for reasons of financial prudence and enabling multi-incident/collaborative working. Practicalities need considering such as ease of access to important locations. In addition, some local communities often prefer to have the investigation team located as close as possible to them and this might help provide them with reassurance.

Accommodation has to cater for adequate case management and IT systems access, briefings facilities, report writing, vehicle access and parking, and secure exhibit storage. A sterile or separate area may be required if the viewing and examining of abusive and indecent material such as indecent images of children (IIOC) is involved. In more widespread investigations, use can be made of temporary satellite rooms, often in neighbouring areas, fitted with case management system (CMS) connection and remote access telephone/video teleconferencing capabilities (VTC). In the early response phase, makeshift facilities may have to be utilised until a suitable MIR is identified and available. If so, the management of any transfer and administrative movement needs to be carefully coordinated so as not to cause too much disruption.

An early function of an MIR is to gather, analyse, and record all the original material generated during the initial response phase. Often this involves staff no longer directly engaged on the enquiry and steps need to be taken to collect the material they hold at the first (de)briefing held. It is vital to safeguard the integrity of this information, in particular first-hand accounts from key witnesses and any significant comments made by suspects, together with any other relevant material, such as emergency calls, fast-track CCTV footage, automatic number plate recognition (ANPR) hits, and exhibit continuity. All this information needs to be collected, logged, and processed through the MIR.

Most if not all MIRs revolve around an IT-based supporting CMS but such a system must not be allowed to dictate the progress or pace of the enquiry. Its

---

[5] See section 1.3.1 which cites 'confidence, professional courage, nerve and self-belief' amongst the list of core qualities and skills of an SIO.

role is to assist in the administration and recording processes and to improve effectiveness and management of information; which is hugely important to the success of an investigation. The SIO and their management team must adopt a disciplined approach towards management of the CMS at all times and introduce monitoring and review mechanisms to check the work the MIR staff are producing through the system. The CMS is a valuable support tool but the SIO and investigation team run the enquiry.

An effective incident room will require the allocation of key roles and functions. Certain systems such as HOLMES have designated roles around which the system operates. These can be replicated in similar systems and are outlined as follows.

Key Roles in a HOLMES-type MIR

SIO	Has overall responsibility for the enquiry and MIR, eg allocation, final 'sign off' or 'referral' of any allocated actions and reports.
Deputy SIO (DSIO)	Responsible for the above in absence of the SIO, plus any other tasks as nominated (eg dealing with sensitive intelligence).
Office Manager (OM)	Manages MIR staff, ensures systems, procedures, and effective running of MIR are maintained. Implements SIO instructions and monitors high-priority actions, reads and assesses all reports and documents, and approves these for filing. Maintains awareness of all developments and informs the SIO.
Receiver	Usually the most up to date in respect all material coming into enquiry as it passes through them first. They assess, prioritise, and determine the urgency of information, and identify important developments and opportunities.
Action Manager (AM)	Manages and allocates actions. Must have current knowledge of staff workloads, skills, and experience to inform allocation decisions. Examines actions allocated, referred, for referral and pending lists, and recognises priorities.
Document Reader (DR)	Reads and examines all statements, officers' reports, interviews, and other documents (eg personal descriptive forms (PDFs), house-to-house (H2H) questionnaires) for precise detail. Decides where additional actions need to be raised to progress the investigation in line with the SIO's policy and direction. Assesses importance and priority of documents, producing a summary of contents where necessary.
Action	Raises actions as directed (particularly during (de)briefing sessions).

Writer (AW)	Ensures actions are not being duplicated and the originating authority is clearly outlined.
Indexer (I)	Indexes all documentation as indicated by R or DR, raising actions as indicated, and maintains designated indexes and categories on the database. Inputs results and endorses documents.
Registrar (Reg)	Tasked with registering documents. This could be a separate role if a high-volume messaging system utilised (eg in Cat A+ type incident) to ensure documents are entered onto the database as soon as possible.
Exhibits Officer (EO)	Records and safeguards all property and material recovered and ensures correct packaging, labelling, indexing, and storage of exhibits (see also section 6.9).
H2H Coordinator (H2HC)	Manages all H2H enquiries. Checks documentation and ensures completed correctly with any actions raised. Agrees content of questionnaires, level required, and parameters to be covered. Supervises/briefs H2H teams.
Disclosure Officer (DO)	Examines and is responsible for disclosure of all material in the enquiry. Prepares schedules for prosecutor and edits relevant material prior to service on defence.
File (or case) Preparation Officer (FPO)	Prepares case papers in consultation with SIO, OM, DO, and EO. Liaises with prosecutions team. Arranges storage of all case papers and associated material.
Researcher (or analyst)	Undertakes detailed research to seek out important links and information that may be missed by other more specific office roles. Can be specifically tasked on large enquiries.
Account Manager	Ensures compliance with rules and conventions plus Major Incident Room Standardised Administrative Procedures (MIRSAP). Checks indexing and registration categories and documents.
Typist	Types up documents from original statements, officers' reports, messages, interview transcripts, and other documents, as required.

Role descriptions are further outlined in the *Guidance on Major Incident Room Standardised Administrative Procedures.*[6] It suggests how some roles can be combined (often referred to as 'double-hatting') when resources are limited. For example, the DSIO may be combined with OM or AM; Receiver with DR; DR with FPO.[7]

---

[6] ACPO, *Guidance on Major Incident Room Standardised Administrative Procedures* (MIRSAP, (2005), 18–42.
[7] ACPO, *Guidance on Major Incident Room Standardised Administrative Procedures* (MIRSAP, 2005), 58–9.

KEY POINTS

1. Allocated roles and responsibilities should not restrict staff performing the overarching role of investigator.
2. Incident room staff need a working environment that allows them to concentrate without interruptions or background disturbances.
3. Desks or in-trays that are overflowing with documents (when part of a CMS) may be indicative of inefficiency (and a 'clear desk policy' is always better for security).

7.4 Resource Management

Complex and major crime investigations usually require large numbers of staff, including experts or others brought in to assist. There are considerations such as budgetary requirements (and constraints), technical resources, vehicles, overtime costs, travel and subsistence expenses to consider, in addition to ensuring the correct levels of resources are sustained.

Requests for necessary and essential resources are best made in the early stages. This is to ensure that as much evidence and information as possible is captured and secured quickly, which in the long term will save time and resources and prevent evidence becoming harder to find or contaminated. Enquiry teams can be reassessed and trimmed back later when resource implications may not be as critical. It can also be worthwhile keeping a regular check on what resources are available in advance, particularly when performing 'cover rota' duties.

Effective resource management means getting teams to perform to a higher standard than their numbers might otherwise allow. There are usually only finite resources available and the SIO should record any staffing concerns and when/how they have had to balance investigational needs against (non-)available resources in their policy logs (see section 4.2). This will afford some degree of protection if a formal review comes later. Provided teams are willing, eager, enthusiastic, and dedicated to their tasks, success can still be achieved despite staffing limitations. The key is to *get the most out of available staff* by setting focused, achievable, and realistic priorities.

7.4.1 Factors affecting resourcing

The following list might assist when determining appropriate resourcing levels:

- Internal categorisation (eg murder Cat A/B/C, High-Priority (HP) Operation, etc).
- Volume of work involved (eg number of victims, witnesses, suspects, crime scenes, and material being gathered such as CCTV, digital data).
- Solvability factors (forensic, witnesses, suspects, or passive data potential).

- Complexity (eg organised crime, stranger homicide, specialist area, linked series crime, cultural barriers, unusual modus operandi (MO)).
- Levels of local, (inter)national, political, community, or media interest.
- Major or 'critical incident'.
- Likely cost and competing demands.

7.4.2 Specialist resources and support

Sometimes there is a necessity to call upon specialist resources to assist the investigation. These could come from a multitude of sources, some of the more common being:

- Crime Scene Investigators/Examiners/Managers, and Coordinators (CSIs/CSEs/CSMs/CSCs).
- Forensic (traditional (wet) and digital), fingerprint experts, and service providers.
- Physical search specialists (eg Police Search Advisers/Teams (PolSAs/PSTs), aerial support, underwater search teams, digital media and cybercrime expertise).
- Imagery and photography specialists.
- Intelligence feeders, researchers, and analysts.
- Specialist investigative interviewers (witnesses, achieving best evidence (ABE), or suspects).
- Forensic pathologist, ballistics experts, etc (and/or other specialist resources).
- House-to-house (H2H) teams and coordinator.
- Communications/digital media/data investigators and single point of contact (SPoCs).
- Passive data recovery teams (eg CCTV and ANPR).
- Tactical Firearms Commander (TFC) and Authorised Firearms Officers (AFOs).
- Covert operations tactical advisers, assets, and resources.
- Financial investigators (FIs).
- Child protection and vulnerable persons advisors.
- Other agencies and partners (eg Fire and Rescue Service, health or local authority).
- National Crime Agency (NCA), Europol, and Interpol.[8]

7.5 Enquiry Team Structure

Dependent on the type and scale of enquiry, an SIO needs to consider not just who and what is required but also how their investigation team will be structured. There is no 'one size fits all'; however, it is worthwhile giving some early thought to team structure, and a simple chart is often the easiest way of producing this. There is an example of this in Appendix B.

---

[8] NCA resources are further described in Chapter 10.

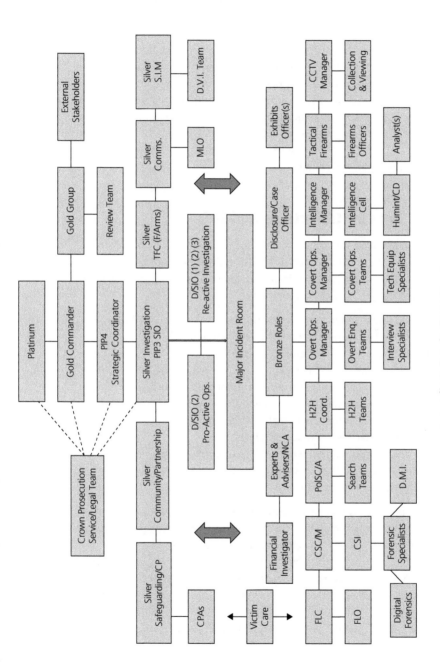

Appendix B Enquiry Team Structure

Delegated areas of responsibility can be assigned to any or all the various tasks and roles, although they should still report back to the SIO, who retains overall responsibility for the investigation. This is a management method that allows important areas of responsibility to be delegated. The SIO can discuss and agree policies and tactics and request regular updates on progress.

Additionally, the SIO needs to be aware that in some cases there may be other parallel investigations taking place. Common examples are Serious Case Reviews (SCRs) when a death enquiry involves a child or young person (see Chapter 15), Child Care Proceedings through the civil courts, Domestic Homicide Reviews (DHRs) held in all domestic homicide cases (Chapter 14), and Independent Office for Police Conduct (IOPC) investigations, eg when a death occurs during or following police contact.

7.6 Enquiry Objectives and ToR

The aims of an investigation need to be clearly defined from the outset. These help ensure compliance with predetermined principles and objectives. They can be listed and included in or referred to in a policy log. A generic list of objectives to choose from follows here.

- Lead and manage the investigation.
- Conduct a thorough and effective investigation.
- Trace, identify, support, and safeguard victims.[9]
- Seek and identify witnesses.
- Establish what and if any criminal offences have been committed.
- Pursue all reasonable[10] lines of enquiry.
- Secure and gather all relevant evidence.
- Identify, trace, and pursue offenders.
- Comply with requirements of CPIA disclosure rules.
- Remain ethically focused at all times and act in the interests of justice.
- Present relevant evidence to the Crown Prosecution Service (CPS).

In some cases, it may be necessary to also draw up some clear terms of reference (ToR). This is essential if the SIO has been appointed to take charge of a complex enquiry that requires specific focus to avoid being overburdened by too many potential offences, offenders, or lines of enquiry. It will prevent the avoidance of doubt or confusion as to what is/isn't or was/was not required of the investigation, ie where it starts/ends, what is in/not in scope, roles and responsibilities, etc. Specific ToR, once agreed, can eliminate confusion as to what was originally decided. They can also be helpful if other units or external agencies

---

[9] Being victim focused is deliberately placed near the top of the list in order to show how important an objective it is.

[10] The term 'reasonable' means just that, ie being rational, sensible, and practical.

become involved, and great benefits can be gained from a ToR document that sets out who has responsibility for what and when, with the inclusion of named signatories.

7.7 **Main Lines of Enquiry (MLOE)**

This is a means of setting and focusing clear investigative priorities that aim to establish facts, find evidence, and arrest and convict any person(s) responsible for the offence(s). A list entitled 'Main Lines of Enquiry' (MLOE or LOE) can be drawn up and referred to in a policy log to ensure it is clear and that everyone is aware of the direction of travel and what the priorities are for the enquiry. This enables the investigation or operation to remain focused and not become bogged down with non-urgent actions and enquiries that may be the product of either an overly enthusiastic or cautious administration or case management process (ie raising too many irrelevant lines of enquiry).

Some main (or key) lines will be obvious that stand out from the information available and case circumstances. For instance, key witnesses who need to be interviewed quickly, or potential exhibits that can be forensically fast-tracked for fingerprints or DNA, or securing and viewing CCTV footage that may provide images of those responsible. By including specific LOE into a priority list assists in prioritising and completing clear investigative opportunities in a process commonly referred to as 'clearing the ground from under your feet'.

When producing MLOE, there is freedom to use all available information and material (eg intelligence) and not just what might be admissible as evidence. Any information relied upon of course must be properly evaluated and analysed to determine reliability, accuracy, and suitability. This rule applies to all sources of information, whether from witnesses, electronic/scientific sources, or other. The ABC principle (see Chapter 3) states:

> **A**—Assume nothing
>
> **B**—Believe nothing
>
> **C**—Challenge/check everything

Setting too many main lines of enquiry can lead to low productivity, enquiry stagnation, and work overload. Being very tightly focused on a specific list of priorities, however, will get the most out of available resources. Determining and judging the relevance and value of available information and making decisions about the best leads to prioritise may have to be done initially very quickly. Thereafter, the list can and must be regularly reviewed as information develops in 'slow time' (fast- and slow-time decision making are discussed in Chapter 3).

The MLOE remain under dynamic review throughout the life of the investigation. There will always be changes to these lines. Some inevitably drop away when completed or are found to be less significant or if the investigation changes direction. Regular references should be made in the policy log to the MLOE with explanatory reasons why they are there. This is a means of showing good control of the investigation and defending reasons for adopting or dropping (non-) significant lines of enquiry.

KEY POINTS

- Main lines of enquiry need the rationale for following them recorded in a policy log entry to explain and justify why they were chosen (see also Chapter 4).
- There should be frequent reviews and re-evaluation as the enquiry progresses and new information and investigative opportunities surface.
- MLOE are a means of getting best use of available resources and prioritising.

Checklist—MLOE examples

- Tracing and interviewing (TI) one or more (particular) significant witnesses.

- Arrest and interview of a named suspect.

- Search (physical) of a particular site or area.

- Obtaining a full profile of the victim N1 ('victimology').

- Forensic/physical scene examination and search of ... (scene number).

- Conducting H2H enquiries (in set parameters).

- Intelligence collection (eg identifying intelligence gaps; subject profiles, biographical profile of associates, their activities, habits, methods; open source intelligence; community intelligence; tactical initiatives).

- Determining 'relevant time', eg likely time of incident.

- Determining movements of all persons at scene (1) (between x and y).

- Determining movements of victim N1 (between x and y).

- Determining movements of declared suspects (between x and y).

- Conducting TIE (see Chapter 8) enquiries.

- DNA or finger/palm print mass screening (or fDNA techniques).

- Establishing motive—eg sexual, financial, hate crime.

- Researching and analysing potential linked crimes or precursor incidents.

- Making use of a communications strategy (eg media appeals).

- Passive data recovery and viewing strategy.

- Victim management strategy.

- Use of a specific overt or covert proactive tactic.

- Use of an anniversary reconstruction and/or road checks in locality.

- Making use of specialist assets, eg National Crime Agency (NCA).

The enquiry team needs to be kept fully informed on what is included in the current list and kept up to date with any amendments or additions (except 'sensitive tactics'). The list should be displayed in a prominent position and/or communicated to everyone on the team (and version-controlled if and when it changes).

7.8 **Messages and Information**

Most major enquiries produce an influx of information to the investigation and if not, this needs to be queried. All information will need capturing, recording, analysing, and evaluating. *The effective management of information is of paramount importance to the success of an investigation.* That one, vital piece of information that can help solve the case and save hours of time, financial cost, and resources *must* be identified and actioned as quickly as possible. Therefore, an effective system must be in place to handle all communications (eg calls, messages, and information) that enter the enquiry. Valuable time will be lost, information overlooked, progress compromised, and possible sources of information discouraged if information is not managed promptly and effectively.

The usual method of logging messages containing information is via standard message forms (printed or digital). These need to be instantly recognisable (eg in a HOLMES-type system there are green, pre-printed forms known as MIR/6) and include all the details of the information, the originator, time, and date received, and what has been done. These messages are the lifeblood of an enquiry and must be monitored and checked on a regular basis (daily as a minimum). Circulation systems must enable every message to be forwarded directly to the SIO so they can always see them.

A significant piece of information may be contained within a message and the incident room staff and SIO must be able to readily identify important information. Therefore any messages containing investigative information should not be left lying around, eg on desks, in a tray, or within a computerised database, without being properly assessed.

Enquiry team members need to know what information they are expected to bring quickly to the attention of supervisors, who in turn must quickly know what to do with it, and when and how to notify the (D)SIO rather than waiting for it to pass through administrative processes. That one vital line of enquiry gleaned from a message or report containing significant information cannot be left ignored when it could be actioned promptly.

KEY POINTS

1. If there is a large volume of messages, criteria for prioritising through high, medium, and low ratings can be introduced and clearly marked on them. If in printed format, the gradings need attaching clearly so they stand out (eg with brightly coloured labels or tags).
2. The effective management of information is of paramount importance to success.

7.9 Action Management

Actions are defined as 'any activity which, if pursued is likely to establish significant facts, preserve material, or lead to the resolution of the investigation'.[11] The term 'action' means doing something or performing an activity. It is one used extensively in serious crime investigation and referred to in MIRSAP.

Actions are numbered documents (usually produced from within a CMS) that contain specific instructions or directions to perform tasks. They serve as a means of recording, allocating, performing, and managing workloads and operational activity that drive the investigation (usually denoted as A1, A2, A12, etc).

Actions detail instructions, a course of action, to whom it has been allocated, time and date, its origin, and a space for entering the outcome. Each one passes through various supervisory checkpoints and roles within the MIR before finally reaching the SIO, who must make a decision as to whether to file it as complete, return for rework, or raise further tasks arising from it.

MIRSAP Guidance

Actions are generated from information gathered during the investigation and may be requested by any member of the major incident room. Actions are raised once authorised by any of the following: SIO, D/SIO, Office Manager, Receiver, and Document Reader. Actions can be raised and registered by any of the indexers. Each action is given a unique reference, consecutive numbers prefixed by the letter 'A'.

---

[11] ACPO, *Practice Advice on Core Investigative Doctrine* (NCPE, 2005), 77.

7.9.1 **Action management**

Action management should ensure that each action:

- Refers to one specific line of enquiry only.
- Does not contain multiple instructions.
- Contains sufficient detail to inform the enquiry officer of exactly what is required.

Associated documentation must be made available to complete the task. Action results completed by enquiry officers should contain:

- Enquiries made to trace the subject or perform the task on the action requirement.
- Information which is not recorded in any accompanying documentation.[12]

Raising, allocating, resulting, and reviewing of actions is the process by which all team workloads and activities are organised and managed. Actions are generated from information received or gathered during the investigation and should be raised and authorised only by specific persons within the enquiry, usually the SIO/DSIO, Office Manager, Receiver, Document Reader, or nominated Action Writer at SIO instruction (ie during briefings/debriefings).

Once allocated, actions must be properly supervised, a function normally undertaken by an Action Manager. If done incorrectly, the efficiency of an enquiry will suffer. All allocated actions must remain under constant supervision regarding:

- to whom they have been allocated and why.
- workloads/numbers of actions each staff member has been allocated.
- length of time allocated (usually fourteen days is sufficient time to complete medium-/low-priority actions).
- whether the actions are achievable.
- skills/training or experience required to carry out the tasks.

It is worth considering the acronym SMARTER, which means all actions/ tasks are:

S	Specific
M	Meaningful
A	Achievable
R	Realistic
T	Time-specific
E	Ethical
R	Recorded

[12] ACPO, *Guidance on Major Incident Room Standardised Administrative Procedures* (MIRSAP, 2005), 84–5.

The Action Manager must maintain an awareness of team workloads and match skills and experience to tasks. They need to apply effective management skills to avoid potential problems caused by staff abstractions and ensure actions are completed in a timely and efficient manner.

7.9.2 Action abbreviations

The following abbreviations can be used when creating actions (eg on a HOLMES-type CMS):

TIE	Trace/Investigate/Evaluate (see Chapter 8)
TI	Trace and Investigate
TST	take statement
TFST	take further statement
RI	re-interview
OBT	Obtain
ENQS	make enquiries
NOMINAL	person who is allocated a sequential number (eg N12)
UF	unidentified female
UM	unidentified male
UU	unidentified unknown
PDF	personal descriptive form
AQVF	alibi questionnaire verification form
M	message form (eg M14)
A	Action
HP	high priority
MP	medium priority
LP	low priority

7.9.3 Prioritising actions

Priority levels need assigning to all actions raised and allocated. Each one should be assigned a high, medium, or low priority. The parameters for these priorities are agreed by the SIO and recorded in the policy log. Suggested parameters are as follows:

High Priority (HP)	Fast-track actions requiring immediate allocation and completion within a tightly defined time frame.
Medium Priority (MP)	Actions that relate directly to a main line of enquiry.
Low Priority (LP)	Actions that may not currently support a main line of enquiry and may not ordinarily be allocated as a matter of routine.

Not all actions are to be given the same priority, eg high or medium, as this defeats the object of prioritising and organising workloads. The whole point of prioritising is to enable the investigation team to devote their time and effort to the most important lines of enquiry. All decisions and markers should be regularly reviewed throughout the investigation.

7.9.4 Early action management

In the early stages, most major investigations require relatively standard types of actions being raised and allocated for conducting important enquiries. To speed up the investigatory process various templates can be used containing a bank of generic actions to consider to kick-start the enquiry. These are often referred to as the 'first 50, 60, etc (or "x" amount) bank actions'. They are pre-prepared to facilitate swift allocation and registering, and to act as aides-memoire.

The sooner a list of actions is raised and allocated, the easier and quicker it is to keep pace with and manage the initial investigation. A pre-prepared list or system that is readily to hand can prove invaluable. In the initial stages, a fully integrated CMS may not be immediately available, in which case a makeshift version may have to suffice. Having a bank of pre-prepared actions available will also facilitate any subsequent back-record conversion (when the system has to catch up with activity that has already taken place but not yet inputted) later.

An action management list (or matrix/table/spreadsheet) can be used almost as soon as the SIO takes charge of the investigation. All action details can be entered onto the list in numerical order to keep a record of what activities have been raised, allocated, and completed. As the details of the actions are recorded together with names of whomever they have been allocated to, the list can serve as an ongoing log of all the investigative work that is being/ has been conducted. The list will also make any handover process easier and show what initial actions have or have not been raised and completed. It may be advantageous to appoint an 'Action Writer' to record and populate the list contemporaneously.

The SIO must retain an awareness of any actions being raised on their behalf. Increasing the number of actions increases workloads and, once raised, a decision must be taken as to whether to proceed with them. Only relevant and focused actions that reflect the investigation's priorities and objectives should be raised. Care must be taken to ensure the investigation is not overburdened with tasks that are not going to take the enquiry any further forward. Although once raised, actions need not necessarily be allocated.

Keeping track of what has been done, by whom, when, and where, and what still needs completing can be challenging unless a good action management system is implemented. One can be used during any initial (de)briefing process and the list of tasks continuously updated and logged as information is fed into the investigation. An example of early action raising is presented in the following box.

Case Example—Stabbing Incident (Homicide)

Rachael Davies from 12 Gould Street, heard what she thought were raised voices and loud screaming coming from the direction of 8 Gould Street. Her partner, Sharon Greaves, arrived at her address shortly afterwards and told her she had seen a young I/C1 female with blonde hair standing and crying outside 8 Gould street. She saw an ambulance attend and the medics begin treating a male with stab wound-type injuries who was lying in the roadway nearby. An unknown IC3 male had been trying to administer first aid to the injured male before paramedics arrived. The victim is believed to be an adult male named Winston Brownlow who later died of his injuries.

First × 20 actions to be raised

1. Arrange inner and outer cordons for scene (1) believed to be Gould Street where N1 Brownlow found and treated by ambulance crew (HP).
2. TI +TST from N2 Rachael Davies, occupant of 12 Gould Street, who heard raised voices and loud screaming coming from the direction of 8 Gould Street (MP).
3. TI +TST from N3, Sharon Greaves, who reported sighting of young I/C1 UF (believed to be Siobhan Taylor) who had blonde hair stood crying on Gould Street (MP).
4. TIE N4 I/C1 UF (believed to Be Siobhan Taylor) with blonde hair seen crying outside number 8 Gould Street (HP).
5. Conduct research on the address and all occupants and any previous history of 8 Gould Street (MP).
6. TI + TST from ambulance crew who attended N1 Brownlow and consider recovery of any relevant forensic samples and notes made (MP).
7. TIE and consider suitability for significant witness status N5 U/M I/C 3 believed to be attempting to administer first-aid to N1 Brownlow (HP).
8. Conduct victimology report and personal profile of N1 Winston Brownlow (MP).
9. Establish location of N1 Brownlow's body and make arrangements for treating as a crime scene (HP).
10. Arrange forensic search of 8 Gould Street and consider treating as crime scene.
11. Arrange forensic recovery of all clothing and possessions taken from victim at hospital and obtain an admission blood sample, if applicable (HP).
12. Conduct initial H2H enquiries in the immediate vicinity and within sight and hearing of scene (1) and 8 Gould Street (MP).
13. Conduct initial trawl of Gould Street and surrounding area as per parameters indicated on map (ref D.9) for any CCTV systems (MP).
14. Appoint Family Liaison Officer and fully brief on circumstances and provision of immediate family support and notification of deceased Brownlow's next of kin (HP).
15. Debrief initial responders and arrange collection of unused material (HP).

| 16. Request attendance of on-call Home Office-registered pathologist (MP). |
| 17. Discuss with local policing commander a local community impact assessment (MP). |
| 18. Check for any precursor or linked incidents (MP). |
| 19. Liaise with MLO and draft initial holding statement for any media interest (MP). |
| 20. Set up MIR at suitable local venue that has appropriate facilities and a CMS (MP). |

7.9.5 Fast-track and high-priority (HP) actions

These are the most effective way of prioritising and allocating urgent and time-critical enquiries. The *Murder Investigation Manual* defines fast-track actions as:

> Any investigative actions which, if pursued immediately, are likely to establish important facts, preserve evidence or lead to the early resolution of the investigation ... Fast track actions are often used during the first twenty-four hours of an investigation, but they may be required at other stages, for example, where another scene is discovered, a significant witness is identified, or a suspect is identified. [13]

Fast-track actions can be applied to reactive or proactive investigations irrespective of whether the crime has been committed recently or not. The first chance to obtain material may be the last, so SIOs must ensure that any new information is brought to their attention quickly so that fast-track actions can be raised and allocated when they are most needed and time critical.

Fast-track actions are invaluable for complying with the 'Golden Hour(s)' principles (the initial period where vital actions are necessary). It is, however, important to *review* any fast-track actions that have been allocated or in the process of being allocated. This meets one of the three strands of the important *ABC* principles (C = 'challenge/check everything'). It must be confirmed that fast-track action allocations are based on valid reasoning and sound judgement to avoid the enquiry taking off in the wrong direction. In the initial stages, any critical actions should be reviewed against changing circumstances as and when any new facts and information become available.

A control policy is necessary for how and when updates and result returns are expected on fast-tracked enquiries. There is little point in allocating high-priority actions if they are not completed and resulted quickly. Clear instructions and direction on when and how to report back is key. For example, the SIO may stipulate an update on or completion of fast-track actions to be provided verbally within twenty-four hours (or less), followed by a more formal (eg written report), within forty-eight hours.

7.9.6 Action results

Action results (or reports) are a way of evaluating the outcome of enquiries. They also serve as a means of indicating the effectiveness and competency of

---

[13] ACPO, *Murder Investigation Manual* (NCPE, 2006).

that particular investigation. Thorough, accurate, and methodical reports portray professionalism and underlie success.

Well-presented reports are indicative of a well-managed and professional approach to the investigation. This is important as they contain potentially disclosable material for the purposes of the prosecutor, defence teams, courts, and any subsequent review or public enquiry.

SIOs may have their own preferences and style for the way they prefer action reports to be completed. For the avoidance of doubt, SIOs should spell out exactly what level of detail and quality they expect. This may include guidance and direction on the avoidance of certain vocabulary that is too vague, such as 'assume', 'presume', 'possibly', 'maybe', and phrases such as 'must have', 'obvious that', and 'no doubt that', ie terms that are not sufficiently factual.

Important rules and standards inform enquiry teams what is required, expected, and acceptable. This is particularly important if resources have been assembled or seconded from different external regions, units, or agencies. Letting staff know what is expected of them and setting ground rules is preferable to them not knowing or guessing what the SIO wants.

Checklist—Action reports

- Good reports indicate good investigative work. No amount of rhetoric or waffle can disguise a poor or shoddy approach and outcome.

- The type of language and comments used in social media forums or in text messages should not be included in formal reports. Staff should be reminded that improper/inappropriate phrases and opinions made elsewhere (eg on personal devices and forums) are potentially disclosable.

- Opinions in reports should be avoided, eg 'I don't think this person is telling the truth', whereas observations and evaluations based on fact and evidence can be included, eg 'there are inconsistencies in their account because …'

- Facts should be listed in a clear and logical order.

- Accurate details of times, dates, and places of any work or interviews conducted, plus full details of any nominals referred to should be included.

- Information cited should be accompanied by an explanation as to provenance and a clear distinction made between hearsay, opinion, and fact.

- Any rough notes should accompany reports for the purposes of disclosure (they are also worth checking, as they sometimes contain more detail than the report itself).

- There must be a true and complete account of all the facts and information, whether or not they fit in with any favoured hypothesis.

- Other relevant information should be included, eg exhibits and property seized, relevant documents, and witness statements.

- Clear and concise language must be used. Even if handwritten there should be double-spacing between lines and easily decipherable words and sentences.

- Witness accounts do not need replicating if contained in a formal statement or ABE interview to which reference can be made.

- Beware of staff 'self-validating' important information, not fully complying with instructions, or recording negative results. This may be an indication of work avoidance, trying to get an action filed quickly, becoming demotivated, or even corrupt and improper practice. Checking and challenging for thorough processes is a *must* (ie to avoid missing an offender or important lead who/which is already 'in the CMS' (see also Chapter 12)).

7.9.7 Action reviews

The SIO and their senior managers should hold regular Action Reviews of both allocated and unallocated (queued) actions. Print-outs or saved digital versions from a CMS can be used for this purpose to produce a record which can be timed and dated, with any instructions clearly highlighted. This allows a clear audit trail for checking both action lists/queues and ensures that all priority work is being undertaken in accordance with the SIO's policy. This task may be designated, eg, to the DSIO, depending on their level of experience, the complexity of the investigation, and the volumes involved.

7.9.8 Action filing policy

There is usually a requirement to set an action resulting/filing policy. This directs the level of management checking and supervision of all material passing through the investigation before it moves onto the Disclosure Officer and then gets 'filed' as completed. Normally at least two levels of supervision are required, those being the Office Manager/Deputy SIO and SIO, to read and place their signatures against all actions, messages, documents, and statements which contain relevant material. All other more routine material can generally be left to a single signatory at the discretion of the SIO.

7.10 Current Situation Reports

Current Situation Reports (CSRs) are useful documents usually registered on a CMS containing important details and updates about an investigation when a case is complex and protracted. The objective is to create a report that provides a clear and up-to-date overview of an enquiry at any given stage. This will be useful for briefing staff, including late joiners, review, and cold-case staff should the enquiry remain unresolved.

SIOs can ensure work begins on the preparation of the CSR at an early stage in the enquiry and that it is regularly updated as it progresses. Each and every updated version should be saved, given a further reference number, and if appropriate a 'hardcopy' printed off prior to amendment and registering. Responsibility for creating and maintaining an accurate CSR lies with the SIO or their nominated deputy or case/file preparation officer.

Prior to closure of an investigation, the case officer should ensure that either: (a) the court result is indicated or (b) reference is made to a closing review which summarises the current state of the investigation and what lines of enquiry or actions remain outstanding. It is also useful to make reference to an audit list of case material and location of all stored and archived exhibits and location of important material such as the policy log.

7.11 Disclosure Rules

The Criminal Procedure and Investigations Act 1996 (CPIA) is the UK's mandatory statutory legislation that regulates the procedures for investigating and prosecuting criminal offences[14] which began on or after 1 April 1997.

There are three disclosure regimes by date order:

1. Prior to 1 April 1997—common law
2. 1 April 1997–3 April 2005—CPIA 1996
3. 4 April 2005 onwards—CPIA as amended by the Coroners and Justice Act 2009 (CJA)

CPIA is a key piece of legislation that governs the way investigations are managed to ensure all reasonable lines of enquiry are pursued. It obliges a prosecutor to disclose to the defence any relevant material.[15] A revised Code of Practice (covering England and Wales) under Part II of the legislation governing disclosure was introduced in March 2015. This sets out how investigators are to *record, retain*, and *reveal* (3 × Rs rule) to the prosecutor material obtained in a criminal investigation.

Management of a criminal investigation must take cognisance of legal requirements concerning unused material. It is one of the key challenges facing the prosecution team in any serious or complex case. The SIO (referred to in the legislation as the 'officer in charge of the investigation') has an absolute duty to ensure that disclosure is dealt with in an appropriate, just, and fair way, and that it is compliant with a defendant's right to a fair trial.

---

[14] A 'criminal investigation as defined in the legislation is an investigation conducted with a view to it being ascertained whether a person should be charged with an offence or whether a person charged with an offence is guilty of it.

[15] Material includes internal as well as external and items such as the relevant parts of an investigating officer's notebook/casebook; rough notes taken during interviews or in witness first accounts; communications between specialists and experts, emails, notes of meetings, itemised mobile phone billing etc, or anything else that might assist the defence or undermine a prosecution case.

The SIO must therefore ensure that their chosen Disclosure Officer (DO) has the requisite training, skills, and authority commensurate with the complexity of the investigation to discharge their function correctly. As soon as a criminal investigation begins the following roles must be designated:

1. Investigator
2. Officer in charge of the Investigation
3. Disclosure Officer

It is the responsibility of the *officer in charge of the investigation* (ie SIO) to ensure all material obtained or generated by them during the course of the investigation is retained and recorded in a durable and retrievable format. This includes having regard to whether relevant material may exist in relation to other linked investigations or prosecutions. Reasonable enquiries must be carried out to establish if such material exists and whether it is relevant to the case.

Disclosure failures can have serious consequences for all those involved in the case and there is a duty to ensure any relevant material is recorded in a durable or retrievable format. Information that may not be of particular relevance at a specific stage of an investigation may become relevant later and this needs to be borne in mind in order to comply with disclosure obligations. For example, a number of people present in a particular time and place may state they saw nothing of significance, but what is 'significant' may not become known until much later. Similarly, if developments in an investigation mean that material previously discounted as being irrelevant then becomes relevant, steps must be taken if practicable to recover and retain it (eg material that suddenly undermines the reliability or credibility of a witness or complainant).[16]

The nominated Disclosure Officer examines all material gathered and schedules it. The test to be applied in scheduling is *relevance*. All unused material, however, must be scheduled, regardless of whether it meets the disclosure test. Non-sensitive material is listed on an MG6C, sensitive material on an MG6D[17] (these being the requisite forms used in UK prosecution cases).

---

[16] In 2018 several rape trials collapsed in the United Kingdom due to a failure to disclose evidence such as telephone and social media records, including the case against an undergraduate at Oxford University days before he was due to go to trial for raping a victim who had been sending him emails and text messages contrary to her own account. The media reported a Chief Constable (Nick Ephgrave, Surrey Police) as claiming there was a 'cultural problem with disclosure of evidence, where it is often seen by officers as a thing to be done at the end of an investigation, becoming subsequent to, rather than integral to the investigation. Changing this mindset is an immediate challenge for us.' ('Police Chief admits 'cultural problem' with evidence disclosure', *The Guardian*, 24 January 2018 <http://www.theguardian.com>).

[17] Revisions made to the CPS Disclosure Manual in February 2018 stated that a Disclosure Management Document (DMD) is to be used in prescribed categories of cases (eg, homicide, rape, and serious sexual offences) where prosecutors will seek pre-charge assurance that all material has been revealed for disclosure purposes.

Relevance Test

A relevance test includes anything that appears to have some bearing on any offence under investigation, or any person being investigated, or on the surrounding circumstances unless it is *incapable* of having any impact on the case.

The Disclosure Officer prepares a report to the prosecutor (in the United Kingdom, on a form known as an MG6E) giving their views on whether any material on the schedule meets the disclosure test (anything capable of assisting the defence or undermining the prosecution case). This is a very wide test and as a general rule, if there is any doubt as to whether the test is passed then it should be included in the schedule submitted to the prosecutor.

The prosecutor has responsibility for determining whether the material ought to be disclosed to the defence team. Any material which meets the test of relevance will be disclosed to the defence team, unless an application can be made to a presiding judge for Public Interest Immunity (PII).

Once defence statements have been received, the Disclosure Officer must undertake another full review of the unused material. They then provide a further report (on an MG6E) to the prosecutor indicating whether anything now falls to be disclosed and whether any identified reasonable lines of enquiry ought to be undertaken to assist the defence.

KEY POINTS

1. There is a duty to nominate a fully trained and accredited Disclosure Officer (and an additional deputy/deputies if necessary) who has responsibility for discharging mandatory statutory obligations under CPIA.
2. CPIA places a requirement on the investigation, in particular the SIO to ensure that proper procedures are in place to *retain, record*, and *reveal* (3 × Rs rule) any unused material obtained during the course of a criminal investigation which may be relevant and have some bearing on any offence or person under investigation.
3. Reasonable enquiries must be made to establish whether relevant material exists in relation to other potential linked investigations.

Bibliography

ACPO, *Guidance on Major Incident Room Standardised Administrative Procedures* (MIRSAP, 2005)

ACPO, *Murder Investigation Manual* (NCPE, 2006)

ACPO, *Practice Advice on Core Investigative Doctrine* (NCPE, 2005)

ACPO, *Tactical Debrief: Operation Sumac* (NPIA, 2008)

Flanagan, R, *A Report on the Investigation by Cambridgeshire Constabulary into the Murders of Jessica Chapman and Holly Wells at Soham on 4 August 2002* (HMIC, June 2004)

Conducting TIE Enquiries

8.1 **Introduction**

The term 'TIE' (which usually stands for 'trace, interview, and eliminate') is an abbreviated instruction and a process used as an investigative strategy. It is a tool aimed at identifying those who could realistically be either a witness or offender. The process is an established and accepted technique in the United Kingdom that many law enforcement counterparts elsewhere (eg overseas) do not use. This UK method allows chosen subjects to be allocated a status that fits somewhere in between suspect and witness, whereas in many other jurisdictions they must be designated as either one or the other.

A TIE strategy is generally used only in the most serious cases where there is no clear suspect. They are rarely used in simple cases or 'self-solvers' because they are either unnecessary or too resource-intensive and intrusive; they must be justifiable and proportionate. One of the early decisions an SIO might have to make is whether or not the TIE method is to be used on their enquiry. A decision to do so should be considered carefully and if used should feature in the list of main lines of enquiry (MLOE) referenced in a policy log.

Key components of the process involve creating and populating categories and prioritising individuals identified from information or research. Examples of sources that may provide suitable TIE subjects include general enquiries, house-to-house (H2H), messages, intelligence, search activities, forensic results, analytical work, etc. Once a group of subjects has been identified through defined criteria as being suitable for the TIE process, they become the focus of a range of investigative techniques that assist in evaluating what, if any, connection they have to the enquiry. These usually include alibi checks, interviews to obtain their accounts, and taking elimination samples and fingerprints. In other words TIE subjects are placed under far more scrutiny than other subjects in an enquiry to ascertain what significance they are.

Applying a more thorough and determined process to selected individuals helps not only obtain their accounts, closely examine them, and apply important techniques but also apply useful tradecraft. This includes spotting things that seem out of place (or 'Just Doesn't Look Right'—JDLR principle; see section 5.6) such as nervousness, strange behaviour, odd comments, evasiveness, unusual marks on hands/faces or injuries, missing/broken items, disinfectant or putrid smells in premises.

Although there is no 'one size fits all', TIE strategies can be crafted to fit individual cases and this chapter outlines the basic principles involved. Having a TIE policy is often viewed as being complex and challenging, but when used properly it can be an extremely effective investigative tool.

8.2 **National Guidance**

Association of Chief Police Officers (ACPO, now the National Police Chiefs' Council-(NPCC)) approved the guidance relating to TIEs which, although now somewhat dated, is still used and contained within:

1. *Major Incident Room Standardised Administrative Procedures* (MIRSAP).[1] This standardised the terminology and incident room procedures. It also provided the definition of what TIE officially means: 'Trace, Interview, and Eliminate'.[2] Other important points in this document state that TIE actions should not be returned for additional ones to be raised when verifying the subject's account. Instead, enquiries should be completed in their entirety. The document highlighted the importance of cross-referencing by the MIR to ensure all information available and known relating to the subject is completed (eg if a relative or associate of the subject owns a vehicle type which is of interest to the enquiry). The document also stipulates the elimination codes 1–6 (see section 8.8).

2. *Murder Investigation Manual* (MIM).[3] The manual refers to the problem of overuse of the TIE process, suggesting the lesser option of TI (Trace and Interview) is often more appropriate. The MIM states: *'Being in a TIE category does not mean that individuals are suspected of the crime, merely that the group is one which, in theory at least, could contain the offender … Following en-*quiries, TIE subjects should be regarded as being either eliminated or un-eliminated from the TIE category, not as being eliminated or un-eliminated as the offender.'[4]

3. *Core Investigative Doctrine.*[5] Updated in 2012 and long since incorporated into the College of Policing APP,[6] covered subjects such as prioritisation, elimination criteria, and conducting enquiries. It described the use of categories in order to identify persons to be subjects of TIE action, defining these categories as '[a] group of people sharing a common characteristic which is likely to include the offender.' One paragraph states: 'When carrying out TIE enquiries investigators should be mindful that the subjects may also be potential witnesses … particularly so where they are in a group who may know the victim or offender.' Like Major Incident Room Standardised Administrative Procedures (MIRSAP), the doctrine mentioned the Major

---

[1] ACPO, *Guidance on Major Incident Room Standardised Administrative Procedures* (MIRSAP, 2005).
[2] Confusion has arisen with the TIE acronym sometimes being referred to as standing for Trace, *Implicate*, and Eliminate. Whatever terminology is used, the procedures remain the same.
[3] ACPO, *Murder Investigation Manual* (NCPE, 2006).
[4] ACPO, *Murder Investigation Manual* (NCPE, 2006), 250.
[5] ACPO, *Practice Advice on Core Investigative Doctrine*, 2nd edn (NPIA, 2012).
[6] Authorised Professional Practice; see <http://www.app.college.police.uk/app-content/investigations>.

Incident Room (MIR) six-point code for the purposes of recording elimination. It also stated:

An important principle of TIE strategies is that implication and elimination processes are always provisional and should be rigorously tested against the material to hand and to any new material that later becomes available. It is essential good practice to regard TIE subjects as being either implicated or eliminated from the TIE category, not as being the offender.[7]

8.3 General Considerations

TIE processes are intrusive because they need to be, which may leave those on the receiving end thinking that they are under suspicion. This may conflict with objectives aimed at securing the willing cooperation of individuals, witnesses, victims' families, groups, and communities. Cultural and language barriers may provide further confusion. Therefore, there may be a need to explain the process tactfully (avoiding use of organisational or legal jargon) and what each element means and why it is necessary. Using investigative processes is always much easier when there is willing agreement and cooperation from those involved.

The Human Rights Act 1998 (HRA) is a further consideration when conducting TIE enquiries. Intrusive elimination activities may lead to potential breaches of human rights and the Article 8 right to respect for private and family life. A breach is only permissible if absolutely necessary, proportionate, and justifiable, and in the interests of national security, public safety, economic well-being of the country, prevention of crime and disorder, health, morals, or protection of the rights and freedoms of others (HRA, Article 8). Each TIE criterion needs to be justified and necessary, eg if there are no fingerprints at any crime scene, there may be no justifiable reason to take them as part of the elimination process.

KEY POINT

TIE processes need to comply with the HRA. Designated categories that lead to the inclusion of individuals as TIE subjects and elimination processes have to be justifiable, proportionate, and necessary.

Checklist—TIE enquiry considerations

• Time and resources consumption—two officers are often required to complete.

• Extensive research—required to produce risk assessments/control strategies.

---

[7] ACPO, *Practice Advice on Core Investigative Doctrine*, 2nd edn (NPIA, 2012), para 6.8.7, 140.

- High standards of investigation and checking otherwise mistakes may occur with innocent subjects wrongly implicated or true offenders eliminated.

- Intrusiveness—need to be HRA compliant (justifiable, proportionate, and necessary).

- Closely scrutinised and managed—by SIO and team supervision.

- Accountable—judicial and review processes examine these processes closely.

- Audit trails—must be clear and transparent with links to information sources and reasoning as to how and why they are being conducted.

- Powers and legal basis—care must be taken to ensure that tactics employed are kept within legislative frameworks and not in breach of safeguards such as those contained in the Police and Criminal Evidence Act 1984 (PACE).

- National Decision Model compliant—decision to use should be outlined in policy as per NDM (see Appendix A).

8.4 Meaning of Terms

The acronym 'TIE'—'Trace', 'Interview', and 'Eliminate'—has been around for some considerable time and often gets confused, although it is referred to extensively in major crime investigations and on systems such as the Home Office Large Major Enquiry System (HOLMES). The NPCC Homicide Working Group (HWG) crime business area sub-group commissioned a research project in 2015 which recommended that the meaning of the terms be changed ((2015) 10(2) *NPCC Journal of Homicide and Major Incident Investigation*). The changes are outlined as follows (Table 8.1):

Table 8.1 TIE—Changes in meaning

TRACE (remains the same)	This term remains the first part of the process. It means conducting research on the subject, confirming residence details, description, warning markers, place of work, places frequented, identity, previous convictions, associates, intelligence checks, risk assessments, build profile, etc. The SIO should determine/agree what 'trace' enquiries entail.
INVESTIGATE (changed from 'Interview')	Has a wider meaning than merely 'interview', though this remains an important part of the process. Should include a much wider range of tactical options, eg search/seize material, obtain descriptive details, take samples (eg DNA or fingerprints), conduct surveillance, check mobile and digital devices, obtain communications data under RIPA, look for things out of place (marks, injuries, odd behaviour, changes of routine or appearance), conduct alibi checks, and corroborate movements.

(continued)

Table 8.1 Continued

EVALUATE (changed from 'Eliminate')	Extended to include both 'eliminate' *and* 'implicate' (ie from the category, not offence). Involves analysing results of investigation process, including verification of alibi and application of alibi codes 1–6, assessment of evidence/intelligence/information, and determining relevance of the subject to the enquiry. Can incorporate making recommendations as to what, if any, further action is required or review priority of the action.

8.4.1 'Persons of interest'

The term 'person/subject of interest' (or P/SOI) is sometimes used in investigations. However, the term has never been officially defined or recognised in nationally approved manuals or by the College of Policing. Neither has it been formally included as a category on most case management systems (eg HOLMES).

The term POI could feasibly refer to anyone who sits somewhere between a witness and TIE subject, TI or TIE subject, or suspect and TIE subject. It could also be used to describe key witnesses, sources of information, and those identified by anonymous information and requiring further research. More significantly, usage could be viewed by the criminal justice system as a means of circumventing the legal safeguards of PACE. Also, if an enquiry forms part of a linked series that transcends force boundaries, then non-standard terminology such as 'POI' may cause confusion amongst those who come from different regions.

It seems likely, however, that investigators or agencies who/that prefer to use the term often do so as a substitute for or equivalent of a 'TIE subject'. If so, then a clear explanation as to what terminology is being used and what precisely it means should be given to all those engaged on an enquiry to avoid any confusion or doubt.

KEY POINT

The term 'TIE' stands for a process and instruction, not title or status. Some investigators use the term 'TIE subjects' or just 'TIEs' (eg 'How many TIEs have we got?'). Others prefer to use the term 'Person or Subject of Interest' or 'P/SOI' for short. It is worth clarifying and confirming what the terms in use are/mean when drawing up a policy and explaining to all staff.

8.5 Recording TIE Policy

Devising and introducing a TIE strategy first requires a decision to introduce the tactic into the investigation and requires a recorded policy decision. For example:

Policy Log Entry (Number)

TIE Strategy

Decision:

TIE subjects will be identified, and actions raised for specific groups
(or categories) of persons created under headings considered to be of
significance. These groups are those most likely to contain the offender(s)
or witnesses. The category headings are as follows:

(list categories—see para 7.4)

TIE actions will be raised and allocated for all those falling within the
aforementioned categories and will include a requirement for obtaining
the following:

(eg samples—eg fingerprints, personal descriptive details and DNA
buccal swabs)

Once completed, each action will be evaluated and a determination made
of whether the nominal can be allocated a MIRSAP elimination code
of 1–6.

Reason:

A serious offence has been committed and in the absence of a clear suspect,
a TIE process (trace, investigate, and evaluate) is justifiable, proportionate,
and necessary to assist in determining whether certain individuals are
of interest to the enquiry. This will incorporate an evaluation process to
determine those who may or may not be of significance.

When phrasing TIE policies it is important not to confuse wording or terms. For example, wrongly substituting the term 'subject' for the stronger term 'suspect' will present obvious complications and possible legal challenges. Careful checks need to ensure correct wording is consistently used in official records and documents by everyone connected to the investigation, including the Crown Prosecution Service (CPS). A TIE 'subject' is something entirely different to a 'suspect', for which legally prescribed processes might apply, such as arrest, cautioning, custody detention, legal representation, and formal interview (ie under PACE).

A TIE strategy may include (and perhaps contain within a 'stand-alone' document) any or all the following:

5WH Checklist—TIE strategy considerations

- Why the strategy is required (HRA considerations—justification, etc).
- What the objectives are.

- Who will conduct the enquiries, where the resources will come from, and if any additional resources such as interpreters are required.

- What categories have been chosen and why.

- Who the subjects are and how they fit into the categories.

- What the TIE action allocation policy is (eg how many per officer/team and priority).

- How nominals will be traced, ie what information and research needs completing.

- What the elimination/implication policy and criteria are.

- When, where, and how any interviews are to take place with TIE subjects.

- What the pre-prepared interview plan is (including topics to cover).

- What documentation is required (eg PDFs for all subjects, photographs—full body or facial).

- What samples are required and how obtained (eg fingerprints or DNA buccal swabs).

- What risk control measures apply (eg prior research requirements, always two officers, supervisory officer to monitor).

- What search requirements are necessary (eg premises, property, digital devices, or vehicles and pedal cycles) and the type and extent of search (eg forensic, Police Search Adviser (PolSA) digital specialist) and legal powers.

- What search and seizure policy is (eg clothing, footwear, vehicles, cycles, digital devices, phones, satellite navigation, passwords, gaming systems, etc) and powers.

- What case-specific requirements apply (eg what to check for/deem as crime scene).

- How to deal with refusals-to-cooperate (what the policy states).

- What to do if necessary to caution and arrest (eg reasonable grounds arise from a significant find during search or admission made).

- When action results should be completed and returned for checking.

- When and how outputs/outcomes are to be reviewed and (re)evaluated and by whom.

Some investigations require consideration of case-specific checks when conducting TIE actions, some examples being:

1. Visible checks for offenders who have suffered injuries while committing the offence (eg cuts to hands and fingers when holding a knife blade, scratches on face, recoil marks from a semi-automatic handgun, etc).

2. Checks for marks or injuries from close contact with a fire ignition source or chemicals.

3. Checks for items and environments seen in the background of digital images or social media posts, or indecent images of children (IIOC) and child sexual abuse and exploitation (CSAE) material.

8.6 **Constructing Categories**

A TIE category is a group of people who are likely to share common character-istics with the offender. These depend entirely on the case circumstances. Each category is defined by discriminating factors that match those of significance to or profile of the offender, such as age, gender, ethnicity, description, move-ments, forensic profile (eg DNA or fingerprints), use of or access to locations and types of premises, vehicles, lifestyles, and criminal background, etc.

Because categories are case-specific, the narrower and tightly focused they are, the better; otherwise they may become overpopulated and difficult to manage. For example, not using sufficiently tightly focused time parameters for a category aimed at identifying and eliminating persons who were present at an outdoor urban crime scene may produce too many individuals to interview and eliminate.

When creating likely profiles and characteristics of offenders to include in TIE categories, specialist advice may be sought from experts such as Behavioural Investigative Advisers and/or Forensic Clinical Psychologists. Their academic research and practical expertise can provide a scientific and specialist approach to the selection of characteristics and criteria for determining TIE categories.

Checklist—TIE category examples

- Aged between (x) and (y) years who had access to scene (1) between … and … (time parameters).

- Aged between (x) and (y) years who were within scene (1) or vicinity of scene (1) (as defined) between … and … (time parameters).

- Previous convictions for similar offences and/or modus operandi (MO) (eg knife or sex offences within a defined period and locality).

- Last person to see victim alive, discovered their body, or reported them missing.

- Similar physical characteristics or profile to the offender(s).

- Used or had access to certain type of premises, location, vehicle, or other mode of transport.

- Named as involved (eg via intelligence reports, information messages, or ongoing work via the enquiry teams or other sources).

- Registered (and archived) sex offenders (RSOs) or other dangerous/violent offenders.

- Suffer from a mental health condition and reside within a (named) district.

- Identified by other agencies as being of concern within given locality.

- Recent prison releases or bail hostel residents (including tagged offenders).

- Known associates of or persons closely linked to victim.

- Close relatives of victim.

- Males/females of certain profile residing within ... (parameters and proximity).

- Committed or attempted to commit suicide or self-referred to a mental clinic (within stipulated time and area parameters) post offence.

- Sought treatment for certain types of injuries (eg burns if arson or gunshot injuries if firearms-related) or sexually transmitted disease .

- Any others at the SIO's discretion.

The list of categories relies on how much is known about the circumstances of the crime and profile of the offender. As the enquiry progresses, the SIO can review the validity of each TIE category and, where necessary, adjust or downgrade some of the actions created to just trace and interview (TI).

The SIO needs to be mindful that a separate policy for TIE actions may also be created within a case management system (CMS) such as HOLMES used by indexers and will probably contain details of parameters that define terms such as 'vicinity of the scene' or 'alibi times'. These need to be identical to and mirror those referred to in the SIO's policy file (eg time parameters for TIE of all persons at scene (1)). It should also be noted that this means there could be other defined categories on the CMS other than TIEs and they must not be confused with one another.

KEY POINTS

- As a general rule, the more TIE categories a subject fits into, the more likely they are to be the offender and therefore need to be prioritised.
- A 'catch-all' category of 'anyone else at the SIO's discretion' should not be routinely used without justification and agreement.
- Experts such as Behavioural Investigative Advisers (BIAs); available from the National Crime Agency (NCA)) can be useful for assisting with and providing advice and expertise on drawing up TIE categories and/or scoring matrix.

8.6.1 Defining the 'scene' and 'vicinity of the scene'

In addition to defining a 'scene' for determining parameters and cordons for the purposes of forensic examination and searching (see Chapter 6), a similar process can be applied for TIE purposes. The SIO determines not only what constitutes the parameters of the scene but also the 'vicinity' of the scene. This enables TIE categories to encapsulate a much wider area of significance to the case circumstances, eg to cover entrance and exit routes. For example, a category may stipulate: 'TIE all persons within scene (1)', or 'TIE all persons within the vicinity of scene (1)' within a defined timescale.

8.6.2 Prioritising categories

If there are a large number of TIE subjects/actions they need to be suitably prioritised. Investigative priorities must always remain dynamic and need to be frequently reviewed. They may change by moving up or down the scale of importance and relevance on a regular basis. Regular action reviews (especially TIEs) with the incident room team need to be performed to monitor and determine progress and prioritisation. This also facilitates a check on workloads to ensure they reflect the SIO's requirements and investigative direction.

8.6.3 Scoring matrix

A scoring matrix can assist with prioritising TIE subjects and focusing resources. It can cater for certain criteria that are case specific and provide a numerical score against which a TIE list can be graded. The SIO may wish to enlist the services of key team members to assist with and contribute to the process.

Certain facts and features can be added to the scoring process. For example, in a case which has a positive scene-specific fingerprint or DNA profile, any TIE subject who is not recorded on the respective national IDENT1 or National DNA Database (NDNAD), and therefore not eliminated, can be made an early priority for an elimination/implication process.

The following example relates to a hypothetical case in which an elderly male was found stabbed to death at his home address (scene 1) sometime between 10.00 a.m. and 3.00 p.m. on a weekday. There was no sign of forced entry. He was elderly and believed to stash large amounts of cash at his home address, most of which was subsequently found to be missing. He resided alone and had very few known associates or close family. A scoring matrix for subjects contained within the TIE categories (which would be geographically specific) may look as follows (Table 8.2):

Table 8.2 TIE Scoring Matrix

CRITERIA	VALUE (1–10)	SCORE
Intelligence/conviction for burglary in a dwelling	(5)	
Intelligence/conviction for aggravated burglary in dwelling, violence, or similar offence (eg street robbery, theft from the person)	(6)	
Intelligence/conviction for aggravated burglary in dwelling involving knife/sharp instrument	(8)	
Aged between (x) and (y) and within vicinity of scene (1) between 09.00 a.m. and 4.00 p.m. (on date of murder)	(7)	
Linked to the victim (eg relative/associate)	(5)	
Linked (by offending, intelligence, stop-checks, or otherwise) to geographic location of offence (ie within set parameters)	(6)	
Previous conviction for daytime offending	(4)	
Known to target or select elderly or vulnerable victims	(8)	
Linked to offence through high-grade intelligence	(10)	
TOTAL		

8.6.3.1 Scoring matrix dos and don'ts

DO
- Provide explicit direction on 'operational definitions' of what is meant by each of the terms, eg 'daytime offending' or 'geographic location'.
- Test the matrix to ensure the right persons are achieving the highest scores as expected.
- Seek assistance whenever possible, particularly from a BIA.

DON'T
- Consider it an easy or quick task; weighting scores are vital and if incorrect could waste resources with the true offender being overlooked.
- *EVER* eliminate anyone/anything using this process; it is a means of *prioritisation* only.
- Score everyone with the same points—the idea is to distinguish and prioritise.
- Ever reuse a prioritisation matrix—should be redone on a case-by-case basis.

8.7 Interviewing Subjects

Conducting interviews is a standard TIE process and the method of approach should be prescribed and agreed by the SIO, who may wish to have an input from an accredited PIP2 interview adviser. It may be decided, for example, that all TIE interviews are digitally (video) recorded, or by means of an audio device, or contemporaneously on notes signed by the subject.

These tactics are aimed at preserving the accuracy and integrity of the process, an important factor, as TIE subjects can later develop into suspects or key witnesses. What subjects say during an interview might be used later as vital evidence; particularly when considering the principle that the next best thing to a confession is a provable lie. Equally, what negative answers are provided might also prove important, eg 'I have never met or been anywhere near this person or place'. If the interview is recorded it eliminates any possibility of missing that one piece of pivotal information, provided knowingly or otherwise, during the interview, and the content can be more easily authenticated.

Sufficient time and care should be taken over planning and preparation for interviews to ensure there is consistency and the best approach. A preferred venue for interviews should be considered and it may, for example, be preferable to invite a TIE subject into a more formal venue (eg police station) where there are better facilities and fewer distractions, or other suitable premises where the process can be conducted uninterrupted. Alternatively, interviewing at the subject's home addresses may facilitate an opportunity to meet subjects in their own habitat with an added benefit of being able to observe their lifestyles and living environments, eg spot who else might be hanging around.

Important areas to cover in interviews form an important part of the planning and preparation. Relevant time parameters of the offence/incident (particularly for alibis) and the aims and objectives will guide the construction of an interview plan. If the subject has already been interviewed or their comments have been captured elsewhere, eg on a body-worn camera, this material can be checked by those conducting the interview. TIE subjects can later become important witnesses and be given a relevant status (eg Significant Witness (SigWit); see Chapter 13). The need for interpreters might be another consideration.

It cannot be stressed strongly enough how important the TIE interview process is. The process provides a golden opportunity to assess key individuals and apply core detective skills. What a TIE subject says, how they react, look, their body language, eye movement, or voice tonality, all of which are an offer during the time spent with them, are important. Noticing things about a TIE subject, eg a scratch on their face or any other visible injury (eg to the hands); their physical appearance or (lack of) a strong physique (eg to lift, carry, or dispose of a corpse/mount a physical attack); what their speech and accent sounds like; if they have any peculiar traits; if they become nervous or uncomfortable when certain topics are mentioned; all of this is rich information for the investigation. There are many examples of offenders being caught by savvy investigators who notice important details during a TIE type interview that helps solve the case.

KEY POINTS

1. Negative responses can be captured eg: 'I have not been there', 'I do not know (name)', 'I cannot remember where I was', 'I have never had sexual contact with … '. Such comments can later develop into evidential gifts.
2. The 'I' in 'TIE' stands for 'investigate', which means applying a wide range of detective skills and training, including noting how subjects behave and react during interviews, and the valuable time spent assessing them and evaluating (the 'E').

8.8 Elimination and Implication

One important point to revisit is that 'elimination' has always meant to eliminate from the category, *not* the investigation (see also section 8.2). This is a fact often confused and misunderstood. For the avoidance of doubt, it is repeated once more—elimination means from the *category* and *not* the offence. For example, if an offender's DNA profile is discovered at the crime scene, the elimination policy could feasibly include obtaining DNA samples from all TIE subjects. Any sample that didn't match the scene profile would mean the subject can be eliminated from the *category* of persons matching the profile but not necessarily the offence as there might have been more than one offender. The famous saying goes, 'absence of evidence is not evidence of absence'.

A second point refers back to the terminology mentioned in section 8.4. The term 'eliminate' has previously meant just that in the TIE acronym. However, the process should rightly also provide an opportunity for completely the opposite—ie implicate. Therefore any of the 'standard' terminology used should, for the purposes of an effective investigation, also be construed as including *either* requirement: eliminate or implicate.

In order to eliminate or implicate a subject, it is necessary to set criteria against which to compare. Agreed criteria and accompanying methods will not only help in satisfying the needs of MIRSAP elimination recording criteria but can also be used for the purposes of prioritisation when reviewing inconclusive TIE actions. Care must be taken to ensure the codes and criteria are applied correctly. On a HOLMES-type CMS the elimination categories are as stated in Table 8.3.

SIOs, incident room staff, and supervisors determine and agree from the returned Action report what level of elimination from the list applies. An important point about this criterion is that these markers can be changed depending on new information if it becomes available, for example if an associate changes their initial alibi account or it is disproved.

Table 8.3 MIRSAP Elimination Codes

Elimination Code 1:	Forensic elimination
Elimination Code 2:	Descriptive elimination
Elimination Code 3:	Alibi by independent witness
Elimination Code 4:	Alibi by associate or relative
Elimination Code 5:	Alibi by spouse/partner/common-law partner
Elimination Code 6:	Not eliminated

KEY POINTS

1. Any requirement to obtain samples or conduct checks and enquiries as part of a TIE process must remain under review and be included as a standing agenda item at any forensic strategy meetings or action review meetings to ensure the elimination criteria remains relevant, justifiable, and necessary.
2. A policy directive is required to ensure all samples obtained are examined in a timely fashion, in order to assist in timely elimination or implication of TIE subjects.

8.8.1 Forensic elimination (Code 1)

In the majority of cases there is the potential for a crime scene examination to reveal useful marks, trace evidence, or material against which to eliminate a subject. These might be finger/palm prints, DNA profiles (through the taking of an elimination buccal swab or fingerprints), footwear marks, or vehicle tyre-mark impressions. Other items such as smart phones or other digital communication devices may also allow for a digital examination process to help in the elimination process.

When determining what samples to obtain, it is wise to be initially cautious and obtain them (eg fingerprints and DNA swabs) even though, at the time, no forensic results may be available against which to compare them. This is because some examination results take time to complete and only become known a considerably later when it is too late to obtain samples. However, the justification and necessity requirements need to be clearly outlined if this policy is to be adopted to comply with basic human rights principles.

Whenever tyre or footwear marks are involved, a visual screening policy may prove more practical. This is to help limit the unnecessary seizing, storage, and examination of items that are not clearly similar to the make, style, type, pattern, or tread of those being sought. Expert advice can assist in making this decision and, if necessary, details or photographs against which to compare samples issued to enquiry staff. This process should be supported by Crime Scene Investigators (CSIs) who have more expertise to assess any doubtful tread patterns and check for potential blood or body fluid staining to support the screening process.

The financial implications of taking samples also needs to be borne in mind, as this may be considerable if high numbers of samples are obtained (eg buccal swabs). Costs may include not just forensic examination costs but also the time it takes to obtain samples and the processing time within the incident room exhibit system as well as storage implications.

KEY POINT

Care must be taken when deciding to eliminate against forensic samples found at crime scenes. There may be other offenders involved who didn't leave any forensic traces. This is why the term 'elimination' means from the *category* and *not* the offence. Also, some offenders commit offences (plan, arrange, conspire, incite, etc) without ever being present at the location where the offence took place.

8.8.2 Descriptive elimination (Code 2)

Descriptions of offenders can be obtained from witnesses and CCTV, and height or physique analysis, etc can be used as factors for elimination. A cautious approach needs to be taken, however, when deciding what level of reliability can be applied to the accuracy of any description, particularly when features such as height and build are concerned. This is simply because it is very easy to get them wrong. Unusual physical characteristics such as distinguishing marks or accents can also prove misleading if wrongly assessed or faked by offenders. Personal features such as the colour of a person's skin can sometimes also be difficult to confirm with any degree of accuracy, eg under poor lighting conditions. The claim that a person who is seen to have a walking limp or peculiar gait on CCTV, for example, can prove misleading if they are, in fact, concealing a large or heavy weapon under their clothing.

Descriptions may be included as a requirement in the TIE criteria for the taking of a person's photograph (either facial or full body). This is so that the true description of that person can be used for comparison purposes and the avoidance of doubt.

8.8.2.1 Personal descriptive form (PDF)

The acronym PDF is referred to in MIRSAP and refers to the provision of descriptive detail for elimination purposes and identification. This form provides prompts for obtaining relevant detail, such as vehicles owned and used, and contact details. The contents can be amended be amended if necessary to include other case-specific detail.

PDFs should not be regarded as an administrative burden. Used intelligently they can provide invaluable descriptive information from which analysts/researchers can identify potential suspects and eliminate unidentified persons. SIOs should, at an early stage of the investigation, establish PDF criteria. The completion of PDFs can be time consuming and, therefore, SIOs should avoid the routine, blanket approach of obtaining PDFs unless it cannot be avoided. PDF criteria should be set against known facts, for example, if the evidence suggests the offender was a male in his twenties, the SIO may determine PDFs will be taken from all males interviewed between the ages of 14 and 45 years, thus excluding other males and females. Where PDFs are required, it is essential that a thorough briefing is given to investigators. Particular attention should be drawn to the fact that descriptions and clothing worn relate to the day of the incident rather than the day the form is completed. Similarly, care should be taken when recording details of vehicles owned or used by the interviewee and, where possible, officers should check the facts carefully.

ACPO, *Murder Investigation Manual* (NCPE, 2006), Chapter 10.

8.8.3 **ALIBI elimination (Codes 3–5)**

Alibis are a fundamental part of an elimination process, provided time parameters are very tightly focused. The process can sometimes prove time-consuming and intrusive, as follow-up enquiries invariably involve other people being interviewed. The reliability of alibis is always a major consideration, which is why they are sub-categorised into three further elimination codes, dependent on the relationship of the individual to the subject and significance in terms of reliability.

In some cases, there are localised forms designed solely for the purposes of conducting and recording alibis, with a space for recording not only the personal details but signatures of those providing the information. A policy will be required as to whether a witness statement is to be taken from alibi witnesses, which may extend the process even further but may prove useful at a later stage if the alibi can be disproved or it changes.

8.8.3.1 **Setting alibi times**

TIE subjects can be asked to account for their movements during alibi times set by the SIO. These should coincide with significant events applicable to the investigation and determined by, for example, witness information, CCTV, or, in homicide cases, the 'time of death' indicating when the offence is likely to have occurred.[8] Time parameters may need to be wide enough to include other factors, such as events before or after an incident that may also be significant. Obviously, the wider the times are the more effort is required to alibi a subject over a longer period.

---

[8] For 'time of death', see Chapter 14.

Alibi times need to kept under review and remain flexible to react to information that may reduce or expand the time periods, in which case some individuals who may have fallen within the initial periods may no longer be of relevance.

Enquiry teams should include in the alibi verification of where the TIE subject was during the relevant times and details of any person(s) who can verify their movements, ie alibi witnesses, who have to be seen and interviewed. Their details are recorded and signed by the alibi witnesses as proof of verification. Alternatively, if the witnesses do not confirm the subject's alibi, then it is a good idea to record this fact as a witness testimony.

8.9 **Search Considerations**

Searches might need to be included as part of the TIE strategy to find and seize certain items. The legal power to do so has to be confirmed, which may be by consent, legal power, or court warrant (if there are sufficient grounds and justification). Searches may involve home addresses, vehicles, vessels, or other linked premises/locations (eg garage, land, gardens, adjacent building, work premises). Powers to seize items also needs to be considered, such as under PACE or common law (see also *Ghani v Jones* (1969) in section 6.8.2). Such a search may include seizing items such as:

- Communication/digital devices—check for (in some cases, seize) all communications data devices,[9] such as mobile phones, computers, tablets, laptops, routers, digital recording, and Wi-Fi devices, gaming devices, and all contact numbers, passwords, websites, and email addresses.
- CCTV or other recording devices (eg dashcams).
- Types of clothing, jewellery, foot-, and headwear.
- Items that are specific to the investigation (eg types of adapted weapons, damaged, or burnt clothing).
- Vehicles, vessels, or bicycles.
- Intelligence information (as well as evidence) and links to others, documents, photographs, anything indicating lifestyle, habits, etc.

In some cases where it is known there has been a biological material shed by, say, a victim (eg blood loss) or a firearm discharged (firearms discharge residue), there is a possibility it may have transferred onto the offender or their possessions. Checks for items that might be receptors of such trace evidence can therefore be included in the search process—items such as clothing, jewellery, rings and watches, shoes, mats, and door handles, and bedding. Advice can be taken from a CSI or scientist on what to look for and how to recover it.

---

[9] Sections 50 and 51 of the Criminal Justice and Police Act 2001 (CJPA) grant power when carrying out a lawful search on premises or persons to seize anything for which there are reasonable grounds to believe may be or contain something which it is authorised to search for and it is not reasonably practicable to conduct the examination at the time of seizure from the premises or person.

Instructions and guidance are always helpful on to how conduct searches and an explanation under what authority and to what extent and level. A more thorough forensic-style search may be required with the presence of at least a CSI or Forensic Scientist, digital forensic specialist, or a PolSA-led team, dependent on the circumstances. If so, these need to be planned in advance with the appropriate resources made available (including an Exhibits Officer (EO)) and legal authority if necessary. Like any other search, these must be executed properly, methodically, and within the law (see also Chapter 6).

8.10 **Refusal Policy**

A 'refusal policy' can be agreed to provide guidance in the event of a refusal by TIE subjects to cooperate with the process, eg be interviewed, provide information or samples, hand over items, permit a search, or even provide their details. In the event that this happens, a specific policy will be required.

Checklist—TIE refusal policy examples

1. Ask and note reason and request signature against notes made.

2. Ascertain whether DNA/fingerprints/photograph already held or by other agency.

3. If previously obtained, ascertain level of verification of identity.

4. Create intelligence database entry (eg Police National Computer/Police National Database (PNC/PND) requesting the obtaining of photo/fingerprints/DNA and cross-referencing with enquiry/incident room interest).

5. Consider possible grounds for search warrant/further action.

6. Urgent referral back to the SIO/management team for decision.

Bibliography

ACPO, *Guidance on Major Incident Room Standardised Administrative Procedures* (MIRSAP, 2005)

ACPO, *Murder Investigation Manual* (NCPE, 2006)

ACPO, *Practice Advice on Core Investigative Doctrine*, 2nd edn (NPIA, 2012) <http://wwwapp.college.police.uk/app-content/investigations>

NPCC Homicide Working Group (HWG), (November 2015) *10*(2), 'TIE Practice: Terminology, Tactics and Training' (pp. 21–24) *NPCC Homicide Working Group Journal of Homicide and Major Incident Investigation www.library. college.police.uk/docs/J_Homicide_MII/J_Homicide_10.2.pdf*

9

Managing Communication

9.1 **Introduction**

Over the course of an investigation, an SIO communicates with many different people, groups, and audiences, in many different situations, in many different ways, and for many different reasons. Not surprisingly, effective communication is an essential prerequisite for the role.

There are countless occasions when an investigative and operational leader needs to communicate effectively with and brief their seniors, colleagues, and enquiry teams. Leading and conducting briefings and meetings is one such example, and although a fairly routine task, it is one that must be taken seriously. These are occasions when there is an opportunity to watch and listen to the person who is in charge and for that person to gain the respect and confidence from those they are answerable to and are leading (including victims, the media, and the general public). These are opportunities to raise and maintain morale, provide direction and focus, clear vision, and understanding of what the priorities are and how the investigation is being led and managed.

Effective communication skills need to be developed, constantly honed, and improved. Time is a precious resource and the way in which meetings, for example, are 'chaired' can make a huge difference towards getting the best out of the session. There will be occasions when not just internal but also external attendees are present and they too must feel encouraged to contribute. Communication style and language may need to be adapted so everyone can understand what is being discussed (avoiding organisational acronyms and jargon).

Utilising modern methods of communication is routine for law enforcement and many new enterprising opportunities are now available. Initiatives can include making full use of social networks and digital platforms when making announcements and appeals about crimes and incidents amongst local, regional, and (inter)national communities to encourage a two-way flow of information. There is a much wider variety of means of communicating available these days than in the past, including, of course, the news media, all of which have simultaneously produced fresh challenges for managing and controlling information flows. Nowadays the public themselves can easily get access to and instantly share and disseminate information and images themselves via the media and social media.

This chapter encourages full usage and exploitation of every available means of effective communication, at the right time and in the right way. It has become an essential part of the SIO's toolkit enabling investigation teams to remain positively and effectively connected, internally and externally, with those whose support and assistance they need.

9.2 **Channels of Investigative Communication**

Most investigations contain some form of proactive or reactive communications strategy, and it is not difficult to expand on a list of options available. For ease of reference, two distinct categories of internal and external are now explained.

9.2.1 **Internal communication**

Examples of internal communication channels:

- (De)briefings and meetings.
- Internal circulations such as news sheets, bulletins, emails, and blogs.
- Conferences and presentations.
- Briefing and current situation reports (CSRs), position and consultation papers.
- Intelligence and case management systems.
- Investigative Policy Logs.
- Reassurance messages.[1]
- Contingency (or response) plans.
- Local, regional, and (inter)national intelligence circulations and bulletins.
- Intelligence reports.

9.2.2 **External communication**

Examples of external communication channels:

- Briefings for and meetings with external partners and agencies.
- Media management.
- Social media, digital forums, and networking platforms.
- Websites, eg those specifically created for a particular investigation or case.
- Multi-agency communication protocols and Memoranda of Understanding (MOUs).
- Poster and leaflet campaigns (eg mobile digital notice and appeal boards).
- Reconstructions, anniversary and publicised/targeted appeals.
- Community engagement via public meetings and local policing teams.

Examples offered under these headings are not exhaustive, and a degree of initiative and creativity can be applied to introduce and exploit as many useful communication channels and opportunities as possible. Making the most of what modern technology can offer is a must.

---

[1] An internal reassurance message might be required if a suspect is at large and has threatened to attack officers and/or is regarded as extremely dangerous (eg member of an organised crime gang (OCG)).

KEY POINT

An external communications policy might need to cater for casual or unplanned encounters with the public or journalists by members of the enquiry team, on or off duty.

9.3 Meetings and Briefings

The term 'briefing' usually refers to occasions when investigation teams and the SIO hold structured sessions during which instructions and directions are provided and information exchanged and discussed. These usually occur on many occasions during the course of a complex investigation, or prior to a pre-planned operation (eg for proactive phases such as conducting searches or carrying out arrests).

Briefings and meetings are a fundamental part of a communication strategy and it would be nigh on impossible to manage and control an investigation without them. They are a means by which information is disseminated and shared, ideas, tactics, and hypotheses exchanged, progress discussed, updates provided, tasks allocated, and feedback gained. Matters of interest and de-velopments are discussed, work is assessed and appraised, problems spotted, issues raised, and directions given. Overall, they provide a vital communications link enabling an SIO to engage with their teams, and they facilitate consultation and participation in the decision-making processes that drive the investigation.

Briefings and meetings are a core component of the investigative process. Apart from discussing information and material currently available, they are a forum for collective discussions to establish or fill information gaps in the 5WH matrix. They are an opportunity to share appropriate intelligence and discuss the 'what we know, what we need to know' principle (see Table 3.3).

They also serve as a subtle means of facilitating supervision, accountability, and standard setting. Updates and progress results can be subtly assessed and scrutinised, not just by the SIO but also by their team managers, supervisors, peers, and colleagues. Questions, opinions, suggestions, and requests for clari-fication of concerns and issues that have arisen can and should be encour-aged. The rule that there is no such thing as a 'stupid' question should be emphasised.

These are also opportunities to build good working relationships, engage in consultation, and engender team spirit, gauge morale, and make staff feel valued and part of the investigation management process. Team members who regularly meet face to face get to know each other better, and any new mem-bers, including invited specialists and experts, feel welcomed and made to feel part of the team via these sessions.

KEY POINTS

1. Investigative briefings are an important means of providing, capturing, and sharing information, and engaging with the team. They provide an opportunity to apply effective control and direction—the art of leadership.
2. Staff should be encouraged to contribute and be reminded that there is no such thing as a 'stupid' question.

Briefings and meetings are also an asset to the action/activity management process. Having an action writer/minute taker accurately record the proceedings and decisions is a way of maintaining effective control of the enquiry and providing an audit trail. This allows the case management element of the enquiry to keep pace dynamically and hasten any necessary back-record inputs or conversion.

Regular sessions should be held, and in the early stages of a complex enquiry sometimes twice-daily depending on the circumstances, then perhaps once a day thereafter. All those involved in the investigation should be invited to attend, with the lead generally being taken by the SIO or their nominated deputy. This might include another team and SIO if there is a going to be a handover process.

A high proportion of (de)briefings and meetings involve cases that result in court proceedings, therefore the content of material discussed potentially falls within the ambit of the Criminal Procedure and Investigations Act 1996 (CPIA). It is the responsibility of each individual involved in a criminal investigation to ensure any information that may be *relevant* to the investigation is recorded and retained. This includes observations relating to the investigation and any notes or accounts made/received. All that is said and recorded is potentially subject to disclosure rules, and care must be taken that any information referred to is factually correct.

A useful tactic prior to a team meeting might be to ensure senior managers have discussed and agreed between themselves any key policies or decisions before they engage with the team at a formal meeting. This doesn't mean they cannot change their minds, but it does create a far better impression than if there are any signs of disunity amongst those who are responsible for leading the investigation (and supporting the principles of 'cabinet responsibility'—ie all agreed and giving consistent messages).

The underlying theme and style of a meeting should always be to remain very positive while allowing key issues to be properly aired and debated.

KEY POINTS

- The contents of team briefings and meetings should be recorded accurately, and any relevant information retained for disclosure purposes.

- Signs of disunity amongst senior managers can be avoided by agreeing key policies and decisions before engaging with the team (and all partaking in a degree of cabinet responsibility).
- If a handover from one team to another is involved, the original team should also be invited to attend the initial briefing(s) for the purposes of continuity.
- Focus needs to remain positive—style and tone of delivery is also very important.

9.3.1 **Planning and conducting (de)briefings and meetings**

Generally, all those involved in the investigation or who can usefully contribute should be invited to (de)briefings, whereas meetings are often very specific and focused upon key agendas, individuals, and roles (dependent on the subject matter). If, however, sensitive issues are to be discussed, attendance may need to be more tightly controlled (sometimes through indoctrination processes). They can also be made subject- or activity-specific, such as proactive phases, when not everyone involved needs to be present. Those required to attend should be given adequate notice of the agenda so they can suggest items for discussion and prepare beforehand, particularly if they have inputs or updates to provide.

It is good practice for the SIO to plan and prepare properly prior to conducting (de)briefings or meetings. They need to be armed with all the salient facts and information and be aware of what important areas they wish to cover with attendees. A pre-prepared structure and agenda is essential.

The 5WH format (see Chapter 3) is a useful template in which to structure the way subjects and areas are covered during the session (eg what happened, when, how, who the victim is, why it happened, where, etc), Wherever practicable, useful material, equipment, and props can be used such as association charts, maps, photographs, diagrams, timelines, statements, CCTV, presentation and remote communication devices (eg video or telephony conferencing facilities for those unable to attend in person, although attendance in person ought to be encouraged).

Content and management of the proceedings must be professional. The agenda must be strictly followed, otherwise there is no point in having one, and time management and control is key to staying on track and not spilling over, risking the meeting becoming tedious. There is nothing worse than being locked into a long and arduous briefing or meeting that becomes a 'talking shop' due to ineffective management and control. These sessions need to remain *inclusive* and *focused* with the lead/chair ensuring things stay on track and that everyone is encouraged to actively participate (provided they have something relevant to contribute).

Example Meeting/Briefing Agenda

1. Introductions/welcome/apologies (chair/lead)

2. Minutes of previous session

3. Actions list/updates

4. Outline/update of case circumstances

5. Intelligence picture

6. Key updates (specific tasks/officers/experts/topics)

7. Current and emerging Lines of Enquiry (LOE)

8. Investigation plan/objectives

9. Key investigative strategies

10. High-priority (HP) Actions

11. Key policies and administration

12. Any other business (AOB)

13. Date, time, and location of next meeting

Note: There are also recognised briefing models in the UK police service such as:

- IIMARCH model (information, intention, method, administration, risk assessment, communication, human rights, and other legal issues).

- SAFCOM (situation, aim, factors, choices, option, monitoring).

- The National Briefing Model.[2]

Whichever format is preferred should always focus on and meet the objectives for the investigation/operation.

Venues used for meetings should be adequately equipped, with sufficient room/seating for all attendees to be comfortable so they can observe, listen, and be heard. The chosen venue needs to be fit for purpose. If large numbers are expected, this may pose additional logistical considerations such as the provision of adequate parking facilities. Some establishments have large lecture theatres or conference rooms/briefing facilities that can be utilised, bearing in mind adequate security may be required; and in some circumstances checked for listening devices.

Facilities may also need to be checked for attendees who have disabilities or particular needs; There may be a requirement to show maps, plans, etc, and for basic equipment such as marker boards, flip charts, analytical charts, or projectors that can display visual images such as CCTV, crime-scene shots,

---

[2] ACPO, *Guidance on the National Briefing Model* (NCPE, 2006) and also cited in <https://www.app.college.uk/app-content/operations/briefing-and-debriefing>.

association charts, or digital images. Diagrams and scenes may need to be illustrated to explain, for example, the position of victims and witnesses etc. Good facilities and equipment improve the professionalism of the session and make the content more interesting and easier to see, hear, and understand. At regular intervals, a check should be made to ensure everyone can follow and is following the proceedings and that an accurate record is being made. Good listening skills and levels of concentration amongst attendees are essential.

One way of ensuring information has been fully received and understood is to summarise key points frequently and repeat them back to confirm understanding and encourage further questions. Active listening to facts and details is a fundamental communication skill. Indicators such as body language, atmosphere, and feedback will help gauge levels of attention, interest, concentration levels, and understanding.

Under certain circumstances, meetings and briefings may be audio- or video recorded to save time and preserve accuracy. Such recordings are also useful for briefing those who are, for whatever reason absent. This option is routinely used in major operations, such as those involving tactical firearms teams or for when large-scale resources are being deployed. It is used to ensure detailed information, instructions, and risk assessments are recorded accurately.

Sufficient time should be allowed as some sessions can last as long as one to three hours, depending on their nature, purpose, and content. Allowances should be made for comfort and refreshment breaks. Attention spans dwindle over time and it is important to maintain attention throughout the entire proceedings.

The SIO's role is to lead and manage the session effectively, ensuring everyone contributes and an equal amount of time is allowed for all attendees to contribute if they wish to do so. The SIO should position themselves in the room so they are in the best possible advantage to hear and see everyone and be heard and seen themselves (ie sometimes in the middle and not always at the far end of the table (as in HM Government Cabinet meetings).

Those who arrive with preconceived ideas of particular theories and views should be encouraged to 'suspend judgement' so they can consider alternative opinions of others and different theories and options (as per the investigative mindset; see Chapter 3). There should be no room for speaking over other people or dominating by certain individuals. Everyone must be encouraged to participate *but* the proceedings must be kept on track. *Time management is crucial* to ensure the briefing/meeting does not become tedious nor dwells on irrelevant issues, and the session remains focused and does not go over the allotted time.

An appropriate use of humour is sometimes a good thing as it helps people relax, lifts team spirits, and encourages good listening. However, this does not extend to sarcasm, pessimism, or derogatory and inappropriate remarks, none of which create a good working environment and which might discourage some people from participating.

Interruptions should be prevented and distractions avoided by choosing an appropriate environment with restricted access. A clear notice posted at the entrance should indicate that an important meeting is in progress. The SIO should avoid being called out to see people or answer urgent calls, nominating someone to screen their calls and see visitors on their behalf unless urgent. Attendees should be encouraged to do likewise, switching off all devices such as mobile phones and radios or putting them to silent or vibrate mode.

An important rule, constantly repeated in this *Handbook* is the **ABC** principle (**A**ssume nothing, **B**elieve nothing, **C**heck/challenge everything; see Chapter 3). It cannot be assumed that information provided at a meeting is always entirely accurate or that a task has been completed thoroughly. For example, if a team states they have tried everything possible to trace a TIE subject without success, it should not be assumed that all possibilities have been exhausted (eg making visits early or late in the day and checking neighbours either side of the last known address for sightings or information). It is a good idea to challenge and to probe, and staff will get used to this being the norm and thus prepare properly.

If sensitive or confidential information is to be discussed, it may be necessary to request those present to sign indoctrination (aka confidentiality) agreements. The vetting and security levels of attendees may have to be determined and applied to preserve the integrity and security of sensitive and otherwise protectively marked material.

Checklist

- Select a suitable venue with adequate space, facilities, and equipment.

- Prepare and circulate an agenda.

- Allow sufficient time and manage it strictly.

- Invite the right people and ensure they attend.

- Good positioning for the SIO within the room is essential to manage the proceedings effectively.

- Avoid distractions—eg all communication devices to silent or vibrate.

- Positively lead, control, and manage the session, speaking confidently, and projecting enthusiasm and energy.

- Diagrams, sketches, plans, and digital images can be useful visual aids.

- Content should be relevant avoiding dominating or irrelevant contributions.

- General reports/updates/feedback can be taken randomly throughout the meeting to retain attention.

- Apply the ABC principle—probe, check, and question contributions and detail.

- Remind staff there is no such thing as a 'stupid' question.

- Appropriate humour can be useful as it stimulates morale and encourages active listening.

- Briefings are an opportunity to give praise/recognition, gauge progress, and focus on task, team, and individual needs (see Chapter 2).

- Check levels of understanding of important information and summarise frequently.

- Nominate someone to raise/allocate actions and record accurate minutes and details of attendees.

- Beware of embellishments or domination from those eager to impress.

- Invite relevant people to make them feel part of the team, eg representatives of the Crown Prosecution Service (CPS), forensic scientists, pathologists, and local officers (who can also play an active part by explaining the policing environment, points of law, or scientific evidence).

- If sensitive information is discussed, consider an inclusion agreement or indoctrination.

- Briefings are a good opportunity to instruct personnel on how to respond to the general public or media if asked about the enquiry.

9.4 **Debriefings**

'Debriefing' is a term that can be used to describe a number of different functions. Individuals or groups may be 'debriefed' about what they might know. It might also refer to a post-incident or response procedure used to extract relevant information, for the benefit of the investigation or just from an organisational learning perspective.

Debriefings should be highly focused and aimed at obtaining as much detailed information as possible, eg from a response phase including call takers and handlers. Debriefings can facilitate the obtaining of a chronological breakdown of events and actions as they occurred, who did what, where, why, how, and outcomes. This is an early opportunity to capture important information and evidence post response. Also sometimes known as 'hot debriefs', a wealth of information can be gleaned from what happened during the Golden Hour(s) period when officers may also be witnesses and/or need to hand over vital exhibits, notes, or information.

The primary objective of a hot debrief is to identify what actions have been taken and by whom, and to capture all possible information that can assist the investigation. For example, details of potential witnesses, useful observations, or comments from bystanders, information and opinions regarding possible suspects, suspicious circumstances that may be linked, any persons or vehicles of interest, and important intelligence.

Checklist—Hot-debriefs

- Debrief those who were part of any first response, including call takers/handlers

- SIO ideally leads and the sessions should not be delegated unless unavoidable.

- Attendees should have completed notes, pocket books, etc before attending to avoid any collusion (ie 'pooled memory') and compromising of integrity.

- Relevant documents and exhibits should be handed over to the investigation team.

- Details of actions taken and a résumé of roles should be provided.

- Notes should be made of the process contemporaneously for immediate reference purposes.

- An action or minute taker can simultaneously raise relevant actions *during* the process.

- Recognise the need to debrief those who have been on a long tour of duty and arrange retention and overtime payments if necessary (money well spent!)

9.5 **Report Writing**

There are many occasions when there is a requirement to draft important and complex documents and reports. These come in all shapes and sizes as memoranda, briefings, and current situation reports (CSR), investigating office reports, or position and consultation papers. There are key features and characteristics that typically make some documents more successful than others. This subject is entirely in keeping with the theme of this chapter, one of communication. Some general points and recommendations include:

1. Reports should not be challenging nor verbose literary works of art in order to satisfy the ego of the author. A sensible and pragmatic approach is best using a simple, straightforward, quick-to-read, and comprehensible style.
2. Most documents benefit from beginning with a clear statement of purpose that succinctly sets the context and quickly engages the reader (eg 'this paper explains', 'this report illustrates', 'this document summarises', etc).
3. Consider who the intended recipient(s) is/are to assist in prioritising the content (ie to separate into 'must', 'should', and 'could have' material).
4. Lengthy and complex reports will benefit from an executive summary followed by an introduction, ending with a conclusion and recommendations.

Annexes, appendices, and supplements can provide additional information for reading when there is more time.

5. Careful thought should go into not just the content but structure and layout with good use of headings, bullets, lists, paragraphs, numbering, diagrams, and tables.

9.6 **Media Management**

When flicking through news bulletins at any given moment there is usually a multitude of headlines, stories, and images. Whether they be positive, negative, or simply sensationalist, there is usually an overarching aim to grab people's attention. Unfortunately, bad or shocking news is what most people are drawn to and what reporters and their editors seek most.

The news cycle is now all day, every day, 24/7, churning out news almost instantaneously from a vast array of sources and platforms. The general public also distribute material themselves via the Internet and social media, although these tend to be snapshots or moments rather than continuous or frequent reporting. Mainstream media (MSM) usually set the news agenda through press and broadcasting corporations, but the public can select its own preferred headlines and sources from a variety of information-sharing networks to suit their own preferences and lifestyles. Any of these news sources can have a positive or negative impact on an investigation, depending on the nature of the content and timing of the release.

Journalists and reporters deliberately search for different or unusual angles on stories in order to get the exclusive. Their aim is to obtain and release a headline and story ahead of their rivals. All too often, this includes apportioning or exposing blame towards someone or something (eg an organisation) for 'wrongdoing', asking, for example, when did they know about it? Why wasn't something done before? What has been done now? Why wasn't it prevented? Who knew about it? How could it have happened? Unfortunately, such negativity sells the story.

Consequently, the MSM fulfil an important role in making public bodies, such as law enforcement agencies more accountable, wherever possible being open and transparent is a core tenet of criminal investigation and policing. So any failure to do so may generate suspicion or scepticism from tenacious journalists. A proactive approach to building a good working relationship with the media is always best as it will instil greater confidence in reporters and the public that the investigation team and their organisation have nothing to hide. The best advantage is that keeping the media informed usually encourages more positive reporting about the investigation.

Nonetheless, SIOs and their organisations (usually via corporate communications departments (CCD)) need to be prepared for challenges from negative or instantaneous journalistic and public reporting. They need to be ready to manage the risk of potential intrusion into and interference with their enquiry, reputational damage or disruption, risk to local communities, staff, partner agencies, vulnerable witnesses and suspects, or disclosure of sensitive tactics and operations.

An early objective should be to spot and anticipate adverse reporting and, where possible, try to manage it by mitigating the risk.[3] Being proactive with the media is the best approach as media outlets can be of enormous benefit when steered towards assisting an investigation by publicising appeals, requests for witnesses or information, and reporting accurate not misleading information. This benefits and protects victims, witnesses, and communities as well as the investigation. Managing the media is an important responsibility, and making them a friend not an enemy will depend on how that relationship is handled.

Reporting examples to try and prevent/manage:

- Inaccurate, misleading information (so-called fake news).
- Speculative *links* to other offences/incidents.
- Derisory comments about a location, individual, group, or community.
- Speculative assertions about *motive* or *cause*.
- Incorrect assumptions or facts about victims, witnesses, or offenders.
- Claims about errors or delays in responding or in the overall investigation
- Preventative actions not being taken and the time lapse/difference between receipt of information and action taken.[4]
- Premature naming of victims, witnesses, or suspects.[5]

9.6.1 Initial media management

Not every encounter with the media occurs at a crime scene or incident, yet this is where things may go wrong. There are potential risks as early responders have initial command and control of the investigation and crime scene and may come into contact with the media.

The media tend to be made aware quite quickly when a serious incident or crime occurs and will head for the scene. In some cases, they may even already be there by the time the police arrive, especially if their offices or staff are located nearby. Determined reporters can present awkward challenges for responding officers and investigators, especially if they comprise TV crews, carry bulky or technical equipment, or block or commandeer valuable space,

---

[3] The risk can be either removed, avoided, reduced, or accepted—RARA; see section 3.7.4.

[4] It is a favoured tactic of the media to report on the gap between when information was received and when action was taken, especially if there have been further crimes/victims during that period. An accurate timeline can prove useful to rebut any such allegations.

[5] In December 2010. Christopher Jefferies was arrested as a suspect for the murder of Joanna Yeates. His arrest led to him being named in national newspapers even though he was never charged (the true offender was later jailed for life named Vincent Tabak). Jefferies successfully sued some press publications over the coverage of his arrest and won substantial damages.

and obstruct access and egress routes. Reporters invariably want to try to get as close as possible to a crime scene (and may use drones or high-powered camera equipment) to get the best shots, and they seek out eye-witnesses and information. They like to record events live and activities direct from the scene, which may include police and emergency responders, casualties, victims, crime scene evidence, and sometimes even fatalities.

In order to manage this effectively, secure cordons are a must to lock down the area and keep the media (and general public) out. This is not just to secure and protect the integrity (ISP principle) of the scene but also to restrict the media from interfering with the investigative process. This sometimes necessitates the use of large portable screens or metal barriers to keep certain items and activities out of the line of sight (eg casualties and victims). Of note is that the media have a right to be present at crime scenes, provided they are in public places *and* outside cordons, and there is no legal power to request them to leave or confiscate equipment.

The SIO may need to discuss or negotiate with the media that they not release distressing or unhelpful images or accounts they might have obtained. Broadcasting codes of practice discourage the use of inappropriate images, although there are no formal powers of censorship.[6] Journalists are expected to take their ethical journalistic responsibilities seriously. The editors code of conduct is governed by the Independent Press Standards Organisation (IPSO). The Contempt of Court Act 1981 forbids the use of any publication in the media which may impede or prejudice a fair trial. This, however, only applies during the time legal proceedings are 'active'. Schedule 1 states that criminal proceedings become 'active' at the time a summons is issued or person is arrested without warrant (where a warrant is issued, proceedings cease to be active once twelve months have elapsed without the suspect's arrest.).

KEY POINT

If there is a problem with the proximity of the media and public to a crime scene, cordons should be implemented and placed far enough away in order to comply with the ISP principle.

9.6.2 Media briefing points

Despite cordons, media crews may still attempt to seek and occupy the best (eg high) vantage points to take shots of scenes and surrounding activities. Media representatives come from a wide variety of agencies and although the majority

---

[6] See <http://www.ipso.co.uk/editors-code-of-practice/>. The editors code is a set of rules that newspapers and magazine industry members have agreed to accept. It sets the standards that newspapers can be held to account by IPSO.

may be well known and trusted, other less well known must be treated with caution. If there is more than one crime scene, this may compound matters, and journalists could be more difficult to control.

One option is to arrange a suitable briefing area in which the media can gather. These are normally sited where journalists can still see some degree of activity, but there is less chance of them interfering with the investigation, it can also serve as a place where enquiries can be fielded and formal briefings held; in other words, a place where they can be better managed and controlled.

9.6.3 Holding statements

Issuing an initial holding statement following a noteworthy incident or crime allows the SIO to 'buy some time' while a more informed response is prepared. It is better not to issue information too soon or before information has been confirmed as to what has happened. To do so might also jeopardise an important phase of the operation, eg arrests. Holding statements can include details such as:

1. Confirmation that (named agency) is investigating.
2. General location of where the incident occurred.
3. Initial indications as to the nature of investigation (eg suspicious death or vulnerable missing person).
4. If a death has occurred, arrangements for a post-mortem.
5. If an incident room has been opened, its location/contact details.
6. Initial appeal for witnesses/information/assistance.

KEY POINTS

1. Announcing or discussing specific details with the media in the initial stages of an investigation should be resisted. Limited knowledge, vague or incorrect facts can later negatively affect the relationship with the media and the public. For this reason staff must be instructed not to discuss the case with the media, with all requests being channelled through to the SIO/MLO.
2. Details of victims should be protected, and if deceased, not released until after formal identification and/or next of kin have been notified.
3. There is an option when seeking cooperation from the media to explain if there is an imminent or ongoing proactive phase (eg arrests) that any release of information (eg suspect names) might jeopardise the operation.

9.6.4 Social media management

In most live incidents attracting public attention, there is likely to be instantaneous social media reporting. This can result in information being publicly available before the investigation has even started or, at the very least, is in its infancy. There are many examples where images and details of events that have resulted in incidents requiring investigation have been both witnessed by members of the public and also recorded/photographed by then and uploaded or live-streamed in real time onto social media.

An early investigative response should cater for establishing what information and reporting of an incident has been/is being circulated on social media platforms. Most media agencies have portals that allow material to be uploaded to them quite quickly for later publication on their news bulletins. Having early engagement with the agency's communications team is essential in order to establish what details or images are available in the public domain. This will help in formulating responses, assessing what information is being disseminated and discussed, and aiding the recovery of any material that may assist the investigation.

9.6.5 **Strategic management**

If an incident or operation is deemed to be one that is 'critical' or particularly high profile, then usually a strategic Gold Group (GG) is formed. A Gold Commander and their appointed Group hold an overarching responsibility for determining and agreeing the communications and media strategy. Whilst the needs of the investigation are important, so too is the need to consider the bigger strategic picture for the organisation or agency, which might include any issues of national or political concern.

An early strategic decision might relate to who the best person is to provide media interviews. In the early stages of an investigation, this is often a senior uniformed officer (eg Chief Officer/Gold Commander) or PIP4 (if applicable) who appears in front of the media ('talking head' style) and provides information and/or reassurances to the public. This is very helpful to the SIO as it allows them time and space to get on with their investigation without being interrupted to provide media interviews. If there is an OCG element to the case, then it may be a deliberate tactic to try and keep the SIO out of the public spotlight as part of a welfare risk management strategy.

A strategic media narrative might cover points such as:

- Inform and include key stakeholders and partners.
- Communicate key strategic messages.
- Aid balanced, consistent, and accurate media reporting by providing accurate and timely information and context.
- Provide public reassurance that an effective investigation has been mounted.
- Minimise impact on fear and causes of crime and reduce community tension.
- Provide consistent messages in consultation with partner agencies.
- Build and maintain public and political trust and confidence in policing.
- Protect the reputation of the organisation/agency.

- Ensure external messages link with and support other strategic aims (eg improve community engagement and public reporting, reducing crime and anti-social behaviour, etc).

9.6.6 **Tactical management**

A carefully considered tactical media plan can be a great asset and may cover:

- Adopting a proactive approach by being open and transparent.
- Keeping victims or their next of kin and close family informed in advance of any anticipated media activity and reporting.
- Targeting carefully selected audiences or communities for operational benefit.
- Withholding or restricting key information if beneficial to the investigation.
- Pre-prepared reactive lines— an 'if asked' position if required.
- Delivering key operational messages.
- Helping the public understand what investigators are doing and why.
- Making appeals for specific information (eg knowledge/sightings).
- Making general appeals for information, victims or witnesses.
- Tracing the whereabouts of missing persons.
- Providing reassurance and advice.
- Providing positive publicity for the investigation and organisation.
- Building and maintaining public and political trust and confidence.
- Tracing named suspects.

The plan can be linked to a list of requirements such as filling information gaps, having considered what external appeals are necessary, how they can be communicated and when, where, why, and by whom. Specific investigative requirements can be catered for, such as requests for sightings of a particular person, vehicle, item, or witnesses in general. Operational objectives can form part of the plan such as assisting with the protecting and safeguarding of victims by ensuring their details are kept out of media reporting. Another example might be attempting to trigger something to happen and having resources in place ready to react (eg prompting an offender to reveal an unknown location, eg to move or recover something).

Media tactical plans have to remain dynamic, flexible, and tailored to individual circumstances as events develop and change as the investigation progresses. The plans must cater for and link up with any overt activities or significant or trigger events or activities, eg arrests, searches, execution of search warrants, significant dates or anniversaries, court appearances, potential criticism of enquiry or any connected incidents, in order to generate public interest and support.

However, at certain times during an investigation, it might also be a sensible and deliberate tactic *not* to share information with the media. This may be because the SIO is not ready to provide any details. If so, then a response may have to be prepared just in case it is needed, often referred to as an '*If asked*' reactive position, which means it has been decided in advance what will be said should the media request information.

Targeted publicity can also be used to appeal to the consciences of those who are thought to be shielding offenders or knowingly withholding information. One such tactic is to mount appeals highlighting chosen locations known to be closely connected to potential suspects or witnesses (eg their home address or places frequented).

Nowadays it is not uncommon for reporters to accompany overt operational law enforcement (LE) officers on operations as part of a report or programme. There have been and are numerous 'fly-on-the-wall' type documentaries depicting overt policing operations and activities. This is another potential means of generating good publicity. Controlled, tactical pre-verdict media briefings can also prove effective, with information and material being released under embargoed agreements in order to achieve maximum impact and publicity at an agreed time, while protecting the integrity of the case and court proceedings. These are good examples of working proactively with the media and keeping them on side.

9.6.7 **Media Liaison Officers**

The role of a Media Liaison Officers (MLO; aka 'press' or 'media/corporate communications officer') is to manage media relations on behalf of the investigation and organisation. An MLO links with a wider, more strategic communication strategy while playing an active tactical coordination and liaison role. This is not only for media and communication activities but also for generating positive publicity and promoting and managing the professional reputation of the organisation.

MLOs operate both 'backstage' in facilitating preparation and liaison, and also 'front of house' by acting as an important buffer and conduit between the media and the investigation. Media relations are, by and large, more effective and professional when managed by experienced and trained MLOs. They usually aim to build and draw upon good relationships with reporters and their agencies so there is greater trust and cooperation when required.

MLOs can assist in formulating media strategies and are usually adept at finding the right form of words and choosing the most appropriate methods and timing for communicating with the media. They can also link in with their counterparts in partner agencies so that consistent and joint messages are released, and they frequently participate in Gold Groups.

Creative ideas are often better discussed and developed jointly with the investigation team, and it is the job of the MLO to spot or create media opportunities or use local contacts to improve the deployment of these. MLOs can monitor the media (including social media and the Internet) and gauge reactions, levels of interest, and accuracy of storylines in order to anticipate misinterpretations or negative reporting. This serves as an early warning mechanism to give ample opportunity to react and formulate a suitable response. Knowing what has been or is going to be published or broadcast can be a useful advantage and can positively influence tactical media communications.

Most MLOs have extensive knowledge, training, and media backgrounds or experience. Once involved in an investigation, they should be included as integral members of the SIO's team and be kept briefed and fully up to date as the enquiry progresses (eg by being invited to important briefings and operational meetings). This enables them to maintain an awareness of (inter)national and local reporting and put their knowledge of reporters, contacts, and news agencies to good use. They will also know when there are quiet and busy news periods or other events to consider in terms of the timings of information releases and appeals.

MLOs can also be tasked with monitoring and collating all media (including online) releases for the enquiry team and for disclosure purposes at court. This may become important if, for any reason, legal teams make challenges about what has been stated publicly in the media, particularly when quoting salient facts provided by the investigation team. The material they gather is also generally what is made available to a victim's family and relatives, should the need arise.

Most importantly, they are able to offer support and tactical advice to the SIO to fend off unwanted media interest and attention or help formulate the right context and content prior to any interviews being provided.

Checklist—Role of the MLO

- Providing support and advice to SIOs, PIP4s, and Gold Groups.

- Assisting in developing strategic and tactical communication plans.

- Preparation and dissemination of information for release.

- Analysis and anticipation of media reporting.

- Liaison with and management of journalists, reporters, and news agencies.

- Monitoring, collating, and logging news media information.

- Distributing news media material and arranging proactive and reactive media releases, briefings, and interviews.

- Mediating over and arranging media facilities/opportunities.

- Managing and controlling the media at crime scenes or other significant locations.

9.6.8 **Consideration of victims and close families**

Media reporting can sometimes negatively impact on victims, including their close family/friends and local community. It is not uncommon for reporters to research victims and their relatives and next of kin, and find and approach them prior to the investigating team having had the opportunity to do so. In mass casualty incidents, this intrusion can become problematic and very distressing for those who are unaware of any involvement of their loved ones.[7]

A communications strategy must take account of liaising, consulting, and keeping victims or their next of kin and family informed (and protected from the media) wherever practicable, and *prior* to any information being publicly released. Victim's relatives need to be consulted on releases of information that may impact on them or their reputation or wellbeing and given support to prevent excessive media intrusion.

Sometimes, sensitive facts may have to be disclosed to the media to assist the investigation. For example, if a murder victim had numerous personal relationships, it may be necessary to make it clear why this information is being released, eg to encourage previous partners to come forward for elimination purposes. However, the next of kin and family may not be comfortable with this tactic and it would need careful planning and consultation with the FLOs. Previous convictions of victims, or their lifestyle and background, are other such examples.

KEY POINT

Releasing victim's details, in homicide cases, must only be done on the authority of an SIO. This is to ensure the victim has been formally identified, and that any spelling or pronunciation of their details are wholly correct. Getting these wrong can cause enormous embarrassment and unnecessary distress to their next of kin and close family.

9.6.9 **Media briefings and interviews**

Media briefings and interviews can take different formats, whether for the press, radio, TV, web forum, etc. They can be useful for showing openness and transparency, making appeals or helping to manage sensitive cases and avoiding inaccurate or sensationalist reporting (and the others mentioned at the beginning of section 9.6). They may take any of the following formats:

---

[7] The independent Kerslake Review of the Manchester Arena bombing that occurred on 22 May 2017. Twenty-two individuals were murdered and more than 700 were injured, The Review criticised the media for hounding victims and their families, putting many under pressure to participate in TV interviews. Some journalists impersonated medical staff to gain access to hospital wards; a tin of biscuits had been sent to one ward with a note offering £2,000 for information about the injured. See: <https://www.kerslakearenareview.co.uk/>.

- **Formal**: prearranged, where the interviewer and interviewee is likely to have prepared questions/answers and researched areas to discuss.
- **Pre-recorded**: provides opportunity to pause and re-record comments that haven't come across well or have been presented poorly (provided the interviewer agrees). Sometimes for convenience they are recorded down a phone line or on other types of digital web formats. Main disadvantage is they can be edited, and key messages such as specific appeals or 'hotline' numbers omitted.
- **Live**: more pressurised with only one opportunity to get right and the interviewer can stray from agreed areas and ask awkward questions that are difficult to avoid because the broadcast is 'live'. Favoured method in 'breaking news'-type headlines on 24/7 bulletins.
- **Press conferences** (aka 'media facilities'): traditional method of facilitating a large number of media representatives to watch and listen to the same message and/or interview simultaneously. Useful for significant announcements that are likely to attract lots of media interest. Prepared statements can be read out by victims or their next of kin/ relatives in person. Q&A session can be included at the end.
- **Embargoed:** This is when information is shared with the media on the basis it will not be published or broadcast until an agreed time. These can be used to brief the media in advance of an event such as an operational phase/activity or court result. These are usually managed by an MLO who requests the media representatives to sign a formal agreement that are binding to the terms of the briefing. It enables the media to have their stories ready for when the appropriate time comes.[8]

The best policy is to clarify beforehand what type of interview it is, what questions and topics are on/off limits, and to establish whether it is live or pre-recorded. Live interviews obviously require far more preparation and rehearsal than pre-records. One consideration is not to be caught off guard by so-called friendly or well-meaning journalists who will undoubtedly have their own agendas.

KEY POINT

There is a need to beware of casual approaches by friendly, seemingly well-meaning journalists who try to groom and coerce interviewees into feeling relaxed and 'off guard' and saying something they (and the SIO) later regret. Absence of note-taking or recording devices might betray true intent of producing an inaccurate or distorted report. 'Off the record' interviews must be avoided at all costs. It is much safer to treat everything as being 'on the record'—after all the reporter may be trustworthy but not their news editor.

---

[8] See <http://www.app.college.police.uk/mediarelations>.

9.6.10 **Preparing for interviews**

Establishing who the interviewer is, what they want out of the interview, what topics they intend to cover, how long the interview will last, and likely questions is good preparation. Like all good investigators, journalists make use of the 5WH interrogative pronouns (see Chapter 3). Equally, the interviewee must be clear about what they want to achieve and be aware of any topics they do *not* want to discuss. The key is to have three key topics ready to mention and have them prepared and mentally rehearsed.

If interviewers ambush or spring on an interviewee particular topics or lines of negative questioning, this is when it is useful to apply the tactic of *turning negatives into positives*. For example, if an interviewer comments on how an enquiry is not making any progress, this can be positively turned around by stating how many lines of enquiry have been pursued, numbers of people interviewed, statements taken, searches, H2H enquiries, or forensic examinations and the like have been conducted.

KEY POINTS

- Have *three key messages* handy for quick reference and last-minute rehearsal.
- Think and prepare carefully about the objectives of the interview and rehearse them.
- Don't answer questions on topics that stray out of agreed parameters or are about matters not within the interviewee's knowledge or responsibility (and better answered by someone else).

9.6.10.1 **Using plain language**

This is a very important rule. Plain and simple 'everyday' language comes across far better than organisational jargon, buzz phrases, or acronyms. Frequently used clichés such as 'intelligence-led policing' (ie what does *un*intelligent-led policing look like?) or 'partnership approach' are not easily understood by ordinary members of the public and they sound artificial.

The best advice is to stick to clear, simple, plain, and understandable everyday terms and language the public understand. For example, 'females' are women, and 'males' are men. Everyday language reaches out to the public far better than official terminology or buzz words. The best way to get people's interest and support is by using language they relate to and can understand easily.

Inappropriate language must also be avoided. The use of discriminatory, prejudicial, or exclusive language indicates a lack of professionalism and encourages the exclusion, devaluing, and stereotyping of groups or individuals. Correct terminology is important, together with a strict adherence to organisational guidance and policies.

> **KEY POINT**
>
> Use plain everyday language when talking to the public via the media and avoid internal jargon, clichés, or inappropriate language that may offend. Don't overly think or complicate what you want to say. Keep the message as simple as possible.

9.6.11 **Withholding information**

It is usually advisable to remain totally open and honest when delivering messages and information via the media. However, sometimes it is operationally advantageous and/or entirely necessary and justifiable to withhold certain unique features or information. An example of this is when deliberately not mentioning unusual features of a modus operandi (MO) regarding a specific manner in which an offence was committed, eg how many bullets were fired, blows struck, what part of the body was hit, how a scene was entered or left, what items were taken/left, what type of weapon was used, words uttered to a victim, etc. Another example might be in situations when there is a 'crime in action' such as a threat to life (TTL) kidnap or extortion, and the safety of victims might be jeopardised by the case being reported in the media (as it may inform offenders the matter has been reported to the police).

Tactical decisions on what to say and not say are made early and recorded in a policy decision. To safeguard the integrity of a withholding tactic, the SIO may also have to withhold certain information from the enquiry team to prove it could not have been leaked, either wittingly or unwittingly. The security and integrity of any withheld material may have to be proved to the satisfaction of a court at subsequent proceedings, particularly if an offender or a key witness volunteers information that has been deliberately withheld (therefore increasing its probative value). It may have to be proved beyond all reasonable doubt there was zero possibility that withheld information could have been leaked and therefore was only known by the true offender or witness.[9]

This tactic is aimed at proving the veracity of an offender's guilty knowledge, involvement, or confession. It also helps eliminate those who may wish, for whatever reason, to admit responsibility falsely for or involvement in the offence under investigation and thereby mislead the enquiry. It can also help eliminate other information from intelligence or evidential sources that can be proved to be inaccurate (eg from an informant).

There may be instances where releasing information would breach a duty of confidentiality or contravene statutory requirements, court orders, or national guidance (eg naming rape victims). These need to be carefully considered in line with relevant legislation and guidance. In difficult, sensitive, or exceptional

---

[9] There are nationally agreed embargo guidelines on withholding information from the media during crimes in action.

cases the matter should be referred to a senior grade (eg at Chief Officer level) who would then consider a strategic decision. A 'Gold Group' may need to be consulted (if applicable) to discuss and agree a media and community impact communication strategy. Such is the importance in serious cases, particularly critical incidents, of getting the right message across (or withholding it) in the right manner at the right time (Table 9.1).

Table 9.1 Disclosing v withholding

For (disclosing)	Against
Identifying/locating offenders	Allows for concealment/destruction of evidence
Identifying victim(s)	Renders victims/witnesses more vulnerable
Gaining publicity/witness appeals	Compromises operational tactics
Feed media requirement for information and updates	Negatively affects relationship with the victim/family/ community
Warn public of any threat/dangers	Causes unnecessary fear and distress
Maintain trust/provides reassurance	Dilutes guilty knowledge from admissions
Prompt offender reaction	Gives offender(s) more kudos
Provide crime prevention advice	May create 'copycat' offences
Prevent media speculation	May create more media interest/intrusion
Appeal to conscience	Alerts offender(s) to investigative activity
Correct any misinformation	May affect fairness of judicial process
Trigger activities or comments	Plan/resources needed to respond/capture material

---

KEY POINT

It is more transparent to explain why details are being withheld. For example, saying it might prevent the tracing and arresting of an offender and stating: "*It would impede our investigation so unfortunately we cannot reveal any information at this stage*". This is much better than saying 'no comment' or refusing to answer, which will appear dishonest or untrustworthy.

There are recommendations to be adhered to for withholding the details of arrests, charges, and judicial outcomes. The details of those arrested or suspected of crimes (except in exceptional circumstances, ie when in the public interest, such as the arrest of a prominent public official; or a TTL situation when the suspect has failed to answer bail) should not be named.[10] This is to respect their

---

[10] See findings and recommendations of the Leveson inquiry: <http://www.gov.uk/Leveson Inquiry-Report> into the culture, practices and ethics of the press (published 29 November 2012).

rights to privacy under Human Rights principles (everyone is innocent until proven guilty). Names should be withheld, but generally their gender, age, and vague home locations are released (provided it does not confirm their identity). If a name is released then the CPS should be consulted beforehand because of the impact this might have on their rights to privacy and reputation should they not be charged.

Once a person is charged however, their names can be released in the public domain unless reporting restrictions apply (eg if they are a child or young person). If charges are subsequently withdrawn, this information must also be published as soon as possible. No details about the investigation are released as this would be *sub judice*, which is a good way of answering any queries about enquiries that are awaiting trial. To publish such details would render the individual or organisation in contempt of court.

The names of any victims or witnesses are never released unless the victim consents to being identified of their own volition. The same applies to witnesses, although it would be quite unusual for a witness to want to have their details released, and if this is what they want then it should be viewed with some degree of scepticism as to motive (eg payment by a media organisation).

It is a useful tactic to have preprepared responses to media questions about the various stages of an investigation. These are often referred to as 'if asked' media lines to take (Table 9.2).

Details of court proceedings in progress are often reported in the media although these must be agreed by the prosecutor beforehand. This is done on the basis that it enables greater openness in the judicial process, but needs to be managed under strict protocols agreed with the CPS. Once a person is convicted, most of the information is released in the public domain anyway and at this stage the media may wish to take advantage of releasing information such as the offender's custody photograph, interviews with the SIO, etc, previously provided under an embargoed agreement (see section 9.6.9). This

Table 9.2 Examples of 'if asked' media lines

'If asked' lines on arrest of a suspect	'It can be confirmed officers arrested a male at (location) on (date) on suspicion of (offence). As the investigation is ongoing, no further information can be provided at this stage.'
'If asked' lines on charge	'(Name) aged x years of (general address) has been charged with xx offences and will appear at xx court on xx.'
'If asked' lines on conviction	'(Name) aged x years of (general address) has today been convicted of xx offences and sentenced to xx.' (Comments may then be added if appropriate, by the SIO about the case and offender.)

is advantageous because it will increase public confidence in the criminal justice system.[11]

KEY POINT

Care must be taken when releasing details of vulnerable persons into the public domain. This may increase the risk of harm to them, particularly if they are facing charges that relate to offences against children (see also section 12.7.1)

9.6.12 **Timing of information release**

Releasing information can be timed to produce maximum benefit if, for example, it is linked in to trigger (eg covert surveillance) proactive activities. Any release of investigative material, however, such as images or CCTV, must not compromise witness interviews by contaminating or influencing recollections. It may be worthwhile seeking the advice of a Crown Prosecutor if there is any doubt about the legal implications on identification procedures, eg releasing images or details of possible suspects (although sometimes parts of images can be edited/obscured/pixelated).

For maximum publicity, appeals can be planned to coincide with significant events, such as the arrest of offenders, searches, court appearances, or anniversaries of incidents. Attaching appeals to linked or trigger events can also help generate more media and public interest. The wider news agenda can be anticipated by scanning to see what other newsworthy events or stories are taking place that may compete for publicity. These could be major sporting or noteworthy events, and anything of a national or local political nature that could occupy the headlines. Publication deadlines may be something else to consider, particularly if it is important to include a popular local media outlet that is not published or circulated daily.

As stated earlier, information must not be released about a victim whose next of kin and family have yet to be notified. This is where timing becomes vitally important.

KEY POINTS

- Timing of information, messages, and appeals can link into significant lines of enquiry or proactive tactics.
- Chronological events and developments enhance media attention, eg the arrest of suspects or the finding of crucial CCTV footage.
- Check what other events may be competing for media attention.

---

[11] See also <http://www.app.college.police.uk/mediarelations>.

9.6.13 **Generating media interest**

There are many occasions when it is of great benefit to have the media report on specific aspects of a case. This might be met with reluctance as there are criteria by which news producers and gatekeepers (editors and sub-editors) select events to report. Matters that are judged 'newsworthy' include specific and interesting characteristics of an offence or incident. Some stories or incidents become major headlines immediately, while others are not considered sufficiently newsworthy at all. Both these extremes have implications for a communication strategy either in responding to the media or engaging with them proactively in order to gain their interest in reporting the required messages.

Cases involving serious criminality, such as homicide or suspicious missing persons, usually attract a substantial amount of media interest per se, especially in the first few days. Thereafter, interest tends to diminish, so the challenge in most (not all cases) is to generate and maintain positive media interest and publicity.

The media prefer unusual features or anything that adds value or intrigue to a story. For example: CCTV footage; pictures of offenders; artists' impressions; details of missing articles (eg clothing); reconstructions; bad injuries; personal appeals from a victim's family or close friends; dramatic emergency calls; pictures of raids; or specialist units in action, such as outdoor searches. Such 'extras' make stories more appealing when they are more dramatic and intriguing. Care must be taken, however, not to breach any copyright protection on images, photographs, maps etc, although the media are very adept at getting hold of their own material.

Publicity campaigns can be linked to filling information gaps (5WH method, see Chapter 3), and used to make appeals for information. Some degree of initiative and creativity can be applied in order to gain interest and target the right people (see following).

Checklist—Publicity-gaining examples

- Use of electronic and mobile 'advertising' placards or screens.
- Full-size upright models or 'cut-outs' of homicide victims placed in public places in order to attract attention (eg victim holding or stating an appeal).
- Celebrities and personalities supporting appeals.
- Targeting specific social media outlets and websites popular with certain audiences.
- Targeting specific communities (in the United Kingdom or overseas) eg medical professionals to help identify unusual physical features or deformities, dentists, tattoo artists, clothing suppliers, etc.

- Simple leaflet drops in targeted geographical locations.

- Making regular podcasts about the investigation.

Sometimes, in order to gain publicity, media messages need to be hard-hitting. Here are some examples that have proved useful in major investigations:

- 'We know people saw what happened ... do you want those responsible to get away with it?'

- 'What if he was your brother, boyfriend, or best friend?'

- 'We know people are scared, we can help and work together on this. Don't let the criminals get away with it.'

- 'Please help the police find my killers' (underneath picture of victim).

- 'We believe someone might be shielding the offender(s) through misguided loyalty, and this person could find themselves being prosecuted for a serious criminal offence.'

- 'Let us decide if the information you have is significant or not.'

9.6.14 Staging reconstructions

Crime reconstructions can reignite dwindling public interest and tease out important memories and information. They can provide a dramatic and high-impact method of getting a message across, raising the profile of the investigation, and aiding recollections. They can also be used in internal communication messages, such as during the provision of electronic briefings and presentations about a case.

Programmes such as BBC's *Crimewatch* and similar localised crime-appeal programmes are invaluable for raising the profile of an investigation, revitalising memories, and making appeals. They can reach out to large audiences and are very professional in their approach by using every trick at their disposal to publicise the message investigators want to convey. They adopt a more collaborative approach than merely a reactive news story.

These types of appeals, however, can produce large amounts of information, all of which must be assessed and potentially investigated. This is why large appeals and reconstructions need to be tightly focused.

Well-intentioned but misleading responses from the public can sometimes soak up valuable time and resources. For example, where appeals are for sightings or the whereabouts of suspects or vehicles etc, the outcome might be possible sightings all over the country or overseas, some of which may prove difficult to ignore. Any risk of this occurring needs to be considered and risk managed accordingly.

9.6.15 **Locating suspects**

Where a suspect has been positively identified but their whereabouts are unknown, as a last resort appeals can be made to assist in either locating or requesting them to surrender voluntarily. If this tactic is to be used, then consideration should be afforded to:

1. Protecting integrity of identification evidence (seeking legal advice if necessary).
2. Breaching human rights (eg right to a fair trial).
3. Dangerous individuals gaining added notoriety and publicity.
4. Rendering certain individuals more dangerous through desperation in the knowledge they are being hunted.

This type of tactic is not to be engaged lightly and usually requires authorisation at the highest level (ie Chief Officer). It should be the subject of a decision by a Gold Commander with close monitoring afterwards by a consequence management cell, ie as a critical incident. Criminals can become desperate as the net closes in and in some cases employing this tactic can lead to very grave consequences.[12]

Final Checklist—Media dos and don'ts

The dos

- Work proactively with the media rather than just being reactive.

- Build up good relationships with the media continually.

- Find out what news is already being distributed in the public domain.

- Steer reporters towards reporting the SIO's key messages.

- Prepare and rehearse *three key messages* (keep handy in an *aide memoire*).

- Research any current and 'hot' crime topics that may be quoted by the interviewer.

- Consider the possibility that the interviewer/news agency may be running their own parallel investigation.

- Be clear about the aims and objectives of any media interview.

- Use simple and plain language, *not* jargon or acronyms.

- Don't overly complicate the message. Keep it simple.

---

[12] In 2012, Dale Cregan, a convicted drug dealer and murderer, was sentenced to a whole-life order for four counts of murder including two GMP officers. He had been widely and publicly circulated as wanted for killing two men and attempting to kill three others. In one incident he had thrown a hand grenade at one of his victims. Whilst on the run from a huge manhunt, he lured two police officers, PCs Nicola Hughes and Fiona Bone, to an address in Hattersley, Manchester via a hoax call and tragically shot them both dead.

- Stay relaxed, confident, and *positive, positive, positive* (3 × Ps rule).

- Transform nervousness, anxiety, or apprehension into enthusiasm and energy.

- Check body language—when on camera you are always communicating.

- Stay confident, not nervous—treat interviewer as one individual and ignore all others.

- Use adrenalin and pressure as a stimulant.

- Check appearance, hair, dress, tie, etc (if on camera).

- Check what material/what is happening i in the background.

- Ignore noise and/or any activity taking place somewhere else.

- Look at the interviewer, not the camera (unless told otherwise).

- Be clear about what topics can/cannot be discussed (eg pending court case).

- Steer clear of giving personal views—reinforce official policy.

- Ensure victim/family is/are informed before any releases are made.

- Ensure messages are clear and strong, stating exactly what is needed from the public (ie do not just appeal for 'general information'—be specific).

- Avoid comments that imply guilt or innocence—never discuss the evidence.

- Use cognitive prompts wherever possible (eg such as a major sporting event).

- Emphasise the importance of *all* information, no matter how trivial (highlight the 'It's probably nothing' syndrome (when people believe their information is insignificant).

- Provide contact details of the investigation team (and have them to hand).

- Ensure there is an appropriate (eg answering machine) recorded message and policy for regularly checking the incident room contact system/website.

- Inform the media as soon as a suspect is charged (this helps prevent them inadvertently breaching the Contempt of Court Act and jeopardising the case).

- Consider giving positive prevention advice and offering public reassurance.

- Consult with other agencies involved before making a media release.

- Publicise good work, particularly heroics or important events such as court results.

- Use interesting facets of a case to gain extra publicity and interest.

- Turn any negatives into positives.

- Make full advantage of an MLO.

The don'ts

- Allow inexperienced staff to provide unauthorised information or interviews.

- Fidget, sway, or stare at feet.

Read direct from a document—it looks insincere and unprofessional.

- Stare directly at the camera (unless doing a 'down-the-lens' interview).

- Make 'off the record' comments—any camera/microphone could still be switched on.

- Answer questions on topics someone else is better suited for.

- Disclose any sensitive operational information or tactics.

- Respond with just 'yes', 'no', or 'no comment'—it sounds suspicious (useful alternatives: 'It is too early to say', or 'That will be looked into as part of the ongoing investigation', or 'At this stage we just don't know until we get a fuller picture.')

- Let the interviewer get you to agree with what they are saying.

- Lower your voice or appear disinterested—always look and sound confident.

- Criticise the criminal justice system or other agencies.

- Disclose information that could lead to discovery of victim's identity, age, or location.

Bibliography

ACPO, *Guidance on the National Briefing Model* (NCPE, 2006)
ACPO, *Murder Investigation Manual* (NCPE, 2006)
<http://www.app.college.police.uk/briefing-and-debriefing>;
<http://www.app.college.police.uk/media relations>
Cutlip, SM and Center, AH, *Effective Public Relations: Pathways to Public Favour* (University of Wisconsin, 1952)

10

Investigative Strategies

10.1 **Introduction**

Core investigative strategies are a toolbox of methods and tactics for consideration when producing an investigation plan. Each strategy contributes to the plan to help achieve an overarching objective. The purpose of an investigative strategy is to:

- define aims and objectives of how it will contribute to the investigation.
- identify and outline the most beneficial and appropriate tactics, lines of enquiry, and supporting actions and activities likely to establish significant facts, reveal or preserve evidential material, and lead to the successful resolution of the investigation (taking into account resources, priorities, time scales, cost, achievability, justification, necessity, and proportionality).

Each strategy allows the grouping of certain activities under themes and headings. Some have merited their own chapters in this book, eg searches, managing victims, witnesses, suspects, and pursuing TIE actions, while others are covered in this chapter.

Checklist—Investigative Strategies

- Victim management[1]

- Suspect management[2]

- Witness management[3]

- TIE enquiries[4]

- House-to-House (H2H) enquiries

- Managing crime scenes and searches[5]

- Passive data generators (eg CCTV and automatic number plate recognition (ANPR))

- Intelligence management

- Communication management[6]

- Communications data and social media

- Forensics (traditional and digital)[7]

---

[1] See Chapter 11.
[2] See Chapter 12.
[3] See Chapter 13.
[4] See Chapter 8.
[5] See Chapter 6.
[6] See Chapter 9.
[7] Forensic strategies are not covered in the *Handbook* due to the specialist, extensive range, and complex nature of the subject.

- Financial investigation

- Proactive overt and covert investigation

- Specialist support and expert advisers

Overlaps can occur between various strategies because some, if not most, cut across and complement one another. For example, a strategy to conduct H2H enquiries may also be referred to in a witness trawl strategy, or digital communications data requirements may be included as part of a search strategy. There may also be similarities in policies, for example, geographical parameters for H2H enquiries may share similar boundaries with those for CCTV trawls. Processes, considerations, and even roles may also bear close correlation to each other (eg H2H and CCTV Coordinators).

Investigative strategies should be discussed regularly by the investigation team. Some of the tactical options may require expert advice and support such as Interview Advisers, Media Liaison Officers, Police Search Advisers (PolSAs), forensic and digital evidence recovery experts, or Crime Scene Investigators/ Managers (CSI/CSMs), or any of the other specialist advisers mentioned at the end of this chapter. Clear aims and objectives are agreed and recorded for each strategy and relayed to those responsible for delivering them.

Ownership can be assigned and those with supervisory responsibility are usually best placed to take on large or substantial projects, up to and including a Deputy SIO. Those nominated should be involved in setting the objectives and helping to draw up associated policies, together with agreed terms of reference, aims and objectives, methods, parameters, and staffing and resource levels.

Investigative strategies remain under dynamic monitoring and review to ensure they remain relevant, appropriate, and on course. Investigations are usually fast-moving and frequently require subtle changes in direction and priorities, and investigative strategies need to be adaptable to reflect any such changes.

KEY POINT

Investigative strategies may be delegated to designated staff to project manage who may require various subject-matter experts and specialists to support them. The SIO, however, still retains 'ownership' and responsibility and therefore the right to make any amendments.

10.2 **Strategy Implementation**

Each strategy contains key tactics, actions, and activities. A list of individual key 'actions' can be raised to provide specific detail and instructions aimed at achieving the overarching aims and objectives.

Example 1

Nature of tactical action

'Arrange H2H enquiries and report on precise areas to be covered as authorised by the SIO with a plan outlining the parameters' (H2H strategy and suspect/ witness management).

Example 2

Nature of tactical action

'Arrange fingertip search of scene (1) and obtain statements from officers involved' (search strategy).

Example 3

Nature of tactical action

'Obtain itemised billing for mobile (number) believed used by victim's girlfriend N6 Alice Keegan for period (from x to y) covering all incoming and outgoing calls (communications data, TIE, or suspect strategy).

One option is to record all details of all or some strategies in a 'stand-alone' record or document with relevant action numbers listed alongside each activity. Some agencies have templates available specifically for this purpose. Any such document must be tightly version-controlled, recorded, or registered onto a case management system (CSM) and cross-referenced in the SIO's policy log.

10.3 **House-to-House (H2H) Enquiries**

Conducting H2H enquiries can be used to:

- Identify suspects, witnesses, and victims.
- Gather localised information and intelligence.
- Obtain investigation-specific material and information.
- Support a communication strategy (eg appeal for witnesses, provide public reassurance, or give crime prevention advice).
- Identify passive or digital communications data sources (eg CCTV or Wi-Fi).
- Facilitate a mass screening exercise (eg DNA or fingerprints).

A combination of these is not unusual. There may be case-specific requirements with a list of questions or topics to cover when speaking with house/ premises occupants and visitors.

H2H is a useful tactic for use in most major and serious crime investigations. To be effective, it must be conducted methodically, thoroughly, and without undue delay. For example, in a high proportion of personal crime cases, a victim is known to the offender and resides within close proximity of the place where the offence occurred, and it is entirely feasible a H2H enquiry may quickly uncover their identity.

CASE STUDY—IMPORTANCE OF H2H ENQUIRIES

Amanda (Milly) Dowler was a thirteen-year-old schoolgirl when she was abducted in broad daylight on her way home from school and murdered in Walton-on-Thames, Surrey, on 21 March 2002. Her body lay undiscovered in a rural area until 18 September 2002, and it wasn't until 23 June 2011 that a convicted serial killer named Levi Bellfield was found guilty of her murder. A key piece of evidence was that at the time of the murder, Bellfield resided at an address in Collingwood Place, very close to the point where the abduction occurred. Bellfield lived just fifty yards from where Milly Dowler was last seen but, as the media put it, 'escaped the net when police knocked ten times at his rented flat without getting an answer but made no enquiries of the landlord as to who lived there'.[8]

10.3.1 Location parameters

An SIO needs to be familiar with a crime scene and its geographical location in order to set realistic and relevant parameters for H2H enquiries. It is good practice to visit, walk around, view, and assess the surroundings at key locations. If an H2H Manager is appointed, they should accompany the SIO/DSIO. Each road, street, house, flat, business, or other building and premises of interest needs to be identified and duly noted. Areas where people are known to 'sleep rough', or congregate should also be considered.

A detailed street/area map is useful for marking out the boundaries of H2H parameters, which can later be registered as an exhibit. This is better than attempting to provide verbal or written descriptions of the chosen areas and can be referenced in a policy log entry explaining the reasons why, how, and where the tactic is to be used. Natural boundaries can help determine parameters, such as roads, streets, rivers, walls, pathways, railway lines, natural borders, and fences.

Large areas can be subdivided into zones or phases in order of priority (phase 1, 2, 3, etc). This helps teams understand what the most important areas are to meet the SIO's objectives and allocate their time and resources accordingly.

To help determine parameters, good use should be made of all available intelligence and information. Local officers, PCSOs, special constables, security staff etc and members of the community (ie community intelligence) who may have specific local knowledge can be asked to contribute and add qualitative detail. Looking at a map or location does not always provide sufficient local information to work with; eg knowledge of local short cuts, meeting places, or

---

[8] C Davies, 'Milly Dowler: Did police mistakes let Levi Bellfield kill again?' *Guardian*, 24 June 2011.

locations where vehicles and stolen cars are abandoned. Other resources such as Geographical Profilers[9] can be enlisted to help determine the best parameters and priorities.

KEY POINTS

1. Some addresses included in H2H parameters may have other relevance, eg if associated with significant witnesses, victim's family members, or TIEs. These could be subject to overlapping strategies and actions. It is unprofessional for different officers to keep visiting the same addresses for different reasons at similar times. Good management and coordination can prevent this occurring.

2. Visiting and inspecting a locus is the best method of ensuring no areas or premises are missed, eg Flat 2b hidden out of sight at the rear of or directly above house number 2 (or small take-away or shop); or premises in an adjoining street that have rear windows or CCTV overlooking the crime scene.

10.3.2 **Fast-track H2H enquiries**

A valuable tactic is to conduct early and/or initial H2H enquiries (often called 'flash' or 'hasty') during the 'Golden Hour(s)'. Teams can be quickly directed to premises within the *line of sight* or *earshot* of crime scenes. Even if specific parameters have not been determined, general investigative material can be still obtained sooner rather than later to generate early lines of enquiry. Accurate records should be kept of all premises visited or persons spoken to, including negative responses offered. This is best supported by full H2H when resources allow.

A useful acronym for determining fast-track H2H to assist in considering particular locations is LEASH:

L—Lain in wait (offender)

E—Egress routes

A—Access routes

S—Line of sight

H—Line of hearing

An outline of what questions to ask or what information is required will need to be decided. Until more information is known, in the initial stages, general requests can be produced for information at each address visited and to each

---

[9] Geographical Profilers are available via National Crime Agency Major Crime Investigative Support (NCA MCIS).

interviewee, such as: what did they see? What do they know? What have they heard? Good use of open questions is the best policy to avoid single and closed answers such as 'yes' or 'no'.

KEY POINT

Information obtained during H2H enquiries needs accurately recording and, if possible, should be agreed and signed by the person interviewed and counter-signed by the recording officer. A first account may become important if a subsequent witness statement is required, particularly if the witness disengages with the enquiry or becomes hostile or uncooperative.

10.3.3 Phased H2H enquiries

Phase 1 usually includes visiting all dwellings and premises in the immediate vicinity (eg of Scene 1) as determined by set parameters. These parameters can remain under review and be extended or reduced as the enquiry develops. A policy entry should be made outlining the reasons and specific details of each phase, as the following example shows.

Phase (I) H2H

This is a densely populated residential area in (location) and all these addresses have been deemed as being within the line of sight or earshot of scene (1). It is anticipated there could be a useful level of cooperation from people in this area given the nature of the investigation. The initial addresses for phase (I) are listed below.

1–11 and 2–12 Glendon Court

70–116 and 71–115 Avondale Gardens

2–10a and 10b Castlebrook Terrace

10.3.4 Policy and documentation

A H2H strategy should contain specific instructions and policy that cover any or all the following:

- Identifying, determining, and stipulating geographic parameters.
- Identifying and nominating most appropriate (ideally trained) resources.
- Determining whether a dedicated coordinator role is utilised.
- Providing specific questions and topics to be covered.
- Documentation to be used and completed (eg questionnaires, Personal Descriptive Forms (PDFs), and occupancy details).

- Details of any information *not* to be given out (eg specific details about the incident under investigation or victim).
- Timing of enquiries and number of visits required (eg 'initially two visits will be made, one in the daytime and one in the evening').
- What and how information should be relayed back to the incident room (eg 'all significant information will be passed directly to the Receiver in the form of a message form; any HP information must be relayed to the Receiver and/ or SIO without any delay').
- When formal witness statements should be taken (eg 'statements should be taken in line with the SIO's designated statement policy').
- A 'no reply' and/or 'not at home' policy (eg if no response on the second or third visit, do a leaflet drop, research enquiries by intelligence cell, enquiries with neighbours or occupants of nearby other premises, raise to a T/I action, or simply vary times for return visits—but must *always* include notifying the SIO).
- Consideration of interview advisers to help formulate questionnaires.
- Geographical profiling/analyst to assist with determining location parameters.
- Policy to manage any language or cultural issues.
- Consideration of capturing 'nosey neighbour-' type information to confirm occupant numbers and details.

KEY POINTS

- In multi-occupancy, sublet premises, or transient communities' areas, a policy may be needed for obtaining fingerprints and photographs of all occupants to help confirm their identities and presence (eg where there are multinationals in cramped living accommodation. Note: consider also offences under Modern Slavery Act 2015).
- H2H enquiry questionnaires should be intelligence-led to accommodate specific information requirements, eg where loud voices or screams are believed to have been heard at a particular time and location.

In most UK police forces there are standard forms for recording H2H information, which are usually organised into 'files' for ease of reference, eg a separate file for each street. Having visited all the addresses on the street, the enquiry team endorses the file with the total number of questionnaires produced and the number of those outstanding. The files should contain occupant detail forms and the all-important questionnaires.[10]

---

[10] Sample documents can be found in ACPO, *Practice Advice on House to House Enquiries* (Centrex, 2006).

10.3.4.1 H2H questionnaires

Case-specific questions can be compiled and used as part of a H2H enquiry team package. Open questions are much better than closed ones that require only one-word (yes/no) answers. Questionnaires should be tailored to the enquiry circumstances and regularly reviewed to ensure they are seeking the right information in line with operational needs and that they reflect tactical changes and developments in the investigation.

H2H sample questions

1. Who resides, works at, or frequents these or other specific properties or premises?
2. Where were you between (time/date) and (time/date)?
3. What did you see or hear in the area of (address/location) during these times?
4. What vehicles or people did you see in the vicinity of (location) between (dates and times)?
5. What do you know about an incident that took place at (location) on (time/date)?
6. What do you know about anyone connected to (x) address/premises/location?
7. What knowledge have you of CCTV or other recording devices fitted or used at either this address or nearby (including personal recordings eg on phone camera)?
8. What vehicles do you own, use, or have access to (ie for elimination)?
9. What other information might you have that could assist the enquiry?

Dos and Don'ts

- Questions need wording carefully to avoid using closed formats, eg Q. 'Do you own a white van?' A. 'No' (yet occupant might regularly use someone else's van).
- If using terms such as 'suspicious' (eg 'Did you see anything suspicious?'), the term needs defining as to what it means.
- Sentences should not contain more than one question and topic.
- Point out that it is better to let the investigation team decide if any information they have is useful.

10.3.5 Identifying suspects

Establishing the identity of a suspect or (if known) where they are believed to live, work, or frequent can be a specific use of H2H enquiries. This can link in with any intelligence-led mass screening for DNA or fingerprints. It must be noted, however, that it is not uncommon for close associates or family members to conceal an offender's details or their presence on their premises, or provide misinformation in order to protect them. Therefore, good application of the **ABC** principle is essential.

Usually both suspect and witness enquiries are conducted simultaneously as a means of subterfuge, to avoid alerting potential suspects who may be in the area.

H2H enquiries can be useful at or nearby suspect addresses, eg during arrests or house searches for gaining useful information about their movements, vehicles, habits, associates, that might be of significance to the investigation. Offenders tend to be more careless away from areas where they have committed crimes, and they may make mistakes that are spotted, and the evidence obtained via H2H enquiries.

KEY POINTS

- Offenders tend to be less careful away from crime scenes. This is where they may be seen changing or discarding clothing, dropping or concealing weapons, hiding stolen property or their means of transport, or meeting up with accomplices before and after the offence, etc. These locations can be good places to mount H2H enquiries.
- Always apply the ABC principle—occupants may be protecting offenders.

10.3.6 Identifying witnesses and victims

H2H can be used to try and identify:

- Anyone who may have witnessed something of relevance.
- Victims/further victims (eg in series offences or reluctance/fear to report).
- connected events, such as an encounter, attack, disposal site, getaway vehicle stolen or abandoned.
- People in or around the vicinity of a crime scene at a relevant time.
- Sightings of a victim or offender before or after a significant event, eg along the likely entry and exit routes of the offender(s).
- Sightings of or information regarding relevant items, eg clothing, weapons, or anything else of significance that may have been seen or discarded.
- persons seen elsewhere (eg on CCTV).

10.3.7 Community reassurance

H2H visits can be used as part of an external communications strategy to deliver important messages to the public. Visits can incorporate the distribution of crime prevention or personal safety advice. Any reassurance messages should remain consistent with those contained in an associated media strategy.

Enquiries can also be used to measure and gauge public reaction, and local policing/neighbourhood teams consulted to assist in completing the task.

10.3.8 'Negative responses'

Inevitably, negative responses will be encountered during H2H enquiries and a consistent policy is needed to manage them. There are various options available, ranging from repeat visits (if so, how many, at what times, and by whom?) to contacting occupants by other means, such as phone calls, emails, or leaflet drops/calling cards. While there are resource and time implications for making revisits, this is always the best option as some residents may need persuading or reassurance to respond or engage.

The enquiry team and SIO need to reassure themselves *why* some enquiries are proving challenging and whether there is an underlying and important reason for non-engagement/cooperation or response or unavailability (eg if individuals are protecting the offender). Some further, more invasive tactics may be required if suspicion heightens.

10.3.9 H2H coordinators

In larger investigations, a H2H coordinator is an optional extra member of staff for managing and supervising all H2H enquiries. They can be co-located at a temporary mobile incident vehicle or office located at or near a chosen location/crime scene so they are close to their teams and enquiry locations. Their role is to ensure enquiries are being managed properly, and useful information is accurately recorded and submitted to the incident room, and no further action is taken (eg follow-up enquiries) without prior approval, and that any significant information is fed back without delay.

The coordinator ensures staff engaged on H2H enquiries are kept fully updated and briefed, and that they themselves remain updated by regularly attending enquiry team briefings to cascade information back to their teams. There must be a two-way flow of information between H2H teams and the incident room. It is important their staff remain highly motivated and treated as integral members of the investigation. The SIO can occasionally drop by and speak personally with the coordinator and their teams whenever at the crime scene or in the area to show appreciation for and interest in their task and to stress how important it is. This also presents an opportunity to dip-sample the records being completed and demonstrate visible leadership.

The H2H coordinator is usually supplied with a dedicated communications link (eg mobile phone or office number), details of which can be left at any premises where there is a nil response. This allows people to contact the coordinator directly rather than the incident room to arrange a return visit, etc.

KEY POINT

A temporary mobile incident vehicle/caravan situated at or near an important crime scene can serve not only as a base for H2H teams but also to provide public reassurance and community engagement, making it much easier for locals, commuters, and passers-by to drop in and offer assistance.

Checklist—H2H Enquiries

- Identify key locations for H2H enquiries (eg crime scene, deposition site, exhibit locations, routes taken, suspect's home/place of arrest).

- Identify and record geographical parameters and policy.

- Formulate an investigation-specific questionnaire (using open questions).

- Fast-track H2H enquiries are those during the Golden Hour(s) period, ie anywhere within *line of sight* or *earshot* of the chosen crime scene(s).

- Prioritise and phase H2H enquiries where necessary.

- Determine what recording mechanisms are to be used (eg PDFs and house occupancy).

- Consider form of approach (ie some people/communities may prefer a non-uniformed visit).

- Set a visits policy (eg two evening visits then leaflet drop where no reply).

- Set a 'negative response' policy and review any non-cooperation or engagement.

- Consider extended area for mass leaflet distribution with contact details of team.

- Coincide H2H visits with trigger events, such as arrests or anniversary of incident (eg exactly one week or month after) for maximum impact.

- Mobile incident vehicles are useful focal points for reassurance and convenient bases for H2H staff.

- Administration must be methodical and completed forms submitted in a timely fashion.

- High-priority (HP) information should be fast-tracked to incident room.

- Planning and preparation may be required for 'multi-occupancy-' type premises, language barriers, and foreign nationals.

- Dedicated coordinator role can help manage the process and supervise teams.

10.4 **Passive Data**

The term 'passive data' is one that has been used in both the *Murder Investigation Manual* (MIM)[11] and the College of Policing *Authorised Professional Practice.*[12] It generally means information that is obtained from automated/mechanical systems, hence the term 'passive'. It includes recording equipment such as CCTV and ANPR.

ANPR is one of the largest non-military databases in the United Kingdom with a national infrastructure of approximately 9,000 cameras that capture 25–40 million pieces of data.[13]

The surveillance camera sector is a massive industry that continues to grow, with an estimate in 2017 suggesting that there were between 4–6 million CCTV cameras in the United Kingdom (see <http://www.app.college.police.uk/app/passive%20data%20generators>). The Government-appointed Surveillance Camera Commissioner (SCC) is tasked with ensuring the use of such systems complies with the basic principles of rights to privacy under Article 8 ECHR by introducing a national strategy for surveillance cameras in England and Wales together with regulation under a Surveillance Camera Code of Practice (to ensure that the public retains confidence in public surveillance systems designed to protect and not spy on them).

It is beneficial to determine swiftly what systems and images might be available, locate the owner, access them, and retrieve and analyse the contents. However, the diversity of systems and file formats can sometimes hamper investigations. At the same time, technological advancements are changing the types of data captured. For example, for the London Notting Hill Carnival, the Metropolitan Police have used automatic facial recognition (AFR) recognition for identifying individuals whom they suspect *may* commit offences or may be wanted. Superfast Wi-Fi and mobile connectivity means that such surveillance data can be captured and analysed quickly as the 'Internet of things' has become a reality.

Checklist—Passive Data Sources (Examples)

- Closed Circuit Television (CCTV)

- Communications data

- Images and data (eg captured on computers, laptops, digital cameras, Wi-Fi routers, mobile smartphones, tablets, fitness bands/watches/Bluetooth devices, etc)

- Body-worn video (BWV) cameras

---

[11] ACPO, *Murder Investigation Manual* (NCPE, 2006), 94–5.
[12] <http://www.app.college.police.uk/app/passive%20data%20generators>.
[13] Annual Report of the Surveillance Camera Commissioner 2016/17, see: https://videosurveillance.blog.gov.uk/2018/01/10/the-annual-report-of-the-surveillance-camera-commissioner-2016-17.

- Financial information

- Digital and computerised devices

- Voice-recording systems (eg in business and banking institutions)

- Customer information systems (eg loyalty cards)

- Electronic access systems (eg corporate/security entrances or hotel rooms)

- Automatic Facial Recognition (AFR)

- Satellite navigation and tachographs

- Vehicle-borne cameras (aka 'dashcams')

- Automatic Number Plate Recognition (ANPR), speed and traffic cameras

- Unmanned Aerial Vehicles (UAV), ie drones

- Electronic tagging devices, and fuel cards

- GPS tracking devices (eg covertly fitted to vehicles for/by OCGs)

- Vehicle tracking 'black boxes' (eg those fitted to certain vehicles)

- TV viewing boxes and gaming consoles

- Other devices managed over the Internet (aka 'Internet of things')

Devices, images, data, or equipment need to be seized quickly in order to prevent destruction, loss, contamination, or overwriting. Fortunately, most officers instinctively look for and seize any CCTV they can lay their hands on. This is perhaps as well as passive data as it can provide compelling evidence and must be a priority in most investigations.

There are some practical issues to be mindful of:

- Variety of recording systems and video file formats in existence.
- Storage and viewing of material, ie if bulk data is recovered (Criminal Procedure and Investigations Act 1996 (CPIA) suggests all data recovered has to be checked for any material which is 'relevant').
- Range and type of images vary greatly, and usefulness often depends on the standard of equipment and recordings (eg some systems overwrite and are rotated on a regular basis to make them cost-effective).
- Date and time stamps can sometimes be inaccurate or misleading.
- Audit trails must be strictly maintained, particularly when copies are made, and original seals are broken (ie integrity).
- Some external agencies have strict protocols governing how and when recordings may be handed over.

- General Data Protection Regulation (GDPR) must be considered.
- Integrity of systems must be checked to ensure they have not been the subject of any virus, interfered or tampered with.

CCTV is now discussed in more detail followed by a further passive data source: communications data.

10.4.1 Closed Circuit Television (CCTV)

CCTV can be of enormous benefit and should be routinely sought and treated as an HP action. As well as recording the actual commission of the offence, CCTV may also capture those en route to/from crimes, or engaging in other activities of interest to the investigation. Some recordings may show that an alleged incident did not occur at all, or may corroborate (or not) eye-witness accounts and (dis)prove alibis.

CCTV can show the nature and severity of offences and identify victims, suspects, and witnesses, (in)consistencies in accounts and forensic or scientific opportunities, such as identifying crime scenes, and for corroborating and tracking movements and routes taken by victims and suspects, and in some cases for identifying people who may be following or travelling with them or nearby. Recordings can also be useful post offence to see what offenders or victims are wearing and may subsequently be missing. It can be used for reconstruction purposes, eg to compare a suspect's vehicle with one caught on a camera at a significant time and location. Note: care must be taken not to be overwhelmed by collecting too much material as it all must be analysed.

Some Law Enforcement Agencies (LEAs) have invested in creating special units for finding and/or recovering CCTV footage. These contain specialists who have the right training and equipment. Some have recruited staff who are particularly gifted with powers of recognition and extremely skilled and capable at recognising and spotting people (aka 'super recognisers') in amongst complex and high-volume images.

KEY POINT

Swift evidence is good evidence, but it is not always wise to seize more CCTV footage than is necessary. Being overwhelmed by irrelevant material is best avoided.

10.4.2 CCTV objectives and policy

The following are considerations for including in CCTV objectives and policy.

Checklist—CCTV Objectives and Policy

- Objectives examples:

  o Identify offence commission.

  o Identify related events, significant incidents, and persons.

  o Identify people or things entering or exiting a significant location.

  o Identify routes taken/not taken.

  o Identify victims, suspects, or witnesses and their behaviour, movements, and actions (ie before, during, and after the crime was committed).

  o Assist in the implication or elimination for a TIE category.

  o Corroborate or negate accounts.

  o Identify scenes, evidential items/exhibits, and forensic opportunities.

  o Establish and confirm timescales and for time-lining purposes.

  o Prove association or links to specific items (eg mobile phone usage).

  o Identify sightings of relevant vehicles and who is in them.

  o Identify reconnaissance activities.

Policy considerations:

- Parameters and priorities for trawls, seizure, and viewing.

- Link with a communications strategy (appeals for CCTV recordings and systems).

- Stipulate locations to be checked for systems (eg shops, automatic teller machines (ATMs), fuel stations, town centres, supermarkets, public houses, social clubs, private properties and businesses, public transport areas, car parks, dashcams).

- Determine how checks are made, ie whether a visual check will suffice or link into a H2H-type strategy to ask for any private systems or recordings.

- State what is to be noted, eg camera angle, position, type of equipment (eg if time-lapse or continuous), location captured in the image, and the terrain immediately around it to identify blind spots.

- Where viewings are to be conducted (ie on site to see what is recorded and check if material could be recorded over (taking a copy of the recording might be an option, eg on a smartphone).

- State how accuracy of time and date are to be checked (eg with the speaking clock).

- Legal implications eg powers (eg sections 8 and 19 of the Police and Criminal Evidence Act 1984, CPIA).

- Security and continuity of material seized.

- Resources, facilities, and equipment to be used.

- Disclosure and preparation of CCTV footage for court purposes.

- Analysis, retention, and disposal.

10.5 **Communications Data and Social Media**

Communications data (CD) feature in almost all types of serious crime investigations and the technical complexity of this type of intelligence and evidence is constantly changing and increasing (eg fifth generation (5G)). SIOs need to be able to adapt their investigation strategies to reflect the ways that sources are accessed and that updated technical capabilities and opportunities are used to good effect, eg Targeted Intercept (TI) and Targeted Equipment Interference (TEI), to present the SIO with richer intelligence pictures.

CD as evidence is usually contextual, meaning it is frequently corroborative of or corroborated by other evidence. It can, however, be used for the corroboration of witnesses, to assist with chronology and a sequence of events, help prove association and assist with geographical locations of people and events, support or refute alibis, etc.

Mobile data can take many forms: anything from conventional images, text messages, photographs to voice over Internet protocol (VOIP) and voice over Wi-Fi (VOWI). A broad range of evidence can be retrieved from suspects' and victims' mobile devices. Digital data can be critical in helping create links and patterns in an investigation. In a digital age, there is usually some degree of communication between most people, be they colleagues, friends, family, or associates, using fast-developing applications.

This is something that digital forensic examiners and investigators can use to good advantage. Digital information and data can reveal plenty about activities, life patterns, behaviour, and personal relationships. The tone of a text or voice message can reveal valuable information, as can the retrieval of GPS (Global Positioning System) and IP session data.

Social media is a major communications contributor and facilitator. Most people, one way or another, make some use of social media and the Internet. Digital traces and footprints left by using (meta) data and programme files that store information are a major boost to crime investigation, from posting location information, compiling and uploading data to websites, to tagging or grooming people on social media sites.

Social media examination offers a wealth of information about a person's lifestyle, habits, thoughts, behaviour, movements, associates, intentions, and beliefs. This form of communication doesn't have to involve criminality per se, but it has created new opportunities for criminals to use encrypted and secret communication methods via the 'dark web/net' to commit and arrange criminal activity, identify and trace victims, resolve disputes, cause serious harassment (labelled 'cyber stalking'), and create friends and enemies (eg through online competitive gaming or in virtual themed 'closed' communities).

In some cases, it may be possible to be proactive in preventing or disrupting serious offences being committed with close monitoring of social media sites and activity. As an extreme example, some notorious spree and serial killers reveal their psychological state of mind and criminal intent prior to the commission of mass murder, terrorism, or other acts of gratuitous violence (and in some cases during by live streaming). This is why it is so important to identify what profiles and usage of digital communications an individual has or is using, particularly victims and offenders, and, in some cases, witnesses.

SIOs need to be aware of the rapidly expanding growth and increasing capabilities in speed and functionality of digital devices and applications, especially when considering a communications data strategy. Fourth generation (4G) phones have very fast live data-streaming capabilities that allow videos to be shared over the Internet in real time as they are being recorded. This means recordings made of crimes as they occur can be instantaneously uploaded onto the Internet (eg Brenton Tarrant, who was charged with murdering fifty people at a mosque in Christchurch, New Zealand, in March 2019). The severe implications for this on victims, witnesses, victim's families, relatives, and on communities can be massive, particularly if this occurs at the time of or very soon after a crime is committed and before an investigation begins.

Most investigations will benefit from having communications and digital data specialists who can be tasked with getting the best evidence and intelligence via this important line of enquiry. This should be treated as an investigative strategy in itself under the control and direction of an appointed lead or supervisor with a team that would probably include a Communications Liaison Officer (CLO), Digital Media Investigator (DMI), Communications Data Investigator (CDI), SPoC, researchers, and an analyst. There is also the NPCC DCG (Data Communications Group)[14] and other service delivery agencies and partners who can be consulted for advice.

KEY POINTS

1. The digital dimension needs to be incorporated into intelligence-building and investigative strategies. The key message is 'think digital'.
2. People routinely activate their digital recording devices to record things of interest. This may include initial responders and other significant events at crime scenes. These must be identified and recovered quickly before they are circulated over the Internet.

---

[14] DCG can be contacted via email at: dcgfutures@met.police.uk.

10.5.1 **Types of communications data**

Hard drives, CD/DVDs, USB sticks, and tiny flash drives are not the only places where material can be stored; 'cloud' and 'remote' computing are also possible storage sites. This means physical presence of evidential material may be more difficult to find and secure as this evidence may be in another place or country, rendering it more challenging to find and legally recover.

The existence of 'virtual crime scenes' and encryption are becoming more commonly encountered. The 'Snowdon effect'[15] raised public awareness of the need for privacy. Many application developers and service providers now specialise in 'end-to-end' encryption. OCGs frequently use encrypted devices or 'call spoofing' to hide or disguise their communications, and even younger social media users have become more adept at the ability to encrypt their digital communication and preserve their privacy.

Social networking and Internet usage must be linked with most if not all other strategies mentioned in this *Handbook*. A search strategy, for example, should incorporate looking for digital devices (including boxes/packaging indicating they exist) and gadgets that may store or transmit data, some of which (eg tiny micro Sandisk 'SD' drives) may be difficult to find. Checks should be routinely made at premises for broadband and Wi-Fi connection, and the routers or servers examined. Examples of digital media and communications are:

- Phones and SIM cards, computers (tablets, desktops, and laptops) and printers, games stations, e-readers, browsing MP3 devices, remote- (application) controlled appliances (eg building security cards, utilities, media players).
- Entries and images on social networking sites (that can be made quickly and easily shared *and* deleted via most smartphones).
- Devices containing digital data and memory.
- Use of location-based services to record a device position.
- Wi-Fi systems and routers that facilitate Internet access, some of which retain connection data.
- Cloud storage of digital information (and 'virtual' crime scenes).
- Virtual worlds (eg use of avatars) and 'virtual' financial transactions (eg through bitcoin and other forms of crypto currency).
- Internet Connection Records (ICRs)—now catered for in the Investigatory Powers Act 2016.[16]
- Vehicle on-board computers and Bluetooth devices.

---

[15] Edward Snowdon is an American whistle-blower and former CIA employee who copied and leaked classified information in 2013 without authorisation about global surveillance programmes. This raised the issue of balancing national security against information privacy.

[16] The Investigatory Powers Act 2016 (IPA) amends a number of statutes (eg RIPA 2000) and introduced new powers and restated existing ones for UK LEAs. It enables the targeted and bulk interception of communications data.

Any investigative strategies that deal with victims, suspects, and witnesses usually include background research requirements. Collection plans for this type of information must include detail about online and social media presence (not just criminal activities), and usage of/access to digital media and communications data—eg what applications, social networking, and Internet sites they use, what devices they possess, how, where, and when they access the Internet, and how and where they store digital information and their passwords.

KEY POINTS

1. Most officers carry personal smartphones with access to the Internet and social networking. Advising on (non-) professional usage at crime scenes is essential as well as debriefing those who may have taken images or made recordings.
2. Compiling a digital and online profile of those connected to an investigation should be a routine line of enquiry (open source research is a valuable tool).
3. Search strategies and evidence collection must routinely incorporate digital communication devices, passwords, PIN codes, and storage systems.

10.5.2 Using data evidentially

Most communications data, once obtained, can be used evidentially. Attribution of a device to a specific person or place remains important, ie proving who was using a device at the time of a significant communication and where, or connection with the Internet or Internet account. This can be achieved, for example, through possession or use at the time of recovery, device content and usage, digital forensic examination, open source research, fingerprints, and DNA, CCTV, covert targeted activity, witnesses, or analytical products.

Confidential and covert techniques can prove highly effective and, at times, vital to support an investigation into high-end of high-risk (HEHR) offenders. If any data recovered is required evidentially, there are set criteria to be adhered to (a CDI can advise on the criteria and the process for this and will be involved in the gathering and presentation of the evidence). Communication service providers (CSPs) can provide some types of data that cannot be used evidentially, and the CDI will be able to advise.

The SIO must be satisfied any available data has been fully recovered and interpreted correctly. They should be fully cognisant of their disclosure obligations under CPIA in respect of data obtained from digital forensic examinations (and note, this is a highly controversial point (see section 7.7).

KEY POINT

Communication and digital data devices might also provide traditional opportunities for providing conventional trace and transfer evidence such as blood, fingerprints or DNA (as per Locard's principle, see section 6.1).

10.5.3 Proactive use of social media intelligence

OSINT (open source intelligence) and SOCMINT (social media intelligence) can be used proactively for operational advantages and as part of an external communications strategy, eg for publicising public reassurance or giving safety advice. Social networking sites are used extensively by some of the biggest law enforcement agencies, eg New York Police Department, the US Federal Bureau of Investigation, and UK NCA, all of whom use social media to circulate 'wanted' details, photographs, and information to the general public. Many UK police forces and the NCA do this routinely.

10.5.4 RF surveys

Radio Frequency (RF) propagation surveys can show if the coverage of a cell or Wi-Fi access point provides service at a given location. These can provide compelling evidence that a mobile device either could or could not have been present as a given location at a relevant time. The configuration of networks changes over time so a survey should be completed as soon after an event as is practicably possible. There should be no delay whilst any call data is obtained and surveys inside premises are best done while they are under the control of the investigating team.

10.5.5 Role of Digital Media Investigator (DMI)

A DMI can play a vital role in setting and successfully delivering a digital media strategy. This includes the coordination of covert and overt digital media inputs into an investigation, such as communications data, open source material, eg from the Internet, digital forensic recovery and examinations, and access to external independent experts.

Checklist—DMI Role and Duties

- Creation of initial digital strategy considering all opportunities available.

- Proactively advising on present or emerging tactical opportunities for exploiting any digital media and communications data as investigation progresses.

227

- Awareness of all aspects of the wider investigation and investigative strategy

- Working closely with an analyst (if appointed) to examine data and seek out information and evidence of use to the enquiry.

- Working with expert analysts, SPoCS, open source and digital forensics teams to develop a technology and data strategy within the overall investigative strategy.

- Briefing search teams and officers prior to deployment.

- Deploying to assist search teams, identifying devices that may provide opportunities.

- Advising on and/or managing any 'virtual' crime scenes.

- Performing role of or advising on role of 'Digital Forensics Manager' (similar to a CSM).

- Coordinating covert and overt CD-related activities across the investigation team and the intelligence cell to ensure that the firewall between the sensitive and non-sensitive is maintained.

- Using expert advice of the SPoC, open source, and digital forensics teams in ascertaining what CD to obtain and how best to obtain it in order to streamline the application process and acquisition of specific CD as highlighted in the technology and data strategy.

- Working with the analyst to coordinate their needs from CD alongside other sources of intelligence and evidence.

- Acting as professional applicant for CD and controlling the volume and relevancy of the data requested.

- Advising on exploitation of OSINT and SOCMINT.

- Providing general support for the investigation in the area of digital media.

KEY POINT

DMI assistance and advice needs requesting at the earliest opportunity. Having them regularly engaged with an ongoing investigation as part of the team and tasking them with helping to draw up a digital strategy for agreement by SIO is the best option.

10.6 Use of Intelligence

Intelligence cells may be established quite quickly to capitalise on early research and information development opportunities to meet an operational intelligence requirement (IR). While it is desirable to use resources comprising suitably trained staff, initially this may not always be practicable. It may therefore be necessary to rely on whoever is available with the requisite skills and knowledge to conduct urgent intelligence checks in 'fast time' and feed the required information into the enquiry.

The SIO may want dynamic research to be conducted in order to fill information gaps when seeking and posing the important 5WH questions, such as those mentioned in section 3.8.

10.6.1 **Role of an intelligence officer/cell**

An intelligence officer (or cell) is appointed to collate, evaluate, analyse, develop, and disseminate material as part of the overall strategy. Depending on the scale and type of enquiry, the size and nature of the intelligence potential will vary. In some instances, one person performing the role will suffice; in others, there may be a number of intelligence development officers, dedicated researchers, analysts, and internal assistance from specialist officers from a dedicated intelligence unit from within the organisation. Linkage may be also required across regional, national, or international agencies.

An intelligence strategy, once determined, is outlined either in the policy log or within a separate document. As with all other investigative strategies, this should be regularly reviewed, updated, and version controlled, together with an agreed list of data sources, closed and open, that should be exploited and accessed.

The SIO should insist that an important requirement of their intelligence cell is to be *proactive* as well as reactive in order to be of maximum benefit. They need to be mobile as well as static in seeking information of interest and in liaising with useful contacts from which information can be gleaned. This function involves much more than sitting behind a computer terminal analysing digitally available material on screen. Intelligence officers have to network to seek out useful information, meet and speak with certain people to establish/maintain useful contacts (remaining aware of status drift towards CHIS (Covert Human Intelligence Source). They must ensure that any useful contacts remain aware of their IR, ie the one fixed by the SIO, which remains dynamic as the enquiry progresses.

Intelligence officers' work is limited only by their own imagination. Furthermore, intelligence collection is the responsibility of all investigators, not just those occupying designated intelligence officer roles. Officers who are out and about making enquiries must be encouraged to be alert to collecting information, and look for opportunities to seek useful sources of information and feed it back to the intelligence cell for analysis and evaluation.

One example would be collecting community intelligence at times and locations where potential useful sources of information are likely to congregate, eg parents at school opening/finishing times when locals are dropping off or collecting their children.

Checklist—Intelligence Officer/Cell Responsibilities

- Researching victims, suspects, and witnesses (including social media profiles).

- Researching OSINT and SOCMINT sources.

- Analysing material gathered utilising tools such as timelines/SOE, comparative analysis, maps, flow charts, storyboards, etc.

- Evaluating raw data/material and translate this into meaningful information.

- Contributing to preparing hypotheses and inference development (see Chapter 3).

- Disseminating intelligence in a timely fashion in an appropriate method.

- Preparing intelligence briefings, packages, and updates.

- Contributing to relevant team/management briefings and meetings.

- Providing links with covert assets eg preparing CHIS tasking requests and liaising with dedicated source units, surveillance teams, and technical support units.

- Managing proactive covert activity intelligence products.

- Applying for and analysing communications data (CD).

- Liaising with local, regional, national, and international intelligence units.

- Researching TIE subjects, locations, incident logs, and crime pattern analysis.

- Researching and analysing H2H information.

- Researching significant messages and information received.

- Sanitising information and transferring it into the correct format for dissemination.

- Researching prison intelligence, debriefing offenders, and analysing releases.

- Producing intelligence bulletins.

- Producing charts or useful exhibits and aids for court purposes.

- Attending case trials to highlight discrepancies in witness testimonies.

- Any other intelligence functions at the SIO's discretion.

10.6.2 Role of intelligence cell manager

These role holders are responsible for day-to-day supervision of the intelligence cell and ensuring any relevant or new intelligence is brought to the attention of the enquiry team. They ensure relevant intelligence is disseminated to enquiry teams in a timely fashion and always at briefing sessions or other suitable times, and fresh intelligence is registered within the enquiry (eg on an intelligence or information form for appropriate actions to be raised), and an audit trail is maintained for disclosure purposes.

Wherever intelligence is shared between internal and external agencies, terms of reference or protocols need to be adhered to or drafted and agreed. This may form part of an existing Information Sharing Agreement (ISA) and is a task delegated to the Intelligence Cell Manager.

A consideration is that the intelligence cell is copied into any messages that enter the MIR. An optional function of the intelligence cell is to research the information contained within those messages, eg named subjects, addresses/locations, or vehicles.

An intelligence cell policy must contain suitable terms of reference including the stipulation of when and how intelligence meetings are to be held, for instance on a weekly basis or more frequently depending on the requirements of the SIO and needs of the investigation. Where there are regular intelligence feeds, an Intelligence Officer can be tasked with preparing a running log in simplified format containing a résumé of all available intelligence, together with evaluation codes. This can then be disseminated to the enquiry teams and updated on a daily/weekly/bi-weekly basis for ease of reference.

10.6.3 **Setting the intelligence requirement (IR)**

The SIO and enquiry team should arrange to be in an early position to identify intelligence gaps which need filling to form the basis of the IR (see also Table 3.3). An analyst can be tasked with assisting. An IR should always remain dynamic and focused not only on priorities but also on other key information and research to service the needs of the investigation (eg risk assessments for TIE subjects). An IR remains under continuous review and any amendments duly recorded.

Information overload should be avoided. When requesting information, specific terms and parameters are recorded in a strategy and/or policy log. For example, if a victim had an extensive criminal background: 'the SIO requests all intelligence logs held by (source) that mention the victim between (date) and (date)'.

The intelligence collection plan is part of the intelligence strategy and must be updated regularly to ensure any gaps and additional sources are identified. The collection of intelligence must always remain in accordance with human rights principles, ie justifiable, proportionate, and necessary. Careful thought must go into the selected methods of collection which may need to involve resources required for the intelligence cell, such as an analyst and researcher(s).

An intelligence assessment can be used as a method of ensuring that the SIO's aims and objectives remain focused and on track. This will avoid mission creep and enable priorities to be reviewed in line with the current hypotheses and general direction of the enquiry. It will also assist in focusing decisions about resources, guide operational activities, and ensure compliance with legislation such as Human Rights Act 1998.

10.6.4 **Research levels**

As part of an intelligence strategy, the intelligence officer/cell is required to conduct research for background details of certain nominals (eg TIEs or suspects). Intelligence searches should be conducted according to a grading system (or levels) set or agreed by the SIO. As there are numerous amounts of research and databases potentially available from which searches can be made, a degree of consistency is required. When the research is requested on a nominal (named/recorded subject), the level required should also be stipulated. For example:

Level A: Basic search criteria
Level B: Intermediate search criteria
Level C: Specific search criteria
Level D: Advanced search criteria

Each level becomes more detailed as it rises up the scale. The search criteria can be fixed according to the requirements of the investigation and range from local checks, such as crime-recording systems, the police national computer (PNC), local and internal agency intelligence systems, the PND and CMS, stop/search records, summons/warrants, to open-source research and linking in with agencies such as Her Majesty's Revenue and Customs, finance companies, NCA, Europol, and Interpol. Sensitive intelligence (aka 'red side') may also need to be added for which there will be limited and restricted access.

Nominals for research should be agreed and discussed with and clearly communicated to the intelligence cell. For example, in a case where there is no declared ·suspect, a policy decision may stipulate research is to be conducted on all recorded offenders or individuals who fall into one or more of the following examples, some of which may be included in or as part of a TIE category, eg:

- Convictions for offences involving weapons.
- Convictions for burglary in dwellings.
- Convictions for drug-related offences/sex offences.
- Known to have mental health problems.
- Recorded as a subject for Multi-Agency Public Protection Arrangements.
- Aged between ... and ... and have links to ...
- White males (IC1) who have identifying marks or features.
- Known offenders who have current or previous residence in ...
- Occupants of bail hostels within location of ...
- Registered homeless within postcodes ...
- Males previously issued with harassment warnings in ...

- Male offenders released on licence or serving suspended or community sentences between ... (date) and ... (date).
- Male employees of ... (eg victim's place of work).

10.6.5 Covert sources of intelligence

There is a wide variety of covert intelligence collection methods which cannot be mentioned in any great detail in this handbook due to their sensitive and confidential nature. The tactic of covert intelligence gathering can link up with a proactive covert strategy and is largely governed by the provisions of the Regulation of Investigatory Powers Act 2000 (RIPA) and Investigatory Powers Act 2016. For example:

- Directed surveillance and other covert operations and techniques.
- HUMINT sources (eg CHIS and UC/UCOL).
- Lawful Intercept (LI) and Targeted Equipment Interference (TEI).
- Covert Internet Investigator (CII) tactics.
- Prison intelligence (through Prison Intelligence Officers (PIOs)).
- Communications data (including bulk collection) and targeted interception and equipment interference.
- Technical Support Units.

10.6.6 Sensitive or 'need-to-know' information

'Need to know' is a security principle meaning the dissemination of certain classified material goes no wider than is required for the efficient conduct of the tactic and enquiry. It is restricted to those whom the SIO and the relevant organisation deem appropriate who have the requisite security vetting clearance level. A balance has to be struck between making information widely available to maximise potential benefits and restricting availability to protect the security of sources, techniques, and information. Put simply, there is a distinction between 'need to know' and 'nice to know', and a sterile corridor or firewall must exist between those who need access and those who do not.

Information held on a CMS is mainly non-sensitive, but some information may be protectively marked as official sensitive (Offsen), confidential, secret, or even top secret (TS). Sensitive material usually relates to its source or origin and protection level. For example, information obtained from a CHIS (Offsen or confidential) or some other covert type would usually attract protection in law from general disclosure. This is known as public interest immunity (PII) and means it may be protected (at the discretion of the trial judge) if it can be argued that disclosure would harm or endanger the source, or would be against the public interest in future law enforcement activity (eg compromise a sensitive tactic).

The SIO (in line with organisational and national policy) can stipulate appropriate levels of access to confidential or sensitive material. These decisions can (as always) be recorded in a policy log. A decision might also be needed about where or how to store information that is deemed so sensitive that it needs to be kept in secure storage or system throughout the duration of the enquiry and probably beyond (see section 4.4 on sensitive policy logs). This is entirely at the SIO's discretion.

KEY POINT

Sterile corridors or *firewalls* can be introduced to protect the source and content of covertly obtained (aka red side) material so that strict rules of security and confidentiality are maintained and to act as a barrier to help manage sensitive and confidential material.

10.6.7 **Intelligence logs**

Intelligence logs (aka 3 × 5 × 2 forms) have a restricted handling code accompanied by a risk assessment and stipulated conditions as to the reasons why it may be unwise to disseminate any further or to act on the information. This position can change and logs be regraded in consultation with the SIO and the originator. If this occurs, the CMS should reflect this, showing both ratings, relevant change details, and reasons why.

3 × 5 × 2 Intelligence Evaluation Model (replaced 5 × 5 × 5) (Table 10.1).[17]

Table 10.1 3 × 5 × 2 Intelligence Evaluation Model

INTELLIGENCE	1. Reliable	2. Untested	3. Not Reliable
A. Known directly to the source			
B. Known indirectly to source but corroborated			
C. Known indirectly to the source			
D. Not known			
E. Suspected to be false			
HANDLING CODE			
P—Lawful sharing permitted			
C—Conditional sharing permitted (specify cond.)			

---

[17] On 31 March 2016, the UK Government changed the intelligence Evaluation Model from 5 × 5 × 5 to 3 × 5 × 2.

10.6.8 **Intelligence dissemination and sharing**

It is highly likely there will be an accrual in an investigation of intelligence that is of benefit to other units or agencies, either internally or externally. An intelligence strategy can cater for a means of feeding and sharing (disseminating) useful information to and with other appropriate intelligence systems. The intelligence officer/cell can be tasked with exchanging relevant intelligence with all other interested parties and departments, which should be duly recorded. A risk assessment may be necessary before some types of intelligence are disseminated to ensure they are handled appropriately under the 3 × 5 × 2 system or other protocols (eg via a case specific risk assessment for sending intelligence overseas).

10.6.9 **Intelligence disclosure policy**

Policy is not only required to comply with the CPIA rules but also to ensure *all* material is correctly gathered and, where necessary, sanitised before being listed on the disclosure schedule. Suitable arrangements are required to guarantee that all relevant material is collected or checked for relevance.

Heavy reliance is sometimes placed upon those not directly connected to an enquiry but who search for and furnish all the relevant material related to the investigation from other sources (eg CHIS controllers and/or RIPA Authorising Officer). The SIO must be proactive in gaining their full cooperation for compiling accurate lists and gathering together all the relevant documentation for use by the enquiry, disclosure, and any PII hearings.

Relevant intelligence (including covert or sensitive material, particularly if it comes from other agencies unconnected to the investigation) must be traced, made available, and presented in a suitable format to the Disclosure Officer and Crown Prosecutor/special case worker. Any PII preparatory material and schedules need close supervision, as mistakes tend to prove costly, with the potential to inflict irreparable damage on a prosecution case (ie for failing to disclose or incorrect disclosure).

10.6.10 **Analytical support**

Analysts (and their researchers) are important members of an enquiry team as analysis forms part of the intelligence cycle[18] (direction, collection, collation, evaluation, analysis, and dissemination) that allows intelligence material to be processed. There are a variety of analytical tools they can use that can be applied, such as association charts, consanguinity chains (see section 11.6.3), timelines and sequence of events (SOE), comparative case analysis (including

---

[18] As cited in College of Policing, Research and Analysis (2014) <https:app.college.police.uk/app-content/intelligence-management/analysis/>.

serial offending), subject and risk analysis, mapping, flow and frequency charts, and storyboards.

They can also assist with hypotheses building/testing and inference development to help draw conclusions, making predictions and aiding problem solving and decision making (see also Chapter 3). Analysts can also be utilised for preparing interview schedules and they could even be considered for involvement in any 'downstream monitoring' process.

Once assigned to a case, analysts should attend and participate in operational briefings and relevant management meetings. They can be shown relevant crime scenes in order to familiarise themselves with an offence under investigation and they are ideally co-located within the incident room as they need to become part of the team and have easy access to relevant material and the necessary IT equipment and software. This should not prevent them from having access to their own specialist equipment such as large-format printers located elsewhere.

Whenever practical and as soon as material becomes available (eg witness statements), it should be provided to the analyst so they can begin without delay. Their work can be expertly plotted and charted using specialist software and technology that makes the interpretation of information easier to present and understand. This may eventually form part of the evidential case as an exhibit (ie not just as an intelligence product), and analysts can be treated as professional witnesses. If not used as a witness, they may be invited to attend case conferences, prepare jury bundles of analytical evidence, and, while a case is in session, be on hand to support and advise the prosecution team and analyse the case as it progresses, particularly witness testimonies.

KEY POINTS

- Appointment of an analyst and their ToR are recorded in a policy log.
- Only the SIO/DSIO or intelligence cell manager tasks the analyst/researcher. Other staff must not commission them to do tasks without seeking permission.
- Key is knowing *what to ask* an analyst to do, so a basic understanding and appreciation of what they can produce and the tools and products they have at their disposal is useful.

'To assist in understanding the various strands of the investigation, the analysts developed a time-line document for easy reference. In the event this ran to 99 pages. It was subsequently described by the Principal CPS lawyer as the single most useful document that came out of Operation Fincham.'[19]

---

[19] Sir R Flanagan, 'A report on the investigation by Cambridgeshire Constabulary into the murders of Jessica Chapman and Holly Wells' HMIC, June 2004, Ch 5.72.

10.7 **Financial Investigation**

There are significant benefits from seeking financial information as part of an investigative strategy. This type of information can reveal details about a suspect or victim's lifestyle, financial profile, and the identification and use of significant transactions. It can reveal suspects and witnesses from evidence of them making financial transactions or being present at significant times and locations and also prove motive and association.

Financial information can be developed and analysed to establish patterns and trends, fill intelligence gaps, and contribute to intelligence profiles. The assistance of a Financial Investigator (FI) should be considered in all serious and complex investigations. Financial data may assist in giving an indication of motive, debt, or financial stress. Most people simply cannot exist without leaving behind some kind of 'financial footprint', be they a victim, suspect, or witness. This information can be used to identify:

- Offences (including high end money laundering (HEML)).
- Significant transactions (eg payments overseas through a third party).
- Suspects, witnesses, victims, missing persons (and their location).
- Association with others and/or links to places and premises.
- Location and movements.
- Use of services such as phones, transport, or other amenities and facilities.
- Motives (wealth and debt).
- Use of hard to trace currencies, eg cryptocurrency.
- Lifestyles and habits.

Financial data may have been created in one, two, or all three areas of the Problem Analysis Triangle (see section 3.8.4.5), ie victim, offender, and location. For example, the creation of financial data by both the victim and offender at a certain location may be the evidence that links them together. Third parties who leave some financial data trace may also become useful witnesses.

Financial data may indicate motive, such as personal gain. Valuable lines of enquiry can be developed (eg H2H including business premises) to identify credit/debit card usage (eg to top up a mobile phone) or any other financial transactions, and to examine till receipts in retail premises or the use of ATMs to see who was at or near a crime scene (as suspect or witness).

Searches of premises or vehicles should include checks for financial information that may help build a picture of a person's lifestyle or generate additional lines of enquiry, eg money suddenly going in or out of a bank account or sudden unexplained wealth or debt. There is a vast amount of information available in the financial world, but investigators must have clear objectives when seeking it that are appropriate and beneficial to the enquiry. Vague and non-specific requests, such as 'obtain a financial profile', are not helpful.

> **KEY POINTS**
>
> 1. Sources of financial data can be included as part of H2H enquiries and business/retail premises enquiries, eg details of financial outlets in the area such as ATMs or general stores that have a small cash-dispensing service, and during covert proactive operations.
> 2. Private sector financial intelligence can provide useful operational information.
> 3. Financial intelligence can support all types of investigations.

10.7.1 Suspicious Activity Reports (SARs)

A SAR is an information report on what a financial institution considers to be suspicious transactions, eg money laundering. This information is made available to law enforcement in order to assist investigations and help identify assets that have been obtained through criminality. Local policy usually dictates how this information is collected. The rules for disclosure extend to a wide variety of financial sectors, ranging from high-value dealers (eg in cars and jewellery), tax advisers, and the legal profession, to real estates, security deposit box companies, and gambling agencies.

10.7.2 Proceeds of Crime Act 2002 (POCA)

This legislation provides for the obtaining of production orders, search and seizure warrants, account monitoring orders, customer information orders, and restraint orders (POCA, parts 2 and 8). The orders require the signature of a Crown Court judge. It should be considered in any major investigation where there is an opportunity to seize any assets that may have been the proceeds of crime. The type of information or material that may provide this opportunity needs to be a consideration across some of the other strategies, particularly when searching premises. Part 5 of POCA, for example, provides a power to seize any cash if it is believed to be a means of disrupting any criminal acts (eg drug- or gang-type activity).

10.7.3 Unexplained Wealth Orders (UWO)

UWOs came into effect on 31 January 2018 and are an investigation order and tool that can be issued by a High Court on satisfaction of a number of tests. They add to a number of powers already available in POCA to investigate and recover the proceeds of crime. A UWO requires someone who is reasonably suspected of involvement in, or of being connected to a person involved in serious crime to explain the nature and extent of their interest in particular assets, eg property. The test for involvement with serious crime is by reference to Part 1 of the Serious Crime Act 2007.

Advice on the use of a UWO can be obtained from the NCA as they are one of the 'enforcement authorities' listed as being able to apply for them. This is a new power and it may be worth considering a referral in investigations that reveal large amounts of wealth that appear unusual. They could add to what may be a significant line of enquiry and link to or support a particular dimension or part of a prosecution case.

10.8 **Proactive Investigation**

Proactive (overt and covert) investigation strategies require the initiation of some action rather than say, merely reacting to and investigating a crime(s) that has been committed or on information received. This tactic can be used to generate intelligence or evidence, cater for continuing criminal activity, target suspected offenders, respond to, and deal with a 'crime in action' (eg ongoing serial offending where there is a pressing public interest to detain the offender(s) as quickly as possible), or target a particular kind of criminal activity where the offenders have not been identified.

Proactive strategies are not confined to covert operations such as surveillance. A range of overt proactive options to prevent, detect, or disrupt criminal activity may be available which an SIO might wish to use as a multi-purpose function or as part of subterfuge, displacement, or disruption tactics. Examples include executing search warrants or mounting high-visibility patrols, intelligence-led stop and search or road checks, or specific targeted activity. Other proactive options might include dealing with threats to life (TTL) in kidnap cases or managing dangerous offenders. Complex investigations may require a fully integrated approach with the use of a number of different techniques dependent on the type of investigation and level of crime.

10.8.1 **Contingency plans**

A proactive contingency (or trigger) plan is to prepare for if and when further offences are committed or incidents of interest to the investigation. The aim of the plan is to ensure there is an appropriate response that may include capturing evidence and conducting specific actions required by the investigation. Contingency plans need to include protocols around call-out procedures and notifications for enquiry teams, and any other specific roles and responsibilities, eg Exhibits Officer, forensic examination and physical searching, CCTV viewing and recovery, specialists (eg ballistics examination), and victim and witness care arrangements. All these requirements are likely to be 'Golden Hour' tasks.

The purpose of a contingency plan will differ with each investigation, but generally such plans are put into place for the following reasons:

- To prevent further offences.
- To provide public reassurance.
- To maximise investigative and forensic gathering opportunities.
- To identify and apprehend offenders.

A plan might benefit from being divided into three sections to cover the roles of: (i) call taker (instructions on receipt of report what and who to deploy and notify, where and when); (ii) initial responders (detail regarding what action to take in addition to general response duties and actions required specific to the investigation; and (iii) investigators, in addition to general responsibilities to include what the investigation and SIO may require from them, eg notification and call-out procedures.

Ensuring that a senior investigator and/or the SIO are notified at the earliest opportunity is essential. The whole point of a contingency plan is to reduce the risk of required actions not being completed and in order for them to work they need effective planning and communication. Consideration should be given as to the best way to brief call takers, response officers, investigators, and other specialists that are required. This should be incorporated into a communication strategy.

10.8.2 Proactive covert tactics

Covert investigative tactics can be used for a number of reasons and to meet specific needs and objectives. They may be conducted using human or technical resources or a combination of both. Generally speaking, it is best to obtain tactical advice from those who have sound knowledge of the various options that might be available, particularly those who work in or have good knowledge of serious and organised crime investigations. There are many different options to take, and a degree of creativity is often beneficial to make best use of covert assets and options. They should not always be viewed as a stand-alone intelligence tactic either as they can complement other options, such as physical searching, scene identification, or as part of an arrest strategy.

Preservation of tactics is essential to 'future-proof' their effectiveness and minimise risk of compromise. Knowledge of certain methods is restricted even within law enforcement circles, and this is an equally important consideration for an SIO. Specialist advice and assets utilised have to be made subject to the principle of 'need to know' (as opposed to 'nice to know') and must be carefully managed throughout the duration of the enquiry and beyond.

Added considerations when using covert tactics are as follows:

- They are often resource- and cost-dependent.
- They produce a product that needs properly analysing (which might be a large task with lots of information to manage).
- Products may need to be the subject of special CPS casework and PII hearing.
- Disclosure rules always apply and, despite PII protection, a trial judge might feel duty bound to declare covertly obtained information to the defence (jeopardising or safeguarding the tactic and source).
- Some tactics can be time-consuming and prolong an investigation.
- There is a risk that intelligence gained might be inaccurate and take the investigation in the wrong direction.

- Some criminals are cunning enough to feed misinformation deliberately to an investigation via covert channels to frustrate the investigation.
- Protecting a covert tactic might become burdensome and long term.
- Strict legal provisions need following.

Article 8 of the European Convention for the Protection of Human Rights (ECHR) provides a right of respect for private and family life, and covert investigation at whatever NIM level has to be pre-authorised and closely scrutinised. Any evidence obtained by these infringements is often compelling so defence tactics at trial may seek its exclusion by questioning the integrity of the process and challenging adherence to the procedures. This includes not just authorisation and the actions of operatives but also the disclosure obligations under the CPIA.

Balancing a defendant's right to a fair trial alongside the management of sensitive material is challenging and may necessitate a PII hearing to prevent certain information being disclosed. Early consultation with the CPS is essential.

Covert processes can be time-consuming, requiring tasking and coordination, pre-application feasibility studies, detailed risk assessment, planning for contingencies (including compromise and its consequences), and preparing and submitting requisite authority applications. This is a task often best allocated to the dedicated intelligence cell. The cell is also usually tasked with managing the covert product and is a very important responsibility. This is because intelligence received might be of such significance that, whether correct or incorrect, could take the investigation off in the right or wrong direction. It is often the interpretation of precise wording contained within covert intelligence products that can become crucially important.

Wherever possible, SIOs should anticipate the need for covert activity early and identify relevant issues by querying:

- What is the least intrusive method of securing such evidence or information?
- What are the legal enablers or constraints?
  — RIPA
  — Police Act 1997
  — Human Rights Act 1998
  — ECHR—Articles 2, 6, and 8
  — CPIA
  — Investigatory Powers Act 2016
- What is the time frame for the operation or unique window of opportunity?
- What resources are required (sufficient trained and accredited staff)?
- What equipment and funding are required and available?
- What are the risks to the organisation of (not) deploying the tactics?
- What are the risks to the public or specified third parties?
- What are the risks to the subject of the investigation?
- Will the methods breach ECHR, Article 8(1)?
- What is the justification for breaching ECHR, Article 8(2)?

- What is the risk of collateral intrusion and how will this be managed?
- How will the covert methods be protected at court?
- What specialist advice is required?

It is only by asking and answering these 5WH-style questions that an authorisation can proceed and a tactical plan be developed and implemented.

10.8.3 Human Rights Act 1998 (HRA)

The HRA was introduced to safeguard citizens from intrusions by the state into their privacy and rights. There are, of course, legal powers that allow law enforcement agencies and some other public bodies to breach these rights under certain provisions. There are important fundamental rules that must be clearly understood and followed to ensure that investigations, particularly when covert methods are used, are conducted without unnecessary or unfair intrusiveness.

The most relevant articles are:

Article 2: Right to life
Article 5: Right to liberty and security
Article 6: Right to a fair trial (often cited by defence lawyers during court trials)
Article 8: Right to respect for private and family life
Article 14: Prohibition of discrimination

Human rights principles that are incumbent on all investigations are outlined in the following table (Table 10.2).

Table 10.2 HR key principles

Justification (legality)	The interference with an individual's Article 8 rights is justifiable only if it is necessary and proportionate. This is stipulated in statutory grounds ie section 28(3) of RIPA (prevent or detect serious crime).
Necessity	The breach must be the only and most suitable way to achieve the objective after other alternatives have been considered.
Proportionality	The activities must be proportionate, which involves balancing the intrusiveness of the activity on the subject and others who might be affected. The activity will not be proportionate if it is excessive in the circumstances. This must remain under scrutiny and dynamic review to comply with the principles of the Act.
Collateral intrusion	Refers to the risk of intrusion into the privacy of persons other than those who are directly the subjects of the investigation or operation (third-party damage). Measures to reduce or eliminate unnecessary intrusion into the lives of those not directly connected with the investigation or operation should be included and dynamically monitored. This may include certain sensitivities in a particular area, location, or community.

Source: Codes of Practice pursuant to section 71 of the Regulation of Investigatory Powers Act 2000 (RIPA).

10.9 **UK Specialist Support and Advisers**

Some extremely useful national resources are available in the United Kingdom from the NCA. These assets can be of enormous help and support to a serious or major crime investigation and their use should be considered as early into the investigation as possible (Table 10.3).

Table 10.3 UK NCA specialist support and advisers

Major Crime Investigation Support (MCIS)	Serious Crime Analysis Section (SCAS)
National Injuries Database (NID)	UK Missing Persons Unit (MPU)
Specialist Research Team	CATCHEM database (Centralised Analytical Team
Witness Intermediary Team	Collating Homicide Expertise and Management)
Expert Advisers Database (EAD)	Crime Investigation Support Officers (CISO)
National Search Adviser	National SIO Advisers (NSIOA)
National Interview Adviser	National Family Liaison Adviser
Geographic Profiler	Behavioural Investigative Adviser (BIA)
National Missing Persons Adviser	National Forensic Specialist Adviser
National Vulnerable Witness Adviser	Forensic Clinical Psychologist

These units and resources provide information, advice, and specialist services to crime investigators and UK LEAs. Their core business is focused mainly on serious crimes, such as murder, rape, abduction, serious sexual offences, or other crime-related critical incidents. Support to the SIO and enquiry staff is arranged through regionally based teams with extensive investigative experience, specialist skills, knowledge and expertise. They can be contacted on email at: mcis@nca.gov.uk or telephone: 0345 000 5463.

10.9.1 **International Liaison Officers**

NCA International Liaison Officers (ILO) work with international partners and coordinate UK law enforcement overseas to gather intelligence, conduct operational activity, and can enhance international investigative delivery through a variety of means. They provide international support to operations that includes in-country intelligence collection and research including brokering relationships and agreements with overseas law enforcement agencies. They can also provide advice on ILORs (International Letter of Request), Joint Investigation teams (JIT), Eurojust (European legal body based in The Hague), Europol, Interpol, overseas intelligence dissemination, and extradition proceedings.

They can provide advice on what can and cannot be achieved in a large variety of overseas legal environments and are invaluable assets if an enquiry includes links to other foreign countries, or the use of EAWs (European Arrest Warrants) and Schengen agreements for cross-border surveillance (note that Brexit may affect this).

10.9.2 **Anti-Kidnap and Extortion Unit (AKEU)**

Crimes in action of this type are usually divided into three categories: kidnap, blackmail, or product contamination.

1. Kidnapping. Involves the abduction or holding of a hostage with the intention of extorting money or other concession. The kidnap may be linked to a criminal vendetta, people smuggling, child abduction, domestic incident, or the worst of them all, stranger kidnaps. Increasingly there are international aspects with kidnaps, either reported in the United Kingdom or overseas. A hostage may be located within either but some can turn out to be hoaxes or scams. This may lead to those involved in the hoax or scam being arrested for blackmail.

2. Blackmail. Involves traditional forms of demands and communication but there are new trends using cyber-enabled methods such as DDOS (distributed denial of service) or Ransomware attacks on public and private sector businesses. These are known as cyber-enabled or cyber-dependant blackmail. Reports of sextortion offences have also seen a significant rise and involve offenders targeting victims using social media. This is whereby demands are made for monies to be paid via electronic transfer methods (note: sextortion is not to be confused with 'revenge porn', which has its own specific legislation).

3. Product contamination. These threats are not always specifically food- or beverage-related. Contamination has also included in such things as saline solutions in hospitals. Where a product is suspected to have been contaminated, the case should be treated as a 'crime in action' as there is a likelihood there is an ongoing risk of threat to life (TTL[20]).

Most TTLs require courageous and fast-time decision making (see section 3.2). This involves a necessary willingness to challenge traditional working practices as the focus changes from reactive to proactive and the main objective becomes the preservation of life (and not primarily evidence seeking). This may cause confusion for some inexperienced or untrained investigators who usually see evidence gathering and arrest as the primary objective. The SIO must effectively communicate the right message and directive to teams so they are in no doubt as to what takes precedence.

Use of the correct terminology is also important. One common mistake is to confuse the terms 'hostage' and 'victim', with the former meaning an individual who is kidnapped and the latter the person or organisation to whom the demand is made. There are nationally recognised terms such as colour-coded roles and responsibilities and various titles allocated to key roles and positions.

---

[20] A TTL is deemed to be one that could engage Article 2 (right to life) of the HRA 1998, or where as a result of a deliberate intention, or the criminal act of another a real and immediate threat to either a loss of life, or cause serious harm or injury to another (including serious sexual assault or rape).

An SIO has to know and understand what these are to manage these operations for when specialist resources arrive to assist (note: these are fully explained in manuals used on training courses but are too sensitive to mention here).

The UK NCA Anti-kidnap and Extortion Unit is available to provide strategic and tactical support and guidance to any national or international investigation. Most K&E incidents are usually declared critical incidents and it is advisable to contact the unit for advice at the earliest opportunity. The UK AKEU on-call duty officer is available 24/7 (365 days a year) on telephone: 0207 238 8418, and email at: kidnap@nca.gov.uk.

KEY POINTS

1. The NCA AKEU provides strategic and tactical support to any (inter)national investigation.
2. In K&E operations, the policy log needs to outline clearly the number one priority: *'Preservation of the hostage's life and facilitation of their prompt and safe release'*.

10.9.3 **Expert advisers**

Some investigations may require assistance from experts who are outside the mainstream of forensic support that is readily available. Specialists and experts may be needed for elements of an investigation that are unusual or even obscure and that pose unique challenges. There are experts willing to provide expert opinion on all manner of subjects, such as entomology (insects, for establishing time of death), palynology (plants and botanical links to persons and items), podiatry (examination of feet), archaeology and anthropology (search for and recovery of human remains), knots and rope,[21] clothing, geophysics, facial mapping, diatoms from bodies in water (to establish if person alive when entered water), digital reconstruction, rocks, etc, even plastic binliners (eg when used to wrap or conceal body parts and corpses).

However, the use of 'experts' can pose unique challenges; for example, determining how experienced they are, how current their knowledge is, how many times they have successfully given evidence, what their qualifications are, how they present their evidence, what they have in place for avoiding cross-contamination, and, not least of all, their cost. The MCIS within NCA maintains a national register of experts to assist in sourcing experts in a wide variety

---

[21] In 1976, Gordon Park was jailed for life for the murder of his wife Carol Ann Park. Her body remained missing until 1997 when it was found weighted down in Coniston Water (Cumbria). The body was recovered alongside a piece of Westmoreland slate which an expert was able to match to slate Park had used to construct his bungalow, and a rock recovered by divers matched rocks from the wall. Knots used to tie the body were also matched to those in his house and boat. This specialist evidence became a key feature of the case against him. (aka 'The Lady in the Lake murder').

of specialist subjects. They also keep details of their CVs and information from when they may have been used in the past, who by, when, and how valuable their contribution was. This is to assist in deciding whether to use them or not. The database does not grant accreditation but a lot of the guesswork can be taken out of the process when requiring expertise that is not available through the usual channels.

Bibliography

ACPO, *Murder Investigation Manual* (NCPE, 2006)

ACPO, *Practice Advice on Analysis* (NPIA, 2008)

ACPO, *Practice Advice on Financial Investigation* (NPIA, 2006)

ACPO, *Practice Advice on House to House Enquiries* (Centrex, 2006)

ACPO, *Practice Advice on the Management and Use of Proceeds of Crime Legislation* (NPIA, 2008) <https://www.app.college.police.uk/app-content/intelligence-management/intelligence-cycle/> (accessed 28 July 2015)

ACPO, *Practice Advice on the Use of CCTV in Criminal Investigations* (NPIA, 2011)

Adcock, S, 'Financial investigation: SIO considerations' (2010) 6(2) *Journal of Homicide and Major Incident Investigation*

College of Policing, *Research and Analysis* (2014) <https:app.college.police.uk/app-content/intelligence-management/analysis/> (accessed 28 July 2015)

Harfield, C and Harfield, K, *Covert Investigation*, 3rd edn (OUP, 2012)

NCA (2018) Aide Memoire: 'Senior Investigating Officers' Practice Advice on the Management of Kidnap & Extortion', v.4, accessed via email: kidnap@nca.gov.uk

Victim Management

Being a victim of a crime is a very clinical, very personal and very blunt experience that never leaves you.

Baroness Newlove[1]

---

[1] Baroness Helen Newlove, UK Government Victims' Commissioner, speaking at PIP4 CPD seminar, College of Policing, Ryton, 13 May 2015. Her forty-seven-year-old husband, Gary, had been murdered in August 2007 in Warrington, Cheshire, after confronting a gang of youths found vandalising his car. They kicked him repeatedly in the head and are now serving time for murder. See also <http://www.victimscommissioner.org.uk>.

11.1 **Introduction**

The term 'victim' is used to describe someone against whom an offence has been committed. It can also include close family/relatives, institutions, businesses (eg in economic crime cases), and sometimes distinct or wider communities. These various types of victims could all be on the receiving end of a wide range of criminal acts such as homicide, physical injury, rape and sexual offences, economic crime or fraud,[2] extortion, terrorism, high-value fraud, sexual exploitation, trafficking abduction, and other serious offending. Those who suffer from criminal acts should expect and surely deserve the full support of and help from those investigating and prosecuting crimes committed against them.

A greater emphasis has now been placed on identifying and supporting victims (one of the five building block principles, see section 5.4). High-profile cases, public enquiries, a Victims' Code of Practice (VCOP), and the appointment of a Victims' Commissioner have all made significant improvements in the approach to victim welfare. Nowadays it is expected victims come first and are properly listened to and treated in a respectful, sensitive, and professional manner, without discrimination, and are afforded a fair chance of recovery.[3]

Obligations placed upon the police and other prescribed services by the introduction of the VCOP means it is mandatory for victims, including relatives of deceased persons, to be treated with the utmost respect, professionalism, and dignity. Any failure produces secondary victimisation and litigation possibilities. There is also a risk of reputational damage and loss of public trust and support.

The SIO plays a pivotal role in this, not only in leading the investigation but also in taking a strategic and tactical perspective. Included in this responsibility is ensuring help is provided not only for victims and their next of kin (NOK) but also in enabling local policing and partnership teams to meet their objectives and maintain good relationships, particularly when incidents affect vulnerable or hard-to-hear/reach groups.

There may be some overlap with some of the contents detailed in Chapter 13 as some victims may have dual status as significant witnesses. Nonetheless, this chapter will cover some of the fundamental considerations that form part of a victim management strategy. Having a thorough and robust policy to cover this element of an investigation will significantly assist in strengthening relationships with victims and the wider general public. It is also a good way of raising team morale as investigators are, after all, working hard

---

[2] In the case of a corporate victim, many employees could lose their jobs as a result of a large-scale fraud or cyber attack. Such victims can reach large numbers and sometimes they are spread across large geographical areas.

[3] When drawing up a list of objectives for an investigation tracing, identifying, supporting, and, if necessary, protecting and safeguarding victims is always be placed at the top of the list (see also section 7.6).

to obtain justice for victims of crime. The chapter begins with a look at the use of terminology.

11.2 **'Victims' or 'Complainants'?**

A retired High Court Judge, Sir Richard Henriques, conducted an independent review on behalf of the Metropolitan Police following their handling of a non-recent sexual offences investigation.[4]

This involved allegations made by a person using the pseudonym 'Nick' against people of public prominence (PPP) who had held public office and were named in the mainstream media. The MPS (Operation Midland) stated publicly that Nick's allegations as a 'victim' were being taken at face value and treated as being credible and true.[5] The allegations were later found to be unsubstantiated, which opened up a debate about whether all those who make allegations should, by default, be treated as 'victims' (or 'complainants') while the veracity of their evidence is investigated.[6]

In his report, Sir Richard drew parallels to the UK's judicial process. Prior to conviction, Crown Court judges do not permit a complainant to be referred to as a victim. Sir Richard stated that since the investigative process is similarly engaged in ascertaining facts which will, if proven, establish guilt, the use of the word 'victim' at the commencement of an investigation is inappropriate and inaccurate.

This view, however, is not wholly endorsed by Operation Hydrant (see section 11.5.2) nor the current NPCC lead (Chief Constable Simon Bailey). Their view is that as there is a need to develop a relationship based on trust and belief in victims, using the term 'complainant' would have a significant detrimental effect and undermine efforts to win the trust of victims, particularly those who are vulnerable. Crimes such as sexual violence are notoriously difficult to prove when the case relies purely on one person's word against another. Genuine victims may fear they will not be believed and a great many 'non-recent' victims in sexual assault cases have claimed this is the reason they haven't come forward.

However, prejudging someone automatically as a 'victim' contradicts some of the important principles outlined earlier, eg the ABC, the 'investigative mindset', 'innocent until proven guilty'; 'beyond all reasonable doubt', and the neutrality of the investigator, etc (see sections 2.9, 3.3, and 3.4). Determining

---

[4] See Sir Richard Henriques (31 October 2016) 'An Independent Review of the Metropolitan Police Service's handling of non-recent sexual offence investigations alleged against persons of public prominence'. Available at: <http://www.news.met.police.uk/commissioners -statement-following-sir richard-henriques-review>.

[5] 'Nick' has now been named as Carl Beech after a legal restriction was lifted and he was charged with perverting the course of justice.

[6] H Hamilton and R Sylvester, 'Police ditch practice of believing all victims: Britain's biggest police force has abandoned its policy of automatically believing victims after a series of flawed inquiries into alleged sex crimes' *The Times* 2 April 2018, and F Hamilton, 'VIP accuser Nick charged with lying' *The Times* 4 July 2018.

whether or not a complainant is proven to be a true victim forms a critical part of the investigation process and criminal justice system. Investigators carry a fundamental duty to remain impartial, be objective, keep an open mind, and conduct a thorough investigation by pursuing all reasonable lines of enquiry without favour. A similar rule applies to 'suspects' who cannot and should not be deemed 'guilty' or 'criminals' until the case is proven, and much thought and consideration goes into each and every decision to designate suspect status (see section 12.4). This is why the choice of words or terminology and formal categorisation (complainant/victim/belief, etc) becomes so important.

The police service (and other similar LEAs) is often the gatekeeper in the process of dealing with those who report as 'victims'. They are not the only ones involved in the system, however, as prosecutors and the criminal justice system also have a vested interest in the correct approach and use of any terminology that assumes an account is treated as accurate before an investigation is conducted.[7]

Undoubtedly every person who makes a criminal allegation should be dealt with non-judgementally. They are to be shown every courtesy, respect, and empathy, and must be supported and encouraged. Their accounts should be obtained by appropriately trained and professionally competent staff (ie investigative interviewers). Details they provide, though, need to be checked for factual accuracy and, if possible, corroborated to strengthen the evidence (as with any witness), and investigated expeditiously. Any supporting evidence needs to be diligently collected by skilled investigators.

It is in no-one's best interests to accept automatically any person's account at face value without making further enquiries (be they victim, witness suspect, or informant, etc), particularly if they relate to events that occurred some time ago. It should be emphasised, however, that many people can and do remember every unpleasant experience or attack in minute and accurate vivid detail, no matter how and when it occurred. It is, therefore, clearly important not to cause added distress to genuine victims due to misplaced scepticism or unprofessionalism.

One solution might be to lay down a policy for dealing with persons reporting criminal allegations. The following is a suggestion as to how this might look.

- The term 'victim' will not be automatically applied unless there are sufficient reasonable grounds to support or 'believe' the allegations and facts being reported.
- Empathy, courtesy, care, and respect will always be shown to anyone reporting as a victim.
- There will be no exhibiting of disbelief or scepticism.

---

[7] See also Assistant Commissioner R Beckley (2018), 'Review into the Terminology "Victim/ Complainant" and Believing Victims at time of reporting'. Available at: <http://www.college.police.uk/ Review-into-Terminology-of-Victims>.

- Those reporting as victims will be reassured that their allegations will be taken seriously, and the facts investigated thoroughly, impartially, and promptly.
- Focus will be on the credibility of the allegation, not credibility of the person.[8]
- Reassurance will be provided that the reliability and accuracy of facts provided from any source are routinely investigated and reasonable lines of enquiry pursued.
- Core principles contained within the Victim's Charter and Code of Practice will be followed, including consideration of any emotional and physical welfare needs.

Two final pertinent points on this subject relate to the application of sound and sensible judgement. Firstly, any individuals who have *clearly* been on the receiving end of criminal acts can and should continue to be properly referred to as victims. This would include, for example, those who have suffered at the hands of unambiguous harmful acts such as homicide or terrorism. By way of an example, it would be entirely inappropriate to use the term 'complainants' (or similar) for any of the twenty-two victims who lost their lives in the atrocities of the Manchester Arena bombing on 22 May 2017, or any of the four London attacks the same year (Westminster, London Bridge/Borough Market, Finsbury Park, and Parsons Green). Secondly, terminology should not affect an application of the 'Victims Code' principles for anyone who reports allegations and who may have suffered harm through atrocious criminal acts.

KEY POINTS

1. Complainants should not automatically be called victims. Any accounts provided (including from suspects or witnesses) should be checked for factual accuracy while applying the principles of impartiality, 'ABC' and the investigative mindset (see chapter 3).
2. Applying a blanket policy of 'believing' every person who alleges a crime has been committed may be prejudicial to the principle of conducting an ethical investigation. Credible evidence must always be sought whether it is supportive or contrary to the account that is given.

11.3 **Victims Code and Strategy**

A Code of Practice for victims of crime in England and Wales was published in October 2015 by the Secretary of State for Justice.[9] It forms a key part of a wider Government strategy to transform the Criminal Justice System (CJS) and to put

---

[8] This is also discussed in section 16.10.
[9] *Code of Practice for Victims of Crime: Presented to Parliament pursuant to section 33 of the Domestic Violence, Crime and Victims Act 2004* HM Stationery Office, October 2015. Available at: <http://www.gov.uk/moj>.

victims first. It strengthens an aim to treat victims of crime in a respectful, sensitive, tailored, and professional manner, without discrimination.

Victims can decide if they do not want some or all the information or services they are entitled to under the Code, or that they want to opt out of any of these at a later date. The services on offer are tailored to individual needs and circumstances and can be discussed with whoever is the service provider. It should be noted that victims can opt back into receiving services under the Code at any time while the case is under active investigation or prosecution.

Chapters 1–4 of the Code apply to organisations such as all police forces in England and Wales, the British Transport and Ministry of Defence Police, the Crown Prosecution Service (CPS), and the Criminal Cases Review Commission (CCRC).

Chapter 5, however, applies to agencies that have a narrower remit and specialised roles in the context of criminal proceedings due to them focusing on specific types of crimes or offences. These are agencies such as the Health and Safety Executive, the Serious Fraud Office (SFO), and the National Crime Agency (NCA).

The code contains a list of key entitlements (not all are applicable) to which most victims of criminal conduct in England and Wales are entitled. These entitlements are summarised as follows:

- Enhanced service for victims: (i) of serious crime; (ii) who are persistently targeted; or (iii) who are vulnerable or intimidated.
- Needs assessment to help establish what support is needed.
- Information on what to expect from the CJS.
- Referral to support organisations, if required.
- Information and updates about the investigation and case disposal details (including time, date, and location of any court hearings).
- Make a Victim Personal Statement (VPS), and have it read aloud at court if defendant found guilty.
- Seek a review of the police or CPS's decision not to prosecute in accordance with the NPCC and CPS Victims' Right to Review Schemes.
- Support from a Witness Care Unit (WCU) if required as a witness.
- Arrange a court familiarisation visit, enter through a different entrance from the suspect, supervised attendance and access to the prosecutor to raise any queries about the case (where circumstances permit).
- Be informed of any appeal against the offender's conviction or sentence.
- If offender sentenced to twelve months or more for violent or sexual offence, opt into the Victim Contact Scheme (VCS).[10]
- Apply for compensation under Criminal Injuries Compensation Scheme.
- Receive information about the Restorative Justice Scheme.
- Make a complaint about information and services not received.

---

[10] If an offender is under eighteen years of age, a Youth Offending Team may contact the victim to seek their views prior to sentencing if they are not receiving support under the VCS.

The Code defines a victim as:

1. A natural person who has suffered harm, including physical, mental, or emotional harm or economic loss which was *directly* caused by a criminal offence (in England and Wales); or
2. A close relative (ie spouse, partner, relatives in direct line, siblings and dependents of victim) of a person whose death was directly caused by a criminal offence (in England and Wales).

Enhanced entitlements are also outlined in the Code for victims in certain categories. These include (i) if the victim is one of a serious crime; (ii) is persistently targeted; or (iii) is vulnerable or intimidated (as per criteria of the Youth Justice and Criminal Evidence (YJCE) Act 1999 sections 16–17). In these circumstances, victims are entitled to have (where appropriate) information about special measures explained, be referred to a specialist support organisation, receive information on pre-trial therapy and counselling, and, if a case is concluded without charge, be informed if the case is reopened. A bereaved close relative of a victim who has died as a consequence of criminal conduct is entitled, under the Code, to have a Family Liaison Officer (FLO) assigned (where the SIO deems it appropriate).

A duty to conduct a needs assessment at an early stage falls upon the listed agencies (eg the police) to which the Code applies, and in particular to decide whether victims fall into one of the three priority categories for enhanced services. An SIO would be wise to ensure all their teams are aware of the requirements of the Code and to appoint a suitably experienced officer to act as a Victim Care Officer (VCO) for each victim at an early stage of the investigation, and determine whether they fall into one of the three categories for enhanced entitlements.

11.3.1 UK Government Victim Strategy

On 10 September 2018, the UK Government launched the first ever cross-government Victim's Strategy.[11] The strategy makes clear the specific support victims should expect, beginning immediately after a crime and ending long after any court proceedings. The key elements are:

- Consultation on a revised Victim's Code.
- Consult on a Victim's Law to underpin the Code, including strengthening the Victim's Commissioner's Powers.
- Consult on establishment of an Independent Public Advocate (IPA) to help bereaved families following a disaster.
- Review of the Criminal Injuries Compensation Scheme (CICS).
- Improve communication and support during the parole process.

---

[11] See <http://www.gov.uk/Justice> Secretary Unveils Victims Strategy 10 September 2018.

- Allow VPS at parole hearings.
- Increase in spending to improve services for victims of sexual violence and abuse.
- Greater support for families bereaved by homicide including funding for advocacy.
- Increasing the number of Registered Intermediaries.
- Improving court environments with victim-friendly waiting areas.
- Keeping the unduly lenient sentence scheme under review.
- Improved delivery of the Victims' Code.
- Development of a new delivery model for victim support services.

11.4 **Victim Support**

It can be assumed that victims of serious crimes require significant support and this needs to be a constituent part of a victim management strategy. Support, of course, includes mounting a professional investigation and bringing offenders to justice. Some victims, however, have added trauma of being a witness and providing evidence against their offenders. The Code referred to in section 3 states that they have certain entitlements, such as updates on the case progress. They are often better served by a single point of contact (rather than a succession of different faces) for regular and consistent updates on the progress of the investigation. They may also need support during and following a court trial.

There is no 'one size fits all' for victim support. Some victims may need a wide range of assistance depending on their individual circumstances. In some cases, for example, they may require psychological or emotional support; in others, it may be financial aid or physical protection or a combination of any of these.

In serious and complex investigations, support may be required from specially trained officers such as Family Liaison Officers (FLOs), Sexual Offence Liaison Officers (SOLOs), and Domestic Violence Officers/Coordinators. There are also voluntary organisations that can help support victims. Joint working arrangements and protocols should enable SIOs/investigators to make prompt referrals after an assessment of need, and this has the dual benefit of allowing the enquiry team more time for getting on with their other investigative actions.

11.4.1 **Registered intermediaries**

Registered intermediaries are specialists who help those with communication difficulties. The Code states that although these intermediaries were originally intended to help vulnerable witnesses give their best evidence in court, they can also assist victims when they are being interviewed to help them communicate their evidence. This facility is available via the NCA: telephone 0345 000 5463.

11.5 **Victim Engagement**

Initial responders and investigators are often 'gatekeepers' by being the first officials to interact and engage with victims of crime. This places them in a unique position of being able to help them cope with trauma and restore a sense of dignity, security, and control over their lives. As mentioned in section 11.2, victims will need encouragement and faith that their reports will be taken seriously and fully investigated. The way people cope as victims depends largely on their experiences as to how they are treated soon after a crime was committed. This means being able to share their emotional distress, sometimes vent some anger, and ultimately to feel confident they will be supported (and fully understand 'what happens next').

Helping gain willing trust and cooperation will assist in determining what their needs are or are likely to be. This will largely depend on the type of individual, their background, and personal circumstances (eg the vulnerable such as children and young people, the elderly; those in difficult family and domestic relationships; or with a disability, impairment, mental illness, or language/communication or cultural barriers). Most, however, have similar basic needs, such as the requirement to feel safe, to express their emotions, seek justice, and to have confidence in and understanding of the investigation process. Should they require it, they need to have access to any offers of services such as welfare support or ongoing medical assistance. Establishing rapport and explaining the support and investigative processes in simple terms is key. These responsibilities need handling tactfully in order to convince victims they can fully engage with and trust the investigation and criminal justice processes.

> Police officers gain the confidence of those who complain of sexual abuse ... by the manner in which they are dealt with; namely by the response to the initial phone call, or by an early appointment, by being given a choice of venue for the meeting, a choice of male or female officer, by the manner in which a statement is taken, by receiving regular information and being part of a highly professional process that is fair to both complainant and suspect.
>
> (Sir Richard Henriques, 31 October 2016: Independent Review of Metropolitan Police Service's Handling of non-recent sexual offence investigations alleged against persons of public prominence).

The first experience any victim has with an investigation is one they will never forget, so it needs to be very positive. Being insensitive towards victims is almost the same as inflicting a form of secondary victimisation, whereas engaging with them in a respectful and supportive manner will provide enormous benefit not just to them but the investigation. The SIO must watch out for any (un)conscious bias from their officers, which can stem from poor training or unprofessional attitudes and behaviour.

KEY POINTS

1. Whenever speaking to vulnerable victims, consideration should be given as to who else is present at the time, and who could be a witness or offender.
2. An initial account might be the only one a victim ever offers so this needs to be obtained carefully and recorded accurately.

11.5.1 Historical (non-recent) victims

Some adult victims from historical sexual abuse cases may have been abused as children. There have been a number of high-profile historical child abuse investigations in the United Kingdom that have led to the identification and prosecution of offenders. In these cases, some victims may have experienced being initially disbelieved, dismissed or feeling unable to share their experiences.

Any subsequent victim strategy would need to ensure victims are adequately supported during the investigation. It would also have to cater for and address any ongoing risks to other potential victims who would need to be identified via an intelligence-led approach (rather than illogical ad hoc trawls that may produce false accusations). The best strategy is to reach out to potential victims on a firm intelligence- or evidence-led basis.

When determining how best to make first contact, consideration should be given to whether a registered intermediary and/or appropriate adult should be used or specialist witness interview adviser.[12]

Corroborative evidence is always useful in these cases and SIOs should look to different ways of obtaining it. Despite an extensive period of time having elapsed between report and event, victims may have disclosed about their abuse to others including their own GPs or counsellors. Photographs may have been taken of offenders, providing evidence of supporting events, times, and locations of significance, which themselves may provide useful supporting corroboration if there are unique features being described that may still be available. Diaries kept or mementoes such as letters, artefacts, or clothing might also prove useful for corroboration. Accurate descriptions of locations can often be corroborated and a timeline of events is always a useful investigative tool for historical enquiries.

The following points are worth noting:[13]

- The decision to report by a victim may not be an easy one to make.
- Crucial for non-recent victims to be supported throughout the investigation.

---

[12] The National Vulnerable Witness Adviser is available from the NCA MCIS)
[13] College of Policing, Op.Hydrant SIO Advice, November 2016, Chapter 2.

- Investigation strategy is aimed at prosecuting where there is evidence and exonerating where there isn't.
- The rationale for and means of contacting/approaching victims should be recorded in a Policy Log.
- Conversations with witnesses/victims should be accurately recorded.
- Victims may, in certain circumstances, be informed that other complainants have come forward to strengthen their resolve (SIO to agree).
- Risk of suicide or self-harming risk management plan for victims should be considered.
- Staff who deal with victims may become affected themselves from distressing accounts.
- An overarching staff well-being strategy will be required.

11.5.2 Operation Hydrant

Operation Hydrant is a UK policing initiative aimed at providing effective operational coordination of non-recent child sexual abuse to identify investigative links and provide deconfliction (ie to ensure no two agencies are investigating the same case circumstances). The criteria for investigations that are covered by the operation are:

1. Non-recent investigations—offence occurred more than one year before reported.
2. Institutions—ie large organisations such as schools and children's homes.
3. Persons of public prominence (PPP)—those with celebrity/high-profile status.
4. Live investigations—actively under investigation or progressing through the criminal justice system.

Each investigation registered is entered onto a national database to assist in linking and deconflicting investigations. Police forces and investigating agencies are then alerted where links exist to avoid duplication. The operation can also receive referrals through third parties (eg the National Society for the Prevention of Cruelty to Children) which enhances the intelligence picture and helps develop a national profile for these types of cases.

Investigating non-recent abuse can present significant challenges due to reduced forensic opportunities and difficult memory recall. These cases may also attract significant media interest. SIOs would be well advised to contact the Hydrant team because one of their key roles is to develop best practice and provide a hub for specialist knowledge and expertise. It is not worth taking the risk of getting things wrong when the number one priority is effective safeguarding of children and vulnerable adults, which must remain the top priority in any reactive investigation.

11.6 **Victim Enquiries**

Victims are always to be afforded a high status in an investigation. This is why in a homicide investigation, on a case management system they are usually referred to as Nominal One (N1). They are not only of importance because of their entitlement to support but also because they deserve this high status and they can, of course, can provide vital information to help solve the case.

A victim strategy therefore needs to incorporate a comprehensive support plan together with one that aims to draw out the evidence a victim can offer. This includes details about themselves, their habits, and associations, and lifestyle and behavioural patterns to help provide clues as to why they were targeted and became victims—often referred to as 'victimology'.

Personal and intrusive enquiries and approaches to useful sources of information, such as family, close friends, and acquaintances may have to be made. This process requires tactful management as it may necessitate a search of personal belongings and/or room, house, computers etc to seek out vital information and possessions that may offer up clues. Reasons for doing so should be carefully explained, outlining the routiness of the procedures and how they are all part of the investigation process.

The purpose of victimology is to establish links between the suspect, victim, and crime along with generating investigative opportunities and useful lines of enquiries. Enlisting the services of an interview adviser to plan what is needed in respect of victimology may reduce the amount of times the family or victim may need to be seen. Initial preparations should be based around the 'what we know and what do we need to know' principle (see section 3.7). This will also enable obligations under the Victims Code of Practice to be followed via the correct categorisation of victims/witnesses and applications for any special measures submitted.

Obtaining details about a victim's background, lifestyle, and the sort of person they are/were usually features in the MLOE (main lines of enquiry) and designated a 'fast-track' or HP action. If they are part of a suspicious missing person enquiry, for example, it may be necessary to obtain recent photographs/digital images of them. It is an unfortunate by-product of being a victim that investigators need to delve into their personal life to find clues. What was going on in their lives at the time of or immediately before an offence/incident can and often does generate leads. It may be useful to enlist analytical services to identify and examine links among associates, family trees, movements, timelines, communications data, and social media contacts, etc. In most cases, information seeking to obtain the necessary rich picture about a victim is not restricted to probing close family and relatives. For example, teenagers do not usually let their parents/carers know about everything they do, but this sort of information might be available from their close personal and school friends.

KEY POINT

One good line of enquiry is to ascertain who knows most about the victim. This same person asked, however, could also be the offender and it may be significant if that person has not been seen or made contact with the victim or their family and friends since the incident under investigation occurred.

Checklist—Victimology enquiries

- Full and detailed personal description (most recent videos or photographs).

- Home, work, and previous addresses.

- Occupation(s), trades and skills, education, training, qualifications, employers, and employees.

- Family background/tree, marital status, current and previous relationships/affairs and partners, children, siblings, relatives.

- Friends, associates, and work colleagues (and recent visitors or persons with whom they came into contact).

- Means of transport, vehicles (usage or access), routes taken.

- Level of vulnerability (child or young person, mental illness, disadvantaged, homeless, elderly or infirm, other type of vulnerability).

- Lifestyle, reputation, character, appearance, physical attributes, personality, previous convictions, current and previous levels of criminality, group/gang association or organised crime group affiliation, previous incidents of note, habits, hobbies, (dis)likes, drug or alcohol abuse or other vices, religion, secrets, sexual preferences, risk-taking likelihood, debts, political and contentious views, any extreme behaviour, and use of online forums/websites/dating/chatrooms/social media.

- Routines, habits, daily activities, places frequented (including places of worship, leisure, travel, holidays, overseas visits).

- Timeline of movements, where they've been, who they came into contact with and when, last known movements, when last seen, and what they said or did and their mood at that time.

- Relevant personal possessions, digital devices, smart phones/watches, laptops, tablets, gaming machines, digital fitness bracelets, where they stored money or valuable items, who knew about and had access to their belongings, any missing items or safe/secret storage areas.

- Medical background details of doctor (GP), any illnesses (physical or psychological), levels of fitness and health, surgical operations or other treatments, prescribed medicines, deformities, unusual marks, scars, tattoos or piercings, dental history and details of dentist, cosmetic treatments.

- Specific queries such as, if female, whether they have ever been pregnant or had a termination), sexually transmitted diseases, etc. Note: it is important that this is recorded properly, including consideration of section 41 of the Youth Justice and Criminal Evidence Act 1999—restricting evidence or questions about their previous sexual history, subject to exceptions for rape and sexual offences.

- Digital and online profile information, social media usage, devices, storage (eg cloud computing) virtual communities and sites used/visited, identities used, and passwords.

- Financial profile, banking details, accounts, savings, valuables, investments, debts, regular payments, earnings, loans, credit/debit cards, recent transactions.

- Any details of a Will or personal insurance.

When searching premises connected to a victim (eg one that is reported missing or deceased), it may be necessary to compile a full inventory of each and every item. This will enable the list to be checked against any items later found to be missing. The SIO may want to use a Police Search Adviser (PolSA)[14] for managing the search. The search can also include looking for association through forensic trace evidence (eg on bedding), which is particularly useful if close associates and sexual partners are of interest. House-to-House (H2H) type enquiries around the premises and areas associated to a victim can also prove useful in building information about them.

KEY POINTS

1. Examining a victim's bedding and mattress may reveal DNA evidence to show possible sexually partners.
2. H2H enquiries can be utilised to assist in gathering information about victims as to their lifestyle, movements, visitors, habits, associates, reputation, etc.

11.7 **Family Liaison**

In some cases, victim support needs to extend to immediate families. According to the VCOP (see section 11.2), close relatives of deceased victims are also entitled to receive services as victims of serious crime. Close relatives are defined as: spouse, partner, relatives in direct line, siblings, and dependants of a person

---

[14] The role of a PoLSA is described in Chapter 6.

whose death was directly caused by criminal conduct. In law enforcement terminology, support to these persons is commonly known as 'family liaison'.

Family liaison is essential when the investigation involves a homicide, suspicious death, multiple fatalities, major incident, road death, or any incident where it might enhance the law enforcement (LE) management of an enquiry or if deemed 'critical'. This can prove to be one of the most challenging and demanding areas of responsibility. The most significant relationship that an enquiry team develops and fosters is the one with families of victims (especially deceased victims) at what is one of the most difficult and distressing time of their lives. Expectations, demands, and accountability levels are understandably extremely high. In some cases, the families of victims can become quite demanding and sometimes difficult to manage, but regardless of this they still need to be offered answers as to what has occurred. These are responsibilities that must be managed conscientiously throughout the course of an investigation and, in some cases, well beyond, regardless of any judicial outcome.

The MoJ Code of Practice for Victims of Crime (2015) states:

> In addition to the entitlements outlined above (i.e. paragraph 11.2), if you are a bereaved close relative of a victim who died as a result of criminal conduct, you are *entitled* to: (i) have a Family Liaison Officer (FLO) assigned to you by the police, where the Senior Investigating Officer considers this to be appropriate. This will happen in the majority of cases; and (ii) be offered accessible advice on bereavement and information on available victims' services by the police.

11.7.1 Family liaison strategy

A family liaison strategy links into a victim management strategy and should appear near the top of an MLOE list. An effective and comprehensive strategy must be recorded as policy and include all aspects of the FLO relationship and tactical planning for maintaining close contact with the victim's family and keeping them apprised of progress and developments. An overarching objective should be to increase benefits to the investigation by servicing the needs of the family with information and support.

A core component of the strategy is to keep the family continuously updated whenever and wherever possible. Victims' families need accurate and regular information on progress of the investigation, plus answers to any queries they may raise. A likelihood is that these will be similar to the type of 5WH questions the enquiry team are working on (eg what happened? Why did it happen? Who did it? How did they do it? Why our relative? etc).

Families are heavily reliant on the investigation team for accurate information, otherwise they may have to depend on rumour, gossip, news reporting, and social media. Public conjecture and supposition are helpful to neither them nor the investigation, but inaccuracies can be corrected provided they are spotted swiftly. Mutually interdependent lines of communication must exist so the family can report what information they are receiving.

Checklist—Family liaison strategy

- Analyse needs, concerns, and expectations of the victim's family to identify relevant and realistic actions in the context of their human rights.

- Gather material from them in a manner that contributes to the investigation and preserves its integrity (eg victimology).

- Two-way information flow will assist both the needs of the family and those of the investigation.

- Adopt and apply the principles of the Victims Code, including facilitation of care and support for the family (themselves secondary victims).

- Secure and maintain trust and confidence thereby increasing the likelihood of a more positive contribution to the investigation.[15]

11.7.2 Family identification and notification

Identification of a victim's family is to be considered in the broadest sense. It generally includes partners, parents, guardians, children, siblings, members of the extended family, and any others who may have had a direct and close relationship with the victim. This can, however, become complicated by split marriages, ex-partners, and children dispersed across geographic locations, or when a victim is associated with particular cultural or lifestyle diversity.

Under the Code of Practice for Victims of Crime, families are entitled to nominate a spokesperson to be a single point of contact to receive information. However, if the family cannot choose a family spokesperson, the SIO must choose one, which can be a difficult task. If there are divided families, more than one set of FLOs may need to be appointed in order for the obligations under the Code to be satisfied.

11.7.3 Death notification

In a death investigation, every reasonable effort has to be made to locate and notify the deceased's NOK as quickly as possible. Any attempted, failed, delayed, or unsuccessful attempts need to be recorded with reasons. Particulars regarding completion of the task should also be recorded, in particular the time, date,

---

[15] These points are also cited in ACPO, *Family Liaison Officer Guidance* (NPIA, 2008), 5–6.

place, and method employed. This is to prevent any accusations of either no or late notification at a later stage.

The task of notifying NOK or close family relative about a death can be quite a difficult and traumatic task to have to perform. If the death is being treated as suspicious, it is even more challenging than if the death was not and is a task usually best left to the police or investigating agency. This is a fast-track action to eliminate undue delay and prevent the NOK[16] finding out via their own means (eg rumour, gossip, news bulletins, or through the rapid spread of information via digital media and social networking systems).

Other pressing matters might seek to occupy the SIO's attention, such as scene management, witness interviews, or arresting suspects, but notification of the death *must* remain one of the most important. Even if the media withhold details or have some uncertainty about a deceased's identity, there are many ways a dead victim's relatives can find these details out for themselves before the investigation team get chance to inform them. By making their own enquiries, the NOK may begin contacting emergency services or attend at scene cordons, hospitals, or enquiry desks seeking information. If so, they need to be managed tactfully, respectfully, and quickly.

Variables such as timing (the 'when' 5WH question) as well as confirmation of the victim's details and the NOK and their geographic position, state of health, and determining who to inform and order of priority all place specific demands on the notification planning. SIOs need to determine how these problems are to be overcome. Also, consideration needs to be made regarding the selection of those who are to deliver the message.

Generally, where there is a spouse, they or if a child, their parent should be notified first and their wishes regarding other notifications respected. This can get complicated in fragmented families and relatives, so any choice of one over another may need to be justified and explainable. A consanguinity[17] chain may assist in determining who should be notified and in what order of priority.

The way this task is performed will almost certainly influence any future relationship between the enquiry team and the family/relatives of a victim. When, where, and how the message is delivered, what is said, to whom, and by whom are key factors. After all this is a moment in their lives they will never forget.

Attempts should be made to establish if there are likely to be any specific requirements such as interpreters for non-native English speakers or allowances for disability. Those who deliver the message must be well prepared and able to cope with the subsequent response, which may range from raw emotion, anger, disbelief, and shock to an outpouring of grief.

---

[16] 'Next of kin' refers to the person or person's most closely related to an individual by blood, marriage, or legal ruling.

[17] Consanguinity refers to blood relations and being from the same kinship as another person or descended from the same ancestry.

The manner in which the message is delivered clearly needs to be done tactfully. For instance, having a liveried police vehicle pull up outside a relative's address may not be appreciated and privacy should always be respected. If, however, using 'plain-clothes' officers to deliver the message, they need to identify themselves convincingly.

The wording and manner of the notification is what really matters. There is little point in being vague or trying to make the news sound any less devastating than it actually is. Saying a person 'is no longer with us', or 'has passed away', or using religious terminology is generally best avoided. The deceased person's NOK need to hear exactly what has happened so they are in no doubt of what has occurred, eg *'I am very sorry to have to inform you that (name) is dead/or has been killed'*. Simple language and straightforward terms are what work best to ensure there is an avoidance of doubt.

Before delivering the message, the family should be seated (to prevent accidents) and clarification sought as to where the officers should sit (so they don't choose the wrong place, ie the victim's regular chair). They should be asked how they wish the deceased to be referred to and, when leaving, the delivering officers should impress on them to have confidence in the investigation. Before leaving, the family should be informed of exactly what happens next, why, and when, and who their liaison officers are and how to contact them.

KEY POINTS

1. Many families claim being informed about the death of their loved ones is the most traumatic event of their lives, and those who deliver the message say it is one of the most daunting tasks to perform. Careful thought and planning need to go into managing the process—it is a moment that will never be forgotten.
2. Agreeing and recording details of how the death message is/was relayed is an important task. An appointed FLO must be certain about exactly what message is/was delivered, how, to whom, when, etc.

11.7.4 Family Liaison Officers (FLOs)

The appointment and role of the FLOs are recorded by the SIO and form part of the family liaison strategy. Their role is not to comfort or counsel relatives but to assist and support them wherever possible, and, most importantly, assist the investigation. The family's main requirement is usually for the investigation team to resolve the case quickly and arrest any offenders, news of which tends to give the most comfort of all. What is important, also, is that the primary role of a FLO is that of an investigator.

FLOs should maintain a comprehensive log of all their dealings and involvement with the family and meetings and instructions from the SIO. Some police forces and agencies have log books designed specifically for this purpose with carbonated tear-out sheets; some also use digital versions. However, the log books are developed and used, it is important they are frequently updated and submitted so the incident room and the SIO can have early sight of the contents.

FLO logs must be kept relevant and focused, checked, and properly scrutinised. There is usually a space for a supervisor's signature on the log and the SIO should nominate a person to maintain close supervision of the content. This is usually the responsibility of an appointed Family Liaison Coordinator/Advisor (FLC/FLA), if appointed. FLO logs may become disclosable to agencies such as the Independent Office for Police Conduct (IOPC) and/or subsequently the family, who may put their own interpretation on the meaning of any entries made. For this reason, the logs are not the place to record opinions about personalities and individuals.

An important part of the FLO role is a requirement to obtain details for an ongoing family/police *relationship assessment*. The FLO should continuously update the SIO so that a critical assessment of the relationship can be monitored throughout the investigation to check there are no emerging or anticipated problems. The FLO should also comprehensively record any complaints or concerns the family may have and bring them to the attention of the SIO at the earliest opportunity.

The FLO should, in consultation with the SIO, FLC, and interview advisor, discuss any special measure applications needed to be applied for should any of the family members be identified as vulnerable, intimidated, or key/significant witnesses. This is to comply with the obligations set out in the Victims Code.

A further important role of the FLO is to obtain a VPS from an appropriate family member. This is seen as a significant opportunity for them to outline to a court the true effect that a loss of life has had on their lives. This document is normally placed before the trial judge prior to sentencing of an offender and either read out in court or referred to when passing sentence.

The amount of detail provided to a family must be determined on a case-by-case basis, although a summary or overview of the evidence is normally sufficient. However, care must be given when a close family member is also a significant witness in the case, which may restrict discussion and contact with that individual.

A pre-trial meeting with the family is normally held with the FLO and maybe even the SIO present to discuss the court process and the presentation of evidence at any forthcoming trial. It is important that the family do not discover a significant or distressing piece of evidence for the first time during the trial itself. Care must be given to avoid discussing evidence with a family member who is also a significant witness in the case. Meetings with the family normally continue throughout the trial process and at its conclusion, usually with the SIO, Crown Prosecution Service (CPS), and Crown Counsel when issues and procedures can be discussed and explained in more detail (these are obligations set out within the Victims Code).

It must be remembered that the role of an FLO is not an easy one. They will be meeting regularly with traumatised and often very emotional people who will listen intently to everything they are told. The SIO must recognise the importance of the role and hold periodic meetings with their FLOs and FLC, in person, to maintain a direct communications link and monitor their welfare. This is in addition to their regular contact with an appointed FLC (if applicable).

Checklist—Role of the FLO

- Act as conduit between the SIO, enquiry team, and victim's close family.

- Ensure families are included as partners in the investigation and provided with as much timely information as possible.

- Ensure families are treated appropriately, professionally, with respect, and in accordance with the Victims Code.

- Obtain detailed and accurate information about the victim (victimology).

- Keep the family updated on progress and any significant developments or events (eg arrests, searches, finds, provided SIO has agreed to disclosure).

- Provide reassurance the investigation is being conducted diligently and expeditiously.

- Facilitate practical support as and when required.

- Feed back any concerns the families have for their own personal safety and welfare.

- Arrange and escort them for formal identification of a body.

- Convey any requests for organ donation to the SIO.

- Ensure they are aware of any material taken from the body that has been preserved for further examination.

- Gather antecedent information and identification evidence (FLOs don't usually interview family members as key witnesses/TIEs (unless in exceptional circumstances).

- Record information and intelligence provided and submit to the incident room.

- Offer victim/family information and advice regarding supporting agencies and facilitate access to medical services for severe trauma cases.

- Closely monitor and apprise SIO on relationship between family and investigation.

- Deal with requests or complaints, eg visiting the crime scene.

- Liaise with coroner and assist in the arrangements for release of the body.

- Consider funeral arrangements and refer to SIO for arranging attendance, eg SIO/DSIO, plus delivery of flowers (if appropriate) and a suitable message of condolence.

- Liaise regarding any known media issues and try to protect them from unwarranted intrusion.

- Notify them of any intended media releases in advance of being released.

- Assist in liaison with any statutory body involved in investigating the circumstances of the death, eg IOPC, Serious Case Review, or Domestic Homicide Review.

- Implement agreed exit strategy (which normally includes a handover meeting with a victim support agency) in line with the SIO's policy.

- Maintain or resume contact with the family prior to and throughout the criminal justice process including any appeal processes, judicial review, coroner's inquest, or reopening of the investigation.

- Act as a conduit between the SIO and CPS to ensure the family are made aware of any changes or reduction in charges made.

- Where appropriate, obtain a VPS.

- Update the SIO and FLC re any matters that would impact on their role and duties.

11.7.5 **FLO appointment**

In selecting and appointing an FLO, a number of factors need consideration:

- Role is as an investigator so ideally, they should be PIP level 2 trained and accredited.
- Needs of the family should be considered wherever possible, eg use of officers who reflect the culture, lifestyle, religion, or gender of the victim (as far as is practicable), or, for example, appropriate staff when dealing with a child murder, a non-English-speaking family, a gay/lesbian/transgender victim, etc (although beware of any temptation to match culture and lifestyle at the expense of training and skills—competence comes first as the FLO can be supported by cultural specialists etc if necessary).
- FLOs are usually deployed in pairs, with one taking the lead role. It is not always essential that both should be present on each and every visit, unless corroboration is required or a risk assessment requires it.
- Scale and nature of the incident—there may be a need for multiple FLOs because of multiple victims and the level of media/political attention (and resilience to cover leave commitments, etc.
- Training, previous experience, and frequency of recent deployments.
- Current workload, commitments, and availability (especially if not full-time FLOs).
- If the FLO themselves have suffered any recent bereavement or trauma.
- If there is a 'suspect' in the family, what additional risks this poses.

- If they have previously arrested family members or have had previous contact and links with them, or reside or work nearby.

11.7.6 **FLO deployment**

FLOs are deployed at the earliest opportunity after a risk assessment. If a fully trained FLO is not immediately available, then experienced officers may be temporarily allocated the responsibility to liaise with the victim's family to commence an initial line of communication and support (as a Golden Hour task) until such time trained FLOs can be deployed. Those nominated to undertake this important task should treat this as their primary role and not become involved in other investigative tasks nor finish duty without notifying a supervisor to arrange a handover.

During the Golden Hour(s) period, the victim's family are at their most vulnerable and distraught. It is a time when they will form early and lasting opinions about the investigative response and handling of the case and the very people they are putting their hope and faith in to resolve their case. Therefore, they need to be treated with the utmost sensitivity and given support *as quickly as possible*. This is also a time when their relative (husband, wife, son, daughter, etc) may be lying dead within a protected scene or area where the family cannot enter and whom they cannot (at that time) see, touch, or hold. If this is the case, the reasons for this (ie scene protection and preservation) *must* be tactfully explained to them.

If the SIO is not in a position to make early or initial contact with the family in person, eg due to competing operational demands, they should personally brief those who are to ensure they know exactly what is required, the importance of the task, and to explain reasons for SIO's non-appearance. This briefing should be recorded in a policy log.

KEY POINTS

- The victim's family needs to be notified without delay. If trained FLOs aren't immediately available, the task must be nominated to someone else under the SIO's direction (a Golden Hour task).
- The SIO should aim to make personal contact with the family as soon as possible to establish a good early relationship. If there are multiple victims, all the families need to be treated the same and similarly visited.
- If the family are not allowed to see or touch their deceased relative, ie for reasons of scene preservation, the reasons for this must be tactfully explained.

11.7.7 **FLO briefing**

Recognised good practice is for the SIO to meet and brief the FLOs prior to their deployment, discussing in detail the family liaison strategy, incorporating details of previous contact, their likely expectations, and how they will be managed.

Checklist—FLO briefing

- Current known details about the circumstances of the incident and what is already in the public domain, eg rumour, media reporting, and social networking.
- What the family already know or might know.
- What information can be given to them.
- Background details of family and victim (including cultural, lifestyle, and religious details).
- Known tensions or breakdowns in the family.
- Where the deceased lies and, if within a protected scene, why the family cannot enter and see them.
- Whether formal identification of the victim has been completed, by whom, where, how, and current location of the body, viewing procedures, and facilities.
- Investigation set-up and details of incident room, contact numbers, names of SIO/DSIO.
- Whether any arrests have been made.
- Whether a post-mortem has been completed or when one is scheduled.
- Precise details of what can be released about cause and manner of death.
- Whether the family can visit, see, or touch the body, what restrictions there are (if any), and what are likely timescales for release of the body for burial purposes.
- Whether anything known about the victim's lifestyle, drugs, convictions, etc and how any sensitive details are going to be handled (eg circumstances and nature of the victim's death and revelation of a lifestyle the family may be known).
- Role and responsibility of the coroner.
- If the deceased person was not alone when the incident occurred and/or if they were with other members of the same family, the FLO must be made aware of the location and condition of these individuals.
- Relevant fast-track tasks/actions (eg victimology, items required, etc).
- Reporting chain, and support mechanisms (eg SIO, DSIO, FLC).
- Expectations, attendance at briefings, regular contacts, submission of reports/logs.

11.7.8 **FLO welfare**

Being an FLO is an arduous and emotionally draining role. There is a statutory duty of care to ensure the safety of all officers and staff, including FLOs. The SIO should complete and record a risk assessment which includes control measures to cover risk or potential risk caused by people, action/activity, location, and environment. Like any other risk assessment, this remains under dynamic review. There is usually an approved template for this process that should be agreed and signed by the SIO/DSIO.

The SIO has an ongoing responsibility to manage the welfare of their FLOs. Regular contact and meetings should always include checks on their wellbeing and they should be encouraged to report any emerging problems immediately.

11.7.9 **Suspect/TIE subject in the family**

If there is the potential for a suspect (or, in certain circumstances, a TIE subject) to be among members of the victim's family, there will be an increased level of risk. Regardless of local policy or preference that may stipulate the required numbers of FLOs to be deployed on an investigation, if there is a suspect 'in the family' it must *never* be a single FLO deployed in these circumstances— two FLOs must be assigned, for safety reasons.

When deployed under these circumstances, care must be taken to ensure the FLOs don't stray into a role which is similar to that of a covert human intelligence source (CHIS). FLOs are always overt investigators and subject to the requirements of the Police and Criminal Evidence Act 1984 (PACE), the Criminal Procedure and Investigations Act 1996 (CPIA) (disclosure rules), the Regulation of Investigatory Powers Act 2000 (RIPA), and human rights considerations. The SIO may therefore need to plan ahead for how any intelligence and evidence gathering is going to be managed which results from the FLO's interaction with a family which contains potential suspects.

Decisions should be duly recorded regarding the deployment of FLOs in these circumstances. The level and amount of disclosure of information given to both the FLOs and the family must be controlled and reviewed to prevent undermining the prosecution case. FLOs should not be utilised for the purposes of arrest or searching. If it is necessary to apply a TIE process to a subject who is a member of the victim's family, the method of approach will need to be reflected in the FLO strategy (although the FLO should not normally partake in the TIE process).

KEY POINT

If there is a suspect in the family of the victim, two FLOs must always be deployed, for safety reasons.

11.7.10 **Media intrusion**

If journalists and news reporters are keen to report on a serious and 'newsworthy' incident, they will undoubtedly try their level best to interview and photograph family and friends of the victim. In some instances (eg high-profile cases), the media could become a major problem, with high levels of intrusion and interference, and even harassment and distress to close relatives possible (see also section 9.6.7). At other times, the family may enjoy and encourage media attention, something that also warrants close monitoring and controlling wherever possible.

The SIO, FLOs, and MLO (Media Liaison Officer) must anticipate in advance and act quickly to control any likely media intrusion to the family and relatives of the victim. The family must be given support and protection, and any statements or media appeals made by the family should be tightly controlled in order to prevent any compromise of the SIO's communication and media strategy.

The family may also approach or be approached by people who wish to act on their behalf, such as solicitors, local leaders, or community interest representatives. The SIO should be aware that sometimes well-meaning people can disrupt or affect the important communications link between the enquiry team and the victim's family. Intermediaries may also have a different agenda to the family and/or police. While the family's wishes are always of uppermost importance, the SIO may wish to outline their concerns and seek advice from local policing commanders and/or a Gold Commander or independent advisory group (IAG) wherever possible.

11.7.11 **Family interaction**

The SIO should make contact and arrange to visit a victim's family (alongside the FLOs) as soon as practicable. The importance of the personal touch cannot be overstated. It is always best practice to develop and nurture the relationship with a victim's close family to ensure their needs, hopes, and expectations are fully considered. This relationship must be dynamically maintained and reviewed throughout all stages of the investigation, covering significant events such as:

- initial response and media coverage
- media headlines on progress and details of the case (particularly if there is criticism of the investigation)
- significant overt activities such as multiple searches
- arrest of suspects
- release or charging of suspects
- release of a victim's body
- funeral arrangements

- court appearances and pre-trial issues
- criminal trial phase (conviction or acquittal and sentence tariff reviews)
- Coroner's court hearings
- post-trial issues, (renewed) media coverage, and appeals
- long-term contact arrangements
- referral to external review bodies (eg the CCRC or IOPC)
- cold case re-investigation
- similar offences that may occur, particularly in the same area/city/town

It should be stressed to the close family that the FLOs are important members of the enquiry team. If the SIO does not acknowledge this, it may be that for the rest of the enquiry the family will want to engage only with 'the boss' and unnecessarily try to commandeer the SIO's valuable time. The FLO is a vital link between the SIO and the family, and this is what they are trained for and how it should be. This does not prevent the SIO/DSIO from visiting the family regularly as and when appropriate, but the family should not directly contact the SIO. If this happens, the FLO has been bypassed, which is incorrect.

No opportunity should be wasted in cultivating and maintaining a good relationship, creating a good impression, and keeping the family involved (such as helping to distribute publicity posters) and regularly updated. One suggestion is for the FLOs to offer and arrange a guided tour of the incident room and to meet members of the enquiry team, remembering to remove things the SIO may not wish the family to see (eg details of sensitive lines of enquiry, suspects, or post-mortem photographs). Once arranged, staff should be briefed beforehand and guided on what they can and cannot say if asked.

Another option is to let the victim's family meet and have a discussion with certain members of the enquiry team or specialists. For example, if a large-scale search has been arranged, eg for missing items, the family may be allowed to meet the search teams (eg underwater search teams) to hear first-hand the efforts that were made and how the operation had been conducted.

11.7.12 Managing expectations

High hopes and expectations that offenders will be found and charged quickly are common, and care must be taken not to raise the expectations of the victim's family and relatives. This is particularly important if the case is complex or likely to be difficult to resolve quickly (ie not a self-solver).

The SIO can easily become drawn into a moral obligation to solve a case through a mixture of professional pride and emotional pleas from the victim's family. Failure to do so will naturally produce disappointment and sometimes resentment if good news is not quickly forthcoming.

While the SIO should *never* appear pessimistic or negative about the likelihood of a successful outcome (3 × Ps principle, see section 2.6), they must remain completely honest and realistic regarding any difficulties and complexities of the investigation. The fact is that some cases are hard to solve, and for one reason or another, securing that vital piece of evidence may not happen as quickly or easily as envisaged.

The SIO and CPS should ensure the family is made aware of any changes to or reduction of any charges made. This will normally be undertaken at a confidential meeting with the family, often chaired by the Crown prosecuting counsel to ensure full consultation and explanation of the rationale behind any decisions to be made. This will be particularly relevant if reducing a charge, for example from murder to manslaughter (which might be based on a statutory defence such as 'loss of control' or other defence on the grounds of 'diminished responsibility'). Clearly, any reduction in the category of offence(s) listed on the indictment will have a significant effect on any likely sentence, therefore a careful and clear explanation of the legal position and rationale should be tactfully provided.

11.7.13 Needs of family versus needs of investigation

There are occasions when information cannot be passed on to the family for fear of compromising the investigation or operation. For example, when planning to deal with suspects or staging arrests, details of which need to remain confidential to safeguard the element of surprise and maximize evidence recovery opportunities. On these occasions, it is entirely understandable and justifiable not to inform the family beforehand.

The aim should be to strike a balance between the competing needs of the investigation and those of the family. In consultation with the FLO and/or FLC, there should be a plan for briefing the family so as not to risk any potential compromise of the investigation, and a draft prepared of an explanation for use at a later stage as to why the information was withheld. If explained that withholding information was for the good of the investigation, families usually understand. As usual, the decision and procedure should be recorded in a policy log entry with accompanying reasons.

11.7.14 Subsequent post-mortems and body release

Early release of a victim's body is always of primary concern to a bereaved family, and the SIO and FLO should have this uppermost in their thoughts. An import element of any investigation is the completion of a second (or subsequent) post-mortem, which the coroner may authorise at the request of a defence legal team following a suspect being charged. In cases where no offender has been identified or charged, a further independent post-mortem may be ordered to be conducted within twenty-eight days.[18]

The SIO and FLO should actively pursue an early resolution to all post-mortem examinations and ensure that the body can be released to the family in order to allow the funeral to take place as speedily as possible. It is vital, however, that they are made aware of any material or samples taken from the body for further examination. Families should be asked if they wish to wait to receive the body complete, which could take a long time in some cases, eg if a separate detailed examination of an internal organ is required. In paediatric cases, delays may be even longer (see Chapter 15). In order to address this the FLO can obtain a written authority from the family as to their decision, ie. either to return or dispose and to include their preferred means of doing so. Close liaison with the coroner in relation to the Human Tissue Act should be maintained and any records relating to actions on behalf of the coroner submitted into the incident room for registering and retention.

11.7.15 Returning personal possessions

The return of property such as personal possessions (eg jewellery) is something that can comfort a grieving family. The SIO and CSM/forensic experts should expedite and prioritise the examination of any victim's personal possessions so they can be swiftly returned (provided they are not required as court exhibits). The reasons for any prolonged retention of personal items belonging to the victim may need to be explained to the family. It should also be considered how the family would like property to be returned, eg cleaned and properly presented. Health and safety issues need to be taken into account.

11.7.16 Family liaison exit strategy

An exit strategy is usually considered alongside an entrance strategy, ie entry level contains a list of objectives, and when these are achieved an exit is considered. Victim's families often become very attached, close to, and reliant on their designated FLOs. However, it is not in their long-term interest for recovery and moving on with their lives to maintain a permanent contact. Resource requirements, in any event, would not permit such contact to continue.

Exit tactics, nonetheless, need careful handling to avoid damaging relationships. It becomes a gradual process, planned well in advance and conducted tactfully rather than abruptly. Good use can be made of other supporting organisations after withdrawal of the FLOs. It is worth pointing out quite early on that the FLO will at some point have to return to normal duties, although in some instances it may be a long time before this actually happens.

---

[18] See Home Office Circular 30/1999 Post Mortem Examinations and Early Release of Bodies.

Where a trial is pending, the case officer who has eventual responsibility for the case file process (normally an experienced investigator) can be substituted to keep the family updated with progress and developments in the case (including any post-trial contact). However, the FLO will be required to assist the family during the trial process and be available to support them at court, for example if they wish to sit through the trial.

11.7.17 Family Liaison Coordinators and Advisers

Family Liaison Coordinators (FLC) are those who have received relevant training and are responsible for the strategic or tactical support to FLOs and SIOs. The FLC can assist in appointing FLOs and, in particular, matching the right FLO, with due regard to their skill and experience level, to the case. They can assist in providing advice around complex cases or multiple deployments and can help with drawing up a risk assessment and contacting support organisations both locally and nationally. They can be tasked with managing and briefing FLOs during times when the SIO is fully committed.

The FLC is briefed by the SIO who in turn tasks the FLOs directly on the aims and objectives set out in the agreed strategy. The management of documentation should be supervised by the FLC to ensure the timely feed into the incident room of any statements, log books, and updates to risk and relationship assessments. The FLC should monitor the performance of the FLO and report on any adverse impact on family liaison.

11.7.18 National Family Liaison Advisor

This UK NCA-enabled role is aimed at providing operational support to forces and agencies in relation to all family liaison matters. They can help in complex investigations and where there are suspects within the family or other sensitivities, and for advising on overseas-based complex family liaison cases. They can also assist in the development and delivery of family liaison strategies at both strategic and tactical level. They can be reached via the National SIO Advisor or through the Major Crime Investigative Support (MCIS) at the NCA.

11.8 Independent Advisory Groups (IAGs)

Law enforcement has acknowledged the benefit of seeking community advice and guidance on policing issues (including serious and complex crime investigations) that may cause concern to local people and communities. This can be arranged through processes that make use of IAGs (aka Independent Reference Groups (IRG)). They are widely acknowledged as an effective means of consulting and working with members of the community to solve problems and in particular deal effectively with potentially contentious issues or critical incidents that might present ethical or reputational concerns.

These were introduced following criticism outlined in the Macpherson Report[19] of 1999 into the death of Stephen Lawrence. It highlighted the need for law enforcement to engage with black and minority ethnic communities in order to provide feedback on how policing policy affects those communities. IAGs have since been regularly used across the United Kingdom in the role of a 'critical friend' to build and form an effective means of maintaining trust and confidence.

IAGs are usually made up entirely of volunteers from members of the public who come from a variety of backgrounds. They have an interest in law enforcement and policing matters and their effect on communities, and they can offer independent advice (as their title suggest). Guidance given by the group, however, is non-binding and the group does not become involved in operational decision making or respond to complaints; there are other mechanisms to meet those requirements.

IAGs can be formed to represent specific locations or themes, such as vulnerable young people, or they can be more strategic (eg the Strategic Independent Advisory Group (SIAG)), which may cover matters of strategic and force- or agency-wide significance. It is advisable to listen to the enabled insights that can be gained from these volunteers and act on the advice given (and if not, explain why not). Their use neatly links into the Code of Ethics (see section 2.9) and can assist in diffusing challenging community tensions that some investigations might generate.

The role of an IAG in a homicide investigation is contained in section 18.4 of the *Murder Investigation Manual* (MIM):[20]

> To review the investigative strategy and advise the SIO on relevant diversity issues which may impact upon, or be affected by, the crime itself and any subsequent police action. In addition to providing investigators with an understanding of community issues they may, in some instances, act as a conduit to the community to prevent rumour or misinformation from damaging the investigation and the police relationship with the community. SIOs should, however, exercise caution if attempting to use the IAG as a means of communicating with the community. IAGs act as a voice for the community and the role of community members is to represent particular social groups to the police. Attempts to reverse this role and turn IAG members into police representatives within their own community may cause significant difficulties for the individuals concerned, and impact on their willingness to participate.

---

[19] The public enquiry following the investigation into the murder of Stephen Lawrence in 1993, resulted in the Metropolitan Police Service acknowledging that some incidents, even if managed properly can have a significant negative impact on the confidence of the victim, their family, and the community. W Macpherson, *The Stephen Lawrence Inquiry* (1999). Available at: <www.assets.publishing.service.gov.uk/government/uploads/system/ ... data/ ... /4262.pdf>

[20] ACPO, *Murder Investigation Manual* (NCPE, 2006).

11.8.1 IAG objectives

Each LEA will normally have their own objectives for IAGs. Listed below is a summary of the most common:

- Assist in improving the quality of service provided to all members of the community by offering independent advice on certain aspects of investigations.
- Assist in identification of institutional discrimination with recommendations on how to tackle such issues and promote diversity and equality.
- Have a good understanding of the needs, wants, and assets of the communities they are representing.
- Inform on issues that affect local communities.
- Work towards improving and building on constructive relationships between communities and the LEA.
- Help towards increasing the public's trust and confidence.
- Advise on critical/major incidents.
- Act in accordance with the Code of Ethics.

An IAG member can be a useful asset in the progression of the investigation, but the SIO/Gold Commander must confirm their objectives. Groups must clearly understand what their role is and is not; for example, to become directly involved in the investigation or become compromised as to confidentiality, particularly if they are obtaining their own information (in which case they may stray close to CHIS status).

Advisers can provide guidance on cultural issues relating to the community concerned, advise on communication with family members and witnesses within the community, and provide strategic advice on policy, including the impact it may have on a particular group. They are not, however, investigators, mediators, advocates, or intermediaries. An adviser should not be asked to speak to witnesses or be allowed to attend a crime scene during the early stages of an investigation without the approval of the SIO. In all cases a risk assessment should be considered and recorded in order to ensure the safety and welfare of the adviser.

An IAG adviser should not:

- Visit a crime scene during the initial response stage of an investigation without the express permission of the SIO (if agreed, a risk assessment should be recorded beforehand).
- Speak directly to witnesses or attempt to persuade them to give evidence.
- Speak to the media (eg to validate any tactical methods).
- Make enquiries or investigate themselves.

See also <http://www.collge.police.uk/Independent> Advisory Groups, 'Considerations for advice for the police service on the recruitment, role and value of IAGs, 2015.

11.9 **Critical Incidents**

The term 'critical incident' (CI) is used to describe any incident where police action (or inaction) may have an impact on the confidence in the police of victims, their relatives or the wider community (see following). Like all areas of policing and law enforcement, criminal investigations must seek to secure and maintain the respect and approval of the public, which means also securing their willing cooperation.[21]

There are very few murders or serious crimes that do not fall into the category of a 'critical incident'. Early recognition and declaration as such will ensure the correct command and control procedures are activated to assist in dealing with the incident more effectively. The term 'critical' is deliberately broad and may apply to a local area and/or a whole police force, agency, or region.

Other incidents, local or national, such as the arrest of CSE offenders, high-risk missing persons, political interest, or law enforcement errors and misdemeanours may be included. It is the personal perception that matters; some seemingly minor criminal acts may assume enormous significance to members of the public. Traumatic events and high-profile events can affect entire communities (such as the mass fatal shootings carried out by Derek Bird in Cumbria in 2010, and the abduction and murder of five-year-old April Jones in Machynlleth, Wales in 2012), producing feelings of insecurity and vulnerability.

Critical incidents are often the consequence of serious or major incidents. The event itself is dealt with operationally, using the policy, procedures, and tactics laid down for each type of incident. A critical incident response incorporates this, but also enables an SIO and their agency to deal with all the other aspects of the incident and the context in which it occurs.

The decision to declare a critical incident can take place at any time during the various phases of an investigation. This identification may occur as early as the first contact received by a call taker. It may also be applicable and appropriate when the incident is being attended either by the initial officer or later by an SIO. It is a means of focusing on all the 'critical' aspects of an incident and consequent decision making, eg how family liaison support or community impact are to be addressed and managed effectively (Figure 11.1).

Definition of 'Critical Incident'

'Any incident where the effectiveness of the police response is likely to have a significant impact on the confidence of the victim, their family, and/or the community.'

(<http://www.app.college.police.uk/Critical Incident Management>)

---

[21] See C Reith, The nine principles of policing. In *A Short History of the British Police* (London, OUP, 1948)

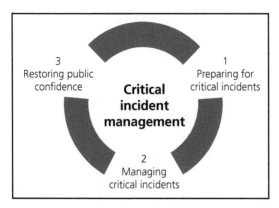

Figure 11.1 Three phases of Critical Incident Management

Deeming an incident 'critical' requires the application of professional judgement. If it is decided the status applies, then the circumstances are given special priority and consideration as to how they are managed and controlled. Basically, any incident, pre-planned or spontaneous, can become a CI and early recognition through community intelligence, environmental scanning, internal communication processes, monitoring of media outlets, and situational awareness will assist in making an assessment of public reaction. Each incident is assessed on its own merits and when such a declaration is made, the response plan needs to identify the cause and strategy swiftly in order to rebuild public confidence.

It may be that as an investigation develops and more information becomes available, the decision to deem an incident 'critical' will need to be reviewed and monitored continually. An example is when community confidence in the police response or the incident itself drops and becomes critical as the investigation develops. As a general rule, certain circumstances can become a critical incident at any time, ie the present, the future, or even the past.

Of crucial significance to the SIO is that a central theme in preventing or managing a CI is effective decision making in difficult situations (see NDM explained in Chapter 3). This includes acknowledging decisions that might include key decisions that require careful planning for events that may develop into a CI. For example, if there is a history of tension between the police and local community with tensions running high, the potential for any activity such as searches and arrests may have a significant impact on public confidence if not planned and managed effectively. This is when good use of 'situational awareness' (see section 3.2.5) becomes vital in decision making.

11.9.1 PIP Level 4 Advisers

A Gold Commander who has overall responsibility for managing the response to a CI may wish to utilise a PIP4 accredited investigator (see section 1.5) to provide support for the strategic and tactical management of the investigation. This offers the opportunity to have a suitably qualified and experienced individual take responsibility for the strategic decision-making element of an investigation while providing advice and investigative support to both the SIO and Gold Commander.

They provide a much-needed middle tier of management and expertise that fits in between the SIO, chief officers, and senior commanders, taking pressure off the SIO who is then able to get on with the tactical elements of the investigation. Policy logs and good record keeping are vital elements for both the PIP4 and SIO, including the Gold Commander, in a CI-type situation.

11.9.2 Community Impact Assessments

In most cases of homicide and other serious crime cases, or where an incident has been deemed 'critical', a Community Impact Assessment (CIA) should be drafted. They are applicable to any pre-planned as well as spontaneous or unexpected activities and events that may also be identified as potential critical incidents, eg arrests being made in high-tension or sensitive areas, or in consideration of 'not guilty' court case verdicts. Local situational awareness allows any feelings of tension and vulnerability to be gauged as well as economic, political, and social factors that can impact on communities.

A CIA is a means of applying an important element of 'consequence management' on community relations. The purpose of the CIA is to cater for and manage the impact, particularly on those of a minority or vulnerable make-up. The impact of an incident or investigation is dependent on a range of factors including the interrelationships that may exist between areas that make up a community, thus creating a range of potential hot spots in which impacts and tensions may develop and emerge. Some particular incidents can and do lead to high levels of fear and tension and, in some cases, a backlash and victimisation of those perceived to be connected.

Checklist—CIA considerations

- Identification and assessment done in collaboration between stakeholders/agencies.

- Risks to vulnerable individuals and groups need assessment and management (using threat × harm = risk principle, see section 3.6).

- Primary responsibility is that of the local policing Commander.

- A CIA must be considered early, particularly with certain communities (an 'initial assessment' being made usually within four hours of discovery).

- Assessment of community confidence needs covering.

- Concerns of a victim's family need to be adequately and sensitively addressed, as they may represent a valuable mediating influence within the community.

- It is crucial that the impact assessment is based on evidence and intelligence, is objective, and capable of withstanding scrutiny.

- Community intelligence needs developing to feed into the preceding point.

- Consideration of forming IAG to assist.

The CIA should remain a standing item on the SIO's management team agenda.

The assessment is informed through effective community engagement and consultation with IAGs and community representatives, partner agencies, and local policing teams. The completion of a CIA is a strategic means of considering the extent of any adverse effects on communities and recording what actions are taken (if any) to reduce and manage or control the impact from a policing and partnership perspective, thereby maintaining public trust and confidence.

It is very important to work alongside the local policing commander, who has a wider responsibility for engaging with the community. The local commander will not want to damage working relationships or partnerships that will have been carefully nurtured. Unfortunately, critical incidents arising from some types of high-profile investigations have the potential to upset the equilibrium and disrupt everyday business. In many scenarios, the response phase to a major or critical incident can be relatively short in comparison with the recovery phase, which in some cases can take weeks, months, or even years.

11.9.3 **Community impact statements**

A community impact statement[22] is a short document illustrating the concerns and priorities of a specific community over a set time. The statements (under section 9 of the Criminal Justice Act 1967) can be taken by the investigation team and be either:

1. Generic: information relating to a range of offences or anti-social behaviour (ASB) identified by the community as being of local concern, including details of harm and impact that these maters have had on them. Once obtained, the statement can be used for a range of similar offences.
2. Specific: information relating to a specific offence or incident which has been identified by the community as being of local concern. The statement can illustrate the impact and harm on the community arising from the specific offence.

---

[22] See <http://www.cps.gov.uk/legal-guidance/community impact statements.

The purpose of the evidence is to provide relevant and useful additional information about the impact that crime or a particular incident has had/is having on a particular community. It is intended to influence charging and prosecution decisions, sentencing, and restorative justice and reparation interventions. A community impact statement can be used alongside an existing VPS.

Bibliography

ACPO, *Family Liaison Strategy Manual* (NPIA, 2003) as amended by ACPO, *Family Liaison Officer Guidance* (NPIA, 2008)

ACPO, *Murder Investigation Manual* (NCPE, 2006)

ACPO, *Practical Advice on Critical Incident Management* (NPIA, 2007)

Beckley, R (2018) Review into the Terminology 'Victim/Complainant' and Believing Victims at time of Reporting, CoP, Ryton. (<www.app.college.police.uk/app-content/critical-incident-management>)

College of Policing 'Op.Hydrant SIO Advice', November 2016

<http://www.college.police.uk/Independent Advisory Groups>, 'Considerations for advice for the police service on the recruitment, role and value of IAGs', 2015

<http://www.app.college.police.uk/Critical Incident Management>

Hamilton, H and Sylvester, R in *The Times* (Monday 2 April 2018), 'Police ditch practice of believing all victims: Britain's biggest police force has abandoned its policy of automatically believing victims after a series of flawed inquiries into alleged sex crimes' <http://www.cps.gov.uk/legal-guidance/community-impact-statements>

Ministry of Justice, *Code of Practice for Victims of Crime: Presented to Parliament pursuant to section 33 of the Domestic Violence, Crime and Victims Act 2004* (HM Stationery Office, 2015; available at: <http://www.gov.uk/moj>)

Macpherson, W (1999) The Stephen Lawrence Inquiry. (see <www.assets.publishing.service.gov.uk/government/uploads/system/ ... data/ ... /4262.pdf>

Ministry of Justice, 'Getting it Right for Victims and witnesses' Consultation paper CP3/2012 (HM Stationery Office, 2012)

Reith, C, 'The nine principles of policing'. In Oliver and Boyd (eds), *A Short History of the British Police* (London: OUP, 1948)

Suspect Management

12.1 **Introduction**

One of the five building blocks (see section 5.4) for investigations is the identification of those suspected to be responsible for committing the crime. This incorporates a number of interconnected processes such as identifying and designating suspects, planning arrests, gathering investigative material, securing evidence, managing custody and detention procedures, conducting interviews, bringing charges, and building a case file. These are processes that require careful operational planning, with consideration of:

- Methods of identifying suspects.
- For what, when, why, where, how, and who is to be arrested (see also section 12.7.2).
- Legal powers and organisational policies.
- Maximising physical, digital, and forensic search and evidence recovery.
- Managing detention arrangements and custody time limits.
- Planning, preparing, and conducting investigative interviews.
- Reviewing investigative material that has been obtained.
- Charging and processing procedures.
- Determining what evidence is relevant for disclosure in a prosecution case.

The focus of this chapter is to cover significant tactical elements of suspect management. It begins with the identification and arrest of suspects. There is an examination of the issues surrounding a decision to declare 'suspect' status, the making and timing of arrests, detention and interviews, and recovering forensic evidence from suspects, charging, and bail, including some practical points on ways to conduct effective, proactive suspect hunts. Some useful case examples are also cited within the footnotes.

12.2 **Suspect Identification**

Suspects can be identified through a variety of methods such as witness interviews, forensic evidence, passive data collection (eg CCTV), admissions, information and intelligence, analytical work, proactive overt or covert work, financial investigation (eg following the money), or just simple, prompt actions taken at or near a crime scene. Any one or more of the main lines of enquiry (MLOE) or investigative strategies and tactics may point to the identity of a suspect(s).

The SIO may wish to produce a policy that outlines various methods in which suspects (if not already known) can be identified. Some of these may appear similar, if not identical, to those discussed in Chapter 13 for identifying witnesses.

Checklist—Suspect identification examples

- Initial response—prompt and decisive action.

- Physical searching around the scene(s) locality and road checks.

- Witness and covert human intelligence source (informant).

  (CHIS) information.

- Matching descriptions through identification.

- Victimology enquiries.

- Conducting TI/TIE enquiries.

- House-to-house (H2H) enquiries.

- Forensic searches and examinations/results.[1]

- Other types of physical searching and digital examinations.

- Passive data analysis.

- Communications and social media analysis.

- Information and intelligence.

- Checking custody, prison release, stop/search, and medical data.

- Financial investigation.

- Proactive overt and covert tactics.

- Offenders 'in the system' (see section 12.3).

- Offering rewards (see section 13.3).

- Checking local hospitals in case an offender has sought medical treatment, particularly if sharp weapons, fire, or explosives are involved (eg wounds, scorch or burn marks to skin, eyebrows, etc).

- Checking if offenders may have committed suicides or attempted to do so post offence (being aware they may have chosen obscure/distant locations).

KEY POINTS

- Some offenders revisit the site of their victim's attack or body concealment/deposition, or attend their funeral or burial (eg out of curiosity, guilt, or morbidity).

---

[1] Never assume a person with previous offending has had their DNA or fingerprints taken and entered onto a UK database as they may be registered in another country.

Tactics can be devised to capture these moments for the benefit of the investigation.[2]

- 'Lone wolf-' (lone actor-) type offenders have their own personal motives, and although rare, tend to be well organised and not easily identifiable through conventional means.[3]

12.3 Suspects 'In the System'

There are a number of cases (some high-profile historical ones) in which details have been known and loaded to a case management system but where the offender has not been recognised.[4] Linkage has not been made or the importance and significance of the information has simply gone unnoticed, which can and sometimes does occur. Human error, shoddy work, information overload, lack of resources, or just plain incompetence can lead to a vital piece of information not being identified nor properly investigated.

The longer a case continues, and the more information is accumulated, the greater chance that an offender's details and evidential links exist within an enquiry system. Having to manage large amounts of information increases the chances of an important piece of detail being overlooked or incorrectly assessed.

There are various ways in which this can occur. For example, elimination criteria could wrongly exclude someone if the description used to eliminate against is too prescriptive (eg an offender is described as between 5'8" to 5'10" and a TIE subject who is 6'0" is wrongly eliminated). An important clue or piece of vital information can be missed because enquiries have not been followed up properly, eg the sighting of a suspicious vehicle has not been investigated, enquiries to check an alibi have not been done, or the tracing of and speaking to a certain individual who is deliberately being evasive have not been completed, etc. It may just be that a piece of information has not been linked to the case or given the right priority, which is why it is important to (re)check detail meticulously.

---

[2] Colin Ash-Smith stabbed to death Claire Tiltman in January 1993 and attended her funeral a month later. He was convicted in 2014 after a change in the law allowed the use of evidence of bad character. He had gone on a spree of attacks against women across Kent during midnight walks armed with knives hunting for victims, and bragged about his attacks in his diaries.

[3] Ukrainian-born student Pavlo Lapshyn murdered seventy-five-year-old Mohammed Saleem in April 2013, while acting alone with a motive of racial hatred. He would have been difficult to catch had he not tried to cause an explosion at a mosque soon after committing the murder.

[4] For example, the 'Yorkshire Ripper', Peter Sutcliffe, case or Operation Minstead, featuring a masked sexual predator from south London, dubbed the 'Night Stalker', aka Delroy Grant. He was convicted of a series of sex attacks and burglaries over a period of seventeen years (possibly 600 victims) and was arrested in 2009. He could have been caught ten years earlier as there was information about his car being sighted near one of his crime scenes in 1999, but this wasn't investigated properly. Grant went on to commit many more offences.

Long-running, complex (unsolved) enquiries are particularly susceptible to this problem. The way to avoid it happening is by applying rigorous management and review processes and by paying critical attention to detail. Thorough checking, re-examining and scrutinising all data that has been collated with careful assessment of the resulting actions and results submitted by enquiry teams is required at all times, particularly if there has been changes in staff or a dip in morale. High standards of professionalism and thoroughness must be insisted upon by the SIO and their management team to reduce any possibility of mistakes. Checking, closely supervising and quality-assuring all information, messages, reports, action results, priorities, and relevance and elimination decisions is to comply with the ABC principle (Assume nothing, Believe nothing, Challenge/check everything). Sloppiness *must* be avoided at all costs.

KEY POINT

The importance of incident room staff being able to work effectively, focus, concentrate, and forensically study each and every minute detail and item that comes into the enquiry cannot be overstated. Distractions such as noise, disruptions, excessive visitors, inadequate premises and equipment, and a poor working environment need to be identified and managed properly to avoid mistakes.

12.4 Designating 'Suspect' Status

Using the correct terminology is vitally important to investigations (also mentioned in section 11.2). There are various terms that mean entirely different things in the eyes of the law, the media, and the public. The term 'suspect', for example, is precisely what the name suggests and is used for labelling those who are *suspected* of committing a crime. They are individuals who are under consideration of formal criminal proceedings.[5] This does not mean they are guilty because everyone is considered innocent until proven guilty, including suspects. Completely different terminology is used for those who have actually committed the crime (and been found guilty); they are known as offenders or perpetrators. The difference between suspect and perpetrator recognises that a suspect is not *known* to have committed the offence whereas the perpetrator is one who is known to have done so (ie by admission of guilt or found guilty in a court of law).

Usually the term 'suspect' is only applied when there are reasonable grounds to suspect (not believe) a person's involvement in an offence. Those who are granted this special status will not yet have been formally charged. Once they

---

[5] See The Code for Prosecutors, 8th edn October 2018; available at: <http://www.cps.gov.uk/TheCodeForCrown Prosecutors>.

are they will become an accused person and a *defendant,* meaning they have been charged (or summonsed) and will face criminal prosecution. These terms need to be managed and used carefully as they impact significantly on a person's status (internally and externally). The media are obliged to observe a person's privacy by not naming (see section 9.6) them when they are merely a 'suspect' (although they sometimes do), but once they are charged and formally appear in court they are entitled to do so (as it is then in the public domain).

Designating someone as a 'suspect' in an investigation is a defining moment. It amounts to a formal declaration the enquiry team is focusing on a particular individual (or individuals). Such a decision is only made when there is sufficient justification and sound rationale backed by supporting investigative material (see section 12.11.3). The decision needs to be recorded in a policy log.

Becoming a designated 'suspect' affords a person certain legal protection and privileges (ie under the Police and Criminal Evidence Act 1984 (PACE)), such as the right to legal advice and being administered a caution before questioning. This means it is important to declare suspect status when there are sufficient grounds for doing so and sometimes for not doing so to avoid possible accusations of circumventing a person's legal rights.

Suspect status is usually declared when there is:

- tangible evidence or investigative material to link a person to an offence, eg physical/forensic evidence, eyewitness testimony, CCTV.
- circumstantial evidence of sufficient strength to provide reasonable grounds for suspicion based on known facts or information.
- strong intelligence supported by properly graded and evaluated material (ie using the $3 \times 5 \times 2$ rating system).

If too many suspects are declared, arrested, and eliminated, it may give the impression that investigators have little or no idea of who is actually thought to be responsible (aka a 'fishing expedition'). This can also produce contradictory or undermining evidence when the real offender(s) is/are eventually arrested, charged, and face prosecution. Formal declaration of a suspect is invariably seized on by the media and local community because it is seen as a highly significant development. Hopes and expectations rise at the prospect of a successful outcome, and if too many people are being brought in as suspects and released without charge, this can be viewed quite negatively.

When the time is right and there are grounds for doing so, the SIO should be bold enough to make a decision and declare a person a suspect. In a long-running enquiry, this will lift the morale of victims, their family, the local community, senior officers/politicians, and, most importantly, the enquiry team.

When making decisions about declaring suspect status, it is important to be consistent. This means the same criteria and standard must be applied to all potential suspects to show there has been consistency in approach to the decision making.

KEY POINTS

1. Correct terminology is important. Suspects are not to be confused with offenders or perpetrators, nor the term 'subject'. Misinterpretations should be quickly corrected.
2. A person is only a suspect until they are formally charged with a criminal offence, at which point they become an 'accused' or 'defendant'.
3. Being a suspect protects a person's legal rights; not granting the status may lead to accusations of circumventing legal protective processes.

12.5 Suspect Background Enquiries

The word 'suspectology' has crept in to compete with its partner term, 'victim-ology'. The study of suspects is nothing new, as research into a person's background, history, and behaviour has always been a fruitful tactic. It can assist, for example, when considering a motive and answering the 'why' question. The background of a suspect helps establish why a person might have targeted a victim, eg if they held a grudge against that person. Why a particular location was chosen might also link in with where a suspect lived or can be linked to at some stage in their lives.

A study of patterns of behaviour can give indications of key changes in a person's mood or habits and routines, which may be a link to their criminal offending. For example, a person who regularly calls or texts their partner and, following their disappearance, doesn't attempt to make any contact at all, or if a suspect disappears after an incident or changes their routine, eg in order to avoid attention. For this reason, an intelligence requirement is to establish who is not where or doing what they should be post offence.

12.6 Legal Considerations

Amendments to PACE made by the Serious Organised Crime and Police Act 2005 (SOCPA) mean arrests can be made for any offence provided certain conditions apply. For an arrest to be lawful, the arresting officer must have:

1. Reasonable grounds to *suspect* an offence has been committed, and the person committed it, or they were in the act of committing, or were about to commit the offence; *and*
2. Reasonable grounds to *believe* ('believe' demands a higher standard than 'suspect') arrest is necessary for one or more of the specified reasons (known as the 'necessity test') to:
   (a) ascertain the person's name;
   (b) ascertain the person's address;

(c) prevent the person causing physical harm to themselves or suffering physical injury;

(d) prevent loss of or damage to property;

(e) prevent an offence against public decency;

(f) prevent an unlawful obstruction of the highway;

(g) protect a child or vulnerable person;

(h) prevent any prosecution being hindered by the disappearance of the person in question;

(i) allow a prompt and effective investigation of the offence or of the conduct of the person in question.

The prompt and effective investigation condition may be satisfied if there are reasonable grounds to *believe* that the person:

- made false statements or statements that cannot be easily verified;
- may steal or destroy evidence;
- may intimidate, threaten, or make contact with witnesses; or
- needs to be interviewed to obtain evidence.

Where the suspected offence is indictable, this condition may justify arrest if there is a need to:

- enter and search premises occupied or controlled by the person;
- search the person;
- prevent contact with others or take fingerprints, footwear impressions, samples, or photographs for comparison purposes.

12.6.1 Code 'G' of PACE

PACE (Code G) requires more detailed consideration of the necessity test. Arresting officers must consider facts and information tending to indicate the person's innocence as well as their guilt (including whether any use of force was lawful and reasonable), and any practical alternatives to arrest, such as street bail or conducting a voluntary interview. Each case is decided on its own merits according to the circumstances existing at the time, using professional judgement and discretion concerning the necessity and proportionality of arrest. The importance of recording decision making for future scrutiny cannot be overstated.

Necessity to arrest and necessity to interview are two separate things. If an arrest is not considered necessary, suspects can still be interviewed voluntarily (ie not in custody) under caution. Code G clarifies the situation in circumstances where a 'volunteer' leaves the interview before its conclusion, having been told (under Code C) they are not under arrest and are free to leave at any time. Leaving the interview, however, could justify arrest (under Code G) if there is a necessity to continue questioning, but this has to be judged on the circumstances existing at the time.

Voluntary interviews can be planned and conducted as thoroughly as for any other interview of a person in custody (under arrest). Attendees should not be treated with any less consideration than an arrested person. It is the interviewer's responsibility to ensure any vulnerability is identified and appropriate safeguards put in place, including any requirement for an appropriate adult, interpreter, etc. Voluntary attendees also have an absolute right to outside communication and legal advice.

12.7 **Planning and Preparation**

Arrest activity is sometimes referred to as 'executive action' and may require a specific operation of its own, depending on size and scale. If practicable, it is preferable to prepare and produce an operational plan beforehand. A research (profile) package is also useful containing all the suspectology-type details (see section 12.5). In addition to the usual name, date of birth, description, photograph, etc this will include a detailed analysis of known associates and criminal background, modus operandi (MO), and any warning indicators. This task is often delegated to an intelligence officer/cell within the enquiry team.

Background information on suspects may show links to other premises or locations, such as where they work or frequent. These may need to be included in planning for searches or activities (overt or covert) aimed at tracing and locating them. The profile should contain information such as previous bad character, outstanding case files, previous offending, current intelligence, lifestyle, associates, and similar factual evidence. Interviewers may later wish to introduce this information during the interview process.

Making arrests for serious offences usually attracts media and public attention (although as stated in section 12.4, suspects should not be named until formally charged). This may present an opportunity to elevate the status of the investigation and re-engage with those from whom information is required. Any witnesses (or other victims) who have been previously reluctant to come forward may now do so upon news of an arrest. Planning should cater for any such investigative opportunities created.

12.7.1 **Duty of Care**

Article 2 of the Human Rights Act 1998 (HRA) states everyone's right to life is enshrined in law. This includes suspects, and means investigators have a duty of care to those who come under suspicion for criminal offences (who could conceivably be innocent). Sometimes it may be necessary or even essential to conduct a risk assessment prior to, during, and after activities such as an arrest in order to meet a duty of care to suspects.

Some suspects may have problems occurring in their personal lives, such as a mental health, debt, or domestic concerns. They may even be a person who is in the public spotlight and becomes prematurely named by the media (aka person of public prominence (PPP)) when they fall under suspicion. Certain types of offences and their gravity, or the nature of the person's status may render them particularly susceptible and vulnerable. Any accusations of serious sexual offences, eg rape or child abuse (non-recent or otherwise), or sexual exploitation/possession of indecent images of children (IIOC) may raise the level of risk. Allegations of these types of crimes can leave some individuals feeling isolated or desperate. This may be caused by adverse media publicity, strong feelings of guilt, shame, reputational damage or negative reactions from their close families, relatives, colleagues, friends, and communities.

A duty of care extends to all suspects and includes a responsibility for managing potential risks of suicide or self-harming following Law Enforcement Agency (LEA) intervention. In some cases, this may have to extend to collateral effects on those closely related to them (eg their spouse/partner or close family). It has been proven that there is a link between suicides and spells in custody or immediately following law enforcement contact.[6]

Potential risks can be identified from intelligence profiles to identify and introduce appropriate control measures. This *must* include relevant information about a person's medical history (physical and mental) or if they have previously self-harmed/attempted suicide. It should also include details about their immediate family and close relatives who may, as described earlier, be equally vulnerable. If the offence is one that may create a suicide risk due to the individual's occupation (eg if they are in a position of trust (PoT)), this should be included in the research. This information is required not only to manage the physical arrest phase but also their safe detention during time in custody and after release.

There are agencies that can assist if risks are identified. If, for example, there is a suicide risk, then a healthcare professional is often better qualified to make an assessment (eg community psychiatric nurse or from an NHS Liaison and Diversion Unit) than, say, a police officer. An individual's own family and doctor are also good sources of information and for providing support. Organisations such as the Lucy Faithful Foundation (LFF)[7] can offer good independent help and advice.[8]

---

[6] See R Teers, 'Deaths during or following police contact: statistics for England and Wales 2013/14', IPCC research and statistics series: Paper 27 (2014).

[7] See <http://www.lucyfaithful.org.uk>.

[8] There is published guidance available produced by the NPCC and NCA on how to manage the risk of suicidal ideation from online offenders on the CoP APP website.

> **KEY POINTS**
>
> - A duty of care extends to suspects, and adequate risk management should be part of arrest planning.
> - Trigger points may render suspects vulnerable to self-harming or suicidal ideation such as when returning on bail, a court hearing, or media release.
> - Bail can be refused if there are reasonable grounds for believing detention is necessary for a person's safety and protection.

12.7.2 Arrest team briefings

Those involved in arrest operations, including specialists such as Crime Scene Managers/Investigators (CSMs/CSIs), should be fully briefed beforehand by the SIO or nominee. An operational 'order' or briefing document is useful to have circulated beforehand (eg using a recognised structure such as IIMARCH or SAFCOM[9]).

Effective communication through briefings usually has a positive effect on the success of the investigation (see Chapter 9). Questions about roles and responsibilities should be encouraged and covered at a briefing. All documents and records used and referred to are subject to disclosure rules and care must be taken to ensure briefing material is not inadvertently left at any target premises or elsewhere (eg in vehicles or in public places).

An operational plan and policy log entry justifying an arrest strategy may benefit by inclusion of 5WH topics such as:

- Who—is the person being arrested?
- What—are they being arrested for and primary objectives?
- Why—are they being arrested (justification)?
- Where—will the arrest take place?
- When—will the arrest take place: exact time, day, and date?
- How—will the arrest be conducted?

These topics can be expanded to cover and explain further detail, such as what searches are to be conducted upon arrest, what forensic considerations need catering for, where suspects will be transported to, by whom, and how, what the reception plan is at the custody suite, and who the interview teams are.

Checklist—Arrest and search operation

1. Command and control (eg Gold, Silver, Bronze (GSB)).

2. Operational objectives.

---

[9] IIMARCH—information, intention, method, administration, risk assessment, communications, human rights; SAFCOM—situation, aim, factors, choices, option, monitoring.

3. Details of investigation/current situation report.

4. Risk management identification and control measures.

5. Details of the suspect(s) and recent identification details (eg photographs).

6. Details of premises and others expected to be present (eg vulnerable people such as children).

7. Relevant intelligence and information.

8. Legal powers (premises entry, arrest, and search).

9. Security and preservation arrangements while operation in progress.

10. Search plan and items seizure: what is sought, and exhibits management.

11. Intelligence-gathering requirements (request for intelligence (RFI)).

12. Contingencies for dealing with unrelated offences.

13. Neighbourhood checks, eg House-to-House (H2H) around site of premises targeted.

14. Detainee transportation, custody reception, and interview.

15. Fast-track action management (arising during operation).

16. Administration (eg warrant administration and search records).

17. Roles and responsibilities (arrest and search teams).

18. Risks assessment and control measures.

19. Communications (radio channels and contact numbers).

20. Disclosure requirements and instructions.

21. Community Impact Assessment and/or media control.

22. Debriefing arrangements/review of operational learning.

Silver control-type facilities or command and control centres are useful to have in place for managing some major arrest operations. Local policing teams can compliment this by being tasked to assist with managing any community impact issues. A Gold Commander may be required to cater for any strategic policing matters (depending on the scale of the operation) and their likely consequences.

Arrests and searches provide opportunities to conduct other enquiries, including speaking with others at or nearby any premises to be visited (if applicable) who could be witnesses or have useful information. Neighbours and visitors may be spoken with see if they have any knowledge, such as suspect movements, habits, associates, and vehicles used. This might include conducting targeted H2H enquiries at adjoining premises.

12.8 **Timing of Arrests**

Usually the sooner suspects are detained, the less chance and opportunity there are for them to commit further offences, destroy or contaminate vital evidence, harm any victims, or interfere with witnesses. There may also be financial and resource-saving benefits in reducing costs by avoiding lengthy investigations. A duty of care for protecting the public has to be an overriding factor.

Where there is an opportunity to make an *early arrest* based on available information, then usually it should be made. The closer to the time the offence was committed the arrest is made, the greater an opportunity there is to recover fresh and uncontaminated forensic evidence or any other useful items or material by using the element of surprise. It also prevents offenders from disappearing or concocting alibis. An arrest phase provides victim and/or community reassurance, increases faith in the investigation and prevents any temptation for anyone to try to 'take the law into their own hands' (vigilantism).

However, the most advantageous time, date, and place to make an arrest will depend on individual circumstances. There are a number of key factors that could influence the decision. For example, coinciding an arrest operation simultaneously with a tactic to try to approach potential witnesses, who may be withholding information for fear of intimidation. There may also be a practical consideration of having to trace a suspect's whereabouts in order to effect the arrest or complete covert work to locate or 'house' (attribute to premises) them beforehand.

The 'Golden Hour(s)' principle suggests offenders who are spoken to closest to the time of their offending are more likely to make mistakes when fabricating stories because they have had less chance to prepare and are less confident. It is a fact that people are more likely to be truthful when interviewed soon after their offending. This is also a time when they are less able to claim they 'cannot remember' what they were doing or where they were at the material time, because the time difference between offence and arrest is minimal.

In summary, an early arrest decision may have to take account of a number of factors:

- Level of risk the suspect poses to victims, witnesses, or the general public.
- Likelihood of them committing further offences.
- Likelihood of them destroying, concealing, or falsifying evidence and impeding the investigation.
- What further evidence gathering is necessary.

There are, of course, other ways in which to conduct searches to locate evidence without the need to make formal arrests, such as under a search warrant.

12.8.1 Delaying arrests

It may be advantageous to delay an arrest if to do so would facilitate other tactics or enquiries. Delaying may also reduce the need to pre-charge bail a suspect or release them under investigation (RUI) and provide a better position from which to conduct a meaningful interview and reduce delay in bringing a case to court (as the evidence will be ready to meet the Full Code Test (see section 12.5.1).

Another reason might be if there are multiple suspects and it is better to make simultaneous arrests to limit opportunities for offenders to dispose of evidence or collaborate with others after being alerted. A delay, therefore, may be necessary to synchronise multiple strikes. One more reason might be to enable suspects to unknowingly 'assist' by leading the investigation team to evidential locations or where victims have been concealed (eg in murder, missing person, or kidnap cases).

KEY POINT

A recorded policy decision is required to explain the reason and justification for a delay in making an arrest. It remains under continuous review and may have to be defended if an offender commits further offences or places victims, the public, communities, or staff at greater risk of harm that could otherwise have been prevented. Keeping a timeline will assist to manage the risk.

One of the complications when delaying an arrest is that suspects can be disadvantaged if they are not being afforded their statutory rights (ie being cautioned and allowed access to independent legal advice) should they be spoken to in the normal course of an investigation. Once deemed a 'suspect' a person should not be interviewed until being properly cautioned as either a voluntary attender at a police station or under arrest. Adequate control measures should prevent this from occurring.

Checklist—Suspect arrests

1. Arrest, reception, and detention

- Nominate appropriate arrest team (decide if independent or part of interview team).

- Determine exact wording of arrest.

- Decide if arrest will be video recorded (if so, ensure it is reviewed afterwards).

- Determine custody suite (convenient location with good interview and downstream monitoring facilities) and if separate locations (or separate wings/custody areas) for multiple suspects.

- Determine mode of transport to custody office (independent staff are usually best to avoid accusations of interference en route; vehicle will need searching beforehand and afterwards).

- Ensure correct procedures followed for recording unsolicited comments/significant statements and these comments are not encouraged by escorting officers before they receive legal advice at the police station. If they make them of their own choice that is another matter, and the comments should be recorded (see section 12.8.2).

- Custody staff are briefed so they know reason and correct wording for the arrest, grounds for detention, and any risks identified, eg any known medical history.

- Duty custody detention review officers should be briefed in advance.

- Appoint custody liaison officer to coordinate activity (particularly if multiple arrests).

- Plan for recovery of forensic exhibits and biometric samples from suspects and nominate people **un**connected with enquiry to obtain them (*avoiding cross-contamination—sterile areas/cells*).

- Ensure swabbing and sampling kits available (eg blood/drugs/firearms residue kits).

- Plan for recovery of suspect's clothing and footwear—ensure replacements are available.

- Consider suspect's religious beliefs/faith considerations and plan for appropriate replacement clothing, dietary, and religious requirements.

- Plan for medical examination of suspect and brief/debrief the medic involved (consider body mapping).

- Plan for early recording of any injuries or unusual features.

- Plan for rapid fingerprinting/identifying of suspect.

- Ensure adequate communications link between arrest team, custody suite, and incident room/SIO to monitor progress and make dynamic decisions.

- Ensure all details of information provided by detainee (eg addresses, intimation details) and possessions are relayed to incident room for appropriate decisions and actions (eg mobile phone examination, house/vehicle key checks, diaries).

- Arrange home address search plan and consider treatment as crime scene (if not done so already) and any other linked locations of interest.

- Consider family liaison strategy, media, and community impact regarding details and news coverage of the arrest.

- Plan for custody extensions and warrants of further detention (WOFD).

- Consider duty of care and risk management of suspect if released.

2. Arrest Debrief agenda

- Comments and replies made, including significant statements.

- Details of persons present and visitors.

- Potential witnesses and sources of information.

- Search results and exhibits seized.

- Fast-track actions required.

- Investigative material and intelligence gathered.

- Completion and collection of evidential statements from all staff involved before going off duty and relevant disclosure (Criminal Procedure and Investigations Act 1996 (CPIA)) material.

- Administration—eg notes completed and any search records.

- H2H results and documentation.

- Welfare/health and safety issues.

- Risk assessment review and evaluation.

- Wider safeguarding issues for vulnerable persons, eg children.

- Victim, local community, and media impact and information assessment

- Collate any operational/organisational learning.

12.8.2 Significant statements

As a general rule, suspects should not be formally interviewed other than at a police station or other authorised place of detention (PACE, Code C, 11.1). An interview is defined as the 'questioning of a person regarding his/her suspected involvement in a criminal offence'. If, however, a suspect becomes talkative and spontaneously comments about the offence they are suspected of without prompting, or insists on providing unsolicited comments, and after a caution has been administered, their comments should be accurately recorded. Voluntary comments or 'significant statements', as they are known, may contain vital information or evidence about the offence under investigation. Denials can also form part of a subsequent interview plan when considered in the context of other evidence.

A significant statement includes anything that appears capable of being used in evidence against the suspect and, in particular, an admission of guilt (PACE, Code C, 11.4A). The term derives from Part III of the Criminal Justice and Public Order Act 1994:

> A significant statement or silence is one which appears capable of being used in evidence against the suspect in particular a direct admission of guilt or a

failure or refusal to answer a question or to answer it satisfactorily which may give rise to an inference.

Suspects should be asked to sign a record of any such statement after reading and agreeing it as a true and accurate record. A refusal to sign should itself be recorded, together with the reasons why, including aspects that the suspect considers incorrect.

Officers can be pre-briefed to record any significant statements and unsolicited comments, and maintain a contemporaneous record until the suspect has been booked into custody. Any comments can be of value to subsequent formal interviews, and denials when arrested also form the basis of a challenge when presented later. If arresting officers are wearing body-worn video (BWV) cameras, these might be proven even more effective.

KEY POINT

Few individuals remain silent or composed when informed they are under arrest for a serious criminal offence. What they say and how they respond should be accurately recorded. Wherever practicable, suspects should be allowed to comment after being told they are under arrest, allowing a suitable pause before being led away.[10] An option is to video-record the arrest which will provide more impactive evidence.

12.8.3 Urgent interviews

Legal frameworks state that arrested persons must not be 'interviewed' except at a police station. This is unless delay would be likely to lead to:

- interference with or harm to evidence connected with an offence.
- interference with or physical harm to other people.
- serious loss of or damage to property.
- alerting other suspects not yet arrested, or hindering the recovery of property obtained as a consequence of an offence.

If any of these criteria is satisfied, an 'urgent interview' may be conducted, ie questioning to locate and recover a victim, missing person, weapon/firearm discarded by a suspect before anyone finding it comes to any harm. Critical questioning must cease once the relevant risk has been averted or the

---

[10] When Ian Stewart (fifty-six years) was being arrested on suspicion of the murder of his fiancé and children's author Helen Bailey in April 2016, he enquired whether the officers had been in his garage. This is precisely where her body was later found, buried in a cesspit under concrete together with their pet dachshund, Boris, after having been suffocated to death and falsely reported as a missing person ('Murderer of children's author found guilty and sentenced to 34 years'; *International Business Times* 23 February 2017. Available at: http://www.ibtimes.co.uk).

necessary questions have been put (PACE, Code C, 11.1). Urgent interviews should therefore not be used to ask evidential questions about other lines of enquiry

When planning arrests that might involve urgent interviews, there should be consideration of practicalities such as the method of recording, eg contemporaneous notes or portable recording/audio equipment. Seeking advice from an interview adviser beforehand is always a wise option.

When a detainee requests legal advice at a police station, they cannot be interviewed until they have received it, unless the above grounds apply, and authorisation has been provided by a Superintendent grade or above (not necessarily independent of the investigation). To do otherwise would attract critical analysis of procedures during court proceedings and could prove fatal to the evidence being relied upon and maybe even the entire case itself (see Christopher Halliwell, 2011[11]).

KEY POINTS

- At the police station, after legal advice has been requested, urgent interviews *must* be authorised by a Superintendent (or above) using the caution 'You don't have to say anything but anything you do say may be given in evidence'. This means adverse inferences cannot be drawn from the interview.
- Urgent interviews are very infrequently used except in the most serious cases such as serial murders, suspicious missing persons, kidnap, abduction, and terrorism cases (ie crimes in action or threats to life (TTL)). They are likely to be closely scrutinised by legal teams and the courts.

12.9 Suspects as Crime Scenes

Suspects are always potential crime scenes because they can be a rich source of evidence to help prove or disprove their guilt. Time scales between incident and arrest will always vary in each case but as stated earlier, the sooner the arrest and detention, the better the chances of trace evidence recovery.

Apart from fingerprints, DNA, clothing, and footwear, suspects are able to provide a wealth of forensic evidence from transfer of hair, blood, semen, paint,

---

[11] Swindon taxi driver Christopher Halliwell led the SIO to the concealed bodies of missing persons Sian O'Callaghan and Becky Godden-Edwards, whom he had murdered and buried at separate rural locations. The trial judge ruled that his contemporaneously recorded confessions, taken by the SIO while out on site, were done without requested legal representation. They were ruled inadmissible because an 'emergency interview' had been conducted without Halliwell being allowed access to a solicitor. An IOPC enquiry found the SIO guilty of gross misconduct, despite him having located the bodies of two murder victims whose remains might never have otherwise been discovered.

soil, gunshot residue, chemical substances, drug traces, glass fragments, fibres, pollen, etc. Arrests need to capitalise on such evidence recovery opportunities that may link suspects to crimes. This should be factored into any pre-arrest planning.

It can be advantageous to obtain samples or seize clothing from a suspect at the point of arrest rather than waiting until arrival at a custody centre. Firearms discharge residue, for example, needs to be recovered as quickly as possible after a firearms-related incident, and in some cases the covering of exposed areas such as the suspect's hands is necessary to increase the likelihood of success in recovering necessary evidence. Advice can be taken on all forensic recovery matters and contamination avoidance from an expert such as a CSM/CSI during the planning stage.

It can also prove useful to have suspects examined by a medical examiner soon after arrival at a custody suite. Checks can be made for blood, cuts, bruising, scratches, burn marks, or other injuries (eg marks on the hand from the recoil firing mechanism of a semi-automatic handgun). A full body-map profile may also be completed and any marks found recorded and photographed. A medical examiner should be debriefed afterwards to see what, if any, comments the detainee made during their examination.

Policy Log Example—Suspect Evidence Recovery Plan

Decision: All persons arrested on suspicion of being involved in the offence of (x) will be subject to the following evidence collection plan:

- Full-length photographing in clothes in which they were arrested

- Medical examination

- Swabbing of hands and any blood or injuries

- Clothing and footwear seizure—to be taken over paper

- Blood and urine samples to be taken

- Hair combings, hair samples, and fingernail scrapings to be taken

- Detainee (suspect) to be kept under constant observation and placed into a sterile cell until such time that forensic capture is complete

Reason: To identify and seize any potential marks, injuries, or other forensic evidence that might prove beneficial to the investigation.

It should be noted that if any third party brings or sends any items such as clothing to the custody suite for a detainee, those items should also be checked to see if they are of significance to the investigation.

12.9.1 **Strip searches**

A strip search is the removal of more than a person's outer clothing. It can be authorised by a Custody Officer when considered necessary to remove an article which the detainee would not be allowed to keep because it may present a danger to themselves/others, might be used to assist escape, or, more importantly to the investigation, be evidence relating to an offence. The conduct of strip searches is covered by PACE Code C, Annex A.

12.10 **High-Risk Suspect Hunts**

Some investigations require time, effort, and resources to locate, chase down, and arrest outstanding suspects, particularly if deemed to pose a threat to public safety. A high-level search operation might mean that a 'crime in action' is in progress requiring a proactive as well as reactive strand to the investigation.

Typically, these occur in cases involving kidnap and abduction, terrorism, serial homicides, high-risk suspicious missing persons, serious physical, or sexual offences where multiple attacks and victims are continuing, or any case where a dangerous offender has gone 'on the run'. Whenever named suspects pose a high-level risk to public safety, there will be an urgent operational objective to track them down quickly and bring them in for questioning.[12]

These can prove quite challenging due to managing the risks and widespread public and media attention, effectively placing the SIO in the eye of a storm. They are always time-critical and become more intense and critical the longer they continue. In high-level, proactive arrest operations (particularly those involving dangerous and/or armed suspects), large amounts of assets and resources are usually required. These may include covert surveillance, arrest and search teams, mobile armed search teams (MAST), firearms tactical intervention/arrest teams, intelligence cells, specialist communications data advisers, hostage negotiators, coordinators from other regions, forces, and agencies, media advisers, and most probably the Regional Organised Crime Units (ROCU) or National Crime Agency (NCA).

These are critical incidents and likely to impact on public confidence and therefore require very skilful operational dynamic management. A separate (eg Silver) control room with a designated GSB command and control structure will be required with the SIO (and/or PIP4) and/or their nominated deputy playing a key role in not just tactical operational decision making but also reporting to Gold and their strategic meetings.

---

[12] Operation Purple Wave in Brentford, West London, in August 2014 was such an example, when missing fourteen-year-old teenager, Alice Gross, was murdered by a missing Latvian suspect named Arnis Zalkalns. Neither could be traced until a huge police operation later led to two bodies, both the victim and suspect (murder/suicide), being found apart some weeks later.

Such operations require fast-time control, management, and rapid decision making (see section 3.2) with the essential communications structure, case management system, and necessary assets and resources at the ready. They are dependent on resilience and support from the host force (maybe even mutual aid), not just the investigative arm, through the SIO/DSIO plus enquiry team, all of whom are likely to be working around the clock.

Any firearms, explosives, or noxious/biological substances are an added challenge if believed involved or used/carried by the suspect(s). An accredited Strategic and/or Tactical Firearms Commander (SFC/TFC) might be required to command and manage any Authorised Firearms Officers (AFO) deployment. Planning and preparation for any 'strike arrests' must be properly coordinated with the SIO/DSIO working closely alongside the TFC to ensure that evidential needs of the investigation are considered and included in the planning phase.

Checklist—High-risk suspect hunts

- If suspects are armed and/or deemed highly dangerous, public safety is always of paramount importance, followed closely by the safety of officers and then suspects.

- Contingency plans need to be prepared for when arrest(s) are made, such as nominated hospitals for any casualties (including suspects).

- Vulnerable persons connected to the investigation might require added (possibly armed) round-the-clock protection while dangerous individuals or gangs remain at large (eg to avoid reprisals, etc).

- Suspect management, evidence collection, and interview plans need preparing in advance of arrests being made (see section 12.7).

- SIO works closely alongside other Silver commanders who might have separate roles and responsibilities (eg TFC) to ensure the needs of the investigation are catered for wherever possible.

- If GSB structure utilised, the SIO should insist on having their role and responsibility (and that of others in the command structure) clearly outlined and agreed, preferably recorded and agreed by the Gold Commander, so ensuring there are clear lines of accountability and everyone knows who has responsibility for what.

12.10.1 Change of mindset

Crimes in action and high-level suspect hunts amount to an investigation becoming proactive rather than merely reactive. The mindset of the SIO and their enquiry team needs to recognise the subtle change in priorities. Public safety and locating and arrest of a dangerous suspect become the main priorities over and above the preservation and recovery of evidence. Intelligence that can assist in making a speedy arrest has to take precedence over traditional investigative considerations, such as gathering and preserving evidence or conducting forensic tests.

As an example, if a mobile phone is recovered the analysis of which could quickly reveal lines of enquiry to help locate a suspect, then a dynamic decision is required as to what takes precedence (forensic evidence versus fast-time intelligence). This is where the dynamics change, ie from a traditional reactive investigation to a proactive one to save life and control risks. If the public are at risk, the operation becomes a 'fast-time' enquiry and reacting to developments and creating arrest opportunities takes precedence, therefore the phone's contents would have to be analysed quickly (at the risk of reducing fingerprint or DNA sampling opportunities) to try to locate any victims or offenders.

An SIO needs to adjust and adapt their aims and objectives to a much faster tempo of proactive decision making, actions, and requirements (section 3.2). Objectives and directives need to be effectively communicated to all the teams to ensure everyone is aware of what might be, for some, a completely different and more high powered working environment. These new objectives need to be communicated properly, ie prominently displayed for everyone to see in order to convey a clear message.

KEY POINT

There is no luxury of 'slow time' (see section 3.2) for decision making when public safety is in jeopardy.

12.10.2 Contingency/trigger plans

Where there is a high-level suspect hunt and a crime in action, it is good to have a prepared plan for when a suspect is found and detained. This will otherwise occur at the least convenient time when it is more difficult to get hold of key resources. There may be more than one area to cover in the plan, eg forensic recovery, search, and seizure. As a general rule, there should be at the very least recorded policy and direction as to what any development should trigger as and when it arises. This may include the items in the following checklist.

Checklist—Contingency plan

- SIO/DSIO (and/or nominated on call officer) to be notified without delay.

- Rapid deployment and effective management of suspect detention and associated evidence gathering, samples, and preservation.

- Scene(s) to be identified, secured, and protected (ISP), confirmed, and quality assured by a CSI supervisor (CSM).

- Implementation of pre-arranged physical search and forensic examination.

- Communications strategy and media liaison plan.

- Exploitation of any fast-track evidence-gathering opportunities such as CCTV.

- Initial suspect interview plan (eg emergency interview to save life).

- Early H2H enquiries.

- Community impact assessment.

- Notify/brief FLOs (where appropriate) and media liaison officer.

- Brief PIP 4/Gold Commander.

12.11 Detention Times and Warrants of Further Detention

Planning and preparation takes cognisance of how long detention proceedings are likely to take in order to plan for exceeding mandatory custody time limits. This should identify in advance which (PACE) duty senior officers are likely to be tasked with the responsibility of considering extending any custody time limits and/or authorising the taking of intimate samples. This will enable them to be briefed and prepared with the case and likely requirements in advance.

Custody time limits need close monitoring throughout the entire period of detention. The use of a live running 'timeline' of events and activities for each and every detainee is helpful plus a nominated officer to assume responsibility for monitoring and updating it. Ideally, this is the same person who is nominated to supervise and manage the detention and interview process on behalf of the team to ensure everything runs smoothly and efficiently. This information can then be used as the basis for any warrant of further detention (WOFD) applications at court (sections 43 and 44 PACE) for detention to increase from thirty-six to ninety-six hours and illustrate how enquiries are being progressed diligently and expeditiously.

With WOFD, wherever practicable the SIO/DSIO should appear in person to make the application. If delegated, the person who attends court to apply for the warrants must be fully briefed and made aware of all the relevant circumstances of the investigation and any likely areas of contention. If they are not directly involved with the investigation, they must be invited to team briefings post-arrest and be kept updated on evidential finds or intelligence updates. It should be noted that at these hearings the defence legal team may wish to try and extract information about the investigation and evidence which may not yet have been declared in formal interviews.

Checklist—'WOFD'

- Applications are made at the time officers are sworn to give evidence. This is important when managing applications involving multiple suspects who are appearing separately, to ensure their detention time does not expire before the application commences.

- If granted, the time of the WOFD commences when it is signed by the magistrate.

- Planning a WOFD should consider the logistics and time frames involved, eg it is often prudent to make early applications, taking account of the court's availability.

- Applications are authorised by a Superintendent or grade above.

- Contingencies should include a 'wash-up' interview with the suspect(s) before the WOFD application is made to ensure all critical questions have been put to them in case further detention is refused.

12.12 Suspect Interviews

Investigative interviewing plays a big role in arrest and detention strategies. While there are specialists and advisers who may assist in professionalising the process, the SIO *must play an active role* in not only devising and agreeing a suitable interview plan but also in its implementation, supervision and dynamic/flexible/adaptable management.

The selection of appropriately skilled officers for conducting suspect interview(s) needs careful thought. It is not just a case of choosing someone who is trained and 'next on the list' but rather choosing people based upon their skills, experience, and suitability. Reserve officers can be chosen and on standby in the event of unforeseen circumstances arising.

Investigative interviewers fall broadly within three different categories which are:

1. General interviewers (eg serious and complex investigations).
2. Specialist interviewers (eg child interviews) and those trained and competent in serious crime suspect interviews.
3. Interview advisers (strategic adviser and coordinator for SIO).

Not all major and serious crime investigators are accredited as per the list above, so the selection of the right staff to conduct interviews is vitally important. Often a combination of three of the categories may be required in a major investigation (ie 1, 2, *and* 3).

The interview process is a phase where detailed and careful planning is required which needn't wait until the time of arrest. Once a suspect is identified, planning can commence immediately highlighting key investigative material that can be used in any subsequent suspect interview.

A briefing should be provided to interview teams (particularly if they are not completely conversant with the investigation) and, if necessary, they should be given a familiarisation visit to the crime scene(s). This may be of assistance if admissions are made or detail provided by the suspect that requires an appreciation and awareness of significant locations.

Aims and objectives for interviews are agreed and separated into 'phases' if there are different areas to cover. Separate objectives can be set for each phase, eg if there is DNA evidence that puts the suspect at the scene or with the victim, the aim of the first phase may be to establish whether the suspect denies ever being in contact with the scene or victim. When the DNA evidence is revealed during later phases of the interview, it then makes it far more difficult for the suspect to allege innocent contact.

Disclosure items need to be agreed and decided, and the structure and timing of the disclosure process may be crucial for getting the most out of an interview. Whenever investigative material is put to the suspect (eg witness evidence, DNA, or fingerprint evidence at a scene), the timing, method, and wording of any disclosure becomes extremely important. A separate officer to deal specifically with all the disclosure for the interview can be appointed to remove this onerous responsibility from the interviewing officers.

It is good practice and sometimes essential to 'downstream' monitor interviews on a visual or audio link, depending on what equipment is available. Suitable custody facilities can be selected that provide the best possible facilities. The SIO and Interview Adviser (if applicable) should be within easy reach of the interview location so that any matters arising or developments can be easily and speedily discussed.

An interview plan *must remain flexible* throughout the process, which is why the SIO/DSIO needs to be involved. It may be important to review, restructure and amend the interview plan as things progress because of things said/not said by the suspect or admissions made, or changing attitudes and opportunities. Some training methods tend to focus on delaying all 'challenges' (as per the PEACE model)[13] to the end of the interview. This may not always be the best approach if there is an opportunity to get a good point across at the right time and maintain the momentum and focus on a particular topic or line of questioning. To summarise, while interviews need to be structured, they should also remain flexible depending on the circumstances and how the interview develops.

12.12.1 **Initial accounts**

Before a detained suspect is interviewed to an agreed plan and structure, or during the first interview, it is beneficial to put to them the allegation and ask

---

[13] PEACE is an acronym that stands for Preparation and planning; Engage and explain; Account clarification and challenge; Closure; Evaluation.

for their account or explanation. This provides an early opportunity to offer any important information, such as admissions or details that could eliminate them or help identify co-offenders. It is unlikely any significant 'challenges' will be used during this phase of an interview strategy so very little or no planning is required.

This type of interview is useful if it is going to be a delay before a detainee suspect is formally interviewed, eg if they are arrested spontaneously and an interview plan and team is yet to be prepared. During the first interview a detained suspect can be given an early opportunity to provide an account (provided it is conducted at a police station under the proper provisions of PACE with a solicitor present, on tape, etc) that could lead to important information being disclosed (which could be to their own benefit as well as the investigation).

KEY POINT

An initial interview of an arrested suspect in custody is aimed at giving them an opportunity to provide an early explanation in response to the allegation. This is entirely different from conducting an 'urgent interview' and may assist in quickly implicating or eliminating them from enquiries.

12.12.2 Preparation and planning

The planning of a suspect interview takes cognisance of a number of factors. While flexibility is always key, a structure is needed which is agreed by the interview adviser and SIO.

Based on a timeline of events around the incident under investigation, various planned phases can be split into three distinct periods, as shown in the following (Table 12.1).

Without these phases, interviews can stray off track, whereas the structure ensures they remain focused on specific times and events. This is important if it is necessary to compare and contrast accounts from multiple suspects concerning their movements, actions, etc within similar time periods. These periods are explained as follows:

Table 12.1 Three interview phases

BEFORE EVENT	DURING EVENT	AFTER EVENT
(relevant time parameters)	(relevant time parameters)	(relevant time parameters)
Topics to cover	Topics to cover	Topics to cover
Investigative areas	Investigative areas	Investigative areas

1. **Before**: Investigative topics to be covered within this phase help establish potential motives and significant lines of enquiry. This is often referred to as 'background' but it does not always follow that this has to be historical. It may include key times and dates leading up to the commission of the offence where it is important to investigate any degree of planning or pre-cursor events that took place. Topics that could be included are lifestyle, associations, character, ownership of items, and use of websites. Relevant topics are identified during the course of the investigation and informed by the nature of what other material has been covered. For example, in the case of forensic samples recovered from a crime scene (including victim), it must be established whether a suspect had legitimate access or had been in contact with them prior to the incident.

2. **During**: This is where an interview usually begins and where the guilty are most likely to feel uncomfortable and vulnerable. It contains the most significant detail relative to the offence and where accounts need closer probing. It is also, of course, the best place to allow early accounts and detail to be introduced by innocent persons. Relevant time parameters might have to be set wide enough to cover this period. Depending on the circumstances, this may include a time that captures events immediately leading up to and away from the offence in question.

3. **After**: Topics relevant in this phase are determined by the timing of the arrest of the suspect. For example, if arrested at the scene or relatively soon afterwards, there will be no 'after period' as the time parameters for the 'during' phase should incorporate this. However, if there are several days between the commission of the offence and the arrest, then this is a key area to be covered. A suspect may well have made admissions to others, or their activities may generally differ from their normal behaviour. They may have even taken steps to cover up their involvement, eg by disposing of property. In the case of a historical enquiry, this is still an important area but the level of detail that would be expected to be covered will have to be more realistic.

12.12.3 Challenges

This is a phase that requires careful thought and planning as to how it is man-aged, what material to introduce, and when to introduce 'challenging' material. Carefully selected key investigative material can be introduced at a crucial stage in the interview and a suspect asked for comment and explanation, affording them an opportunity to comment.

This should not be an opportunity for case theories or suggestions to be intro-duced but can include topics and areas of significance that may be at odds with what has been stated (or not) by the suspect. It is important that the strength of the material is not misrepresented or overstated, and it is made abundantly clear what is being alleged. For example, it may be an account from a witness, a CCTV image, social media data, or forensics that place the interviewee at a crime scene.

12.12.4 Investigative material

Mention of 'investigative material' is frequently made throughout this chapter and in other areas of the book. The CPIA definition of 'material' states: 'Material of any kind including information and objects which are obtained in the course of a criminal investigation and which may be relevant to the investigation.' Potential sources from which investigative material can be obtained include:

- Victims
- Witnesses
- Suspects
- Locations and crime scenes, eg forensic and digital material
- Property recovered from searches
- Passive data generators, eg CCTV, communication devices, computers, financial records
- Intelligence sources.

In criminal investigations, there is usually an aim to seek and gather investigative material to progress the enquiry. If a prosecution follows, the material may or may not become evidence. Therefore, when dealing with a suspect's legal adviser prior to or during an interview, it is advisable to resist using the term 'evidence', eg when asked what 'evidence' the enquiry team has that implicates their client in the offence for which they are to be interviewed. This is because at this stage it will be uncertain what will/will not be treated as evidence until formal agreement by the CPS.

KEY POINT

When dealing with a legal adviser prior to a suspect interview, it is advisable to use the term 'investigative material' instead of 'evidence'. The former covers a far wider range of possible sources than the latter that may/may not become evidential material in any subsequent prosecution case.

General Checklist—Suspect interviews

- Prioritise and coordinate interviews (if multiple suspects).

- Facilitate a briefing and scene familiarisation visit for interviewing officers.

- Agree nature of allegation and any 'points to prove'.

- Have 'suspectology' detail available.

- Consider any requirement for interpreters.

- Examine records/tapes of previous interviews with suspect(s).

- Check custody records for relevant information provided by suspect.

- Consider any 'significant statements'/pre-interview comments.

- Consider what 'investigative material' is to be used during interview.

- Consider monitoring of interviews.

- Consider initial interview to gain suspect account.

- Decide on structure and the three phases (see table earlier).

- Determine what disclosure will be provided, how, when, and by whom, and content and format of pre-interview briefing (legal adviser).

- Determine what exhibits required for interview/sign labels for continuity.

- Review arrest strategy (impact on interview process).

- Note any requirements for 'appropriate adult'/potential mental health issues.

- Consider witnesses (vulnerable/intimidated/significant) and impact on disclosing their evidence.

- Consider all legal issues (custody time limits/WOFD).

- Identify objectives and areas for clarification (ie SIO's agenda).

- Plan for introduction of 'challenges' for key investigative material.

- Consider use and timing of 'special warnings'.

- Determine 'no comment' or 'prepared statement' interview strategy.

- Have staff and necessary resources on standby for fast-track actions

- Determine whether separate interview required for evidence of 'bad character' (under 'previous misconduct' provisions of Criminal Justice Act 2003).

Checklist—Post-interview considerations

- Debrief interview team(s).

- Analyse and evaluate interview comments and responses.

- Analyse and evaluate information from interview(s).

- Assess what impact any information provided has on the enquiry.

- Ensure any necessary fast-track action(s)/further enquiries are actioned.

- Consider and review further interview strategy.

- Consider welfare of suspect/interview team(s).

- Maintain close liaison with/update CPS.

12.12.5 Intelligence interviews

The objective of an intelligence interview is to obtain information about criminal activity other than the offence(s) for which a suspect has been arrested. Intelligence interviews do not fall within the PACE definition of an interview and are not conducted under caution or recorded. They are sometimes also called 'offender debriefings'. Most organisations have individual policies for balancing the integrity of an investigation in progress whilst exploiting the opportunity to obtain potentially actionable information from an intelligence interview.

Considerations include not conducting the interview until after the investigation phase has concluded, using different officers to those connected to the investigation (usually intelligence staff or CHIS handlers) and managing the content of the custody record so the safety of a detainee who agrees to an intelligence interview is not compromised.

12.12.6 National Investigative Interview Adviser

In complex cases involving multiple suspects or where witness testimony is likely to be key, the services of the NCA National Investigative Interview Adviser and their cadre of deputies can be called upon to assist as Subject Matter Experts (SMEs). They are available to provide advice and guidance on the interviewing of suspects, victims, and witnesses across a broad range of criminality with particular reference to legal codes and national standards. This includes:

- Advice and support in establishing interview strategies in accordance with national guidelines.
- Advice and support regarding planning and preparing interviews.
- Analysis of interviews.
- Analysis of written statements.
- Debriefing of overall interview process.
- Assistance in reviewing interview processes.
- Assistance in maximising the interview products in subsequent processes.

The adviser works closely with SIOs and interviewing officers to develop bespoke interview strategies. They also contribute to the implementation of the NPCC Investigative Interviewing Strategy, incorporating development of the Professionalising Investigations Programme (PIP), and the delivery of training.

12.13 **Charging and Bail**

There comes a time in the investigation, probably when the interviewing of a suspect has been completed, that a decision must be made whether to charge or release a suspect without charge. A decision may be required as to whether any further action is required at all because in some circumstances they are no longer considered a suspect. They may have been eliminated or there may just be insufficient evidence to implicate them (commonly known as 'no further action' or 'NFA').

The decision to charge and prosecute an individual is a serious step and one that affects not just the suspect, but also victims, witnesses, investigators, and the general public. It is not to be taken lightly, recognising the ethical principles mentioned in section 2.9 applicable to all criminal investigators not to be influenced by bias or prejudice and act in the interests of fairness and justice. The SIO remains responsible for managing the investigation and making any decisions around starting and concluding them. They must also decide when the time is right to charge a suspect, ie when they think they have enough evidence to approach the CPS for a charging decision. In making this decision a balance needs to be struck between unnecessary delays and premature charging, and the Crown prosecutor who ultimately makes the decision to charge will rely upon one of two tests.

12.13.1 **Full Code Test**

Prosecutors can only agree the commencement of a prosecution case once it has passed both stages of the 'Full Code Test' (FCT). The only exception is when the Threshold Test (TT) may apply (see section 12.13.2). The two stages of the FCT are: (i) evidential; and (ii) public interest. Of significance is that the test can be applied once all *reasonable* lines of enquiry have been pursued. This means that it can be applied even if there are outstanding enquiries, provided the prosecutor is satisfied further evidence or material is unlikely to affect their decision. The SIO will still have to convince the prosecutor there is a realistic prospect of a conviction, no matter how serious the case might be.

For the case to meet stage (i) of the test (evidential sufficiency) four points need to be considered:

1. Whether the evidence is admissible in proceedings.
2. If the evidence is reliable (as to accuracy and integrity).
3. If the evidence is credible (are there any doubts?).
4. Whether there is any other material that might affect the sufficiency of evidence.[14]

---

[14] The fourth requirement has been added to support more adequate disclosure practice and enable the prosecutor to be made aware of any material that may impact on their charging decision *before* being made

For the case to meet stage (ii) of the test (public interest), a prosecutor must be satisfied there are public interest factors in favour of proceeding with a prosecution. The points to consider are as follows:

1. Seriousness of the offence
2. Level of culpability and involvement of the suspect
3. Level of harm to any victim
4. Age and maturity of the suspect at the time the offence was committed
5. Impact on community
6. Proportionality
7. Likelihood of harm to any information source

> **KEY POINT**
>
> The FCT can now be applied before an investigation has concluded, but only if the prosecutor is satisfied further material is not likely to affect their decision.

12.13.2 Threshold test

The 'threshold test' (TT) can be applied in exceptional cases where the criteria for the FCT has not yet been met. This is where the seriousness or circumstances of the case justify an immediate charging decision. There are five conditions:

1. Reasonable grounds to suspect guilt.
2. Further evidence can be obtained to meet realistic prospect of conviction requirement.
3. Seriousness of the case justifies an immediate charging decision.
4. There are sufficient grounds to object to bail.
5. It is in the public interest to charge.

If this test is applied, the SIO can expect to have to be proactive in securing any requisite further evidence within an agreed timescale and that the full code test will be applied once that material becomes available.[15]

12.13.3 Post and pre-charge bail

Once charged, a decision has to be made by the custody officer whether or not the defendant (noting the change in term from suspect to defendant) is given bail to attend court at an appropriate time and date, or if they are to be remanded in custody. This decision will depend upon a number of factors but there is a general presumption that there is a right to bail under the Bail Act 1976. Conditions can be imposed on police bail such as ensuring the defendant

---

[15] See CPS (October 2018) 'The Code for Crown Prosecutors' 8th edn, <http://www.cps.go.uk>.

surrenders to custody, does not commit further offences, does not interfere with witnesses, obstruct the course of justice, or for their own protection (or where they are a child or young person, for their own welfare).

If, however, outstanding enquiries are required before a charging decision can be made, it may be necessary to release a suspect on pre-charge bail. Putting a suspect on bail and releasing them from custody enables conditions to be placed on them to help manage a risk of them committing further offences or interfering with victims or witnesses. Under the Policing and Crime Act 2016, changes for pre-charge bail came into force in the United Kingdom on 3 April 2017. Historically, no time limit or judicial oversight was ever given. Some individuals spent months or even years on pre-charge bail with little or no legal safeguards, hence new legislation has been introduced containing statutory safeguards for increased accountability and scrutiny.

This change has meant there is now a presumption of release *without bail* in all cases where no charges are yet brought, unless certain criteria such as necessity and proportionality are fulfilled. Where they are, a twenty-eight-day period of pre-charge bail can be granted by an Inspector with a further extension to three months by a Superintendent. Any additional bail thereafter must be granted by a magistrates court (Note: this only applies to pre-charge bail. There are no time limits placed on those who are *charged* and bailed to appear at court).

Inspectors, Superintendents, and other authorising officers (or 'designated' or 'appropriate' decision makers) can authorise an applicable bail period (ABP). This is the window of time within which a custody officer can set and vary bail. The applicable bail period commences the day after the arrest and any extensions must be authorised prior to expiration of the current period (retrospective applications are not allowed).

If a case is deemed exceptionally complex, the Appropriate Decision Maker (ADM), in the police service an Assistant Chief Constable (ACC), can authorise bail extension up to six months, provided they consult with a 'qualifying prosecutor' in the CPS and the decision maker has reasonable grounds for:

1. suspecting a person is guilty of a relevant offence; and
2. believing either (i) further time is needed to make charging decisions; or (ii) further investigation is needed of any matter in connection with a relevant offence; and
3. believing a charging decision or investigation is being conducted diligently and expeditiously; and
4. believing bail is both necessary and proportionate (as per Article 8(2) ECHR).

The ABP clock is suspended while a case is with the CPS for a charging decision and it starts again if they require further investigative work. It stops the day the case file is sent to the CPS and starts again the day the CPS sends its request back for further work. A further point of note is that there is a duty to liaise with the suspect or their legal representative before any decision is made to grant pre-charge bail. This is so they can be afforded an opportunity to make representations.

12.13.3.1 Necessity Test

Section 34 of PACE has been amended to require that pre-charge bail is only applicable if any or a combination of the following conditions are met:

1. Failing to surrender to custody.
2. Committing further offences.
3. Interfering with witnesses or otherwise obstructing the course of justice.
4. For their own protection, or if child or young person, for their own welfare.

12.13.3.2 Proportionality Test

Authorisation for pre-charge bail is only proportionate if:

1. It is not arbitrary or unfair.
2. Restriction is strictly limited to what is required to achieve (ie legitimate public policy).
3. Severity of the effect does not outweigh benefit to the community that is being sought to protect.

If pre-charge bail is granted, then the interim activity prior to return date will need managing, as will compliance with any conditions that have been imposed in order to manage risks. Records will need to show, if further extensions are applied for, that the investigation is being managed expeditiously and diligently.

Decisions should be taken in line with the broader narrative around compliance with Code G of PACE and the necessity test to arrest and the determination whether an arrest is necessary and a 'voluntary interview' is more appropriate. These are matters an SIO needs to plan and prepare for in advance and to become part of an overall suspect management strategy.

12.13.4 Release Under Investigation (RUI)

If the criteria for pre-charge bail (as above) is not met, there is an option to release a suspect as being 'under investigation'. A category has been created on the Police National Computer (PNC) to reflect such a status.

The following points are worthy of note:

- No time limit is set as to how long a person can remain in this category (whereas with the bail option there is).
- No conditions can be imposed (whereas with bail you can) to help manage any risks.
- Subjects in the category can be re-arrested at any time following release once fresh evidence becomes available.

Liaison with partner agencies might be helpful to share risk intelligence and support decisions. RUI is probably not a safe option if there are specific known risks to victims or witnesses where conditional bail might be safer. Suspect suicide prevention might also be a consideration (see section 12.7.1). Any decisions and supporting rationale should be recorded in a policy log.

Where RUI is utilised, the investigation should still be progressed with due diligence and expeditiously (eg officers being away or off on sick leave are probably not sufficient justification for the investigation not to make progress). The RUI process, if utilised, should always feature as part of any ongoing case reviews and with management oversight to ensure matters are being progressed. In cases where no further action (NFA) is taken, the suspect should be formally notified.

KEY POINT

In accordance with all other advice in this *Handbook*, it is recommended to record any decisions (using the NDM) as to whether pre-charge bail or RUI are/are not appropriate and how any risks to victims, witnesses and suspects (eg suicide or vigilantism) will be monitored and managed.

Bibliography

ACPO, Practice Advice on Core Investigative Doctrine, 2nd edn (NPIA, 2012), 105
CPS (October 2018) The Code for Crown Prosecutors 8th edn, <htto://www.cps.go.uk>
Teers, R 'Deaths during or following police contact: statistics for England and Wales 2013/14', IPCC research and statistics series: Paper 27 (2014)

Witness Management

13.1 **Introduction**

Witnesses are one of the most fundamental and pivotal assets in any investigation as their evidence can play a significant role in the progress and outcome. .The term 'witness' relates to anybody, except a suspected offender (see under section 63 YJCA Act 1999) who is likely to give evidence at court. However, the definition is not restricted to direct eye or ear witnesses; it can include those who provide circumstantial evidence to implicate or eliminate suspects and testimonies provided by professional (eg. investigators) and expert witnesses.

Victims can also be witnesses if they provide valuable information about crimes committed against them. A person reporting a crime should always be treated as a potential witness, as should call takers/handlers and initial responders who may be the very first to corroborate, see, hear, or receive vital evidence at an early stage in the investigation (ie during the 'Golden Hour(s)').

Encouraging members of the general public to come forward and provide testimonies, however, is not always straightforward. Fear and mistrust can become difficult barriers to overcome, particularly if there is little or no chance of finding evidence from other sources such as forensics. Any assistance from willing witnesses must therefore be managed carefully so as not to lose their willing cooperation. This chapter covers some of those important processes.

Witnesses are defined in section 63 of the Youth Justice and Criminal Evidence (YJCE) Act 1999 and section 52 of the Domestic Violence, Crime and Victim's Act 2004 as:

> any person (other than a defendant) who has witnessed conduct in relation to which they may be called, or proposed to be called to give evidence in relevant proceedings, which includes anything which might be, has been or could be referred to in evidence given in relevant proceedings by another person.

13.2 **Tracing Witnesses**

A main line of enquiry is usually to capitalise on all opportunities to trace, interview, and take statements (TI/TST) from potential witnesses. Influential factors are likely to be the circumstances, location, timing of the incident, and type of victim, offender, and community. This information indicates the type of witness likely to be available and where they might be found. For example, offences that occur in the early hours of the morning may point towards delivery staff, night workers, party-goers, taxi drivers, and trades people who are likely to be around at that time of the day.

Like any other area of investigation, a degree of initiative and skill is required. One of the core competencies of an investigator is the ability to communicate with different sorts of people and diverse communities (see also Chapter 9) in order to root out facts and information and win their trust. This may occur at crime scenes, during general enquiries, on visits to houses, shops, and premises, over the phone, on social media sites, or during overt activities—basically at every opportunity. Each case is different but the principles remain the same; investigators must be encouraged to be proactive and alert in looking for opportunities to find, communicate with, and obtain evidence from witnesses.

Scientific methods are available that can assist in identifying witness-seeking opportunities, such as analysing association charts to indicate people and places linked to victims and suspects. Anonymous reports from people who have offered information can also be examined closely; for example, when listening to recorded calls directed into enquiry teams for background clues on likely identities or places of origin. Some witnesses make contact and withhold information until they gain sufficient confidence, eg stating they have 'heard something' when they have actually seen it.

KEY POINT

Activities to trace witnesses must begin quickly when people are willing and co-operative, events are still fresh in their minds, and their evidence is uncontaminated. Feeling strongly about reporting what they know or have witnessed may reduce over time or if third-party influences dissuade them.

Checklist—Witness identification tactics

- During the initial response phase (including briefing officers engaged on crime scene cordons for potential witness approaches). If details refused, descriptions should be noted (including vehicles) to help trace them or use questionnaires (pro formas) to record details when there are large numbers of individuals to manage.

- Deploying evidence-gathering/mobile visual units at scenes to record those present, particularly where large numbers are involved.

- Checking journalist reports/websites for witness indications

- Recorded and uploaded details of incidents from the phone/cameras onto social media forums by the general public.

- Making appeals with positive messages and reassurance about protecting welfare and confidentiality.

- Publicising a public hotline, contact method/number/website.

- Using software programs that can identify who is active on social media platforms and commenting about incidents under investigation.

- Appeals through other means, eg at public meetings, high-visibility patrolling, street briefings/surgeries, distributing posters, leaflet drops, and electronic billboards (in appropriate languages).

- Conducting house-to-house (H2H) enquiries.

- Conducting TIE enquiries (may reveal witnesses as well as suspects).

- Passive data collection (eg CCTV, ANPR, body-worn/vehicle-mounted cameras).

- Checking financial transactions in specific areas to see who might have been present (eg using ATM machines or making purchases).

- Enquiries in local public places (eg shops, bars, transport routes to/from scene)

- Locating a mobile incident vehicle at or near an important location/scene.

- Staging reconstructions, road checks or anniversary events as appeals.

- Using cognitive prompts (eg offence occurred when important sporting event played, or at time of popular TV programmes).

- Via a family liaison strategy (see Chapter 11).

- Community liaison, local officers and partner agencies.

- Intelligence gathering (eg use of covert human intelligence source such as human intelligence/covert human intelligence (HUMINT/CHIS) tasking.

- Placing intelligence markers on records of potential witnesses.

- Searching premises or important sites and locations.

- Analysing related incident logs and messages, listening to call-handling recordings and having them transcribed to ensure all detail is analysed.

- Tracing anonymous callers.

- Challenging allegiances to explore opportunities with a view to potentially changing them (eg partners or associates of suspects).

- Offering rewards.

- Using offenders who are also witnesses.

13.2.1 Offenders as witnesses (SOCPA)

Witnesses can sometimes be found amongst offenders and defendants. Sections 71–75 of the Serious Organised Crime and Police Act 2005 (SOCPA) provide useful legal options for using persons who are offenders to support a prosecution case. These are:

- Section 71—granting a conditional immunity from prosecution for assistance.

- Section 72—providing a 'restricted use undertaking' option for information an individual provides for a prosecution or investigation.
- Section 73—powers for a court when sentencing persons who plead guilty to take account of their undertaking to assist an investigation or prosecution.
- Section 74—powers for the person sentenced to be referred back to court for discounted sentence when they assist an investigation or prosecution.
- Section 75—when sentencing under section 74 courts can exclude people from court or impose reporting restrictions.

These sections are often used for offenders who provide evidence against the higher pedigree of serious and organised criminals or terrorism groups. Interviews with 'assisting offenders' is a highly specialised area. Close consultation with nominated high-level Crown Prosecution Service (CPS) personnel, risk assessments, resource- and cost–benefit analysis and detailed planning[1] are required.

13.3 Offering Rewards

Consideration of offering a reward to the public for information, either by the police or following a request from a third party, eg a news agency, can be used in some situations. This is only likely to happen in the most serious and grave cases, particularly if they remain unresolved.

Every case has to be judged on its own merits, and before embarking on a reward policy the SIO must fully appreciate the pitfalls. An obvious one is the impact this could have on the credibility of the witness if they were to claim the reward. The value of their evidence would have to be balanced against a motive of seeking financial reward, which would be heavily scrutinised and could have an adverse effect on their motives and integrity.

The CPS should be consulted in every case where a reward is considered or offered or indeed claimed, clearly outlining the criteria stipulated for payment and the full circumstances of how the witness came forward. This also applies to any payment made to informants should they later become prosecution witnesses.

All policy decisions made around the use of rewards must be clear and transparent, recognising all the pros and cons of using the tactic and how they are managed. It must be proved beyond all reasonable doubt that the highest professional and ethical standards have been applied—for example, clear details being outlined as to what criteria must be met before a reward payment is considered, which is usually for information leading to the arrest and conviction of the offender. Details will also be required of when a payment will be made, usually not until the conclusion of all court proceedings, including appeals.

---

[1] The UK National Crime Agency has a dedicated 'debriefing' unit that can be consulted for advice and guidance when considering using this useful piece of legislation.

Whenever the tactic is used, the motives of the witness claiming the reward are always going to come under close scrutiny, and their honesty and credibility. Where such a witness claims a reward, this fact *must* be disclosed to the prosecutor, who decides about how it is to be accounted for and disclosed to the court.[2]

KEY POINT

Offering rewards sometimes has the potential pitfall of motivating people to provide inaccurate, misleading or false information that may undermine an investigation. The best approach is to proceed with caution when using the tactic and seek corroboration wherever possible.

13.4 Initial Contact and Accounts

The manner in which investigators approach witnesses from the point of first contact, during interviews and through to the conclusion of the case can have a significant bearing on if and how they provide supportive evidence (as referred to in section 11.5). Making initial contact with witnesses is not just confined to the early stages of a 'live' enquiry but also during re-investigations such as historical or 'cold' cases.

Members of the investigation team and any others who may come into (initial) contact with witnesses must fully appreciate the impact their actions, attitude, behaviour, and approach (communication) styles may have. First impressions count immensely and influence how a witness perceives they will be treated and dealt with throughout the entire process; maybe even unsettling them and their decision to help and cooperate. It may take a long time to win back their faith and trust if they have a bad experience at the hands of those they first encounter. Inappropriate or ill-considered methods of dealing with witnesses may hinder the investigation and lose a vital source of evidence. This point must be stressed to all staff engaged on the enquiry team.

KEY POINT

Locard's rule, 'every contact leaves a trace',[3] is equally applicable to the impact investigators have on witnesses. First impressions count and may influence their

---

[2] See *R v Rowe, Davis and Johnson*, aka 'The M25 three', Times Law Report 25 July 2000. The three defendants successfully appealed against their convictions for murder, causing grievous bodily harm and several robberies on the night of 15–16 December 1988. In the original trial, the prosecution case had failed to disclose that a reward had been paid to the main prosecution witness who was also initially treated as a police informant.

[3] See section 6.1.

> decision whether to offer (or not) information. The initial 'contact' they have with those they first come into contact with *must* be a positive one.

Procedures described later in this chapter for interviewing certain categories of witnesses and victims may require the use of special facilities and recording equipment. These interviews, however, cannot always be arranged instantaneously, as trained staff and resources may not be readily available, but resourcing and facility delays *must not* prevent witnesses/victims from providing valuable initial accounts. These enable an assessment of their information and contribute to a decision on what category and status they might be assigned (ie significant, intimidated, or vulnerable). Their information may also be needed quickly to help in identifying crucial high-priority lines of enquiry/fast-track actions, for example:

- Early arrest of an offender.
- Identification of a crime scene.
- Recovery of material evidence that might otherwise be lost or destroyed.
- Save life.
- Prevent commission of further offences.

Any initial questioning should be by way of a brief account, avoiding gathering great detail until a later, more formal interview is arranged. Officers should try to avoid prompting and not use leading questions, limiting themselves to gaining what is absolutely necessary. The accounts should be recorded accurately with comprehensive notes taken and, wherever possible, signed by the witness afterwards. A note should also be made of responses, persons present, and the time, date, and location of the interview. The demeanour of the witness and any other relevant information should also be noted.

Such an initial account opportunity might occur in the 'Golden Hour(s)' period when people are first spoken to by officers attending the scene or during searches or H2H enquiries, in which case witnesses should be separated to preserve the integrity of their evidence.

Any information recorded will be needed by subsequent interviewing teams, prior to conducting the witness interview, and referred to in any subsequent statement or witness account. There will be a requirement to check carefully for inconsistencies or alterations with any formal interview and the initial account. This is particularly important in relation to any description or identification of suspects and vehicles or words spoken and comments made.

If first accounts are recorded by response officers on body-worn video cameras (BWVs), it is important these recordings are properly reviewed *before* making decisions about matters like witness categorisation, lines of enquiry, etc.

KEY POINTS

- Obtaining initial accounts complies with the 'best evidence' rule and 'Golden-Hour' principles.
- Initial accounts, accurately recorded, can be obtained using open questions without much prompting or probing (eg 'Tell me ...', 'Explain ...', or 'Describe ...'). These minimise the risk of influencing what witnesses have to say.
- Discrepancies between initial accounts and more formal witness interviews must be identified, as they can undermine reliability and accuracy.

13.5 **Evidence Credibility**

Reference was made in section 11.2 about an avoidance of prejudging any person (or their information) as a 'victim' and always applying important principles without favour such as the 'ABC', the 'investigative mindset', and maintaining neutrality (all outlined in Chapter 3). These same rules apply to potential witnesses, who might be victims too.

For an account to be evidentially useful it must be reliable. Determining whether or not a witness is being truthful or indeed whether they have recalled facts accurately forms a critical part of the investigation process and criminal justice system. Investigators must always remain impartial and objective, maintain an open mind, and conduct a thorough investigation by pursuing all reasonable lines of enquiry without favour. This includes (wherever reasonable) checking any information provided by a witness and seeking corroboration, which can serve to strengthen (or weaken) their evidence. Carefully scrutinising the veracity and accuracy of an account provided is a fundamental investigative requirement.

This may include checking the integrity of the person providing the account. Part of the process may have to involve establishing a person's background to see if there is anything that could affect their reliability or credibility. Finding out if they have any link to the victim or suspect can be a useful line of enquiry. These are queries that will be put to the test under cross-examination in a legal setting so it is best to find the answers out beforehand.

It also assists in determining what level of reliability can be placed on the evidence and person supplying it (eg whether they might have a motive to be malicious or untruthful). These enquiries need to be made tactfully, of course, and in a manner that doesn't dissuade the person from providing an account and in accordance with the principles of the Witness Charter (see section 13.15).

Conducting background enquiries is a process sometimes known as 'witnessology' in the same way as 'victimology' or 'suspectology'. An example might be where a witness has previously made false accusations or allegations, or has numerous convictions for dishonesty. It is best to know this information in advance to determine the likely significance of a person's evidence and before any judicial proceedings that might follow.

Seeking independent corroboration is always the right way. Making an objective assessment of the evidence details will help determine if a person is providing special or particular knowledge that only they could have known through an honest and trustworthy observation. Getting the chronology of events right and having them corroborated should be an early activity in the enquiry, and any genuine errors rectified as early as possible.

If a witness is a specialist who is required to give expert opinion, it is important to know how they have 'performed' in other judicial cases, ie under cross-examination, and whether any adverse or praiseworthy comments were made by a trial judge or reported in the media or by the case officers. Fortunately, the United Kingdom has the benefit of the Specialist Operations Centre (within NCA) that maintains an Expert Adviser's Database containing information about registered 'experts' in a large variety of disciplines. This database includes details of any previous cases in which they have been involved, and their credibility and reputation as a witness from the viewpoint of investigators who have knowledge of them.

13.6 **Protecting Witnesses**

Some cases have witnesses whose evidence becomes critical and who are likely to be at substantial risk of harm from those or their cohorts against whom they are giving evidence. If this is the case, a duty of care is owed to them, and most forces and agencies, and in some cases local authorities, have in place arrangements for offering support to witnesses which operate on a sliding scale, depending on the perceived level of threat. Witnesses, however, should never be offered any incentive, inducement, or guarantee to provide a statement of evidence on promise of special treatment. In addition, the general rule is that any support provided must not significantly increase their current living standards.

Witness support measures are usually highly confidential and cannot be explained further in any detail. However, when considering potential candidates for a support scheme, an SIO may wish to consider the following:

- Gravity of their testimony.
- Whether they contributed to their own predicament.
- Background and make-up of their family.
- Assessing the risk using the T x H = R method (see section 3.6).
- Whether they or their immediate family have a criminal record.
- Level of support required and who it includes (eg extended family).

Expert advice should be sought from specialists on witness protection tactics and at the earliest opportunity. Witness support units usually require a structured assessment and application process, due to resource and financial implications that could potentially, in extreme cases, extend over the lifetime of the witness.

In some cases, overt or covert tactics may be required to protect witnesses. An example of a covert tactic might be an ongoing assessment of risk through HUMINT sources who could be tasked with an RFI (request for intelligence) for establishing if any and what type of risk there might be to certain witnesses.

Victims who are also witnesses may need support from an appropriate victim support scheme. Support may also be required for witnesses who are 'secondary victims' because of the traumatic effects of what they have seen.

KEY POINT

Care should be taken when recording witness statements not to include personal information of the witness or victim unless absolutely necessary for the investigation. Written statements should only include personal information if it is relevant evidence to the investigation. This is in accordance with Article 8 HRA 1998, the General Data Protection Regulations (GDPR) and Data Protection Act 2018.

13.6.1 Offering protection

Investigators should not openly comment on particular tactics for protection that have been provided for witnesses or concerning any operational element of their support. To do so would risk compromising sensitive tactics and the very people whom the arrangements have been designed to protect.

However, public statements contained within a communications strategy can include a message that reinforces a commitment to protecting witnesses aimed at encouraging people to have confidence in stepping forward. It is advisable to seek advice from an expert such as a Media Liaison Officer (MLO) or Witness Protection Officer who can assist in devising the most suitable wording. SIOs should aim to send out a positive message of how they and the investigating/ prosecuting authorities are jointly committed to supporting witnesses and victims, and, if appropriate, mentioning some high-profile local cases where this has been successful.

13.6.2 Anonymity orders

Part 3, sections 74–97 of the Coroners and Justice Act 2009 (CJA), Chapter 25, which came into effect on 12 November 2009, allows for the application to a court for an 'Investigation Anonymity Order'. This is an order made by a Justice of the Peace (JP) in relation to a specified person prohibiting the disclosure of information:

1. that identifies the specified person as one who is or was able or willing to assist a specified qualifying criminal investigation; or
2. that might enable the specified person to be identified as such.

13.6.2.1 Qualifying offences

An offence is a qualifying offence for these purposes if it relates to either (a) murder, or (b) manslaughter, and the death was caused by one or both of the following:

1. Shot with a firearm.
2. Injured with a knife.

Under the Act it is an offence for a person to disclose information in contravention of an Investigation Anonymity Order, and a person guilty of this offence is liable on conviction on indictment to imprisonment for a term not exceeding five years or a fine, or both. A person who discloses information to which an Investigation Anonymity Order relates does not contravene the order if:

1. disclosure is made to a person who is involved in the specified qualifying criminal investigation or in the prosecution of an offence to which the investigation relates;
2. disclosure is made for the purposes of the investigation or the prosecution of an offence to which the investigation relates;
3. disclosure is in pursuance of a requirement imposed by any enactment or rule of law; or
4. disclosure is made in pursuance of an order of a court.

13.6.2.2 Conditions for making an order

A JP may make an 'Investigation Anonymity Order' if satisfied that a qualifying offence has been committed and there are reasonable grounds for believing that the following conditions are satisfied:

1. The person likely to have committed the qualifying offence is a person who was aged at least eleven but under thirty at the time the offence was committed.
2. The person is likely to have been a member of a group engaged in criminal activities in which it appears that the majority of the persons in the group are aged at least eleven but under thirty at the time the offence was committed.
3. The person specified in the order has reasonable grounds for fearing intimidation or harm if identified as a person who is or was able or willing to assist the criminal investigation.
4. The person specified in the order is:
   (a) able to provide information that would assist the criminal investigation as it relates to the qualifying offence; and
   (b) is more likely than not, as a consequence of the making of the order, to provide such information.

Witness Anonymity Orders are different from Investigation Anonymity Orders, but they fall under the same Act. They are an order by a court that requires specific measures in relation to witnesses in criminal proceedings. This is to ensure the identity of the witness is not disclosed during or in connection with court proceedings. The kinds of measures that may be required in relation to a witness include one or more of the following:

1. The witness's name and other identifying details may be:
   (a) withheld; and/or
   (b) removed from materials disclosed to any party to the proceedings.
2. The witness uses a pseudonym.
3. No questions are asked that might lead to the identification of the witness.
4. The witness is screened to any specified extent.
5. The witness's voice is subjected to modulation.
6. The order will not allow the witness to be screened so that they cannot be seen by:
   (a) the judge or other members of the court (if any); or
   (b) the jury (if there is one).

KEY POINTS

- If anonymity measures are used, careful management of information within the enquiry team and case management systems is required to ensure the measures and identities are not compromised.
- A Witness Anonymity Order is required in addition to an Investigation Anonymity Order if it is necessary for the witness to give evidence in court.

13.7 **Reluctant Witnesses**

A reluctant witness is one who has evidence to offer but is reluctant for a variety of reasons, eg in communities where there is a mistrust of the police or where there is fear, hard-to-reach minorities, language and cultural barriers, or vulnerable persons. Criminal groups and organised crime gangs (OCGs) can also make it highly risky for genuine witnesses to come forward. Alternatively, witnesses may just have a lack of understanding of what is involved or be reticent due to witness apathy—a 'not wishing to get involved' attitude.

For those who are in fear of intimidation, an approach needs to be planned and executed that demonstrates an unquestionable intent to safeguard their welfare and eliminate any potential for compromise. This can be achieved using effective measures and tradecraft, eg similar to those used in CHIS (informant) handling by arranging covert meeting places and not visiting their home addresses. Such measures, once adopted, however, must be recorded within a 'sensitive' policy log (see Chapter 4) to ensure confidentiality and security and maintain the integrity of the process.

Officers with good interpersonal communication skills are usually the best choice for approaching and 'handling' reluctant witnesses as these attributes can make all the difference in securing willing cooperation. Careful thought and planning, together with research of the individuals concerned, their background, previous dealings with law enforcement, finding someone they have trusted before, etc can prove very effective. Trusted third parties, such as some community leaders, members of independent advisory groups (IAGs), family, friends, and relatives, or local authority support units, for example, can sometimes help break down barriers of mistrust or apprehension.

KEY POINT

A record and audit trail of all policies, tactics, approaches, and contact with witnesses are required to avoid any transgression or breach of process accusation. It is optional to use a separate policy log for each witness, including a sequential record of events of all contact and communication between them and the enquiry team.

13.7.1 Summonses and warrants

As an extreme measure, paragraph 4 of Schedule 3 to the Crime and Disorder Act 1998 provides a power to bring reluctant witnesses before a magistrates' court either by summons or warrant, to make a deposition before the court. This should only be considered in exceptional cases where:

1. A person is already charged with the offence in question.
2. The witness has provided information that is of value to the prosecution case but has refused to provide a witness statement.
3. The procedure does not place them at unacceptable risk if the evidence is produced, which cannot be mitigated by special measures (eg anonymity, screens).

13.7.2 Hostile witnesses

Hostile witnesses are those who are believed to have witnessed an offence, part of an offence, or events closely connected with it, but who are openly opposed to assisting the investigation process.[4] This could be due to their

---

[4] Ministry of Justice, *Achieving Best Evidence in Criminal Proceedings: Guidance on Interviewing Victims and Witnesses, and using Special Measures* (Office for Criminal Justice Reform, 2011), para 2.144.

lifestyle, criminality, relationship with the alleged offender, and/or intention to appear as a defence team witness. Some hostile witnesses simply refuse to cooperate whilst others provide false or misinformation intended to support a false account or completely mislead the enquiry team.

Where a hostile witness consents to be interviewed, this can be recorded in accordance with the significant witness procedure. Where a hostile witness claims not to have any information to assist the investigation, every effort should be made to record this too as 'negative' statements can prove useful if the individual or their evidence resurfaces at a later stage.

13.8 Witnesses as Crime Scenes

Some victims and witnesses need to be treated as crime scenes, eg if they come into close contact with offenders or evidential items (eg vehicles or weapons) or there is any potential for the cross-transfer of material such as fibres, DNA, fingerprints, or body fluids. This includes occasions where witnesses attempt to detain offenders, or come into close contact with them before or after an offence is committed.

It will require tactful handling if a witness is to be treated as a crime scene and, for example, subjected to swabbing or have their clothing or possessions seized. There has to be recognition of maintaining their willing support and cooperation, particularly if they need to be subjected to some form of forensic process or examination.

13.9 Investigative Interviewing

Investigative interviewing relates to the process of witness (and suspect) interviews that are methodically undertaken and recorded. This type of interviewing can:

- Direct the investigation—leading to the prosecution or release of a suspect.
- Support a criminal justice process.
- Increase public confidence in, and credibility of, the investigating team.
- Prevent the loss of critical material.

Consideration needs to be given to the (dis)advantages of, and necessity for, recording (video or audio) certain types of interviews with particular categories of witnesses. This is to protect the integrity of the process, enable the witness to recall events freely without interruption or contamination, and provide a 'best-evidence' product. It can also provide strong and compelling evidence in cases where a witness becomes a suspect. On the negative side, it can be overly resource and time consuming.

13.9.1 **Interview advisers**

In the United Kingdom, there is a cadre of nationally accredited interview advisers who are best involved in an investigation at the earliest opportunity. Advisers can assist in determining appropriate strategies and methods to conduct interviews and guide decisions on correct categorisation of witness and their interviews. They help take some responsibility away from the SIO by 'managing the process' for them in a similar way to how a Crime Scene Manager (CSM) might oversee a scene examination. Advisers can also help select the most appropriate trained staff for conducting interviews and manage and support them throughout the process. As always, any final decision around policy and tactics always rests with the SIO who should not be dominated by overly enthusiastic advisers.

Those selected to conduct interviews should be trained to PIP level 2 within the corresponding National Occupational Standards (NOS) competency framework (see Section 1.5). Consideration may be given to their relevant competence, background, and experience, having regard to the nature of the offence under investigation and any individual welfare issues that may arise (eg child death investigations, domestic violence).

KEY POINT

SIOs should satisfy themselves that investigative interviews are being conducted in accordance with their own requirements and remain in full control of the process. 'Advisers' are what their title suggests and they are there to advise. Any final decision always remains with the SIO.

13.9.2 **Witness interview strategies**

A witness interview strategy is a high-level overview of the policy, objectives, and process in the context of the overall investigation. It is not to be confused with an interview plan, which tends to be more tactical in nature. The strategy is usually discussed and agreed through extensive consultations between the SIO, Interview Adviser, and nominated interviewers.

A general witness interview strategy should adequately cover most witness interviews in any enquiry, the components of which are:

1. Witness categorisation:
   - Vulnerable.
   - Intimidated.
   - Significant.
   - Other (ie none of the above).

2. Management of initial contact:
   - Purpose (eg to obtain initial brief account or to aid categorisation).
   - Process of initial contact (eg under achieving best evidence (ABE) guidelines).
   - Relevant briefing material (eg source of witness information).
3. Method and rationale for prioritising interviews:
   - Interview adviser to provide assessment of their importance (particularly if multiple witnesses).
4. Method for coordinating interviews:
   - Strategies for minimising repeat interviews (particularly for certain types of witnesses such as those in vulnerable communities, Child Sexual Abuse and Exploitation/Modern Slavery and Human Trafficking (CSAE/MSHT) victims, etc).
5. Resources:
   - Skills or knowledge of interviewers required
   - Location and means of gaining access to interview suites and recording equipment

Circumstances may arise in which a more specific strategy needs to be developed for an individual witness. Such a strategy tends to be the result of either:

1. The likely nature of their evidence (eg importance to the investigation, inconsistencies with other material, reluctance, vulnerability, or hostility); or
2. Communication challenges (eg young, traumatised, incapacitated, learning, speech, or language difficulties).

The components of a specific witness interview strategy are:

1. Witness assessment:
   - Category or categories the witness falls into.
   - Capacity to give informed consent to an interview.
   - Likely significance of their account (based on initial information and assessment).
   - Likelihood of (non)cooperation.
   - Practical considerations (eg medical/psychological condition).
2. Sources of advice:
   - Subject-matter experts.
   - Anyone who knows and understands the witness.
   - CPS in context of 'early special measures discussion'.
3. Information important to the investigation:
   - Matters of general investigative practice, including:
     — comprehensive account.
     — points to prove.
     — case law (eg *R v Turnbull and Camello* (1976) 63 Cr App R 132).

— other persons present at time of any observation.

— anything mentioned to third parties post incident.

- Case-specific material, including:

— probable location of any items used in commission of offence.

— significant evidential inconsistencies or omissions.

— nature and background of any relationship—witness and suspect.

— anything that might impact on credibility (eg alcohol or drugs taken).

— information regarding likely witness intimidation.

— background information to support a 'bad character' application (subject to the necessary gateway provision with the consent of the trial judge).

— anything specific to the nature of the incident.

KEY POINT

Some types of incident may highlight specific areas to cover with witnesses. For example, fire investigation experts might wish to establish if a witness saw any flames and if so what colour they were, if any popping or banging noises were heard, what colour and direction the smoke was blowing in, if any doors or windows were seen open, or any smoke alarms heard.

13.9.3 PEACE model

The PEACE model of interviewing remains a recognised framework for conducting interviews with victims, witnesses, and those suspected of offences. It has been around since 1992 and has a proven track record of success. It provides a straightforward structure to stages of the interview process. The acronym stands for:

> **P**—Planning and preparation
>
> **E**—Engage and explain
>
> **A**—Account, clarify, and challenge
>
> C—Closure
>
> E—Evaluation

13.10 Witness Categories

Witnesses are generally divided into one or more of the following groups, which dictates how interviews should be recorded as well as any consequences for how evidence might be given during any trial process:

1. Significant/key.[5]
2. Vulnerable (YJCE, section 16).
3. Intimidated (YJCE, section 17).
4. Other (Criminal Justice Act 1967, section 9).

13.10.1 Significant/key witnesses

Significant witnesses (aka 'SigWits'), sometimes referred to as 'key' witnesses, is the category most likely to be encountered during investigations. It is a responsibility of the SIO to identify and/or confirm those witnesses afforded 'SigWit' status. This decision can be recorded and incorporated within an overall witness strategy. In some cases, it may also be necessary to explain why a witness has *not* been granted 'SigWit' status to pre-empt questions which may arise later.

DEFINITION OF SIGNIFICANT WITNESS

Significant witnesses are defined in ABE[6] as those who:

1. Have or claim to have witnessed, visually or otherwise, an *indictable offence*, part of such an offence, or events closely connected with it (including any incriminating comments made by the suspected offender either before or after the offence); and/or
2. Have a particular relationship to the victim or have a central position in an investigation into an indictable offence.

There is *no* statutory provision for recorded interviews with significant witnesses to be played as evidence-in-chief; however, this does not prevent defence teams from asking a court for permission to play some or all of the recording in support of their case, eg to challenge the integrity of the process.

There can be a temptation to concentrate on obvious types of witnesses who may fall into this category, such as those who observe a crime being committed. There may be other suitable recipients for this status who are less obvious, such as initial emergency responders to a crime scene, who may observe important events and circumstances. However, the category still needs to be applied sensibly. Interviewing a large number of witnesses as 'significant' can be time-consuming and resource-intensive. Having numerous witness products to transcribe and reproduce in documentary format can have a detrimental impact on

---

[5] Ministry of Justice, *Achieving Best Evidence in Criminal Proceedings: Guidance on Interviewing Victims and Witnesses, and Guidance on Using Special Measures* (Office for Criminal Justice Reform, 2011).

[6] Ministry of Justice, *Achieving Best Evidence in Criminal Proceedings: Guidance on Interviewing Victims and Witnesses, and using Special Measures* (Office for Criminal Justice Reform, 2011), para 1.25.

the enquiry team and hinder the management system from keeping pace with a fast-moving enquiry.

KEY POINT

SigWit interviews take time to transcribe in order to produce a useful product. One solution is to request investigative interview summaries soon after interviews have concluded to assist in providing sufficient details of what a witness has said.

Significant witness interviews are visually (video) recorded unless the witness refuses. Alternatively, they may be interviewed on audio-recording equipment (with consent). If both methods of recording are refused, written notes and a statement may be taken, including an explanation that the interviewee has refused video or audio recording with accompanying reasons.

As the recording cannot be used as evidence-in-chief, any evidential material captured needs to be transferred into a format acceptable to the courts, usually in a Criminal Justice Act, section 9 witness statement (Form MG11). This is achieved by reviewing the recording and compiling a statement to be read and signed by the witness. This should be completed as soon as possible after the interview to avoid the witness being unduly influenced prior to reading and signing. The signing process does not require recording unless new or changed information is revealed.

The purpose of the SigWit interviewing process is to preserve and protect the *integrity* and *accuracy* of the process, rebutting suggestions that a witness may have been unduly influenced or coerced. It should also allow for an increase in the amount and quality of information gained. The only occasions when pre-recorded visual evidence can be used as evidence-in-chief is when the witness meets the definition of 'vulnerable' or 'intimidated', and playing the recording enhances the quality of their evidence. However, on some occasions a significant witness may feasibly change status, moving into either of these categories and then become eligible for consideration of special measures, as explained later.

13.10.2 Vulnerable witnesses

Vulnerable witnesses are those defined by virtue of their personal characteristics as recommended in *Speaking up for Justice*,[7] plus those defined as vulnerable as a result of their youth.

---

[7] Home Office, *Speaking up for Justice* (HM Stationery Office, 1998).

DEFINITION OF VULNERABLE WITNESS

Defined by section 16 of the Youth Justice and Criminal Evidence Act 1999[8] (YJCE):

- Child witnesses (under eighteen years).[9]
- Suffering from a mental disorder (as defined by the Mental Health Act 1983, as amended by the Mental Health Act 2007).
- Significant impairment of intelligence/social functioning (learning disability).
- Suffering from physical disability.

Courts must take into account the views of the witness in determining whether they fall into this category. Additionally, when determining whether the quality of the witness's evidence is likely to be diminished in these circumstances, the court has to consider the likely completeness, coherence, and accuracy of the evidence (YJCE, section 16(5)).

Child witnesses (under eighteen years by virtue of section 98 of the CJA) are automatically 'vulnerable' by their age. A previous sub-category of 'child witnesses in need of special protection' relating to sexual and violence offences has been removed, meaning all witnesses under eighteen years of age are on an equal footing, regardless of the offence. Section 100 of the CJA amended sections 21 and 22 of the YJCE by making it a rebuttable presumption that a child witness will give their evidence-in-chief by means of a pre-recorded interview and that they will be cross-examined via live television link.

Subject to the permission of the court, a child witness may now 'opt out' of giving their evidence by video recorded interview or by live link or both. If they do so, there is a presumption that the child witness will give their evidence from behind a screen.

13.10.3 **Intimidated witnesses**

Complaints in cases of sexual assault fall into this category (by virtue of section 17(4) of YJCE), as in these types of cases there is the likelihood the victim will know their offender. Included here might be those who witness specified gun and knife offences (section 17(5) as inserted by the CJA), and other cases, such as domestic violence, stalking, crimes motivated by race, religion, homophobia, and those which are gang related or involve repeat victims or vulnerable persons. Some families of homicide (or other serious crimes) victims might also fall into this category by virtue of the *Code of Practice for Victims of Crime* (see section 11.3).[10]

---

[8] As amended by the Coroners and Justice Act 2009.

[9] Section 16 of the YJCA defines a child witness as being under the age of eighteen years.

[10] Ministry of Justice, *Code of Practice for Victims of Crime* (HM Stationery Office, 2015).

DEFINITION OF INTIMIDATED WITNESS

Section 17 of the YJCE defines intimidated witnesses as:

Those whose quality of evidence is likely to be diminished by reason of fear or distress owing to:

• Nature and alleged circumstances of the offence.
• Age of the witness.
• Where relevant:
— Social and cultural background and ethnic origins.
— Domestic and employment circumstances.
— Religious beliefs or political opinions of the witness.
• Behaviour towards the witness by:
— The accused.
— Members of accused person's family or associates.
— Any other person who is likely to be either an accused person, or a witness in the proceedings.

Section 101 of the CJA gives complainants to sexual offences greater access to video recorded evidence-in-chief in Crown Courts (not magistrates' courts), but each case must be considered individually and no assumptions made. Some complainants to sexual offences may prefer to give evidence from behind a screen so the defendant cannot see them on the video link; others may prefer to see the alleged offender in open court.

13.10.4 Special measures

A Court of Appeal judgment in the case of *R v R* (2008) EWCA Crim 678 overturned the phased implementation timetable for special measures for vulnerable (YJCE, section 16) and intimidated (YJCE, section 17) witnesses as set out in Part 2 of YJCE, notably visually recorded evidence-in-chief and live TV link.

The effect of the judgment is that *vulnerable* and *intimidated* witnesses are both now eligible for the following special measures in magistrates' (including youth) courts and Crown Courts:

• Use of screens (section 23).
• Live TV link (section 24).
• Giving evidence in private (section 25).
• Removal of wigs and gowns (section 26).
• Use of visually recorded interview as evidence-in-chief (section 27).[11]

---

[11] Video-recorded cross-examination is the last of special measures in PartII of YJCE Act to be implemented. It was previously available to s16 'vulnerable' witnesses in some UK crown courts (Leeds, Liverpool, Kingston upon Thames). From3 June 2019, it is also available to s17(4) 'intimidated' witnesses at the aforementioned crown courts and to vulnerable witnesses at Bradford, Carlisle, Chester, Durham, Mold, and Sheffield.

Vulnerable witnesses are also eligible for the following special measures:

- Communication through intermediaries (section 29).
- Use of special communication aids (section 30).

The legislation suggests that access to special measures depends on a three-stage test:

1. Whether the witness fits the definition of either vulnerable or intimidated.
2. Whether any of the special measures are likely to improve the quality of the witness's evidence.
3. Which of the available special measures (or combination) are most likely to improve the quality of the witness's evidence.

Even though some witnesses may be eligible for these measures, different witnesses have different needs. It is a matter of judgement and is ultimately for the court to decide, based on a consideration of these needs as well as the circumstances of the alleged offence and the interests of justice, as to which special measures may be appropriate in any given case.

13.10.5 Early special measures discussions

The CPS should be informed of the potential need to make an application for special measures through an 'early special measures discussion'. This used to be called a 'meeting', but it has been recognised that it does not need to happen in person and can be, for instance, over a phone or other communications link. Practical guidance in relation to early special measures discussions is described in CPS guidance.[12]

Early special measures discussions consider how such witness evidence will be presented at court. It is important these discussions take place either before or as soon after any interview as possible, so that a witness statement can be prepared while their memory remains fresh. Preparing a statement later risks exposing the witness to unnecessary anxiety and may be counterproductive, as some of their information becomes distorted due to memory fade or contamination as time passes.

13.10.6 Visually recorded interviews as evidence-in-chief

The use of visually recorded interviews as evidence-in-chief (YJCE, section 27) is not routine practice and should be viewed as an exception rather than the rule. The overarching aim is to maximise the quality of the witness evidence, which in some cases might mean that other special measures, such as live evidence-in-chief from behind a screen via television link, is of more assistance.

---

[12] <http://www.cps.gov.uk/publications/docs/best_evidence_in_criminal_proceedings.pdf>.

Where an interview is video recorded with a view to being played as evidence-in-chief, consideration should also be given to the guidance set out in *Advice on the Structure of Visually Recorded Witness Interviews*.[13]

KEY POINT

If eligible, a court must determine whether any of the special measures would be likely to *improve the quality of the witness's evidence*. If so, the court must then decide which of those measures, or combination of them, would be likely to *maximise the quality of the evidence*. In arriving at its decision, the court must take account of the witness's own views and the possibility that the measure might inhibit the evidence being tested effectively.

13.11 Witness Intermediaries

An intermediary is a communication specialist whom courts approve to communicate to a witness questions that the court, the prosecution, and the defence team may ask and to relay responses. Intermediaries can assist in all stages of the criminal justice process from investigations and interviews, through pre-trial preparations for court to trial.

Checklist—Role of witness intermediaries

- Assist in victim/witness interviews and trials when a witness has limited expressive and/or receptive communication abilities.

- Evaluate abilities and needs of the witness and establish rapport.

- Provide advice on how to obtain best evidence from the witness (eg types of questions to avoid, types of questions most likely to elicit an accurate response, duration of the interview, frequency of breaks from questioning).

- Rephrasing questions the witness does not understand.

- Helping to communicate any responses.

- Assisting in pre-trial preparation of the witness.

There is a witness intermediary team based within the NCA who can provide support in the use of Registered Intermediaries and offer advice on interview

---

[13] ACPO, *Advice on the Structure of Visually Recorded Witness Interviews* (National Strategic Steering Group for Investigative Interviewing, 2013).

strategies. They can be contacted by email at on email: mcis@nca.gov.uk, or telephone: 0345 000 5463.

13.12 Witnesses Who Admit Criminality

Some witnesses admit to their own criminality during the course of an interview. This can be anticipated in advance from knowledge and research of the victim, their initial account, lifestyle, background, character, and nature of their evidence (ie witnessology).

Interviewers should be prepared and briefed during the planning phase so they know how to respond should the situation arise. A policy can be prepared, encompassing consultation and agreement with the CPS, outlining what the procedure is to be. Depending on the extent of criminality admitted, the CPS will advise on setting a threshold for what is/not in the public interest to pursue and what is serious enough to warrant further investigation.

13.13 Role of Confidantes

The term 'confidante'[14] is given to particular types of witness and means those in whom offenders have confided. Some witnesses obtain information about a crime because offenders admit to them what they have done. This is generally to a family member, partner, work colleague, or fellow associate or criminal, or to victims' families or associates.

A number of investigative strategies mentioned in other chapters could include an added requirement to attempt to identify opportunities to uncover 'confidantes'. For example, an intelligence strategy (covert and overt) could cater for the identification of those who are likely to have had an opportunity to witness anything said or done by an offender. This may involve some degree of analytical work to highlight likely candidates by examining lists of suspect's partners, relatives, friends, colleagues, or associates. It could also include identifying and profiling those who might be classed as having strong morals and consciences that render it difficult for them to maintain secrets and loyalties for any length of time.

Another example is in a communications strategy. Appeals for seeking help and information could be designed to reach out to those who may not even know or believe they have information of any value, but could in fact be confidantes who hold vital evidence about an offender. This option still applies even when a suspect has been identified and arrested. Those who possess such information, however, may have very close personal ties with the offender and any approach will have to be planned very carefully.

---

[14] Mentioned in P Stelfox, 'Role of Confidantes' (2006) 2(1) *The Journal of Homicide and Major Investigation*.

341

A victim support/family liaison strategy may present a further option. Given that in some crimes, the offender and victim are known to each other, it is entirely feasible their families and associates could be confidantes of the offender. In which case it would be important that staff (eg FLOs) are alert to the possibility and able to recognise opportunities that may be of advantage to the investigation. Information acquired about the victim and their lifestyle and contacts will facilitate the analysis of further potential confidantes.

In an interview strategy, interviewers should be aware that suspects may reveal facts and detail about their movements pre- and post-incident and with whom they came into contact. Consequently, they may make disclosures that could lead to the identification of confidante-type witnesses. This information might not be volunteered unless the right questions are asked.

Finally, there is the area of what are known as 'cell confessions', ie offenders in custody who make admissions to other inmates. The golden rule is that these must be viewed with a degree of scepticism as to reliability and credibility of the 'witness' and their motives. However, it may be that any information and intelligence gleaned about close associates or movements and lifestyles from suspects and convicted offenders can help identify further confidante-type witness-seeking opportunities.

13.14 Using Interpreters

In some cases, it may be necessary to utilise the services of an interpreter to interview certain witnesses. There are important guidelines and frameworks to follow and some useful ones are listed below. Interpreters:

- Identities should be verified (eg on arrival).
- Should be separated from members of the public and anyone connected with the case.
- Should be supervised at all times when conversing with witnesses.
- Should only work in the language in which they are fully qualified.
- Whenever possible translate statements *immediately following the interview.*
- In ABE interviews, the wording of resulting statements must be checked to ensure their version is what the witness actually said or meant.

13.15 The Witness Charter

The Witness Charter[15] (revised December 2013) from the Home Office Ministry of Justice sets out the standards of care that can be expected by a witness to a crime or incident in England and Wales. The Charter applies to all witnesses

---

[15] Ministry of Justice, *The Witness Charter: Standards of Care for Witnesses in the Criminal Justice System* (HM Stationery Office, 2013), available at <http://www.gov.uk/moj>.

of a crime and to character witnesses but not expert witnesses. It outlines the standards and sets out the level of service that witnesses should expect to receive at every stage of the criminal justice process, through to giving evidence at trial and any post-trial support.

It is aimed at ensuring every witness receives a level of service that is tailored to their individual needs so that they are more likely to stay involved with helping the case and attending trial to give evidence. The document is essential reading in developing and maintaining adequate knowledge for performing the role of an SIO.

13.16 **Victim Personal Statements**

A Victim Personal Statement (VPS) is a statement written in the victim's own words. It is different from one that is a written or recorded account of what happened to the victim. The VPS can be taken at the same time as a witness statement, but can also be taken at a later stage to:

- explain the effect the crime is having (or had) on the victim's life physically, emotionally, financially, or in any other way.
- express concerns about intimidation from a suspect.
- express concern about the suspect being granted bail.
- request support from a Victim Support Scheme.
- request compensation.

A VPS[16] forms part of the case papers and is sent to the defence legal team. All victims have the opportunity to make a VPS if they wish, and it is very important they are offered every chance to do so. Bereaved relatives or partners in homicide cases and parents and carers, where the primary victim is a child or vulnerable adult, can also provide a VPS if they so wish. The VPS is basically a person's opportunity to express their feelings and describe the effect of a crime *in their own words*.

Bibliography

Ministry of Justice: *The Witness Charter: Standards of care for witnesses in the criminal justice system* (HM Stationery Office, 2013) <http://www.gov.uk/moj>)
Ministry of Justice, *Code of Practice for Victims of Crime: Presented to Parliament pursuant to section 33 of the Domestic Violence, Crime and Victims Act 2004* (HM Stationery Office, 2015 <http://www.gov.uk/moj>)

---

[16] See Ministry of Justice, *Making a Victim Personal Statement: Victims Have a Right to Explain how a Crime has Affected Them. A Guide for all Criminal Justice Practitioners* (HM Stationery Office, 2013). Available at: <https://www.gov.uk/government/publications/victim-personal-statement>.

Ministry of Justice, *Making a Victim Personal Statement: Victims have a right to explain how a crime has affected them. A guide for all criminal justice practitioners* (HM Stationery Office, 2013)

National Investigative Interviewing Steering Group, *Advice on the Structure of Visually Recorded Witness Interviews*, 2nd edn (ACPO, October 2013)

NPIA, 'Offering monetary rewards: A useful investigative tactic when trawling for witnesses' (2011) 7(1) *Journal of Homicide and Major Incident Investigation* <https://www.gov.uk/government/uploads/system/uploads/attachment_data/file/183366/witness-charter.pdf>

Stelfox, P, 'Role of Confidantes' (2006) 2(1) *The Journal of Homicide and Major Investigation*

14

Homicide Investigation

14.1 **Introduction**

The unlawful taking of a person's life with criminal intent is and always has been the most serious crime against humanity. That is why the investigation of homicide is the supreme challenge and responsibility for a criminal investigator, and one which carries a huge professional and moral obligation. It also comes with an enormous amount of prestige, respect, and professional kudos, and can define a career. There is, however an expectation that all homicides will be solved and murderers caught quickly and punished. Failure to do so can attract negative comment and criticism, not to mention increased public risk and fear.

Unsurprisingly, it is the identification of a homicide that can sometimes prove equally as challenging. For this reason, sudden and unexplained deaths occurring outside medical settings require a form of investigation to confirm what caused the death and whether it was natural, accidental, or suspicious. Although most of deaths result from natural causes, investigators have a duty to ensure there is no likelihood of failure to recognise malicious intent or criminal involvement. With over 55 million people dying around the world every year—two per second[1]—the percentage of those occurring at the hands of a murderer remain relatively small. Nonetheless, murders do occur and those responsible must be caught. Enter the SIO.

Suspicious death and homicide investigation are complex and part of a risk-oriented business, not just for the individual but also their organisation. This comprehensive chapter has been compiled with a view to help explain and unravel some of the core investigative responsibilities and processes. It aims to provide the foundations for building essential areas of knowledge and good practice that will need to be considered when embarking on the greatest challenge and responsibility that can be bestowed on a senior investigating officer—homicide investigation.

14.2 **Categories of Death Investigation**

Terms may vary across different agencies and organisations but, generally speaking, death investigations can be separated into four categories:

1. Deaths that are expected (disease or natural causes, eg old age).
2. Deaths that are sudden, unexpected or accidental (non-suspicious).
3. Special procedure deaths (see below list).
4. Unequivocal homicide or suspicious deaths.

---

[1] Cited in Professor Dame Sue Black, *All That Remains: A Life in Death,* (Doubleday, 2018).

Category (1) deaths are usually accompanied by a death certificate signed by a medical practitioner(s) with very little or no investigation required. Category (2) are those handled by a coroner and sometimes assisted by the police (eg when the death is accidental), and a potential requirement for an inquest.

Category (3) might attract what are sometimes termed 'special procedure investigations' because they merit a higher level of response and more thorough investigation due to their nature. Hence, they might include early notification and involvement of a senior detective (Investigating Officer (IO)/ Senior Investigating Officer (SIO)) to assume responsibility for supervising or conducting the investigation. Special Procedure deaths might include any of the following:

- Unknown identity of the deceased.
- Child deaths (see Chapter 15).
- Unnatural deaths in healthcare settings.
- Police or prison custody (or other lawful detention institution).
- Illicit drug-related.
- Certain types of road traffic collisions (eg if police pursuit related).
- Locations away from home of the deceased or their close relative.
- Any outdoor locations.
- Water or drowning.
- Apparent suicides.
- Fires or fire-related.
- Industrial or agricultural accident/work-related.
- Human remains, dismemberments, body parts, or bones.
- Vulnerable persons.
- Persons with prominent public profiles (PPPs).
- Ministry of Defence establishment deaths
- Deaths on railways or other forms of public transport.
- Aircraft/air accidents.
- Critical incidents.
- Unusual or disturbing features (eg insecurity/damage at the premises where body found).

The aim of a category (3) investigation is to improve the management of the risk by providing more thoroughness, eliminating mistakes, and ruling in/out any possibility of criminal involvement. These types of deaths are often more difficult to judge and prone to more scepticism and suspicion because of the circumstances in which they occur, the types of individuals involved, and the higher degree of risk. Such cases carry a more substantial level of accountability and are likely to attract public and media interest.

Category (4) deaths speak for themselves and require consideration of most of the procedures outlined in this *Handbook*.

KEY POINT

Initial responders or investigators who respond to and deal with a sudden death, whatever category they might be and about which they have doubts, should always be encouraged to seek advice and a second opinion from a more senior detective and/or SIO.

14.2.1 Official categories of murder

Category (4) deaths are usually afforded official categories as per those listed in the Murder Investigation Manual (MIM).[2] These are useful to know, although they tend to relate more to command, control, and resourcing than decision making. Nonetheless they are widely adopted and regularly used in terminology and policy (Table 14.1).

It is advisable to try to make an early objective and mature assessment of the scale, gravity, and complexity of the circumstances under investigation. However, this might not be initially possible, particularly at the initial response phase but may become clearer as more information is gathered.

Table 14.1 Categories of Murder (MIM)

Cat. A+	Homicide or other major investigation where public concern and the associated response to media intervention are such that 'normal' staffing levels are inadequate to keep pace with the investigation.
Cat. A	Homicide or other major investigation which is of grave concern or where vulnerable members of the public are at risk, where the identity of the offender/s is/are not apparent, or the investigation and the securing of evidence requires significant resource allocation.
Cat. B	Homicide or other major investigation where the identity of the offender(s) is not apparent, the continued risk to the public is low, and the investigation or securing of evidence can be achieved within normal resourcing arrangements.
Cat. C	Homicide or other major investigation where the identity of the offender(s) is apparent from the outset and the investigation and/or securing of evidence can easily be achieved.

---

[2] ACPO, *Murder Investigation Manual* (NCPE, 2006).

14.3 **Equivocal Deaths**

Equivocal (ambiguous or uncertain—opposite of unequivocal, meaning explicit and clear) deaths are those that are the most vulnerable to misinterpretation. They can present uncertainty about what caused a person's death as the circumstances and evidence are either unclear or vital information is missing. In which case, difficulty may be experienced in making a firm categorisation based upon an initial assessment as to what happened and what might be the cause and manner of death. For this reason, they are deemed 'equivocal' deaths.[3] How they are dealt with may be catered for by local policies and procedures.

In order to assist with an assessment, some local policies may advise initial responders make a brief examination of a deceased's body to check for obvious wounds, injuries, or recent trauma. Any visual inspection, however, should only be made of exposed areas of the body such as head, face, neck, and forearms, provided it appears safe to do so and protective gloves are worn. Any touching, moving, or disturbance of a body must be kept to an absolute minimum and, if it can be avoided, a body should *never be turned* or subjected to any other significant movement that might allow body fluids to be released (eg out of the nose or mouth) and frustrate evidential examination.

Visual inspections are never totally conclusive. Sometimes and in some circumstances, they may reveal obvious tell-tale signs such as wound injuries, marks (eg around the wrists), blood, bruising, or weapon marks. Even so, only a pathologist during post-mortem procedures can confirm the true cause of death. What might assist is paying close attention to information such as the condition of the deceased, their state of dress, or any disruption to a scene at the time of arrival and subsequently (that might have been caused legitimately, ie by medical staff). This is extremely important in order to prevent misinterpretation if, for whatever reason, this information is not available at a later stage.

Some causes of death, such as strangulation and suffocation, poisoning, lethal drugs administration, or internal bruising and bleeding caused by blunt trauma, for example, are difficult to detect externally, even on an examination table. In equivocal (uncertain) death situations, when in doubt, a safer (risk-management) option is to arrange the forensic removal of the body to an accredited mortuary and securing/retaining the scene until more information is known and a post-mortem (which may have to be a forensic type) has been performed in order to provide more conclusive answers as to cause of death (COD).

---

[3] It may be difficult to determine with any accuracy what is thought to have happened, and in turn describe it to others. Remember that terminology is important, so avoid the use of the term 'victim' until the facts become clear. This is a topic covered in section 11.2

KEY POINT

For safety and preservation, the minimum standard when dealing with a body is to wear a face mask and two pairs of disposable gloves and to make a record of counter contamination measures (eg scene entry log). Remember Locard's principle: *'every contact leaves a trace'* (see section 6.1)

14.3.1 Gathering and analysing information

Information will be needed to ascertain what may have caused a death. The process of seeking and analysing information helps determine how and why a person died. Making good use of the interrogative pronouns, 5WH (see also section 3.8) provides a structured approach to obtaining and collating the necessary information. A list of potential queries/actions can be raised relatively quickly after information gaps have been identified that will assist in determining what happened, why, when, where, and how a person died.

Checklist—Homicide 5WH questions

- Who is/are the deceased (ie detailed victimology) and how was identification confirmed?

- When and where were they found?

- Who certified death, at what time, where, and when?

- What appears to be the cause and manner of death?

- What evidence suggests anything other than a natural or accidental death?

- When did death occur (rigor mortis, dated articles lying around, eg dated mail and newspapers around or behind the front door)?

- Who are their next of kin? (When and how were they told? What were they told and who by? Where are they now? What support have they been given?)

- Who is/are the deceased's spouse, partner, relatives, close friends, or associates?

- Where does the deceased reside and with whom? (Where are they now? What do they know about the death? What background information can they provide?)

- When was the deceased last seen alive? By whom? Where? Under what circumstances?

- What medical treatment has been administered? Why? By whom? Who has debriefed them and what did they say?

- Who else has examined/checked or disturbed the body?

- What significant possessions have been found (eg wallet/purse/mobile phone)?

- How was the body found? Where (location, position of body, etc)?

- Who found the body? (What is their relationship to the deceased? What is their background and character? How, why, and when did they find it? What have they said in their initial account?)

- What condition was it found in (eg obvious signs of injuries, marks, attack/defence injuries, missing/mutilated body parts, drug misuse, suicide indicators, missing or disturbed items, damage to property, signs of a struggle, or entry/exit points)?

- What arrangements have been made for ISP[4] the scene(s)?

- What clues or information is available (eg suspects, witnesses, intelligence, previous attacks, CCTV, crime recording data)?

- What is noticeable at the scene (eg theft, disturbance, forced entry or insecurity, signs of search, missing items, clean-up, blood distribution corresponding to the position of the body)?

- Where has death taken place? (What signs are there of the deceased having died elsewhere, eg mud on their clothing, drag or scuff marks, blood trails?)

- Why was the body not discovered sooner? What was the deceased doing leading up to their death?

- What is known about their last movements, moods, problems, and behaviour?

- What other recent activities or events might be linked to their death?

- What could be a motive for criminal intent?

- Who has informed the coroner and what have they been told?

- Who else has been informed or requested?

- What enquiries have been conducted?

- What other information is available?

---

[4] ISP—Identify, Secure, and Protect. See section 6.2

KEY POINTS

1. Equivocal deaths are more challenging than other deaths and effective decision making can mean the difference between preserving or destroying evidence. If the category of death is unclear, a thorough assessment must be made remembering there is only one chance to get it right, which is why the MIM states: *'If in doubt ... think murder!'*
2. Offenders associated with a victim may anticipate coming under close scrutiny and may deliberately *stage* the crime scene to make it appear something else happened, eg a burglary gone wrong. This is to divert attention away from themselves. Offenders who are strangers to their victims however, need not stage the crime scene as they believe they will not be immediate suspects.

14.4 **Preservation of Life**

Section 5.4 makes reference to the Five Building Blocks Principle, one of which is the 'preservation of life'. Initial responders to a sudden death of any description must first check whether there are any signs of life and, whenever possible, administer first aid and seek emergency professional medical assistance as an overriding priority. Some people can and do appear deceased because their vital life signs are barely visible, eg in hypothermia cases.

Law enforcement and other non-qualified responders are not medical experts and must always refer to those who are. Fortunately, in some cases death may have already been certified or be patently obvious and undisputable due to heavy decomposition, skeletisation, vital body parts missing, when deeply submerged in water, or buried. In order to administer first aid or check for vital signs of life, some movement of or interference with the body may be necessary. This may involve attaching medical devices, special equipment, or physical movement. These processes can interfere with and contaminate forensic evidence collection opportunities and leave extra marks and traces that need to be explained. Defibrillators, for example, leave heavy bruising around the chest area. Therefore, it is important to debrief medical practitioners who have been involved in initial responses and accounts obtained of:

- Who notified them?
- How they gained access to premises?
- How they administered any medical treatment (what treatments, equipment, dressings, or drugs were used and why) and where the body was upon arrival and its exact position (face down, on side, etc)?
- What condition the deceased was in?

- Who was around or with them?
- What their initial assessments and findings were and what equipment, packaging, or dressings they left at the scene?
- What actions they took and what, if anything, was found, noticed, moved, or removed on or from the body or surroundings in which it was found?
- Who certified death and at what precise time was this done?
- What notes, details, sketches, or photographs were made/taken?
- Who they saw or spoke to or what they were told or heard?
- What they know about the deceased's medical history and doctor's details?
- What else was noticed that might be of use to the investigation?

Healthcare or medical professionals can be asked for an opinion as to what may have caused the death, based on their medical training, knowledge, experience, and assessment. They may have noticed something that, though not conclusive, may help provide an early *indication* as to what may have been the COD. They should *not* be encouraged, however, to begin examining the body after death is certified as this may interfere with forensic examination processes required later.

KEY POINTS

1. An overriding responsibility is to preserve life. Some interference may be inevitable in order to discharge this duty and conduct a meaningful assessment. It should be kept to a minimum and any disturbance ascertained and noted.
2. Identification of the deceased for notification of the next of kin is also a priority, provided it poses no threat of forensic/investigative conflict.
3. Once initial responders recognise the circumstances as being a special procedure or suspicious death they must withdraw, protect the scene, and summon specialist resources.

14.4.1 **Certification of death**

Only qualified and competent healthcare professionals can formally declare and certify a person to be clinically dead (aka pronouncing life extinct (PLE)). Medical doctors, paramedics, and pathologists are the only people who can legally perform this task. The precise time and date and by whom death is certified is important information and one that is used as a starting point for establishing 'relevant time', ie significant period when death might have occurred. The person who makes the official determination of death must record the reasons of how they have done so and the exact time and date.

Confirmation or pronouncement of death is completed before any further steps can be taken, ie forensic examination of the body. Once this has been done and treatment and resuscitative efforts have ceased, jurisdiction passes to the investigation.

14.4.2 **Examination of critical victims**

Advances in medical knowledge and treatments mean that victims who suffer severe trauma injuries can receive improved levels of treatment and can survive. More and more victims are being treated and kept alive on ventilators and life-support machines despite their injuries being severe and potentially life-threatening.

In severe cases, medical diagnosis may indicate there is little chance of survival. If suspected criminal acts are involved the option may exist for allowing a victim to be examined by a forensic pathologist while still alive. This may prove a delicate issue for their close family and friends, who are likely to be suffering from emotional trauma and who may not wish their loved one to be examined in this way. It would require informed consent from the next of kin but there may be an option for having a medical expert conduct an external examination pre-death (avoiding using the term 'Forensic Pathologist'). Any such examination could prove beneficial to the investigation, but it would have to be performed tactfully and not interfere with any treatment.

14.5 **Time of Death (TOD)**

When a person dies at home with their family around them, or in a hospital setting with medical or emergency services close by, recording a reliable time of death is relatively straightforward. When there are no reliable witnesses, however, and a body is discovered alone, the requirement to establish time of death accurately becomes more difficult and it often has to be estimated.

Estimating a 'time since death' (TSD), or 'time death interval' (TDI) tends to be a contentious scientific area in the pathological sense. In the majority of cases it is preferable to rely upon factual evidence, such as witness testimony or other material such as CCTV, if available. Having an estimated or calculated TOD is a valuable piece of information (and in some cases supporting evidence) which links into a number of investigative strategies for setting time parameters, eg conducting alibi enquiries.

Traditional clues are usually found and utilised, such as the time and date the deceased was last seen alive, dates on unopened (e)mail and other dated items such as newspapers found at their home address, plus information about their movements, appointments, routines, last use of mobile phone, and other intelligence. There could be useful observations such as if outdoors, changing weather conditions post-mortem, eg rain or snow, when under-neath the body is dry.

There can be associated complicating factors, such as the environment a body has been found in, inclement weather, freezing or hot temperat-ures, indoor heating, air conditioning, chemicals, submersion in water, ice, or peat bogs, insect and animal scavenger disturbance, plus the amount of time taken to find the body; any of the latter can aggravate the task of establishing TOD.[5]

Post-mortem changes can assist when estimating TOD as corpses go through different stages which are as follows:

- Pallor mortis (paleness of death—starts within minutes).
- Algor mortis (coldness of death—when the body starts to cool down).
- Rigor mortis (stiffness of death)
- Livor mortis (blue colour of death—gravity makes blood pool at lowest level and creates lividity marks).
- Putrefaction (bacteria consuming cells and tissues and gas production such as methane, which causes bloating).
- Decay and eventual skeletisation (only bones, teeth, and possibly some hair and nails remaining only).

A list of potential scientific methods for calculating time of (or since) death follows:

1. Temperature. Algor mortis (post-mortem cooling) is based upon a steady core body temperature prior to death, presumed approximately 37°C. However, any temperature-based method needs to account for the mul-tiple variables that are experienced in crime scenes, such as the effect of different items of clothing and the number of layers worn, the variety of ventilation or artificial heating, activity engaged in prior to death, and even the physical position of the body. Submerged bodies and exposure to fires can also alter core body temperatures. One method used is based on loss of body heat following a rectal temperature reading. A common calculation used in this process is based on the work of German scien-tist, Henssge, using a graphical model known as a Henssge Nomogram.[6] A number of issues have since arisen, however, which cast doubt on the re-liability of the calculation. As a result, in February 2012, the Home Office Forensic Pathology Specialist Group (FPSG) wrote to all registered patho-logists requiring them to exercise great care when using this calculation to

---

[5] So-called body farms in the United States have been created where human remains are left out in the open to study the decomposition process

[6] C Henssge, 'Death time estimates in case work: the rectal temperature time of death nomogram' (1988) 38 *Forensic Science International*, 209–36.

give a time of death. This should now only be treated as a broad estimate stating that:

(a) time range may be useful in focusing an investigation but should not be used to establish a range in which the murder was or was not committed; and

(b) time period established by the model should not be used to exclude a suspect from the investigation.[7]

2. Rigor mortis. Muscular rigidity begins quickly but is only observable after three to six hours. It can last up to thirty-six hours before diminishing. This may be affected by the temperature of the environment, the degree of muscular activity prior to death, and the age of the deceased.

3. Morphological changes. In the absence of blood circulation, red blood cells settle under gravity and livor mortis (hypostasis) develops. The progression of decomposition, however, will depend on factors such as the health of the deceased prior to death, the effects of drugs or medications, the ambient environment (temperature and humidity), extent of animal and insect activity. and degree of peri-mortem trauma.

4. Muscular excitability. This is determined by external electrical stimulation of muscle groups and requires very specialised equipment that is not widely available.

5. Gastric contents emptying (gastroenterology). This method assumes that gastric contents are digested at clear predictable rates. The theory is that if the time of the last meal eaten is known, the extent of gastric (eg stomach) emptying can assist with an estimated time of death. This will depend on the type of food ingested (eg fat content), the physiological and psychological status of the deceased (eg degree of stress or fright), and consumption of alcohol or drugs misuse.

6. Ophthalmological changes. This includes analyses of vitreous humour and the chemical constituents of the fluid within the eye (eg changes in potassium concentration).

7. DNA and ultrastructural changes. Assessment of DNA and denaturation could provide a method of time of death estimation, as cells begin to break down with the onset of cellular death. Like other methods, the rate is affected by variables such as ambient temperature, exposure to ultraviolet light, and humidity.

8. Entomological methods. The study of insect lifecycles may be helpful, as blowflies such as green and bluebottle flies and their larvae (maggots) have a predictable lifecycle. Temperature, humidity, manner of death, and the presence of drugs within the body may affect the results.

---

[7] Dr J Adams, 'Estimation. Interim Report to the Forensic Science Regulator' Forensic Pathology Specialist Group (December 2011).

9. Botanical methods. The use of plant growth through the study of palynology (pollens) and botany assume the seasonal-specific pollen species adherent to articles of clothing or parts of the body, especially within interred remains. Rootlet infiltration of remains can similarly help with identifying perennial plants through their growth stages.[8]

14.6 Cause and Manner of Death

From an investigation perspective, the medical cause of death (COD) is the pathological condition which caused the death, ie the reason why a person died. Heart attacks, gunshot wounds, and skull fractures are all causes of death. They are the diseases or injuries that alter the victim's physiology and lead to death. This can be differentiated from the *mechanism of death*, which is the physiological change or variation in the body's workings that cause a cessation of life (eg brain trauma such as cerebral contusion into the brain, or subdural or epidural hematoma which is around the brain). In some cases, there might be more than one mechanism of death.

The phrase *manner of death* (MOD) tends to be used as a legal and administrative term. It refers to the root cause or sequence of events that lead to death and is generally divided into five categories:

1. Natural (process or disease).
2. Accidental (unintentional or inadvertent actions/unforeseeable events).
3. Suicide (intentional and caused by the deceased themselves).
4. Murder/homicide (caused by a third party).
5. Unascertained or equivocal (cannot be determined with reasonable certainty).[9]

Just as causes of death may involve different mechanisms, they can also have several possible manners. For example, a gunshot wound cannot be a natural death but can be a homicide, suicide, or accident; or where a person who has heart disease is assaulted in the street and as a consequence suffers a heart attack and dies, the cause of death would be heart attack and the manner homicide (ie unnatural death).

The medical cause of death and pathological interpretation as to manner of death play a role either in the verdict determined by the coroner or the outcome of any subsequent criminal proceedings. However, a Forensic Pathologist may not always be able to determine the manner of death. For example, in a case where a cause of death is determined by the Pathologist, eg as a head injury, the manner of death may have to be determined by a coroner's verdict

---

[8] Taken from Dr B Swift, 'Methods of time since death estimation within the early postmortem interval' (2010) 6(1) *Journal of Homicide and Major Investigation*, 97–107.

[9] These deaths are when a coroner cannot accurately determine the appropriate category.

aided by an investigation. The conclusion could be that there was a fall without third-party involvement and verdict of misadventure (eg a person who falls down a flight of stairs accidentally), or alternatively unlawful killing if they were deliberately pushed (from a pathological perspective, it is usually difficult to determine whether someone has fallen or was pushed, therefore this evidence would have to come from elsewhere, eg a witness, CCTV, reconstruction, etc). Therefore, sometimes in order to establish the manner of death, a combination of an investigation and pathological findings is required to complete the evidential picture.

14.7 **Forensic Pathology**

The word pathology derives from Greek words for disease and knowledge. In modern usage, pathology means the scientific study of disease. It is a wide-ranging medical specialism and includes the work of microbiologists, haematologists, chemical pathologists, and immunologists. There are predominantly two categories of pathologists involved in post-mortem examinations: Histopathologists and Forensic Pathologists.

Although there are nineteen different specialties of pathologists, the majority are histopathologists, who examine microscopic samples of human tissue to determine disease. Some histopathologists assist coroners to conduct non-forensic post-mortem examinations in cases where the death is not suspicious, but the coroner needs to identify a medical cause of death. The pathologists who are concerned with the investigation of suspected homicide are called 'Forensic Pathologists'.

The first port of call for assisting in cases where homicide is suspected is a Forensic Pathologist who is registered on a list held by the Home Office. These are known as 'Home Office Registered Pathologists' (HORP). They provide a 24/7 service to the police and coroners in 'suspicious' death cases. They are specialist medical practitioners who undergo additional training in forensic pathology once they have fully qualified as doctors. HORPs must be registered with the General Medical Council and hold a licence to practice within the United Kingdom. They must also be members of the Royal College of Pathologists. Once practitioners have the necessary qualifications, they may follow the application process to seek inclusion on the Home Office Register.

HORPs can assist with the investigation of suspicious deaths, as opposed to their non-forensic colleagues who may be employed to establish identity and cause of death in non-suspicious cases. Under existing legislation (Coroners and Justice Act 2009), both Forensic and non-Forensic Pathologists are instructed to conduct post-mortem (PM) examinations by one of Her Majesty's coroners. Although the legal purpose of a PM is to identify the deceased and determine the cause and surrounding circumstances of death, a forensic PM has an additional purpose, which is the collection of evidence. HORPs are trained in the collection of forensic medical and physical trace evidence from the deceased and in giving expert opinion in court as to the cause of death.

When dealing with a death scene and medical advice is required to determine the cause of death, or there is a need to retrieve forensic trace samples from the body, a Forensic Pathologist can be called upon to assist and advise. This is always best done with the agreement of a coroner. The Forensic Pathologist can advise on body recovery to ensure that vital trace evidence is not lost when the body is moved to the mortuary.

When all the results of tests are collected, the Forensic Pathologist produces a report for the coroner and a witness statement for the investigation. This is not necessarily the end of their involvement, as they may be asked to advise the SIO and prosecuting team throughout the investigation by attending meetings and case conferences as well as giving evidence at court.

Checklist—Role of Forensic Pathologist

- Attend crime scenes, liaise with SIO, and Crime Scene Investigators (CSIs), forensic providers, and other experts (eg fire investigators).

- Make observations of the body and the context in which it was found.

- Assist with identification.

- Assist with the estimation of TOD.

- Contribute to the formulation of a forensic strategy for evidence recovery from the body, including prior to removal to the mortuary.

- Advise on what samples should be taken.

- Advise on a strategy for safe removal of a body to the mortuary.

- Advise on what samples should be taken from people dying in hospital.

- Carry out full external and internal examination of bodies and coordinate the imaging of any wounds or injuries with a measurement scale by a photographer.

- Advise on what additional tests are required before, during, and after the post-mortem, eg X-rays, histology, toxicology, ballistics.

- Provide information to help initiate early lines of enquiry.

- Advise on health and safety issues in relation to the scene of the discovery of the body and the personnel involved in the examination of that scene.

- Identify risks of contamination and possible control measures.

- Advise on what other experts may be required, eg paediatrician for child cases, radiologist and/or ballistics expert for firearms and explosives cases, odontologist for dental examinations.

- Provide full briefing to the SIO post-examination and communicate provisional findings to the coroner.

- Provide a detailed witness statement to include not only cause of death but also an interpretation of circumstances surrounding the death.

- Attend briefings as and when required and meet with the prosecution team prior to trial to discuss pathological findings.

- Provide evidence in court.

- Provide opinions on non-fatal wounds and/or suspicious circumstances.

KEY POINT

A Forensic Pathologist can be asked what they are ruling out as well as what they are ruling in, which may give an indication of what has *not* occurred, eg a natural death.

14.7.1 **Attendance at crime scenes**

After initial contact by the SIO, a Forensic Pathologist usually confirms that the coroner has been notified and has authorised their involvement. Once authorised, they have the option to attend and assess the crime scene. If they decide to do so (and more often than not it is better they do), it is best the SIO requests their attendance themselves rather than delegating the task to someone else (e.g. more junior). This places them in a better position to begin liaising with the pathologist and striking up a good working relationship. The initial call also allows for a preliminary discussion about the circumstances of the case and for the Pathologist to make initial suggestions for managing evidential recovery around the body.

Having a Forensic Pathologist personally attend the scene assists teamwork. Early interaction between all specialists and experts and the investigation team is what forms a solid partnership. Once they have received an initial briefing from the SIO, the Pathologist has an opportunity to examine the scene and deceased in position, clarify and check information from those present, and provide on-the-spot advice where there is doubt as to whether to treat the death as suspicious or not. Their on-site advice is vitally important when formulating body and evidence forensic recovery tactics.

KEY POINT

It is advisable to build a good early relationship with the Forensic Pathologist. Contacting them personally is a good start rather than delegating the task to others, particularly if the initial call happens to be at an unsociable hour.

Checklist—Pathologist initial briefing

- Confirm details of the SIO/DSIO.

- Provide details of the CSI and CSM, and any other specialists involved.

- Known health and safety hazards together with contamination issues.

- Details regarding the deceased (identity, medical and social history).

- Reasons why the death is being treated as suspicious or unequivocal.

- What has occurred since body discovery (eg any disturbance by members of the public, initial officers attending, relatives, or medical staff).

- What relevant material or information is available and whether they can have access to it (eg photographs, CCTV footage, or witness statements).

- Details of what is known about injuries on the body or weapon used.

- Condition of the body when found (eg rigor mortis, decomposition, insect activity).

- Any assessments made by other experts.

- Priorities for the investigation

- Contact details of relevant individuals.

- Any other relevant information.

The pathologist's initial briefing may need to be refreshed if and when necessary, eg when further information becomes available, eg CCTV recording of an attack. This includes time after the post-mortem has been completed. Information inevitably changes as the investigation ebbs and flows and this allows the Pathologist to review their initial thoughts and findings.

KEY POINT

- If in any doubt as to cause or manner of death, a Forensic Pathologist should be requested. They are the experts at interpreting circumstances, injuries, marks, medical conditions, etc and crime scenes.

14.8 **Initial Tactical Meeting**

Any advisers and specialists required can be brought together for an initial tactical meeting. The meeting might include a Forensic Pathologist, CSC/CSM, Scene Photographer, forensic experts, fire investigators, and any other specialists such as ballistics experts, entomologists, palynologists, anthropologists, and archaeologists (just who is required may not be ascertained until a scene walk-through/assessment has been completed).

It may be necessary to recognise and agree the varying jurisdictional and disciplinary roles and responsibilities that apply to the various specialists. The meeting can be arranged either: (i) at the RVP near the cordon; or (ii) at some other suitable location, such as a police station, incident room, or mobile incident trailer or command vehicle. Ideally, the meeting should take place be *prior* to any examination of a body/bodies.

At this point the SIO can clarify specific responsibilities, share appropriate preliminary information, and establish the aims and roles of each specialty. It can be agreed who is/are responsible for the collection of specific types of evidence and the order of priority. All team members should identify how they are going to record any samples/exhibits they may take and clarify how these will be processed, ensuring the designated Exhibits Officer (EO) is informed.

This is an opportunity to discuss jointly the circumstances of the death and make important decisions and policies on how to enter the scene, approach the body, and determine what samples are required, as well as how the body/bodies will/are to be recovered, protected, removed, and transported, and what imagery and recording requirements are necessary (eg still photography, digital or high-vantage-point shots). The tactical plan should be recorded either in a policy log or stand-alone record. Once agreed, the plan should be countersigned by all those involved in the decision-making process.

KEY POINTS

1. Initial tactical meetings and briefings allow for a factual information exchange. This includes confirmation of roles and responsibilities, time factors, information known, and approach/examination strategy.
2. More than one tactical meeting may be needed as the examination progresses and further information is revealed.
3. A list of all those present should be made and, if at a scene RVP, a record of their times of arrival and departure (which can prove useful if any costs incurred by the use of experts have to be met).

14.9 Conducting a 'Walk-Through'

A 'walk-through' or scene assessment[10] provides an opportunity to gain an overview of the overall scene. This is usually the first opportunity to locate and view the body, identify valuable and/or fragile evidence, and determine initial investigative procedures for a systematic examination and processing of the scene and body (also a crime scene). It enables a reassessment of scene boundaries, making adjustments where necessary, and allows viewing of the deceased in position. The SIO should decide who is required to be included when the scene 'walk-through' is conducted. The CSI/CSM, photographer, and Forensic Pathologist are usually included. Information from witnesses and other sources is useful to have available prior to and during scene assessments to help put things into context.

The usefulness of making an early recording and photographing of the body and scene at this point cannot be overstated. It creates a permanent record and preserves essential details of the body position, appearance, identity, and surroundings. The images also enable the sharing of information with other members of the team.

Scene assessments and walk-through processes should be subject of a debriefing process to help participants, specialists, and the SIO share information, thoughts, and ideas. This will help determine the evidence examination and recovery plan and clarify key roles and responsibilities.

KEY POINTS

- When conducting a scene assessment, evidence of indicators such as drag or movement marks on the body or ground can be checked and any other post-injury activity.
- Information from medical staff or initial responders who may have disturbed or moved the body and left items at the scene is useful to have prior to a walk-through.
- Health and Safety considerations can be (re)considered during this phase (see also section 6.10)

14.10 Evidence Recovery

The initial tactical meeting and scene assessment should influence what, where, when, why, and how samples are to be taken, and by whom. This includes any clothing that may have to be removed and the necessary protection of the

---

[10] Scene assessments are also covered in Chapter 5.

body's head, hands, and other exposed areas, as deemed appropriate. Tapings, combings, swabs, and scrapings of exposed surfaces may be required in order to prevent loss or contamination of potential evidence when the body is being physically lifted and transported to the mortuary.

Bodies can, and do, discharge bodily fluids when disturbed, which can obscure or contaminate trace evidence, particularly from open wounds and orifices. Extreme care must be taken when examining and (re)moving evidence and the body or body part. A proper chain of custody and continuity of exhibits and evidence needs to be recorded, detailing meticulous processes and records about the preservation, collection, and handover of all evidence to ensure the integrity of any evidence recovered.

The deceased's valuables and property can be secured to ensure correct processes are followed and for eventual return to their next of kin. Evidence on or near the body must be protected to ensure it is available for further examination or evaluation. This may include drugs and paraphernalia, digital devices, and any cash and valuable items, the existence (or non-existence) of which may in itself provide useful information for the investigation.

Detailed photography of the deceased as they are initially found prior to any external examination is important at this stage. When the body is eventually moved, this will also include photographing the surface beneath it using measuring guides where appropriate. These are matters to be discussed with and agreed by the SIO and the other specialists involved, eg CSI and Pathologist.

14.10.1 External body examination

At the right stage and time in the examination and evidence recovery phase,, the process of an external body examination will be required, taking into account the single-most important piece of evidence at the scene is the deceased's body. This is why it is so important to hold a 'tactical' meeting and even a further one once the initial assessment has concluded to agree the process, as there may only be one chance to get it right. After photography, records should be made to include:

- position of the body.
- external physical characteristics.
- existence of marks, scars, and tattoos/piercings.
- state of dress/undress.
- presence or absence of any items that appear relevant.
- presence or lack of blood, bodily fluids, injury/trauma, petechiae, etc.
- evidence of any treatment or resuscitative efforts.

Dependent on the initial outcome of the external examination, and providing any of the above is feasible depending on the circumstances, it may be necessary to make a further evaluation of the need for further forensic specialists. The body or any other pertinent evidence may be in a fragile state, so none of the above may be possible or advisable.

14.10.2 **Ante-mortem body specimens**

A Code of Practice[11] that provides guidance on what material should be considered for recovery at the scene by a CSI prior to any post-mortem procedures is useful to be aware of:

1. Tapings from exposed body surfaces and uppermost surfaces of clothing (where it is considered likely that trace evidence will be shed on manipulation). If clothing is not to be cut away, the manipulation of the body required to remove clothing may dislodge or contaminate trace evidence; clothing should not be removed until specimens have been taken from head and hands.
2. Combings of head hair, beard and moustache hair, and pubic hair.
3. Plucked hairs from these sites, each sample being representative of the range of hairs present at those sites.
4. Where objective evidence of chronic drug use is relevant to the case, a pencil thickness of head hair, cut as close to the scalp as possible and the cut ends wrapped in foil.
5. A swab or swabs from mouth and teeth.
6. Taping from the hands where any foreign material is recognised; taping must be taken before fingernail scrapings or cuttings.
7. Scrapings from underneath the fingernails of each hand, or fingernail cuttings, using appropriate equipment provided or approved by the CSI or the forensic scientist. Sampling from hair and hands where the death may be related to firearms or explosives must be made using only a 'gunshot residues and explosives sampling kit' approved by the relevant forensic science laboratory, and preferably with advice from a forensic scientist.
8. Swabs from any moist areas on the body surface where the possibility exists that such moist stains have arisen from a person other than the body. Where there is possibility of sex-related crime, swabs will be taken from those areas where semen or saliva may be most likely considered to be present (face, neck, nipples, and hands).
9. A swab or swabs from the perianal skin, taken before a swab or swabs from the anus.
10. A swab or swabs from vulva and low vagina, taking care to avoid contamination of the latter from the initial swabbing of the former. These swabs must

---

[11] Code of Practice and Performance Standards for Forensic Pathology in England, Wales and Northern Ireland, published by the Home Office, the Forensic Regulator, Department of Justice and the Royal College of Pathologists, January 2012.

be taken after swabbing the perianal skin and anus (to avoid leakage during the course of the vulval swabbing).

11. A swab or swabs of injuries that may have resulted from contact with another individual where the skin from that individual may have been shed, eg swabbing of the skin of the neck in postulated manual strangulation.

In each instance, appropriate control swabs must be taken. Multiple swabs from a single area are numbered by order of their taking.

KEY POINTS

- Forensic trace work on external or exposed surfaces of a body will almost certainly be completed prior to pathological examination. This may slow the body recovery process down and create some delay but will form part of the forensic strategy.
- If ligatures or bindings are involved, the rule is not to undo or cut any knot. This is to enable a 'knot expert' to examine how the binding has been constructed.

14.11 Removal and Identification

Once the necessary on-the-spot examinations and samples have been completed, a body (or body part or parts) can be prepared for removal and transportation. Like everything else, this is done only after agreement by the specialists present on the best way to perform the task and will depend on the case circumstances and condition or location of the body. Other considerations may include controlling onlookers, ensuring a safe passageway, and maintaining the dignity of the process.

External parts of the body, such as the head, hands, and feet, are usually covered with plastic bags. Moving a body is a meticulous and delicate task in order to avoid bodily fluids and other evidence being disturbed, lost, or contaminated. Once ready, the body is secured in a sealed and labelled body bag. The body bag *must not be disturbed or opened* until the SIO, CSM, and Pathologist are present at the mortuary and it has been agreed to do so (this is a crucial rule with which to comply).

The movement of bodies and body parts from a scene requires tactful handling, including sometimes concealing the location and exit route to prevent journalists and morbid onlookers viewing or photographing and recording the removal process. Body transportation should be managed skilfully, employing professional personnel (eg undertakers) who have the correct training, skills, equipment, and most appropriate vehicles and clothing/uniforms to convey the body to a mortuary, something essential to maintain the dignity of the dead and for their next of kin, families, and relatives.

> **KEY POINT**
>
> 1. If a body is removed prior to, or with/without supervision, a check must be made to ensure no injuries have been caused while being handled and transported, eg by undertakers removing a body from a limited access location. If witnessed by officers or other professionals, this information must be relayed to the SIO.
> 2. A body bag is sealed at the point of removal and *must not be opened or tampered with* until the SIO and their team of experts (ie pathologist and CSI) agree it is appropriate to do so.

14.11.1 **Continuity and identification**

When being removed from a crime scene, a body needs to be 'identified' to those transporting and receiving it, eg funeral directors, mortuary staff, and the Forensic Pathologist. This duty is performed before any post-mortem takes place. This is to ensure there is continuity of identification from the crime scene to mortuary with the body being accompanied in order to supervise and protect the chain of continuity and make the handover complete. A body is an important exhibit and the integrity of its handling and movement is no less important than any other key piece of evidence. Identification procedures should continue when the body bag is first opened and immediately prior to any further examination or autopsy taking place.

Evidential continuity identification is made by those who observe the body at the scene, whereas personal identity identification is performed by a relative or person who knew the deceased. In practice, the latter process is conducted at the mortuary, usually in a suitable viewing room once the external examination of the victim has been completed and all necessary external swabs and samples have been taken. The body is then externally cleaned up and made as 'presentable' as possible.

A post-mortem can be temporarily suspended while the viewing and identification are completed, provided this is not going to interfere with any examination process or contaminate evidence. This procedure has the following benefits:

- Allows formal identification without having to wait for a full post-mortem to be completed.
- Allows relatives of the victim an early opportunity to see and identify their relative, and most are always eager to do so, which should be respected wherever possible.
- Enables a viewing before any further medical interference with the body.
- Provides an opportunity to establish and foster positive relationships with the deceased's family.

This part of the process needs managing sensitively and tactfully, and all options and arrangements should be discussed with the Family Liaison Officer (FLO) beforehand. Other considerations may be important, such as the state of the body and distress seeing it may cause. If the victim is a young child, and even in other cases, the family may want to touch or hold them (some cultural beliefs may also need considering). If so, this will require careful management and supervision with the Pathologist and CSM to ensure there is no compromise of the post-mortem and forensic examination process (this is covered in section 15.8).

KEY POINT

'It is best to let relatives decide for themselves whether or not they wish to see the remains of their family members. Many opt to do so and will be caused undue stress if they are not allowed the opportunity.' Lord Justice Clarke: Inquiry into the Marchioness disaster on the River Thames, 1989.

14.11.2 Methods of identification

Accurate early identification of the deceased is a top priority. An unknown nameless body presents one of the biggest problems for an investigation and identification is *the* imperative, regardless of how much time has elapsed since death. This must be done as quickly as possible so the next of kin can be notified (it is not recommended that they find this out themselves, eg via social media alerts) and the circumstances of the death properly investigated.

In most cases, identification is achieved through family members, witnesses, or local information. Using one's initiative is also recommended, eg, checking personal possessions such as a mobile phone on or around the deceased (provided this will not compromise any forensic procedures that are required) as this may reveal a caller's details. Sometimes, however, the process can become complicated by mutilation, advanced decomposition, dismemberment, or extensive injuries. Known relatives or friends of the deceased may also prove difficult to contact or trace to attend and confirm identity.

Checklist—Methods of identification

- Name of deceased (personal identity).
- Relatives, witnesses, or information (eg through enquiries and appeals).
- Personal effects/possessions (eg clothing, jewellery, documents, digital devices/cell phones, keys, driver's licence, credit cards, security passes, receipts, etc).[12]

---

[12] Remain alert to 'rogue' personal effects that might belong to someone else.

- Physical characteristics (physical identity—sex, age, stature, hair, tattoos/piercings, surgical operations, implants, scars, physical irregularities, body modifications).

- Ancestry and nationality (or race).

- Facial identification (visual, photographs, facial reconstruction[13]/forensic artist, facial image analysis, or iris recognition).

- Fingerprints (Ident1 and NDNAD[14] (biological identity).

- DNA obtained from Guthrie cards retained by the National Health Service (taken at birth for every child born in the United Kingdom since 1950s and used to test for genetic conditions).

- Missing person checks locally and through the UK Missing Persons Unit.

- Forensic anthropology.

- Odontology (dental records, teeth, gums, contents of oral cavity).

- Dental enamel (to help pinpoint place of birth).

- Osteology (study of the human skeleton—a sub-discipline of anthropology).

- Biological samples (blood, biochemistry, toxicology).

- Radiological imaging (for use in osteology, odontology, and facial reconstruction).

- Computed tomography (ie CT scans for two- and three-dimensional imaging).

- Podiatry (using foot analysis for diseases, walking gait, abnormalities, etc).

- Environmental information (specialist examinations to identify likely environment within which a person lived, eg stable isotope fingerprinting to identify geographic region, or pollen, soil, and botanical samples).

14.11.3 Senior Identification Manager

A Senior Identification Manager (SIM) is appointed (often by a Gold Group) in cases where there are mass or multiple fatalities, eg in civil disaster-type incidents. A SIM is also useful where there is any requirement for a specialist officer

---

[13] In 2013, dismembered female remains comprising of head, torso, and limbs were found in a shallow grave on Costorphine Hill in Edinburgh. The only clues were recent cosmetic dentistry (done in Hungary). A facial reconstruction likeness produced by craniofacial expert Dr Caroline Wilkinson was circulated via the media and recognised by a relative in Dublin in Ireland as Phyllis Dunleavy. She had been staying in Edinburgh with her son, James Dunleavy, who claimed she had returned to Ireland. He was subsequently arrested and later pleaded guilty to her murder (Operation Sandpiper).

[14] Ident1 contains finger and palm prints of over 7 million UK ten-digit prints. The UK NDNAD (National DNA Database; est.1955) is the largest national DNA database in the world. Over 6 million profiles are stored representing nearly 10 per cent of the UK population.

to help positively identify deceased and oversee the process on behalf of the coroner (Procurator Fiscal, in Scotland). A SIM is usually accredited to the same standard as an SIO, ie PIP level 3 (and often an experienced SIO themselves) having been additionally trained in line with national disaster victim identification (DVI) practices. When engaged on an operation they usually maintain their own policy log.

Any case in which there are a number of deceased (eg victims) and/or body parts and dismemberments can benefit from the engagement and appointment of a SIM. Specialist and complex tasks and processes can be managed by a SIM to help improve the professionalism of the approach using (inter)nationally recognised and agreed standards.

There doesn't need to be a national disaster to benefit from involvement of someone in the role. There are numerous serious crime cases in the United Kingdom and overseas where a SIM has been appointed to assist the investigation. For example, Operation Abnet, the 'Jigsaw murder' of Jeffrey Howe whose dismembered body parts were scattered across five different locations throughout Leicestershire and Hertfordshire in March 2009; Operation Bridge, in which Derrick Bird shot dead twelve people (mostly chosen at random) then turned a gun on himself in Cumbria, June 2010; and the 'Crossbow Cannibal' murders committed by Stephen Griffiths in Bradford, where a victim's body was dismembered into eighty-one pieces and deposited in a local river in 2010.

A more recent example can be found in Operation Northleigh, the fire in Grenfell Tower in North Kensington in London (14 June 2017), in which seventy-two people died. The SIO worked in close collaboration and consultation with the appointed SIM. The relationship between the SIM and SIO became a big factor in the successful identification of all the victims and management of a very challenging and complex large-scale major incident investigation involving the tragic loss of many human lives.[15]

In cases such as the aforementioned, the close working relationship between the SIO and appointed SIM is extremely important. The needs of the overall investigation always remain uppermost in the mind of the SIO, but it must be recognised that the responsibility for recovering and identifying victims through DVI work usually must take precedence. The rule to follow is: DVI first, forensic scene examination second. Any information on cause and manner of death gleaned from the examination of fatalities may have a wider impact on public safety, and this must take priority over the immediate needs of the investigation (eg in the Grenfell Tower case: if further deaths could be prevented from unsafe building design or materials used on similar tower blocks).

---

[15] Highlighted during Op. Northleigh presentation by the SIO at the National Homicide Working Group Conference in Leeds, November 2018.

Checklist—Responsibilities of a SIM

- Victim/deceased recovery.

- Post-mortem identification procedures.

- Casualty Bureau functions.

- Family liaison.

- Ante-mortem evidential harvest.

- Ensuring integrity of identification.

- Reconciliation (forensic matching).

- Recovery, collection, and storage of forensic evidence.

- Recovery and storage of personal property belonging to deceased.

- Liaison and co-working with SIO.

- Setting identification criteria in consultation with the coroner.

- Overseeing setting up a temporary mortuary.

- Management of repatriation process.

- Maintaining a policy log.

14.12 **Post-Mortem Procedures**

Powers to authorise a post-mortem examination and remove a body to an appropriate location for examination are held by the coroner (contained within Coroners and Justice Act 2009). When arranging a post-mortem, there are some important considerations, as follows.

Checklist—Arranging post-mortems

- Coroner needs to authorise a post-mortem *before* it takes place.

- Coroner needs to know and be kept informed of time/place of post-mortem (in some instances they may wish to attend).

- If a suspect has been arrested or charged, their legal team may wish to have a representative present (or subsequent post-mortems if there are multiple offenders).

- Mortuary chosen needs to be placed on alert that a forensic pathological post-mortem is due so they have sufficient time to prepare the examination, viewing rooms, and equipment (suitable time and date should be agreed).

- Deceased's medical notes and/or hospital records, X-rays, etc if taken initially to hospital (eg A&E unit), must be obtained and made available for the Forensic Pathologist to examine before they conduct the post-mortem.

- Details of all treatment and drugs prescribed or administered to the deceased and any such items or information recovered from the crime scene or address.

- Details of infectious diseases or chemicals, such as HIV, Hepatitis B, or chemical/biological agents, must be communicated to anyone who has or may come into contact with the body, eg mortuary staff.

- Deceased's social history and lifestyle (eg if drug abuser, sexual orientation, reputation, etc) will be useful.

- The EO arranges necessary bags, labels, sample buckets, fingernail-cutting, hair-combing, and plucking kits to be ready and available (evidence-gathering equipment), although usually the CSI team will have this equipment also.

14.12.1 Attending post-mortems

In most cases, the SIO personally attends post-mortems. This is to observe first-hand any significant findings and participate in discussions as the examination proceeds on all matters that may affect the course of the investigation. In some cases, the task may be delegated owing to competing demands or other important matters that may take precedence or need attending to, being mindful of the length of time it takes to undertake a post-mortem (usually no less than three or four hours).

A compromise might be for the SIO to attend at the beginning and return before completion in order to discuss the findings personally with the Pathologist. Progress reports can also be received remotely (eg. over the phone) as the examination progresses, which is still not as good as being there in person to observe the process. There is no hard and fast rule but suffice it to say, wherever possible the SIO should normally insist on being present throughout this very important process. Many times during post-mortems questions arise and important decisions are required as the examination progresses. A body is a key exhibit and clue in the investigation.

Checklist—Persons required at post-mortems

- SIO (or designated deputy)

- Senior Identification Manager (SIM—if applicable)

- Forensic Pathologist

- Mortuary technicians/assistants

- CSM/CSI

- Crime scene imaging staff/photography experts

- Other experts as required (radiographers, ballistics, paediatricians, anthropologists, biologists, toxicologists, palynologists, odontologists, etc)

- Principle Exhibits Officer

Post-mortem procedures (and mortuaries) are grim and often gruesome. SIOs must remain wholly professional and detached, and get acquainted and familiar with the surroundings and procedures, remembering their functions and purpose. All senses become aroused by the sights, sounds, and smells that become more and more familiar through experience (although each visit usually produces a few surprises). Experienced investigators cannot concentrate on their work if they are too concerned about the suffering of the dead; if this were to be the case then they could not do their jobs properly.

The unmistakeable stench of putrefaction and insect-riddled or mutilated remains takes some getting used to, but the trick is to try and breathe through the mouth not nostrils, something which can be mastered with experience. It is best to treat the entire process as an anatomic, scientific, and forensic exercise, training the mind to view a body extremely respectfully and as a depersonalised evidential shell. A body can offer up a gargantuan amount of information and evidence to help prove how they met their death. The evidential rewards are plentiful and not many people get the opportunity to see how a complex human body is internally constructed. It should be treated as a privilege to do so.

Those required to be present should be assessed for their suitability to cope with what they will experience during the process. If medical students request to be allowed to attend and observe, this is a judgement call, taking into account any sensitivities or potential risk of leaks of information to unauthorised persons that may compromise the investigation. Medical students are pathologists of the future and need to develop their knowledge and skills.

14.12.2 **PM evidence recovery tactical meeting**

Before commencing an examination, a further tactical meeting (additional to the ante-mortem at the scene) is to discuss and agree the forensic evidence recovery plan for the post-mortem. The SIO leads the meeting, which usually takes place at a suitable venue (eg an office within the mortuary) with all the persons listed in section 14.12.1 being present.

The purpose of the meeting is to discuss and re-examine the circumstances of the case. It is to determine and agree what the primary objectives are for the post-mortem, what samples are to be taken and in what order, what photography is required and when (eg before, during, and after removal of clothing), and whether any X-rays are required (eg to find bullets, pellets, knife tips, etc). Depending on the type of case, the following are the kind of objectives and samples routinely considered.

Checklist—Post-mortem objectives

- Establish or confirm identity of the deceased.

- Assess the size, physique, and condition of the deceased.

- Ascertain cause of death (and manner if possible).

- Determine time of death.

- Determine likely survival time of victim after any attack.

- Conduct injury analysis (amount of force used, type of weapon used, precise method details, sexual assault indicators, any incapacitation, direction of blows and position of deceased at time of injury, which wounds were fatal, whether injuries incurred ante- or post-mortem).

- Establish whether any indication of self-defence or if offenders likely to have been injured.

- Establish/confirm place of death (eg any evidence of movement of body after death, eg drag marks on feet/ankles/livor mortis patterning).

- Ascertain lifestyle of victim (eg drug or sexual abuse, health condition).

- Determine if deceased under influence of drink/drugs/toxins prior to death.

Checklist—Post-mortem samples

- Further DNA swabs from the body from unexposed areas and/or areas not completed while the body was *in situ* at the crime scene (eg swabs of all biting wounds for saliva traces and any other likely areas for gripping/holding traces).

- Oral, vaginal, or penile, and anal swabs, nasal swabs (in special circumstances).

- Fingerprints—identification and/or elimination from crime scene.

- Fingernail scrapings and clippings (if victim has long fingernails, photograph as offender may have scratch marks).

- Head and pubic hair (or other bodily hair) combings and cuttings.

- Blood, urine, stomach contents, and bile (toxicology/time of death/sperm heads).

- Tissue sections for histology.

- Swabbing of exposed fractures for foreign debris (eg head fractures).

- Internal swabs of areas such as the oesophagus (eg for sperm heads).

- Ocular fluid (toxicology and time of death).

- Liver, lung, brain, fat tissue (in special circumstances).

- Botanical swabs/samples (advice required from palynologist).

14.12.3 Health and safety risk assessments

It is in everyone's interests that during a post-mortem process, health and safety principles are adhered to and managed effectively, even when there is a conflict with the expediency of an investigation. There is a very real danger of risk of infection from dead bodies/body parts and any contact, examinations, samples, or possessions taken must be suitably controlled. As a general rule all bodies and body parts should be regarded as being potentially infectious.

A risk assessment should be recorded when the post-mortem tactical meeting is conducted and before anyone enters the examination room. The SIO needs to record this entry into their policy log after consultation with the Pathologist. The mortuary in which the post-mortem is conducted must have adequate facilities to contain infectious risks, ie ventilation and cleansing equipment. In conjunction with the coroner, the SIO and FP can request that a suitable mortuary be utilised.

For health and safety reasons, the SIO should allow only those persons who are absolutely necessary into the examination room. Permitted observers can often be accommodated behind glass screens or in a viewing gallery.

Checklist—Post-mortem risk assessment

- Those in attendance must be in receipt of up-to-date inoculations (eg TB and Hepatitis B).

- Full protective clothing must be worn, ie full-length gown and mask, face/eye shield, waterproof non-slip boots/overshoes, nitrile gloves.

- Any individuals who have any open wounds/cuts/abrasions or skin complaints must be identified and such matters discussed with the Pathologist.

- Drinking, eating, or chewing in the examination room is forbidden.

- Experienced staff should accompany the inexperienced.

- Familiarisation instruction on the layout and facilities of mortuary should be made.

- Any accidents during the process fully investigated and recorded.

14.12.4 Preparation and note taking

It is advisable to be well prepared before going into an examination room at a mortuary, eg armed with suitable note-taking equipment. It is always useful to note what the Pathologist and other experts are saying while the examination is in progress, making drawings/sketches that will assist when back at the incident room (for briefings, etc). Useful sketches of injuries or marks can be made and although photographs will be taken, these may not be immediately available. Anatomical body maps can be used to help indicate the location of significant findings.

14.12.5 Preliminary procedure

As stated earlier, a body bag (in effect an exhibit bag) must not be opened or disturbed until the SIO and pathologist agree, and everyone is ready and present in the mortuary examination room. Once the bag is opened (and checks made to ensure the seal has not been tampered with), the body is externally examined once more before any clothing or possessions are removed. Cognisance should be taken of the ante-mortem examination findings and results, for which the same persons should be present.

The position and condition of any clothing and personal effects, such as jewellery, may reveal vital clues, particularly if a sexual attack has occurred. Any cuts, tears, holes, rips, etc in clothing can be matched with corresponding injuries. Evidence of missing buttons, zip fasteners, etc should be checked. A decision should have been made during the tactical meeting as to how any garment should be removed and recovered in order to capitalise on evidence-recovery potential (eg DNA, blood, fibres, etc), and if/what/how much photography is required during the process.

14.12.6 Completion of examination

A further meeting of all those involved is held once the examination is complete. This is an opportunity to discuss with the FP (and any other experts present) any findings, interpretations, and conclusions. Expert opinions must be supported by plausible rationale (which can and often should be questioned and probed using the ABC principle).

The Forensic Pathologist usually summarises their findings and provides an initial verbal report. It may be, however, that some aspects of the examination are still incomplete. Further tests may be required on samples or parts of the body, eg tests on the brain or toxicology reports from blood, urine, or stomach contents may be required, which must be done separately. Specialist examination of bone fractures may need further analysis. In some instances, a further examination of the body may be necessary to check whether there are any indications of bruising or bite marks that have been enhanced or have surfaced after the passage of time (taking care to distinguish them from artefacts of the removal/post-mortem procedure).

An EO must ensure all relevant exhibits are accounted for, packaged properly, and labelled with correct evidential signatures from the Pathologist and any other expert who has handled them. The list of exhibits recorded should be thoroughly checked with the Pathologist as they too may keep a corresponding record of all items and samples taken.

The Pathologist should be kept up to date with evidential developments that may affect their conclusions. In some circumstances, they may also wish to revisit the scene before reaching any firm conclusions and ask for any additional information, such as copies of witness statements.

14.13 National Injuries Database (NID)

The UK National Injuries Database can assist investigations, pathologists, and medical practitioners interpret injuries and marks on victims as well as with forensic medical issues. The unit is housed within the NCA Major Crime Investigative Support (MCIS) team and can provide support to serious crime investigation in the United Kingdom and internationally.

The NID has the capability to conduct research on their extensive database to provide support and advice in determining the cause and type of any injury found on victims either living or dead. It can also assist with sourcing independent expertise for forensic medical opinions and provide research and expertise in specialist imaging and court presentations.

The work of the unit is mainly victim-focused, and it can be used to search for cases to identify possible similarities between wounds and specific injury patterns, and identify possible weapons. This is particularly useful in cases where the nature of the injuries is unknown and the weapon unidentified, and will help investigators look for the correct type of weapon and who might have access to them. The database currently holds a large number of cases of suspicious deaths, homicides, and serious assault cases, including child abuse, sexual offences, and self-inflictions. It also has extensive scene, injury, and weapon images.

The NID also manages the Operation Marshall database (see section 15.11) for all intrafamilial child deaths within the United Kingdom, and facilitates the technique of image overlay/superimposition for the comparison of weapons and wounds.[16]

---

[16] The NID can be contacted via email: mcis@nca.pnn.police.uk or mcis@nca.go.uk.

KEY POINT

1. If any material is passed onto another agency or a second opinion is sought (eg via the NID), it is common courtesy to inform and liaise with the original Pathologist (or other expert concerned).
2. The NID can help identify injuries and what might have caused them, which is useful for when seeking to narrow search parameters to look for a specific type of weapon.

14.14 **Types of Death**

While it is not possible to go into any great depth or detail about the complexities and wide variety of deaths that can occur, this section offers an overview and quick reference guide to them. These are all specialist and complex subjects in their own right and expert advice should always be sought.

14.14.1 **Asphyxia and strangulation**

'Asphyxia' comes from a Greek word referring to a 'lack of pulsation'. In everyday terms it means death from an interruption of the process of breathing. Asphyxia may be due to suffocation (blockage of airway), strangulation (external pressure on neck), internal blockage, or interference with the movements of respiration. Asphyxia signs can include:

- petechial haemorrhages in the face, eyes, and/or body.
- congestion to the face.
- cyanosis (blue discoloration) of the face.

To complicate matters slightly, these signs can be mimicked by other events, including heart failure, resuscitation, and hypostasis. Therefore, circumstantial or supporting evidence is always useful.

Strangulation is traditionally divided into ligature and manual strangulation. Pressure may also be exerted on the neck using a 'bar arm' or 'choke hold' with a forearm. Ligature strangulation may be carried out using a variety of methods, including ropes, cord, wire, and improvised items or pieces of clothing (such as a bra or tie). Internally, it can cause fractures to the larynx or hyoid bone, denoting trauma to the neck, and internal bruising or haemorrhaging. Manual strangulation can leave fingernail abrasions and localised fingertip bruises to the muscles in the neck (which may be indicative of attempts at defence or panic removal of the ligature by the victim).

14.14.2 **Firearm and gunshot fatalities**

Four factors that affect physical appearance of gunshot wounds on a human body are: (i) type of weapon; (ii) type of ammunition; (iii) range from muzzle to body; and (iv) any intermediate targets. There are some additional considerations for incidents and deaths involving firearms:

- Specialist ballistics expert advice should be considered.
- X-rays are required to locate bullets/projectiles in a body.
- Swabs should be considered for firearm discharge residue from the body (to help determine how far the victim was from the firearm).
- Discharge residues on the victim's hands can help determine if they handled the firearm (eg if suicide suspected).
- Firearms discharge residues should be important forensic preservation/recovery consideration from suspects and their clothing/jewellery/possessions (checks to see if they have any firearms injuries themselves, such as recoil marks on their hands, rival gang or accidental bullet wounds, or adapted clothing to carry and conceal handguns).
- Analysis is required of both entry and exit wounds to help a ballistics expert determine direction of travel of the bullets, the angle the victim was shot from, and in what order the shots were fired (usually done by inserting a rod to indicate angle of direction).
- Recovery and examination of bullets assists in determining whether there was more than one weapon involved, and possibly what type of weapon was used (eg shotgun or automatic).
- In addition to GSR, contact trace evidence can be considered on firearm related items such as DNA, fingerprints, hairs, fibres, organic material, glass, paint, and botanical material or soil.
- Tracing—the systematic tracking of firearms and, where possible, their parts and components from manufacturer to purchaser for the purpose of assisting criminal investigations. The results of tracing can offer valuable intelligence to be used in combating illicit manufacturing and trafficking.
- 'Every gun tells a different story' (NABIS mantra—see section 14.14.2.2).

14.14.2.1 **Useful definitions**

Firearm	Lethal barrelled weapon from which any shot, bullet, or missile can be discharged
Ammunition	Collective term for all items that can be discharged from a firearm
Round	Single ammunition cartridge
Spent casing	What is ejected from semi-automatic firearms, or remains in a revolver cylinder after firing
Shotgun shell	Shotgun cartridge loaded with shot

(continued)

379

Jacket	Covering over the core of a bullet
Cartridge	Live round of ammunition, comprising shell casing, primer, propellant, and projectile(s)
Cartridge Case	Main body of a round of ammunition that contains the components, which is discarded after firing (retains marks from firearm discharged)
Bullet	Missile/projectile fired from a firearm usually made from lead
Fragment	Portion of bullet or jacket
Clip	Device used to store and fire multiple rounds of ammunition together as a unit
Barrel	Cylindrical tube that directs the projectile (rifled or smooth-bore)
Muzzle	End of barrel from which the projectile exits
Calibre	Measurement of barrel diameter and also size of a bullet
Rifling	Spiralling grooves cut into a gun barrel that cause bullets to spin and provide greater accuracy
Gunshot Residue (GSR)	Residues from powder, primer, and projectile, partly expelled during firing and partly remaining in firearm (come into contact with firer, hands, clothing, etc)
Pellet/shot	Small spherical projectiles loaded in shotgun cartridges and some air rifles
Wadding	Plastic or fibre filler loaded in shotgun cartridges
Deactivated weapon	Weapons modified so they can no longer discharge any projectile

14.14.2.2 NABIS (UK)

The National Ballistics Intelligence Service (NABIS) delivers fast-time forensic intelligence as well as tactical and strategic intelligence to tackle all aspects of firearms-related criminality within the United Kingdom.

NABIS provides:

- Database (registry) of recovered firearms and ammunition used in crime or entering police possession. The database provides strategic and tactical intelligence which helps guide law enforcement activity.
- Ballistics comparison capability to link crimes and incidents within twenty-four to forty-eight hours in urgent cases.
- Intelligence Cell tasked with developing, understanding, and disseminating strategic and tactical intelligence to LEAs.
- Regional facilities to test-fire, analyse, and link firearms and materials to other incidents.

NABIS works with the police forces of England and Wales as well as partner LEAs such as Police Scotland, British Transport Police (BTP), Ministry of Defence Police (MODP), MI5, National Crime Agency (NCA), UK Border Force (BF), and the Police Service of Northern Ireland (PSNI). It can be reached by telephone: 0121 626 7114 and email: nabis@west-midlands.police.uk (<http://www.nabis.police.uk>)

14.14.3 Fire deaths

Local protocols usually prescribe how to investigate fire deaths, which should include arrangements for tripartite investigations between the police, fire and rescue service, and scientific experts. Some key considerations are:

- Fire deaths can relate to crimes such as arson, homicide, and robbery.
- Bodies subjected to fire effects can offer up clues about the fire (or explosion) and what occurred before, during, and after.
- When considering a victim's location, position, and condition, fear and panic can cause victims of fire deaths to behave in a way that may seem illogical or unexplainable.
- Fire victims' clothing may reveal important evidence, eg do burn patterns on clothing match those on the body?
- Identification of victims is usually more challenging where fire is concerned
- Post-mortems are also more difficult as fire damage can cover up injuries or create spurious injuries that mimic assaults.
- X-rays might show evidence of shooting, stabbing, or other crimes underneath burn injuries (eg pre-fire damage).
- Key question to ask is whether deceased was alive or dead when the fire took hold (ie to give an indication of whether they were murdered before fire was started).
- If deceased was alive during the fire, there is often carbon monoxide in the blood, soot in the airways, and scorching below the vocal chords.

The presence of flammable liquids and several seats of fire ignition are good indicators of arson. However, meaningful interpretation of these clues is best left to the experts due to the complexity of fire investigation. The SIO will have to rely upon the Pathologist to try to interpret what injuries are visible, if any, on badly burned bodies.

Deaths resulting from fire are generally caused by asphyxiation via the inhalation of noxious gases and fumes such as carbon monoxide. Victims are usually dead prior to the burning of parts of the body flesh. The Pathologist should focus on answering the key question referred to above: whether the victim was alive or dead at the time the fire started or was the fire caused after death (and therefore may have been used to destroy evidence and cover up a homicide.

KEY POINTS

- Section 13.9.2 refers to additional information from witnesses in fire cases.
- If fuel from a filling station is suspected as an ignition source, obtaining control samples from nearby outlets needs to be fast-tracked, as most have frequent deliveries (ie every twenty-four hours). The samples can be used for forensic comparison purposes against identical accelerants at the scene, on victims or suspects.

> • Accelerants can be found in places you least expect them, eg in U-bends of sinks.
> • Position of curtain hooks in residential properties is useful to show if they were open or closed at time of fire (ie if material is missing).

14.14.4 **Bodies in water**

Post-mortems on bodies that have been submerged in water can be complicated because the body is often in a poor condition, and the signs of drowning may have disappeared after a few days. Some pointers to consider are:

• Similar to fire deaths, a key fact is whether they were already dead before they entered the water.
• Typical signs of drowning are foam in the airways and overinflated lungs.
• Spurious post-mortem injuries may be created items in the water, eg by boats, fishing equipment, underwater objects, marine life, or by the deceased's own hands dragging on the bottom of the waterway.

The finding of and recovery from water of a human body/body part(s) poses added challenges to ensure forensic evidential material, and how the body/body part will be preserved during a recovery operation. This requires close liaison between a team of experts and the SIO to put together the best option quickly. Time will be critical to avoid further destruction of the body in the water and if at all possible a contingency plan should be prepared in advance if there is a search phase beforehand.

14.14.5 **Body dismemberment**

Dismemberment is a form of mutilation, fragmenting a human body by severing and removing limbs. Not all dismemberments are as a consequence of criminality. Accidents and misadventure and mass fatalities due to disaster-type events can also cause the detachment of human body parts. When it is as a result of criminal behaviour, however, the case usually attracts interest and public attention; the more deviant or gruesome the death, the more intriguing the story.

For some offenders, dismemberment may be the best option to make a body more manageable and easier to dispose of by reducing it to smaller pieces (usually six—known as 'sites of election' see Figure 14.1). As most murders are unplanned, there is often an element of initial panic in disposing of a body, and this is when the notion of dismemberment might be first considered.

However, bodies and body parts are extremely difficult to handle and dispose of. As with any intention to conceal a crime such as murder, clumsy mistakes result from inexperience. One example is where the perpetrator returns to a deposition site after having second thoughts, or has a 'better idea' and selects a 'more reliable' secondary deposition site(s). This may even lead to body parts being deposited at different locations or at different times, something that

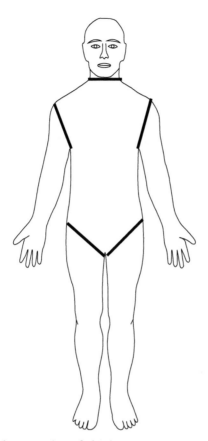

Figure 14.1 Dismemberment sites of election

produces new challenges for the perpetrator in distanced concealment and requiring means of transportation. Another is where a clumsy attempt is made at
shifting body parts away from or out of the location where the dismemberment
was performed (as in the Gemma McCluskie case[17]).

The table below describes several types of dismemberment, each having different motives. Reference cases from the NID (see section 14.13) indicate that
the majority of dismemberments occur post-mortem rather than ante-mortem,
although in a small number of cases it occurs in both. Dismemberment is not to
be confused with decapitation (the removal of a person's head) or evisceration
(disembowelment) (Table 14.2).

---

[17] In March 2012, Gemma McCluskie, twenty-nine-years old, was murdered by her brother, Tony
McCluskie. She had been an actress in the famous BBC soap opera *Eastenders*. Her dismembered body
parts were discovered in Regent's Canal in Hackney in London, starting with a headless torso. Tony
McCluskie was captured on CCTV dragging a heavy suitcase along the pavement containing her remains
and heaving it into the rear of a taxi. Minute blood and body tissue traces were later found in his bath-
room. Note: a learning point in this case was that there is not necessarily a large amount of biological
trace evidence when a dismemberment occurs inside a residential property

Table 14.2 Types of dismemberment

Defensive mutilation	(i) General dismemberment—used to facilitate body removal by disarticulation of the joints to cover up traces of a crime and hinder identification. Most common form encountered. (ii) Localised dismemberment—eg removal of head/hands, to try to destroy a person's identity.
Aggressive mutilation	Where aggression is expressed by the perpetrator to the victim after their death or where the cause of death was dismemberment.
Offensive mutilation	Associated with lust, necro-sadistic murders (religious, spiritual, or ritualistic), to release sexual pressure, fulfil urges after death, or satisfy religious requirements.
Necromaniac mutilation Criminal enterprise	When a body is dismembered post-mortem and the perpetrator keeps a body part as a trophy or fetish (eg genitalia). Dismembered body parts as part of a threat, eg by OCGs as part of rituals or threats to rivals, or in some extortion cases (eg sending human digits or ears to make a point/threat).

In addition to a HORFP, additional specialists may be required, not least to confirm (unless obvious) the parts are human. Forensic Anthropologists or Anatomists may be needed to identify and confirm the remains and to identify the body part. Their expertise can extend to seeing what sort of method, item, or tool may have been used to perform the dismemberment, and if it was a skilled or unskilled operation, plus offer injury interpretation.

The location of where body parts are found should be treated as a crime scene. This further applies to the location where the dismemberment took place. Both will need to be carefully forensically examined for blood, bone, and human tissue traces, particularly splatter and drag/movement marks. Areas such as bathrooms, kitchens, garages, and sheds, ie where there is access to sinks, water, receptacles, tools, and drains, are favoured locations for carrying out this physical task. As there is often little planning involved, offenders then have to decide on a means of concealment and transportation if moving body parts to a suitable deposition or storage site.

The manner of dismemberment might offer clues as to the possible reason for it (see above table). Under careful examination, it may be possible to match a cut or injury to a tool or weapon. Some experts keep records of tool marks used to experiment with and produce matches on dismembered body parts (eg saws that leave unique marks on bone).

Dependent on the state of the remains, once confirmed, it will be necessary to identify to whom they belong. In cases of severe decomposition of a head, experts can produce a facial reconstruction from the skull (including 2D and 3D manual and computerised reconstruction) using the bone structures as a guide. Isotope analysis of body parts may also be possible for indications of diet, lifestyle, geographic origin, and possible geographic movement.

Dismemberment cases may include searching for the items/tools used to perform the cutting and removing of limbs, etc and materials for concealing the parts and activity (eg wrappings, binliners/bags, cleaning equipment, chemicals, cover sheets, gloves, and digging tools). Checking for the purchase and acquisition of the necessary materials (eg at stores, via CCTV, and financial transactions) and looking for the likely place where dismemberment occurred become main lines of enquiry (MLOE).

When human body parts are found important questions will arise and the 5WH process of information gathering can be applied.

Checklist—Dismemberment cases

• What body parts are there?

• Who do they belong to?

• Where were they found? (geographical significance—see section 3.8)

• When, how, and by whom?

• Why was the location chosen and how did they get there?

• How have they been dismembered?

• Why were they dismembered?

• Where did death and dismemberment occur (could be two different activities and locations)?

• Who did the dismemberment (consider profile and skill/physical ability required)?

• Where are the other body parts?

• How did death occur (was the victim dead or alive during the process)?

• What level of skill was required/applied?

• What tools/methods were used?

• What other evidence is available (eg sexual assault/disfigurement/post-mortem activity)?

• How long has the body/body part been there and why wasn't it found sooner?

KEY POINTS

• Some forensic providers provide a service in which images and details of bones and body parts can be emailed to them to provide a quick analysis of the bone or body part to determine origin (ie human or otherwise).

> - The UK Missing Person's Unit maintains a database of recovered unidentified body parts and a missing persons DNA database.
> - Those who dismember human bodies can injure themselves during the process, which may provide useful evidence.
> - Spatters of body fluids can be found even after an area is cleaned. U-bends in baths and sinks are renowned for capturing fragments of bone and tissue.

The head is usually more difficult to remove as the neck is comprised of a series of inter-locking and overlapping bones. The prospect of removing the head sometimes proves too daunting for many, and this may be the point at which bisecting the torso, difficult and unpleasant as that may be, begins to seem preferable. Going for that option is usually a big mistake as the ensuing mess is much more challenging to conceal. While the torso is intact, the internal organs will remain contained within the bodies cavities; but once they are exposed they will leak copiously and create a really noxious stench.[18]

14.14.6 Suicides

The investigative mindset (ie 'keeping an open mind'; see Chapter 3) must be applied when dealing with any 'apparent' suicide. Every sudden and unexpected death, suicides included, must be treated with caution. The basic rule to be applied is: *if in doubt ... think murder.*

There have been countless examples of homicides or false missing person reports having been staged to look like suicides.[19] Careful checks will help spot tell-tale signs such as cord or zip-tie markings around wrists and ankles, strangulation marks that don't match up with the alleged noose, signs of a disturbance or forced entry to the property, or indications the suicide could have been staged or is false (ie false information is provided), perhaps even at the hands of a contract killer. Toxicology results might prove highly significant, eg if incapacitants or stupefying drugs have been administered. Another possible cause might be where the person has been threatened, groomed, or coerced into committing suicide over the Internet.[20]

Note: Suicides cannot be formally categorised as such until a coroner has returned a formal verdict. Until such time they are termed 'apparent' suicides. In apparent suicide cases, there are three points to consider:

---

[18] Quotation taken from Professor Dame Sue Black, *All That Remains: A Life in Death*, (Doubleday, 2018).

[19] Children's author Helen Bailey from Hertfordshire was reported missing in April 2016 as a possible suicide act by her partner. The SIO retained an open mind and diligent enquiries led to her body being found, and that of her dog, Boris, concealed in a well underneath the garage. She had been suffocated. Her partner Ian Stewart was later convicted of her murder.

[20] Dr Matthew Falder (aka '666Devil' or 'evil mind') was convicted in 2018 of 137 serious offences and jailed for 25 years. While he did not physically touch any of his many victims, he lured them through online grooming and blackmail into taking indecent pictures of themselves and doing degrading acts on themselves and then shared them on dark web sites such as 'hurtcore' and 'screambitch'. At least one of his victims attempted suicide.

Checklist—3 × apparent suicide considerations

1. Close proximity to the body of the weapon or means of causing death.

2. Evidence of injuries or wounds that convincingly appear self-inflicted *and* could feasibly and practically have been inflicted by the deceased themselves.

3. Existence of a motive or intent to take their own life.[21]

Some factors are often discounted as indicators of suicide, eg multiple stab wounds to the body. yet it can be surprising how much a person can injure themselves when wholly intent on taking their own life. This might include inflicting stab wounds on themselves. Traditional areas targeted are called 'sites of election' and can include the throat, wrists, chest, and abdomen, or the head if with a firearm. Suicidal gunshot wounds are usually at close range so there should be evidence of firearms discharge residue around the area of the entry wound, but not in every case on the deceased's hand. (Note: sometimes weapons may 'go missing' at suicide scenes due to them either being stolen (eg if in a public place) or removed by family or friends (eg to prevent embarrassment)).

The manner of death is an indicator of motive and intent. For example, putting a head on a railway line or leaping off a tall building. Motive and intent can be established by examining movements, activities, and behaviour leading up to their death—for example, sourcing a ligature (eg rope) and fixings to hang themselves, purchasing flammable materials to set themselves on fire, visiting buildings or bridges from which to jump to their deaths, informing others of their intent, leaving notes, researching suicide websites, a history of failed attempts, significant changes in behaviour, excessive use of drink or drugs, or severe depression and mood swings.

14.14.6.1 Suicide by hanging

Care needs to be exercised when investigating an apparent suicide by hanging to ensure it has not been staged. Tell-tale signs might be more than one ligature mark/line visible on the neck or binding marks around the wrists. These sorts of deaths can, in some circumstances, also be accidental, such as in autoerotic deaths (see below).

Asphyxiation and death frequently occur quite quickly once oxygen is cut off from the brain. The body convulses in an effort to relieve the ligature and some people may try to get their fingers underneath to remove the pressure, thus creating tell-tale scratch marks. Involuntary movements during the process of death can mean that areas of the body such as the hands and legs may become bruised if they come into contact with nearby items or surfaces. These marks should not be confused with defensive wounds or an attack from a third party.

If the person is clearly dead and there is no need for immediate life-saving or medical treatment, nothing should be touched, handled, or disturbed until

---

[21] Aka the 'Ovenstone criteria'—as cited in IMK Ovenstone 'A psychiatric approach to the diagnosis of suicide and its effect upon the Edinburgh Statistics' (1973) (123) *British Journal of Psychiatry*, 15–21.

the body and scene have been fully examined and photographed. If the ligature around the neck has to be removed, the knot or tie should be left intact and any ligature cut made in an area that does not damage or disturb the actual knot.

14.14.6.2 Suicide notes

Suicide notes are indications of suicide, provided they are genuine. Proof they were actually written by the deceased and written voluntarily needs to be confirmed. Any note should be recovered in a manner to preserve forensic evidence, including DNA and fingerprints. Past writings of the deceased can be collected for comparison purposes as there are linguistic specialists who can compare not just handwriting but comparative writing style, grammar, and N-grams.[22]

It is sometimes a possibility that suicide notes (and the means of committing the suicide) have been removed or destroyed prior to law enforcement (LE) involvement. Investigators should be mindful of family members who can, in some circumstances, experience difficulty in accepting the fact that their relative or loved one has committed suicide and can remove or destroy evidence. It has also been known for relatives of suicide victims to accuse the investigation of a cover-up or coming to the wrong conclusion and request a formal review in the hope they can change a coroner's verdict.

Diaries, letters, text messages, communications, and social media data and similar material can be examined for information that may point towards or away from, and corroborate a theory of suicide ideation. Any stated or inferred intention of a person to take their own life and sudden and strange precursor activities become important investigative information.

Recovered articles and material can help contribute towards compiling a 'psychological autopsy' of a deceased. This is a collaborative procedure involving investigators and mental health experts in an attempt to determine the state of mind of a person prior to the fatal act.

14.14.6.3 False reports

Some offenders murder someone they know (eg partner or spouse) then try to stage it to appear a suicide or murder by a stranger. In an attempt to deflect suspicion away from themselves, they make a report (eg emergency 999 call) about having discovered the victim. If they do so, how they act and what they say can provide useful evidential information for (dis)proving their involvement. The contents of any report or call to the emergency services (police, ambulance) can be closely scrutinised for precise wording and detail via a transcript/recording (if available) of the exact words and phrases used.

Studies have shown that when making such falsified reports, mistakes are made by offenders in how they make these calls. It is worth considering that

---

[22] An N-gram is a sequence of items such as syllables, letters, or words in a sample of text.

indications of guilt can be inferred from their choice of words, language, tonality, and general behaviour (eg they may ask for the police and not a medic because they know the person they have killed is dead by their own hand).[23]

14.14.6.4 Murder—suicide

This involves an act in which an individual kills one or more other persons before, or at the same time as killing themselves. The combination of murder and suicide can take various forms including:

- Murder encompassing suicide, eg deliberate car crash, suicide bombing.
- Suicide after murder to escape punishment.
- Suicide after murder as form of self-punishment/guilt.[24]
- Suicide pacts (killing another then oneself by agreement).
- Suicide after killing members of own spouse/partner/family/relatives.

14.14.7 Autoerotic asphyxiation

Autoerotic asphyxiation is the term that describes the use of some form of self-strangulation and asphyxiation to increase or attain sexual arousal and orgasm. Hypoxyphilia involves a person achieving sexual arousal through oxygen deprivation by means of a noose, ligature, plastic bag, mask or other device or equipment. The activity is usually planned, so that there is sufficient time and planning to allow him/herself the opportunity to escape asphyxiation prior to the loss of consciousness. However, due to equipment failures, errors in the placement of the noose or ligature or other mistakes, accidental deaths sometimes occur as there is strong element of risk taking.

These types of deaths can be devastating news for the family and friends of deceased persons. Apart from the obvious grief experienced, they prove hugely embarrassing and it must be borne in mind that, like suicide, those who attend the death scene before the arrival of emergency responders and investigators might wish to remove, cover up, or alter things.

Research shows that an autoerotic death scene can reveal key characteristics that provide clues and indications of accidental death, rather than suicide or homicide.

Checklist—Autoerotic death key features

- Absence of suicide note.

- Victim either totally or partially naked and/or genital organs predominantly exposed.

---

[23] Further details and advice can be obtained from the Authorised Professional Practice (APP) site which has a useful template from the US Federal Bureau of Investigation (FBI) that can be used to check for the signs.

[24] Many spree killings have ended in suicide, such as Derek Bird (June 2010) who killed twelve members of the public in Cumbria then turned the gun on himself.

- If male, dressed partially in women's underclothing.

- Ropes, belts, or other bindings arranged so that compression of the neck could be produced voluntarily.

- Scarf or towel placed around the neck under the rope to protect against rope burns.

- Body, extremities, and/or genitals bound with ropes, chains, or leather.

- Pornographic material (especially pictures nearby).

- Evidence of masturbation apparent (eg semen or vibrators).

- Evidence of repetitive behaviour (eg permanently installed bar, grooves on a rafter or other apparatus).

- Victim suspended by the neck, with feet on the floor, while sitting in a chair or lying in a bed.

- Act appears to have been performed alone, usually behind locked doors or when privacy was assured.[25]

14.15 **Role of HM Coroner**

A coroner is an independent judicial office holder appointed by a local council in England and Wales. Their standard role is to confirm and certify the death of an individual within their jurisdiction. They may also conduct or order an inquest into the cause and manner of death, and investigate or confirm the identity of an unknown person who has been found dead. As soon as a death is deemed suspicious and is placed under investigation, the coroner who covers the area where the body is found must be notified without delay. This is a key function of an SIO.

Under section 1 of the Coroners and Justice Act 2009 (Chapter 25), the coroner has a duty to investigate all deaths where there are grounds to suspect any of the following:

1. Death was violent or unnatural.
2. Cause of death is unknown; or
3. Person died while in prison, police custody, or another type of state detention.

Under section 5 of the Act, the purpose of the coroner's investigation into a person's death is to ascertain:

1. Who the deceased was.
2. How, when, and where they died.

---

[25] Cited in JL Uva, 'Review: Autoerotic asphyxiation in the United States' (1995) 40(4) *Journal of Forensic Sciences*, 574–81.

14.15.1 **Coroner's inquests**

A coroner is required to hold an inquest under the following circumstances:

1. The deceased died while in custody or otherwise in state detention and that either:
   (a) death was a violent or unnatural one, or
   (b) cause of death is unknown.
2. Death resulted from an act or omission of:
   (a) a police officer, or
   (b) a member of a service police force, in the purported execution of the officer's or member's duty as such; or
3. Death was caused by a 'notifiable' accident, poisoning, or disease.

Once an inquest has been held, the coroner sends a report to the Registrar in the district where the death occurred, who will register the circumstances and details of the death. The Registrar then issues a death certificate. Inquests are held in public and may include a jury. This may involve witnesses being called who are legally obliged to attend and may be penalised if they fail to do so. The coroner may record the cause of death as:

- natural causes
- accident or misadventure
- industrial disease
- unlawful killing
- suicide
- attempted or self-induced abortion
- alcohol or drug related
- open verdict

The coroner may also record a 'narrative verdict', setting out the facts surrounding the death in more detail and explaining the reasons for the decision.

14.15.2 **Additional post-mortems and body release**

Coroners have the power to authorise secondary post-mortem examinations to facilitate the early release of a body to the family. Although the great majority of homicides result in swift arrests, delays can occur due to the complexity or difficulty of certain types of investigation, or where there are a number of jointly charged defendants. This may cause undue distress to families and relatives, and SIOs should be keen to seek early completion of subsequent post-mortems.

The main objectives and features (as agreed by inter-agency agreements between bodies such as the NPCC, Coroner's Society, Law Society, and Home Office) for second post-mortems are:

- Reducing delays for release of a body for burial or cremation.
- Limiting the possibility of miscarriages of justice.

- Reducing the incidence of multiple post-mortems (on the same body).
- Where no-one is charged in connection with the death within a month, provision is made for a second, independent post-mortem for use by a defendant in the future.

There is no statutory authority for a person charged in connection with a death to order a post-mortem examination of the deceased. The performance of such an examination, however, is well recognised by the courts. However, any second examination can only be undertaken on the authority of a coroner. The coroner will not release the body unless all those having a proper interest in it confirm in writing that they have no objection to the body being released. Before the proposed release of the body, the coroner will, however, notify their intention to do so, in writing, to all those persons who have not yet confirmed that they have no objection to the release of the body.

14.16 Human Tissue Act 2004 (HTA)

This Act introduced a number of provisions that are of relevance to homicide investigation. These include the following:

- Storage of the body of a deceased for the purpose of determining the cause of death must be on premises licensed for that activity by the Human Tissue Authority unless the storage is incidental to transportation.
- Performance of a post-mortem examination may only take place on premises licensed for that activity by the Human Tissue Authority (see LHA strategy 2018–2021. Available at <http://www.hta.gov.uk/LHA strategy2018_2019>.
- Pathologists undertaking post-mortem examinations must act under the authority of a licence from the Human Tissue Authority authorising post-mortem examinations on those premises.
- Coroners and Justice Act 2009 prevents a coroner authorising a post-mortem examination if doing so would violate section 16 of the HTA.
- Samples may only be taken for the purpose of establishing or confirming the deceased's identity or determining the cause of death if the post-mortem has been authorised by the coroner (in non-suspicious cases).

14.16.1 Taking samples

Samples of relevant material may be taken for three reasons: (i) and (ii) are for identification of the deceased and determination of cause of death and taken under the authority of the coroner (under HTA); (iii) for any material required for prevention and detection of crime or the conduct of a prosecution, (ie suspicious death). The latter are taken through powers to seize evidence under section 19 of the Police and Criminal Evidence Act 1984 (PACE) and under common law. Of significance is that category (iii) activity *is not subject* to HTA restrictions

All samples taken should be recorded by an EO and given a unique identifier. This record should make it abundantly clear which are those samples taken for the coroner and which are those taken for the investigation. Any samples taken at the location where the body was found should also be incorporated into this list.

A criminal investigation into a suspicious death can end in a number of different ways and it is a matter for the investigation to determine, in line with relevant guidance, what must happen to samples seized as evidence (under PACE) and how they should be disposed of. It would be entirely different if the samples were taken and the death not deemed to be suspicious. In which case, the HTA would stipulate they be returned to the family without delay and/or disposed of as deemed appropriate.

Given the possibility of a significant period between post-mortem examination and the conclusion of an enquiry, it may be wise to have made an initial assessment of the need to retain samples soon after examination. The SIO can take account of any views expressed to the FLO in this regard.

Section 39 of the Act allows 'relevant material' to be taken, stored, and disposed of without consent for criminal justice purposes. It is essential, however, that the family are made aware of what material has been taken and the reasons for its retention. The FLO should ensure relatives of the deceased have indicated a disposal option for 'relevant material' seized by police. There are three choices for the family to make:

- Retention of material for review, audit, teaching, research, and genetic counselling.
- Return material to the family.
- Disposal of the material by means of burial, cremation, or other lawful disposal, by the Pathologist/LEA in a sensitive manner.

Generally speaking, small tissue samples, slides, blocks, and swabs make up the majority of retained tissue. However, in exceptional circumstances it may be necessary to retain large body parts, such as the heart or brain. In such cases, the family should be told that an organ or large body part has been taken for additional testing. The family then have the option of delaying any funeral or cremation until the body part can be returned. Such additional testing should be completed as quickly as possible in discussion with the Pathologist around timescales and deadlines for completion. This can then be communicated to the family via the FLO.

If a family proceeds with a funeral before the return of the body part, arrangements for disposal with them can be made as soon as testing is complete. The immediate return of a body part is not necessary if it will affect a prosecution case. At the conclusion of criminal proceedings, the SIO and EO should hold an exhibits review to decide if any 'relevant material' is no longer required and can be disposed of. In some cases, however, it may be necessary to consult with the Crown Prosecution Service (CPS), the coroner, and the convicted person's defence team to ensure any disposal will not affect any appeal/inquest or breach of the Criminal Procedure and Investigations Act 1996 (CPIA).

The future retention of any 'relevant material' taken for an investigation should be done in accordance with the minimum periods established by the Code of Practice issued under the authority of section 23 of the CPIA:

- If an investigation results in criminal proceedings being instituted, all material which may be *relevant* must be retained at least until the accused is either acquitted or convicted, or until the prosecutor decides not to proceed with the case.
- Where the accused is convicted, all material which may be *relevant* must be retained at least until:
  - the convicted person is released from custody or is discharged from hospital, in cases where the court imposes a custodial sentence or a hospital order.
  - six months from the date of conviction.

14.17 Conducting Exhumations

The exhumation of human remains is both intrusive and emotive, but may be the only alternative available to address a specific requirement of an investigation. It can be used as a means to either identify a cause of death, establish or confirm a deceased's identity, conduct a pathological or forensic examination, obtain a forensic sample such as DNA, toxicology, or recover certain artefacts believed buried with a body.

Whatever the objective or necessity, exhumations are usually grim and traumatic occasions for those affected or involved, and should only be embarked upon as a last resort and even then, only after precise planning and preparation. There are many complicating factors to consider, eg if the body to be exhumed is buried underneath other coffins, or where the grave is located and the legal authorities required. Fortunately, these are not the types of activity that occur frequently and there are good lessons and experience to be learned from those that have been conducted.

UK national guidance is available from the NCA containing best practice and advice in respect of exhuming bodies from graves within established UK burial grounds and cemeteries. It contains guidance on:

- Domestic law/authorities and permissions required
- Family liaison
- Media and communication

- Role of the coroner
- Research, planning, and strategy
- Finance and resources
- Health and safety risk assessments
- Site planning and preparation
- Roles and responsibilities (covering all necessary experts and specialists)
- Exhumation process (and checklists)
- Identification and continuity of body
- Transit and mortuary processes
- Re-interment
- Producing an operational order

The guidance is well worth reading if conducting an exhumation and is available via the Police Online Knowledge Area (POLKA) website (Major Crime Investigation Forum), and advice and support via MCIS (telephone: 0345 000 5463).

14.18 Suspicious Missing Persons and 'No Body' Murders

People go missing every day for a variety of reasons including voluntarily, getting lost, under duress, accident, injury, or illness. Some can also go missing due to being victims of crime and in the most serious cases, abduction or homicide. Serious offences such as human trafficking/slavery and criminal/child sexual exploitation could also be the cause.

High-risk, unexplained, or suspicious reports of missing persons require in-depth investigations, and the rule warrants repeating: *'If in doubt … think murder'*. Suspicious or high-risk missings can quickly escalate into critical incidents, particularly if they involve vulnerable persons. The initial response and risk assessment (ie high, medium, or low) to a report of a missing person should be treated with the utmost urgency. This may also present an opportunity to save life and obtain/secure evidence. In the first twenty-four to forty-eight (Golden) hours there is far more chance of finding and saving a missing person and mounting a successful investigation.

Once appointed to take command of a suspicious missing person enquiry, the SIO should review the initial response (such as search strategy) and ensure an effective command and control structure is in place. All necessary resources need to be deployed and fast-track (HP) actions raised, allocated, and prioritised. There will be a collapsing time frame and every second will count.

If a missing person is particularly vulnerable and high risk, eg a young child, the likelihood of interest from the media and public greatly increases.

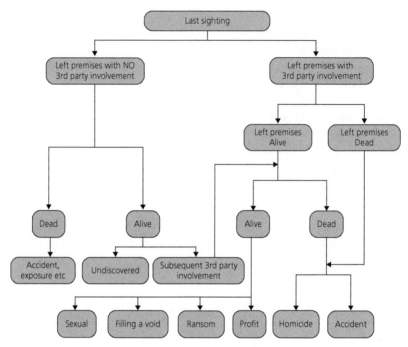

Figure 14.2 Hypothesis tree—missing person enquiries

Source: Alison, L and Rainbow, L (eds), *Professionalising Offender Profiling: Forensic and Investigative Psychology in Practice* (Routledge, 2011)

One example is the case of April Jones, aged five, who went missing on 1 October 2012 in Machynlleth, Powys, Wales. This case was quickly designated a murder enquiry. Prompt and decisive action from a high-level police response and experienced SIO and enquiry team led to the early arrest of a local man named Mark Bridger, aged forty-six years. He was later charged and convicted of the little girl's abduction and murder, but not before the disappearance had rapidly generated a massive amount of inter/national media coverage.

Using hypotheses is one way of applying the NDM to assess the options of what might be the possible reasons for a person having gone missing (hypotheses are a way of testing theories as to what might have happened—see section 3.9.2 and Figure 14.2)

14.18.1 'No Body' murders

Without a body, investigating what happened to a missing person (misper) becomes a lot more challenging. These enquiries often raise suspicion that a serious criminal offence (eg homicide) has occurred if the misper's body cannot be located. Some indications may be obvious, such as an apparent attack site where the victim lived or frequented containing trace evidence such as their blood or human bone/tissue residue.

Circumstances surrounding the manner in which they went missing might be highly dubious. For example, a wife and mother who leaves behind her husband, children, and close friends and family, and disappears without trace, taking no means of support or communication, and has recently been the victim of sustained domestic violence (DV). The circumstances might show her disappearance to be completely out of character with no reason or preparation for her absence, yet the person, body, and remains cannot be found. These types of missing person investigations are often categorised or referred to as 'no body' murders.

KEY POINT

It is always worth a close look at the person who claims to be the last person who saw the missing person alive. Famous historical cases, eg Ian Huntley,[26] have shown how this type of person turn out to be the murderer. One of first HP actions should be to make them a TIE subject (see section 8.6).

A carefully coordinated and planned search (not just physical but also through research) for a suspicious missing person is required not only to try and find them but also prove they are no longer alive. Commencing 'proof of life' (POL) enquiries can have the opposite effect and prove they must be technically dead. To assist these enquiries a template has been designed that is widely accepted as the national standard with backing from the judicial process for conducting and recording POL enquiries.

The template is a reference document containing multiple categories and contacts to be considered for checking agencies and departments that might reveal traces of the missing person. These might include health and local authorities, utility companies, the DVLA, passport office, financial institutions, charities, judicial and employment services. Using this document and method, an SIO can provide a witness testimony to show the extent of their comprehensive enquiries and efforts to trace the missing person, thereby proving they must be in fact no longer alive. (Guidance on conducting of POL enquiries and the template is available from the NCA, telephone: 0345 000 5463).

---

[26] Huntley murdered ten-year-olds Holly Wells and Jessica Chapman in Soham, Cambridgeshire in August 2002. He was the last person to see them alive and gave TV interviews claiming this. He had, in fact, invited the two girls into his school caretaker's home, murdered them, and dumped their bodies in a field near RAF Lakenheath in Suffolk, where they remained undetected until nearly two weeks later. There were 'no bodies' to begin with but the case was quickly treated as a murder enquiry.

14.18.2 **Pseudocide**

This term refers to the act of faking death and usually involves leaving false traces and evidence aimed at misleading others. While extremely rare, there have been notable cases. The British politician John Stonehouse left his clothes on a beach in 1974 to escape debtors; in 2002 a man named by the media as 'canoe man', John Darwin, staged his own death as a canoeing accident and went in hiding in Panama in an elaborate life-insurance fraud. The most famous of them all, Lord Lucan, strangely continues to be 'spotted' in obscure parts of the world.

Pseudocide can be a means of revenge, escape, or to avoid capture and punishment, sometimes prompted by debt, greed, boredom, or fear. In May 2018 it was used as a tactical ploy by Ukrainian journalist, Arkady Babchenko, who appeared to have been murdered by Russian paid assassins, only to reappear the next day live on TV flanked by Ukrainian security chiefs. It was claimed he had staged this to thwart a Russian assassination attempt. There had even been photographs showing his bullet-riddled body lying in a pool of blood.

Usually there should be straightforward clues to be found, particularly around financial transactions (eg transferring large amounts of money before disappearing), setting up new identities, researching the Internet, lifestyle or motive. As there is often a financial motive, insurance companies have acquired plenty of experience at this kind of fraud and they may be a good source of reference for assistance.

14.18.3 **UK Missing Persons Unit**

The national and international point of contact for all missing persons and unidentified bodies/cases in the United Kingdom is the Missing Person Unit (MPU), located within the NCA. It is the hub for the exchange of information and links in with Interpol, Europol, and other international organisations. (Note: When someone goes missing, Interpol posts 'yellow notices' across its 192 member countries to alert LEAs, and 'black notices' are issued when a body is found).

The MPU act as the centre for information exchange and expertise and can assist SIOs through the provision of:

- tactical advice and support on high-risk missing person cases and no-body murders (United Kingdom and abroad).
- response and coordination of law enforcement response to high-risk cases.
- case analysis using its national database (HERMES) of missing and unidentified persons.
- child rescue alert (CRA) system—an investigative tool to alert the public of missing children believed to be in imminent danger.
- access to specialist overseas services through Interpol, Europol, SIRENE Bureaux, and the NCA's international liaison team.

- direct access to the NDNAD, Missing Person's DNA database, National Fingerprint Office, and National Dental Index.
- central hub for linking police and law enforcement agencies, government departments, NHS trusts, social welfare, and non-government organisations.
- provision of information for families and friends of missing persons including a range of factsheets that are available.

The UK Missing Persons Unit are contactable by telephone: +44 (0) 800 234 6034, email: ukmpu@nca.gov.uk and <http:// www.missingpersons.police.uk>.

14.19 **Deaths in Healthcare Settings**

Although rare, these types of deaths are sometimes referred to an LEA (eg by a coroner) if unascertained or suspicious, in which case an SIO is appointed to review all the circumstances (eg 5WH style). A mature assessment can then be made as to what category of death investigation, if any, is appropriate (see section 14.2).

Cause for concern may be raised by a number of sources, including family members and whistle-blowers at the institution concerned or even the media if their attention is drawn to the circumstances.[27]

If it appears there may have been corporate failings, liaison can be made with the Chief Executive of the relevant organisation. However, it must be remembered that this individual may eventually come under investigation themselves and consequently might be extremely defensive or vague with any explanation or offers of assistance. Attempts at obfuscation by vague or unclear responses must be managed by means of a thorough and considered approach to any discussions or interviews.

If deemed suspicious or requiring a special procedure investigation (local protocols may apply), an initial consideration might be to identify, protect, and safeguard further vulnerable persons who potentially may also be at risk, particularly if the death occurred in a residential care home. The Care Act 2014 places a responsibility on local authorities to ensure that vulnerable people are not at risk of becoming a victim of abuse and neglect. Organisational liability under the Corporate Manslaughter and Corporate Homicide Act 2007, and Ill Treatment and Wilful Neglect under sections 20–25, Criminal Justice and Courts Act 2015, and the Health & Safety at Work Act 1974 should also be borne in mind.

In order to reach a decision about any potential criminality or culpability, the SIO will need to gain the assistance of expertise from a CSI and Forensic

---

[27] See K Lay, D Brown, and G Narwan 'NHS ignores whistleblowers despite hospital deaths scandal' *The Times* 21 June 2018. This report covered the story of nurses having reported use of powerful painkillers at Gosport War Memorial Hospital by 'Dr Opiate', Jane Barton, in which over 600 patients died between 1989 and 2000, allegedly through wrongful and unnecessary administration of opioids.

Pathologist, with early consultation with a specialist CPS case worker (especially when examining 'causation'-type evidence). If an assessment reveals sufficient grounds for suspecting a criminal offence has been committed (other than, say, a breach of health and safety legislation), then the police usually assume the lead for the investigation.

In the aftermath of a suspected incident, steps must be taken to secure evidence (as per the ISP principle; see section 6.2). This may include physical, scientific, and investigative material, although this might be difficult if some time has elapsed after an incident is believed to have occurred. In some cases, a sensible and reasonable approach may be more appropriate (eg where an operating theatre or treatment area is concerned).

Checklist—5WH considerations for deaths in healthcare settings

- Who is the deceased?

- What is known to have happened?

- When and where did the death occur?

- What was the cause and manner of death?

- What duty of care was owed to the deceased and by whom?

- What was their medical history?

- What sort of care and treatment had they been receiving?

- What evidence is there for intentional mistreatment rather than procedural error or mistake?

- What evidence is there of criminal intent?

- Who was responsible (individual or organisational failing)?

- What evidence is there of homicide, manslaughter, unlawful act, gross negligence, ill treatment, or wilful neglect?

- Who are the next of kin?

- What have the next of kin been told and by whom?[28] (see also section 14.3.1)

Although rare, there have been cases around the world of medical serial killings, and the perpetrators are sometimes referred to in the media as 'angels of death' (eg Michael Swango MD, American serial poisoner of his patients). A famous UK example is Dr Harold Shipman, who injected his patients with large doses of

---

[28] See also NPCC Homicide Working Group, *An SIO's Guide to Investigating Unexpected Death and Serious Harm in Healthcare Settings* (2015).

morphine to kill them. His crimes remained under the radar despite being the subject of a police investigation, which was subsequently heavily criticised in a public enquiry into the matter as being 'shabby'.[29] This type of serial homicide needs to be borne in mind and SIOs must remain alert (ie investigative mindset) to the possibility to prevent further deaths occurring (*if in doubt ... think murder*). In cases where there is an unlawful administration of drugs or toxins (just the amount of the substance can make them lethal), there are very few obvious physical signs. Obtaining and examining the correct samples and insisting on a forensic pathological examination and thorough toxicology tests are key decisions. Checking career backgrounds of those involved or suspected (suspectology; see section 12.5) might show signs of previous troubling patterns of behaviour or complaints. These could also show an unexpected rise in deaths/illnesses in their patients in locations where they have been previously operating, including overseas.

Checklist—Investigative considerations Healthcare Deaths

- Compile a timeline of any suspected persons to see what their backgrounds are and where they have been previously, overlaying linked or similar incidents.

- Locate/interview victims/witnesses including those who may have moved on.

- Locate third parties who may have useful information, eg drug companies, visitors, consultants, agency staff, paramedics, funeral directors, etc.

- Take wider view on what might constitute a crime scene (eg storeroom, drugs cabinet, digital media/records, relevant company administration).

- Review all hospital/medical records relating to the suspect and victims (ie to see if their death was linked to medical profiles).

- Check pharmacy records for unusual amounts of drugs being dispensed or anomalies in drug inventories.

- Consider forensic post-mortems, exhumations, and toxicology tests (stipulate what drugs or poisons to look for, with reasons offered).

- Check victim profiles for commonalities.
- Check death certificates and coroner's staff/undertakers/mortuary technicians for anything they may have noticed was unusual (JDLR principle), and other related items and material.[30]

---

[29] The Shipman Inquiry by Dame Janet Smith DBE, released 14 July 2003, see <http://www.webarchive.nationalarchives.gov.uk>.

[30] This may include notes, drug charts, anaesthetic machines, instruments, syringes, incineration bins, clothing worn by patient and staff, treatment rooms, samples, staff communication devices, and internal CCTV.

14.20 **Domestic Homicides**

Domestic violence (DV) encompasses physical, psychological, sexual, financial, and emotional abuse involving partners, ex-partners, other relatives, and household members. Domestic disputes that result in death of one of the partners are all too common and account for a vast amount of homicides. In most cases, the initial response phase can quickly identify a perpetrator and the incident then becomes a routine investigation (ie Cat 'C' murder; see section 14.2.1) as the case is a relatively easy 'self-solver'.

However, these deaths are often not as a result of the first incident investigated and are likely to have been preceded by varying degrees or pattern of DV or abuse. Many people, such as family, friends, or neighbours, may have knowledge of previous attacks, together with various agencies such as the police, social services, probation service, and health service, or there may even be previous prosecutions or injunctions.

A necessity is to ensure any investigation benefits from and covers a wide range of background information in order to gather fuller facts for consideration by a court or enquiry. A domestic homicide can trigger a number of other parallel investigations such as a Domestic Homicide Review (DHR), a Serious Case Review (SCR) involving victims under the age of eighteen years, an Article 2 coroner's investigation (Right to Life under the European Convention of Human Rights), or an Independent Office for Police Complaints (IOPC) investigation covering a 'police-involved death'.

These additional implications make what at first appears a simple and straightforward case into a complex and time-consuming investigation. The SIO and their Disclosure Officer should ideally have a good working knowledge and understanding of how third-party material can be sought and examined in order to satisfactorily progress the investigation and fulfil their CPIA responsibilities on disclosure.

14.20.1 **Domestic Homicide Reviews (DHRs)**

DHRs were introduced on a statutory basis under section 9 of the Domestic Violence, Crime and Victim's Act 2004, and came into force on 13 April 2011. They place a statutory requirement on the police to inform the relevant Community Safety Partnership (CSP) whenever a domestic homicide occurs. The chair of the CSP holds the responsibility for establishing whether a homicide is to be subject of a DHR under the above Act, which defines what is a domestic homicide review.

A DHR means a review of the circumstances in which the death of a person aged sixteen years or over has, or appears to have, resulted from violence, abuse, or neglect by:

1. A person to whom s/he was related or with whom he was or had been in an intimate personal relationship, *or*

2. A member of the same household as themselves,

Reviews are conducted with a view to identifying the lessons to be learnt from the death. 'Intimate personal relationship' includes relationships between adults who are or have been intimate partners, or family members, regardless of gender or sexuality.

A member of the same household includes:

1. Any household visited so often and for such periods of time that it is reasonable to regard a person to be a member of it.
2. Any household in which a victim was living at the time of the act that caused the death (ie if a victim lived in different households at different times),

Note: when victims of domestic homicide are aged between sixteen and eighteen years, a Serious Case Review (SCR) should take precedent over a DHR, although a separate DHR could be set up to consider the domestic violence issues (Serious Case Reviews are covered in section 16.14).

14.20.2 **Purpose of a DHR**

A DHR is conducted to:

1. establish what lessons can be learnt from the domestic homicide regarding the way in which local professionals and organisations work individually and together to safeguard victims.
2. identify clearly what those lessons are both within and between agencies, how and within what timescales they will be acted upon, and what is expected to change as a result.
3. apply lessons to service responses including changes to policies and procedures as appropriate.
4. prevent domestic violence homicide and improve service responses for all domestic violence victims and their children through improved intra- and inter-agency working.

Note: DHRs are not inquiries into how someone died or who is to blame. They are not part of a disciplinary process and they do not replace, but will be in addition to, an inquest or any other form of inquiry into a homicide.

Bibliography

ACPO, *Guidance on Disaster Victim Identification* (NPIA, 2011)

ACPO, *Interim Guidance on the Management, Recording and Investigation of Missing Persons* (POLKA, College of Policing, 2013)

ACPO, *Murder Investigation Model* (NPIA, 2006)

Alison, L and Rainbow, L (eds), *Professionalising Offender Profiling: Forensic and Investigative Psychology in Practice* (Routledge, 2011)

Black, Sue (2018), *All that Remains: A Life in Death*, Doubleday, London.

NPCC Homicide Working Group, *An SIO's Guide to Investigating Unexpected Death and Serious Harm in Healthcare Settings* (HWG, 2015)

Dogan, K et al, 'Decapitation and dismemberment of the corpse: A matricide case' (2010) 55(2) *Journal of Forensic Sciences*, 542–4

Journal of Homicide and Major Incident Investigation, vol. 6 Issue 2 Autumn (NPIA, 2010)

NCA, *Exhumation Guide* (Major Crime Investigation, POLKA, College of Policing, 2018)

Ovenstone, IMK, 'A psychiatric approach to the diagnosis of suicide and its effect upon the Edinburgh statistics' (1973) (123) *British Journal of Psychiatry*, 15–21

Practical Guide to Dismemberment cases (National Injuries Database, NCA, 2014)

Rutty G, *Body Identification: Briefing Guide to Assist in Body Identification* (NPIA National Injuries Database, 2009)

Uva, JL, 'Review: Autoerotic asphyxiation in the United States' (1995) 40(4) *Journal of Forensic Sciences*, 574–81

Infant and Child Deaths

15.1 **Introduction**

Sudden and unexpected deaths in infants and children[1] (SUDI/SUDC) are fortunately quite rare but nonetheless extremely distressing and traumatic. They affect parents, carers, families, relatives, friends, professionals, and local communities profoundly. Unlike older and more mature people, healthy infants and children are not expected to die. The vast majority who do so usually die as a consequence of medical or natural causes, such as disease, physical defect, or by pure accident. Unfortunately however, a small percentage are caused by callous and criminal acts of malicious, intentional and gratuitous violence, maltreatment, neglect, physical/sexual abuse, or through the administration of noxious substances or drugs.

Children and infants can be subjected to a wide variety of fatal actions. Amongst these might be deliberately inflicted head injuries, asphyxiation, stab wounds, serious sexual exploitation, assaults and linked activities, hypothermia, dehydration, shaking injuries, methadone poisoning, broken/fractured bones, drowning, burns, crushing injuries, ruptured/failed organs (liver, kidney, etc), and abdominal injuries.

Some children, through no fault of their own, are vulnerable not due to poor health, disease and accident but because they are under the control of callous neglectful parents, carers, or they fall victim to sexual predators. At a tender age, victims are unlikely (and often unable) to question or notice inherent dangers, nor are they in a position to object to lethal and deliberately administered noxious substances.

Child death investigations pose particular challenges due to the hidden nature of tangible evidence and tell-tale signs. Young infants and children's bodies are smaller and more fragile than adults' and therefore indicators of non-accidental injuries are less noticeable. Contact trace evidence in intra-familial child homicides has limited use unless there are specific injuries due to regular contact between victim and offender(s). Traditional methods of investigation are therefore limited because, unlike adult homicides, evidential reliance upon proving contact through passive data, DNA, and fingerprint (trace) evidence is of much less significance given the home-based familial set-up and frequent 'legitimate' contact between offender and child.

Thus, a requirement to diagnose accurately, follow correct procedures, and thoroughly investigate all attendant circumstances of a child death is much more important than in an adult death. This means retaining extra professional curiosity when dealing with any child death and not falling into the trap of jumping to conclusions too quickly (ie applying an investigative mindset). While it is necessary to consider anything that might appear suspicious, there

---

[1] 'Infant', for the purposes of the Joint Agency Response now means up to twenty-four-months of age, and 'child' as not having reached their eighteenth birthday. Baroness H Kennedy QC, *Sudden Unexpected Death in Infancy and Childhood: Multi-agency Guidelines for Care and Investigation* (Royal College of Pathologists, 2nd edn 2016) (The Kennedy Report).

has to be an appropriate balance between conducting a thorough investigation and supporting 'innocent' parents at a difficult time. The welfare of other associated children might also be important.

Baroness Kennedy QC stated that the role of the police was to ensure every child who dies deserves the right to have their sudden and unexplained death fully investigated in order to establish a cause of death and exclude criminal acts. This helps support grieving parents in providing answers and enables medical professionals to understand the cause of death better and create intervention plans to prevent future tragedies.

Every infant and child who dies deserves to be treated with respect and care. Surviving siblings also have a 'right to life' under Article 2 of the European Convention on Human Rights (ECHR). An SIO is entrusted with these responsibilities and concluding or excluding that a criminal act has taken place and helping to record an accurate cause of death. This chapter provides useful guidance for those who might be required to investigate these unique cases.

15.2 Categorising Sudden Infant and Child Deaths

Consideration of the different categories or classifications of child deaths helps determine the type of response and investigation required. Most sudden child deaths usually begin as a Category 1 SUDI/C but they can move up (or down) the scale as information changes. In order of seriousness, every child death that is sudden and unexpected[2] and not medically expected or explicable falls into one of the following categories:

Category 1	Non-suspicious—usually natural or accidental (ie SUDI/C).
Category 2	Suspicious[3]—factors raise the likelihood of a criminal act.
Category 3	Clear evidence of *mens rea* (guilty intent) of homicide or other serious criminal offence (see checklist following).

By definition, Category 1 cases almost always require a less intense response from those falling within Categories 2 and 3. However, a number

---

[2] 'Sudden and unexpected' encompasses all cases in which there is death (or collapse leading to death) of a child, which would not have been reasonably expected to occur twenty-four hours previously, and in whom no pre-existing medical cause of death is apparent (and for which no death certificate of cause of death can be provided. The Kennedy Report, p 10). Available at: <http://www.rcpath.org>.

[3] 'Suspicious' means: 'although there is no direct evidence or grounds to suspect a specific criminal act, there are however factors that raise the possibility a criminal act may have contributed to the death and thereby merit a more detailed investigation of the circumstances of the death' (R Wate and D Marshall, 'Effective Investigation of Intra-familial Child Homicide and Suspicious Death' (2009) 5(2) *Journal of Homicide and Major Incident Investigation*.

of the initial actions will be the same, eg examination of the body, full history from parents/carers, place where the child died, examination and multi-agency background checks, as it is not always apparent at the outset into which category they fit.

Checklist—Category 3-type offences

- **Murder**—contrary to common law.

- **Manslaughter** (including corporate manslaughter, eg deaths in healthcare settings)—contrary to common law.

- **Familial homicide** (causing or allowing a child or vulnerable adult to die or suffer serious physical harm)—section 5 of the Domestic Violence, Crime and Victims Act 2004 (DVCV) (as amended by DVCV (Amendment) Act 2012).

- **Infanticide**—section 1 of the Infanticide Act 1938.

Other related or kindred offences might be:

- **Child destruction**—section 1(1) of the Infant Life (Preservation) Act 1929.

- **Administering/procuring drugs/instruments to procure an abortion or miscarriage**—sections 58, 59 of the Offences Against the Person Act 1861.

- **Exposing a child whereby life is endangered**—section 27 of the Offences Against the Person Act 1861.

- **Concealment of birth**—section 60 of the Offences Against the Person Act 1861.

- **Preventing lawful burial**—concealment of a corpse—disposing of or destroying a dead body.

- **Neglect**—death of infant under three years caused by suffocation while infant in bed with person sixteen years or over who is under the influence of drink or prohibited drug—section 1 of the Children and Young Persons Act 1933 (as amended by the Serious Crime Act 2015).

- **Wilfully assault, ill-treat, neglect, abandon, expose child under sixteen years**—section 1 of the Children and Young Persons Act 1933.

- **Maliciously administering poison, etc or noxious thing so as to endanger life**—section 23 of the Offences Against the Person Act 1861.

- **Attempting to choke, etc so as to commit an indictable offence**—section 21 of the Offences Against the Person Act 1861.

- **Drunk in charge of child apparently under seven years**—section 2(1) of the Licensing Act 1902.

- **Child abduction by person connected with the child**—section 1 of the Child Abduction Act 1984 as amended by the Family Law Act 1986 and the Children Act 1989.

- **Grievous bodily harm or wounding with intent**—section 18 of the Offences Against the Person Act 1861.

Research conducted in 2004 (Bacon Levene, 'Sudden unexpected death and covert homicide in infancy' (2004)_89 *Archives of Disease in Childhood* 443–7) suggested that one in ten cot deaths may occur as a result of murder or neglect, which means one in ten may be a covert homicide. Equally, 90 per cent of these deaths are from medical or natural causes. Safeguards, therefore, need to be incorporated into even level 1-type investigations to preserve evidence in case the initial assessment proves deceptive, the circumstances develop, and the classification needs to change.

This is vitally important when considering procedures referred to in other sections of this chapter that are inappropriate for Categories 2 and 3. For example, in homicide or suspicious deaths, the classification for the investigation changes from a 'SUDI/SUDC' death to a 'homicide investigation', and the place where death is believed to have occurred (eg a child's bedroom) is then reclassified a 'crime scene'. This triggers standard procedures that are outlined in other chapters of this book due to a serious criminal act (although in the majority of cases, unless clearly homicide, the body is likely to have been transported to a hospital Accident and Emergency (A&E) unit and will not have remained in position for forensic examination purposes, as explained later in this chapter). An SIO will also be making early consideration of making arrests, treating witnesses as 'significant', possibly managing the investigation on a case management system, conducting house-to-house (H2H) enquiries, witness trawls, etc.

If there is nothing obvious to suggest a suspicious death or homicide has occurred—*an important judgement call*—the term 'SUDI/C' death is used to describe what is probably a lesser type of investigative response (although still very thorough, and certainly more comprehensive than the standard response to a non-suspicious sudden death of, say, an adult). Category 1 types of death are therefore covered by guidelines outlined in this chapter, while Categories 2 and 3 are investigated in accordance with more conventional (eg homicide-type) investigative requirements. However, even if the death is treated as a homicide, it is still covered by WT 2018[4] and requires a Joint Agency Response (that can provide invaluable information very effectively and promptly to the SIO, eg initial information sharing).

---

[4] WT 2018 (HM Government: 'Working Together to Safeguard Children: A guide to interagency working to safeguard and promote the welfare of children (The Stationery Office, July 2018) is statutory guidance that references the Kennedy Report 2016 cited earlier, therefore placing both reports on a statutory footing.

> **KEY POINT**
>
> Even if there is clear evidence of homicide, a child death it is still covered by WT 2018 guidelines and requires a Joint Agency Response (JAR) identical to that required for a sudden and unexpected death, although the police would take more of a lead role (WT 2018, para 23, p 101).

As stated earlier, child homicides and suspicious deaths are not always obvious or easily recognisable and by their very nature are more difficult to categorise initially. There may not be any obvious signs, such as wounds or fractures. Head and internal injuries, asphyxiation, ruptured blood vessels in lungs, traces of poisoning, abuse, and neglect can be very difficult to detect in young children, particularly infants. Hence, child death procedures have been consolidated to ensure all Category 1 SUDI/C investigations meet a higher investigative standard. This is to provide not only adequate safeguards for sensitive parent management and support but also to ensure every effort is made to establish why a child died unexpectedly and rule criminal offences in or out.

There is, however, a requirement to conduct enquiries more sensitively, one example being the expectation of a more tactful and less obvious use of 'Golden Hour(s)' tasks. Another is the need for a greater multi-professional and considerate approach to the investigation. SUDI/C procedures require a balance between the requirement for carrying out an effective investigation and the need to acknowledge and cater for the needs of the parents and other children who may be affected. For these reasons, a specialist trained investigator and/or PIP3 SIO (who might also be specially trained) should ideally take the lead on child death investigations, particularly when it is unclear what category the death falls into.

In summary, when dealing with SUDC there are five common principles:

- Balanced approach between sensitivity and the investigative mindset.
- Multi-agency response.
- Sharing of information.
- Appropriate response to the circumstances.
- Preservation of evidence.[5]

Four simple questions to aid classification might also be:

1. Why did the child die?
2. What was the cause of death and circumstances?
3. What possible criminal offences have been committed?
4. Who was/were responsible?[6]

---

[5] The Kennedy Report, para 1.5, p 63.

[6] As cited in D Marshall, *Effective Investigation of Child Homicide and Suspicious Deaths* (Oxford University Press, 2012), 35.

KEY POINTS

1. Determining the right category is the starting point when applying correct procedures.
2. Four key questions to assist are: (i) Why did the child die? (ii) What was the cause of death and circumstances? (iii) What possible criminal offences have been committed? (iv) Who was/were responsible?
3. In all cases of SUDI/C, whether suspicious or not, a lead investigator[7] should take charge. It is recommended they attend the location of the body to liaise with the lead clinician and other medical practitioners (ACPO Homicide Working Group, *A Guide to Investigating Child Deaths* (ACPO HWG, 2014), p 9).

15.3 **Factors Increasing Suspicion**

Every case is judged on its own merits but certain facts or circumstances may heighten suspicion. When determining a potential Category 2 death the following might assist as a guide:[8]

1. Child has obviously been dead longer than stated.
2. Blood or vomit on clothes or body, or around the nose or mouth and on the face of the type associated with smothering and physical abuse.
3. Unusual external marks or bruises, ligature, grip or bite marks, burns, scars, abrasions, incisions, petechiae or retinal haemorrhaging in the eyes—symptoms of suffocation or shaking.[9]
4. Presence of foreign bodies in the upper airway.
5. Child appears ill-treated or badly neglected.
6. Inappropriate delay by parents in seeking medical help.
7. Position, surroundings, and condition give cause for concern.
8. Parent's unusual reaction/demeanour/behaviour.
9. Evidence of high-risk behaviour, eg domestic abuse, drug/alcohol abuse.
10. Parents or carers provide inconsistent accounts of events.
11. Mental health issues within the family.
12. Previous unusual illness or recent admissions to hospital.
13. Child is older than twelve months (these unexplained deaths are rare and unusual).

---

[7] Reference to Investigating Officer/Lead Police Investigator is understood to mean a member of staff who has attained the national standard in the field of investigating child deaths (ACPO, 2014).

[8] See also Mayes et al, (2010) 6(1) *Journal of Homicide and Major Incident Investigation*, 77–96, and the Kennedy Report).

[9] The eyes need to be checked quickly as the cornea clouds over after death in a matter of hours, preventing any examination of the retina (Kennedy Report p 86) as a fundal examination or fundoscopy.

14. Intelligence suggests the child has been 'at risk' or precursor incidents suggest this should be the case, eg child or sibling is on a 'child protection' or 'safeguarding plan'.
15. Child or family is known to social care (services).
16. Parent or carer has a criminal record.
17. Another child having died in the family previously.

15.4 'Working Together' and Joint Agency Response

Success of any type of infant/child death investigation relies upon effective co-operation and liaison between the police, essential experts (paediatricians), and other agencies all working together.[10]

Any child death should trigger formation of a team of professionals from a number of agencies, now referred to as a 'Joint Agency Response' (JAR). The police have National Police Chiefs' Council (NPCC) guidelines and some forces or regions have their own policies, as may some of the other agencies and bodies that become involved. Note: LSCB change under WT 2018 to 'Local Safeguarding Partners' (WT 2018, para 1, p 7).

All the relevant agencies share responsibility for an investigation to establish the cause of death and carry a duty of care to the parents and surviving children. An SIO who takes the lead in a criminal investigation will be expected to work alongside highly qualified and experienced professionals, who together must balance the medical, forensic, and all other investigative requirements with the welfare of the parents affected and potential risks to other (and future) children.

An assembled team of professionals will be able to provide the necessary knowledge, expertise, information, and resources to mount a sophisticated joint investigation into why and how a child or young person died. Any sudden and unexplained death must trigger the combination of such resources, with the SIO ensuring there is sufficient trust and confidence amongst the team for an effective and coordinated interagency response, particularly in relation to information sharing.

Each agency and individual will have different areas of responsibility. For example, a paediatrician is likely to focus upon issues that have implications for others, such as infectious diseases, in addition to the cause of death. A coroner, on the other hand will focus solely upon the cause and circumstances of the death, and social services for safeguarding the welfare of other children in the family. These various agendas are intertwined and should be complementary in establishing why a child died, providing parents and others affected with

---

[10] WT 2018 para 1.7, p 17.

support, and quickly identifying and investigating any potentially suspicious circumstances.

Baroness Kennedy outlined some key components for a JAR, and states that despite whatever local protocols may apply, no response is considered complete without these core components:

- Careful multi-agency planning of the response.
- Ongoing consideration of the psychological and emotional needs of the family, including referral for bereavement support.
- Initial assessment and management including a detailed and careful history, examination of the infant, preliminary medical and forensic investigations, and immediate care of the family, including siblings.
- Assessment of the environment and circumstances of the death.
- Standard and thorough post-mortem examination.
- Final multi-professional case discussion meeting.[11]

15.5 **Guiding Principles—SUDI/C**

A number of fundamental principles underpin the work of all relevant professionals, especially responding officers and SIOs, when dealing with all three categories of SUDI/C. These are:

- Sympathetic and sensitive approach to the child's family, with tactful communication.
- Awareness that innocent parents/carers wrongly accused suffer unimaginable grief.
- Retaining investigative mindset as to how and why a child died (a child with seemingly no obvious signs of external or internal injury can still have been the victim of unlawful killing, but the signs may be less detectable).
- Coordinated JAR (see per para 15.4) required including the police, other specialists and service providers who have particular knowledge and experience of child abuse and development (plus WT principles).
- Thorough and meticulous but compassionate approach.
- Preservation of all potential evidence.

As the majority of unexplained child deaths are *not usually* the result of criminal acts, ie Category 1, the response needs to be finely balanced between providing the utmost consideration for the needs of an innocent, grieving family and conducting a thorough investigation into the cause of death.

Child deaths have added sensitivities, complexities, and challenges, both from a professional and an emotive perspective. These events demand a high level of composure, experience and tact, which is why using trained child

---

[11] The Kennedy Report, para. 1.7, p 17.

413

protection/abuse unit investigators is the best option. Amongst the tragedy lies the important task of looking for any factors that may heighten suspicion (see section 15.3 earlier). For these reasons, only the most experienced staff, supervisors, and experienced detectives should manage these investigations, although the first contact is likely to come from less experienced officers whom as gatekeepers and as stated in other chapters, will inevitably create a big impression from the first moment onwards.

KEY POINT

The focus of the investigation needs to be on the rights of the dead child above and beyond anything else. Seeking explanations and/or justice for the child always takes precedent.

15.6 **First Response**

Child deaths are usually reported directly to the emergency services, routed through a call centre. Sometimes they originate directly from A&E units at hospitals. Occasionally a GP (doctor) will be first on the scene and notify the emergency services. Call handlers (as per section 5.5) are responsible for obtaining as much information from the person reporting the death as possible and organising the rapid despatch of medical care to the scene. In most cases, the police are notified simultaneously and may even arrive before medical teams.

If the initial response requires attendance at a child's home address, this should wherever possible, be undertaken unobtrusively. This is in order to reduce or minimise undue attention or distress to the parents and avoid attracting early attention of neighbours and onlookers. Non-uniformed staff using unmarked/plain vehicles are best suited as first responders, provided no undue delay is caused as a result (remembering 'Golden Hour' principles see section 5.3).

Those attending should make an initial assessment of not just the scene and circumstances but also the safety and welfare of any other children connected. Depending upon the circumstances of the death and conditions in which other children are found, it may be necessary to take prompt action to secure their safety and wellbeing (ie safeguarding), a decision usually taken in consultation with other agencies (see Chapter 16).

After initial attempts at resuscitation, the child should be taken directly to a hospital A&E unit (unless obvious and clear signs of homicide). This is because it is less distressing than going to a mortuary (for parents) and ensures all possible resuscitation options have been considered. It also assists parents in allowing them to travel with the child and receive any necessary support from trained medical staff, and permits the initiation of JAR procedures.

At hospital, a consultant clinician is notified by the medical professional confirming fact of death who in turn informs the designated paediatrician[12] with responsibility for unexpected child deaths, and the coroner and police (if not already involved) via standard protocols. The paediatrician usually initiates the information-sharing and planning discussion between the various agencies while the police take care of the investigation on behalf of the coroner (evidence gathering, liaison with pathologist, etc).

The initial investigation into the circumstances of a child's death also includes obtaining information and historical details from the parents (ie medical history taking). This procedure may have already been commenced by medical staff if the body is at hospital. It forms an important part of building rapport with the family, parents, and relatives, and for the purposes of an investigation is an ideal opportunity for exercising essential tradecraft skills and intuition in order to form an early opinion as to whether there may be any suspicious indicators.

It is during these initial stages that views are formed and decisions made about which category the death may fall into (see section 15.2). Professional curiosity is a trademark of all good investigators and must always prevail. The initial response phase is within the Golden Hour(s) period, a time when emotions are running high and people are at their most vulnerable. Offenders in particular are under the greatest levels of psychological and emotional pressure and may make mistakes by giving false and inaccurate accounts and details. This is the best opportunity to gauge reactions, observe the attitudes, behaviour, and demeanour of the parents or carers, and look for any suspicious or disturbing signs or comments, or flawed explanations that do not add up. As with any investigation, the skilful handling of those involved (including significant witnesses), information building, and accurate record keeping are essential during the initial stages (Golden Hour(s)).

A member of nursing staff is usually allocated to handle, support, and stay with the family. In some areas, some of the JAR procedures are undertaken by a designated SUDC nurse rather than a paediatrician. They should begin obtaining initial details from the family and accurately record them. Hospital staff will be fully briefed by the medical crew who attended and conveyed the child to hospital. The SIO should note that these details are highly valuable pieces of information and probably the first account (other than the call to the emergency services) of what occurred. If the circumstances develop into something more serious and suspicious, the medical staff may become significant witnesses for the purposes of determining mode of interview.

---

[12] A designated paediatrician for unexpected deaths in childhood is defined as: 'a senior paediatrician responsible for coordinating responses to unexpected childhood deaths. This is a statutory role, with responsibilities set out in Working Together 2018.' The Kennedy Report, p 12.

Checklist—Initial considerations

- Confirm location of child's body and continuity of movement.

- Lifesaving attempts/medical attention must take precedent.

- Make early assessment and retain *professional curiosity*.

- If obvious criminal offence (eg homicide) apply ISP principle (ie crime scene).

- Locate any nappies, underwear, clothing, or possessions taken from the child/young person (eg by hospital staff).

- Obtain and record details of the person/s who removed any items.

- Treat all items as potential exhibits and package/label separately to avoid risk of contamination (they may later require forensic examination).

- Consider relevant powers (eg to arrest, search, or safeguard).

- Reassure the parents/carers/owners any items seized will be returned.

- Chose words carefully around parents (eg 'suspicious death' or 'crime scene'—better to say 'place where death occurred' and use a child's name rather than saying 'body' or 'it').

- Careful and accurate note-taking of anything heard or seen is essential.

15.6.1 History taking

Once a child has been certified clinically dead, hospital staff normally facilitate arrangements for the parents to be allowed time with their child. This is usually followed by a more in-depth interview (also known as 'history taking') at the hospital with the parents. Wherever possible, the police take the lead (if a Category 2/3 death), with a paediatrician to interpret all medical and parenting issues unless being treated as a non-suspicious death (Category 1: the majority of cases), then the designated paediatrician takes the lead as it will be more medical (rather than criminal investigation) focused. This is probably a difficult judgement call to make and will depend on the individual circumstances. Note: history taking is not just the medical history being obtained but also facilitates the gathering of information for the benefit of the investigation. Much of it will be very sensitive and families may feel extremely vulnerable when asked pertinent questions. Great skill and tact are required to avoid any accusation of value judgement or criticism.

Before approaching the family (ie with the paediatrician) it is vital to discus and agree:

- Who will lead introductions?
- Who will be present?
- Who will take notes?

- If the child will be examined prior to history taking (helps inform professional judgement on whether or not the death is suspicious at an early stage)?[13]

If parents are suspected of criminality, the SIO will have to determine whether history taking should take place at all and instead treat them as 'suspects'. This doesn't necessarily mean parents have to be arrested immediately, but it does mean that once that threshold has been crossed, it will be unlikely that the product of any informal history taking can be used in any criminal proceedings. However, the majority of information will relate to the deceased child and is not contentious.

15.6.2 Teamwork

The initial stages of a response to an unexpected child death might involve a multitude of professionals from a variety of different agencies. The SUDI/C consultant clinician (if in a hospital setting) is a useful resource and should be on hand to offer advice around any child death. There will be a number of professionals involved in the early stages, particularly at hospital, and it should be remembered they need to coordinate their activities to effectively investigate all the circumstances. If there are no suspicions/concerns then a paediatrician will be taking the lead.

Sometimes it can be awkward to challenge professionals but the ABC principle must prevail as even doctors and specialists can sometimes get their diagnoses wrong. There may be a vital piece of information missing and it will need clarifying and agreeing what further information is required. Some medical professionals might also find law enforcement officers' involvement and presence intimidating.

There may be a large number of people involved in the response procedures who all need to act together and operate as an effective team.

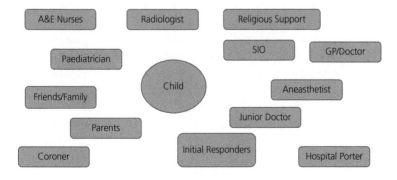

---

[13] D Marshall, The paediatrician's perspective. In *Effective Investigation of Child Homicide and Suspicious Deaths* (Oxford University Press, 2012) p 77.

15.6.3 **Scene management**

Investigators should always strive to preserve the 'place where death occurred' in as pristine a condition as soon as possible after the time of a child's
collapse or upon the body being discovered. An entire house and contents
could be relevant, eg feeding bottles in the kitchen, heating systems (hot/
cold environments), general state of tidiness and cleanliness, toys and food,
etc, and it may be useful to conduct a 'walk-through' similar to that described
in section 14.9.

Depending on the circumstances (it might be possible to securely lock down
the scene), it might necessitate an officer controlling the security of a room
until a thorough combined examination can take place.[14] The lead investigator/
SIO has responsibility for deciding whether to deem the premises a crime scene
and/or request the attendance of a Crime Scene Investigator (CSI) and/or photographer (and any other resources as necessary). There is often a strong case
for CSIs routinely attending all child death scenes as the photographing and
digital recording of the place where death occurred is a way of ensuring there is
permanent record in case the circumstances later develop into something more
serious (eg in post-mortem results such as toxicology).

Vitally important is that where there is no immediate suspicion, the preservation process is handled tactfully and sensitively, particularly in a child's home.
This may, for example, require an explanation as to why it is a necessary process
for the investigation (ie it will significantly help determine why the child died
and is standard procedure). Some parents become highly sceptical of police
procedures and require careful management. There is also a need for parents
(including carers, relatives, and friends) to be dissuaded (and effectively prevented if needs be) from destroying evidential items such as bottles, bedding,
nappies, and residue food and drink, that may prove useful to the investigation. In extreme cases where parents are obstructive, legal powers (eg section
19 of PACE and sections 8, 18, and 32 if arrests have to be made) may have to
be considered.

It is no longer routine practise to seize bedding or a cot or 'Moses basket'
in which a child died and should only be done if there is a good reason for
doing so (eg factors raising suspicion as per section 15.3). It is sometimes
more advantageous for the bedding etc to be left undisturbed so it can be observed where it is by the SIO and SUDI/C paediatrician/nurse who may wish
to attend a joint home visit and assessment. In natural deaths, bedding can
be one of the key items that may hold clues as to how a child died (thickness,

---

[14] The issue of powers to control a scene may arise if no criminal offence is suspected but there is a
duty to investigate (eg Category 1 non-suspicious SUDI/C. This is catered for in Home Office Circular 68/
1955: 'a Coroner or his officer is justified in searching not only the body, but the effects of the deceased
and the premises where the body is found, if there is reason to think the search is likely to lead to the
discovery of evidence bearing on the cause of death.' D Marshall, *Effective Investigation of Child Homicide
and Suspicious Deaths* (Oxford University Press, 2012).

position, etc, eg overheating/airway obstruction), and in many ways there is nothing different between these procedures and standard crime scene procedures regarding identifying and securing/protecting (ISP principle, see section 5.8).

The SIO can conduct a thorough and proportionate scene assessment while in a preserved condition and arrange for any necessary photographs, visual images, measurements, drawings, etc (always a safer measure for providing an accurate record, whatever the circumstances). Other experts and advisers such as a CSI or plan drawer may be required to assist and, if believed suspicious, then standard investigative procedures apply (eg, a Forensic Pathologist to attend, discuss, and formulate a crime scene examination, body recovery strategy, etc 360-degree imaging).

One main difference (repeated again), however, is the requirement to be more sensitive and tactful than usual for the benefit of grieving parents and distressed relatives, especially when in the majority of cases no crime will have been committed. For example, where items are removed parents will need an explanation as to why this is a necessary, ie. standard procedure to assist in establishing how and why their child died.

KEY POINT

When dealing with the place where death occurred (ie potential crime scene), the approach needs to be far more sensitive and tactful for the benefit of grieving parents and distressed relatives.

Checklist—Scene considerations

- Check for evidence of alteration or staging.

- Include all potential scenes, multiple rooms, vehicles, and exteriors of dwellings.

- Check rubbish receptacles and laundry for discarded items.

- Obtain photographs, visual imagery, and scaled diagrams.

- Take measurements of furniture and preserve relevant items.

- Look for possible weapons or objects that may have been used to cause harm (eg smothering—may be pillow or even child's toy), especially if patterned injuries.

- Give consideration for recovering trace evidence (fingerprints, DNA, blood, hair, fibres, etc) on associated articles, weapons, or drugs.

- Check for evidence of soiling, vomit (vomit containing what appears like coffee granules may be blood), illness, colic, messes, or spills (and monitors or devices if a special needs child).

- Seize any documentary evidence, eg life insurance policy on child, diaries, medical appointments or birth/health records, and midwifery papers

- Check for evidence of neglect, quality of caretaking (food, warmth, clothing, etc).

- Check for baby bottles and food containers.

- Check for evidence of drugs, alcohol abuse, domestic problems, debts (stress inducers).

- Paraphernalia used and discarded by emergency responders.

- Potential toxins and medicines.

- Photographs and recordings, DVDs showing child's physical developmental levels (mobile phone recordings/images).

- Childcare books and magazines/leaflets given by hospital after birth advising good practice and key prevention messages.

- Communications data and social media.

- Apply the 'JDLR' principle (just doesn't look right).

15.7 **Role of the SIO**

The SIO links in with first response officers and/or supervision/lead investigator (if different to SIO) to commence the briefing/debriefing processes methodically (see also sections 9.3 and 9.4). One of the first considerations is to confirm the whereabouts of the child's body, which may have been removed to hospital.

A designated paediatrician may need to be informed (if not done so already) to help commence a joint investigation into why and how the child died. If the case is being treated as a Category 2 or 3 death, then stipulated procedures as for any other major investigation usually override all else (eg early arrests, standard crime scene management, conducting significant witness interviews) while still adhering to the principles of 'working together' and a joint multi-agency investigation. The SIO will work alongside a team of carefully selected professionals.

If the child's body lies at hospital, a joint interview will usually be conducted with the parents or carers (previously mentioned as 'history taking'). Consideration on a case-by-case basis can be given as to whether parents are spoken to together or separately. The SIO should view the child's body themselves (preferably in the company of a consultant or designated paediatrician), recording details of any observations. paediatrician body map injuries, marks, bruises, signs of medical intervention, etc. Signs of poor hygiene, nutritional state, and post-mortem staining and rigor mortis that is inconsistent with early accounts given by parents/carers might be noticeable. This information will be useful for briefing the coroner and determining the type of post-mortem to request.

Checklist—Typical 5WH questions

- Who is the child, where are they and their parents now? Who is with them?

- Why has the child died (what is possible cause and manner of death)?

- What category of death has been assigned and why?

- What are the factors that might raise suspicion (see list in section 15.3)?

- Who is/was in charge of treating the child?

- What history taking has taken place?

- Where and when is the death likely to have occurred?

- What has been done to preserve the place where death occurred?

- Who discovered the child and what did they see or find?

- Who reported the death, how, and what exactly did they say?

- Who attended the death scene, what did they find/see/hear (eg paramedics or GP), and how has the information been captured/evidenced?

- Who else might be a witness?

- What explanation did the parents provide? What was their demeanour and attitude?

- Who was the last person to see the child alive and when?

- What was the sleeping position of the child? (Was it different from normal?)

- What was the condition of the child then?

- Who was on the premises where and when the death occurred?

- Who else shared the child's room/bed?

- When was the child last fed, how (eg breastfed), what with, and by whom?

- What was the child's behaviour and condition twenty-four–seventy-two hours prior to death?

- What was the health of the child prior to death (any conditions/medicines)?

- Who was professionally involved with the child or their family (eg GP, healthcare/ local authority, education department, etc)?

- What was the child's living environment like?

- Was an intercom/monitor/other digital recording device in place?

- Who may have posed a threat to the child?

- What evidence is there of neglect/ill-treatment?

- What research has been conducted and intelligence is available (eg on child, parents, siblings, carers, family, or visitors)?

- How many other children live in the same household or family?

- What other child deaths have the family/extended family experienced?

- What, if any, sort of special treatment did the child require after birth?[15]

15.8 **Family Liaison**

Grieving parents can exhibit a variety of reactions such as overwhelming grief, anger, confusion, hysteria, disbelief, or guilt. A key rule, now repeated, is that they should be treated and managed *sympathetically* and *sensitively*, remembering that frustration may be levelled at the police as a manifestation of distress.

The police response and associated activity can in some circumstances prove very distressing to the family, particularly if there are no criminal offences involved. However, the importance and usefulness of a thorough investigation should be explained to them as being beneficial in finding answers to important questions and establishing what caused the death of their child.

Demonstrating sensitivity and tact in handling child death cases does not have to prevent a shrewd and tenacious SIO from being 'compassionately sceptical' or 'professionally curious' about the circumstances under investigation. How an SIO presents themselves externally may have to disguise what they are actually feeling internally: applying the investigative mindset (Chapter 3).

KEY POINT

Wherever possible, bereaved families should have the investigation process explained to them. They should be kept up to date with progress unless this would compromise the investigation, avoiding duplication of information they might be receiving from other agencies.

15.8.1 **Deploying FLOs**

Whatever category of death is being investigated, it may be appropriate to appoint a Family Liaison Officer (FLO) at the earliest opportunity, although this is not always a routine procedure in Category 1-type SUDC investigations. Certain circumstances may influence this decision, such as a high level of media interest

---

[15] See also ACPO Homicide Working Group (Child Death Sub-Group), *A Guide to Investigating Child Deaths* (ACPO, 2014).

and/or intrusion. There may also be added complications in dealing fairly and equally with estranged natural parents who may have other partners. They will require a single point of contact from the investigation team or agency if no FLO is appointed.

It may be decided that in order to ensure the family are fully engaged as partners in the investigation process and/or in order to maintain a sensitive, supportive relationship with them, the deployment of an FLO is beneficial. There may be, for example, a reliance on tests such as toxicology or specialist examinations of portions of the brain leading to a protracted waiting time for the results and outcome. This can be a very unsettling, uncertain, and anxious time for the parents.

During this period, at the same time as providing support, an FLO can be the SIO's conduit within the family and home environment, picking up on any vital clues that may assist the investigation. This is particularly important if there is a greater reliance on circumstantial supportive evidence, especially if a potential offender(s) comes from within or is connected to the child's family (termed 'intra-familial'; see section 15.10), with family dynamics that can change or intensify.

15.8.2 Allowing holding or touching of the body

It is entirely natural for a parent/carer to want to hold or touch the body of their dead child and this is known to help with the grieving process. As a general rule, this is permitted if the death is not deemed suspicious, provided it is supervised by a professional (eg police officer or hospital staff), who should be present during the process.

In most cases it is unlikely that important forensic evidence will be compromised by the tactful and sensible exercise of this activity. It is usually trace evidence being sought if someone else (eg a stranger) other than a person who has legitimate access to the child (eg parent/carer) is suspected of involvement in or having caused the death. Individual circumstances will dictate whether this is applicable. Contact trace evidence in intra-familial homicides, however, has limited use because parents and family members are not unknown strangers and will have had recent and regular access and legitimate contact with the child.

Risk of contamination can be managed, eg if clothing is required for body fluids or interpretation, then seizing prior to contact with the child will suffice. Any concern about the unlikely possibility of post-mortem injuries being caused during this process can be negated by the ability to easily distinguish between ante- and post-mortem injuries. Thus, any external forensic gathering potential should be balanced against the needs of the grieving family. Although ultimately a decision for the SIO, guidelines favour allowing parental contact, provided appropriate control measures are in place.

A supervised contact session, if and when permitted, is something to be agreed between the SIO, CSI (for advice where possible), and hospital staff.

Hospital A&E departments are normally quite used to dealing with unexpected child deaths and experienced nursing staff should be able to arrange for a child to be protected (eg covered in a blanket) and suitably prepared for the parent/carers to hold. Normally the parents are seated to avoid them dropping the infant, and a member of experienced staff (eg a bereavement nurse) is present to ensure parents comply with any tactful instructions or in case they become overly emotional or unwell during the process.

The SIO decides on the appropriateness of this course of action, which will depend largely upon the particular circumstances of the case and degree of suspicion falling on the parents. It is beneficial to discuss the process with an experienced CSI beforehand and/or the Forensic Pathologist/Paediatrician. Once permitted, the parents should be closely monitored so they do not mishandle or mistreat the body in any way.

15.8.3 Requests for mementoes

Requests for mementoes such as prints of hands and feet, photographs, and locks of hair are normally permitted, but in cases where there is a police-led investigation and there are concerns and suspicions, this should not be agreed until *after* the Paediatric Pathologist has fully examined the body. These requests should only be refused (and not every family wants them) if there is good reason to believe it would jeopardise a criminal investigation.

The responsibility for arranging the taking and delivery of mementoes from the body (which is always potentially a crime scene) rests with the SIO. If a decision is made to do so, details of the method adopted and agreed terms must be recorded in a policy log. However, in non-suspicious cases the parents should normally be allowed to leave the hospital with the requested mementoes, as it can be several days before a post-mortem takes place, provided the coroner consents.

Checklist—Family liaison considerations

- Avoid undue criticism of the parents/carers, either direct or implied.

- Don't refer to the child/infant as 'it'—use their proper name.

- Avoid placing children's bodies in body bags.

- Allow parents to see, touch, and hold their child, provided it does not interfere with clinical care or any forensic examination and only in the presence of a professional.

- Deal sensitively with religious beliefs and cultural differences while remembering the importance of evidence preservation.

- Allow parents/carers an opportunity to ask questions and have explained to them what is happening at every stage.

- Allow the parents/carers to accompany the deceased infant/child to hospital.

- Arrange for other children in the household to be looked after.

- In some circumstances it may be appropriate to appoint an FLO depending on the circumstances.

- A supervised contact session with the child can be arranged.

- Mementoes are usually allowed to be taken, provided the SIO and pathologist agree it won't interfere with the investigation and examination.

15.9 **Post-Mortems**

The primary aim of a post-mortem examination in SUDI is to aid the coroner in reaching a decision regarding how the death occurred. Once death is certified, the coroner has jurisdiction over the child's body examination process. As with any adult suspicious death investigation, the SIO liaises with the coroner *beforehand* to discuss arrangements for a post-mortem which are conducted on their behalf.

In child death cases, a post-mortem is always performed by a specialist Paediatric Pathologist. If deemed suspicious, a Home Office-Registered Pathologist takes the lead and conducts it with the Paediatric Pathologist working alongside them.

As with any other death investigation (see chapter 14.12), the SIO provides a full briefing (and it is advisable to keep a record in case of any later disputes) to the Pathologist(s), including the showing of any scene recording or photographs (if available) and any information gathered to inform the process. This process occurs before an examination commences to ensure they have as much detail as possible.

Child post-mortems are different from those conducted on adults, if for no other reason than the bodies being examined are much smaller and more fragile, and important areas cannot be examined or viewed easily. The range of diseases to be considered can also vary from adults, as children's bodies are still in the stages of early development.

Depending on the circumstances, added histological examinations and samples and a wider range of ancillary tests may be required.[16] For example, if 'shaking' or 'suffocation' is suspected, then the brain may need to

---

[16] The Kennedy Report Appendix 6, pp 98–103 lists post-mortem test and sample considerations for child death investigations.

be examined by a Neuropathologist and the eyes by an ophthalmic expert. These added tests may mean the identification of unlawful and malicious acts can be more difficult and/or take longer to detect, and prolong the process.

Obtaining the clinical history of the child in addition to case circumstances will also influence what samples are to be taken and in what priority (ie an intelligence-led approach). Types of tests or examinations that may be considered by the Forensic Pathologist are as follows (or a combination):

- Full skeletal survey and MRI scan
- CT scan (on advice of the Neuroradiologist)
- Paediatric radiology
- Neuropathology—brain/spinal cord examination
- Musculoskeletal pathology—bones
- Ophthalmic pathology—eyes
- Chemical pathology—metabolic diseases
- Microbiology/virology—infectious diseases

KEY POINT

Unlike adult homicide investigations where there may be independent witnesses, child homicides require greater reliance on expert medical evidence. The suspect is also often closely connected to the family (rather than a stranger). These investigations can take much longer to resolve due to the specialist nature of the tests required.

Under the provisions of the Human Tissue Act 2004, a Pathologist can retain only such tissues as required to ascertain the cause and manner of death. The next of kin (ie parents) must be consulted regarding their wishes about the retention of tissue for any further research purposes, and the return to them for burial/cremation or sensitive disposal by other means must be a consideration. It may, however, be in the parents' best interests or that of others for the Pathologist to retain tissue samples, especially when a definitive conclusion as to cause of death has not been reached. However, this may be a sensitive issue and one that has previously caused some degree of controversy. This does not, of course, apply to samples taken for the purposes of a criminal investigation under section 19 PACE (see also section 14.16). Samples may also be retained with permission of the coroner. He/she can authorise retention until an inquest has been concluded.

Category 1 SUDI investigation—Specialist paediatric pathologist performs post-mortem and takes samples on behalf of coroner, which fall under HTA after conclusion of inquest.

Category 2/3 investigation—Paediatric pathologist plus HORP and samples are seized under PACE for criminal investigation with adherence to rules of evidence re integrity of exhibits.

15.10 'Intra-Familial' Child Homicides

This is a term used in certain types of investigation where the offender is:

- Family or extended family member.
- Person living in the same household.
- Person visiting the household regularly.
- Person having care responsibility at the time of the alleged offence, eg teacher, health or youth worker, babysitter, or child minder.
- Carer (where the victim is under eighteen years).
- Carer when the child is in care, eg foster carer or children's home employee.

Section 5 of the Domestic Violence, Crime & Victims Act 2004 (DVCV) as amended by Domestic Violence Crime and Victim's (Amendment) Act 2012 (DVCVA) 'Causing or allowing a child or vulnerable adult to die or suffer serious physical harm', is a useful piece of legislation introduced to create an offence designed to cater for circumstances where there are two or more parents/carers who may be responsible for the death or serious injury of a child and neither accept responsibility, which produces the 'which of them did it' scenario. This offence can still be used for a single defendant if they caused the death/serious physical harm.[17]

Initially, evidence is gathered in order to prosecute for a primary offence such as murder or manslaughter, but where this is insufficient evidence then an offence under section 5 DVCV can be considered. An offence under section 5 DVCV provides that members of a household who have frequent contact with a child under sixteen years or a vulnerable adult will be guilty of an offence if they:

- caused the death.
- allowed the death, if the following conditions are met:
  — they were aware, or ought to have been aware, that the victim was at significant risk of serious physical harm (ie grievous bodily harm under the Offences Against the Person Act 1861).
  — they failed to take reasonable steps to prevent that person coming to harm.

---

[17] Section 6 of DVCVA has special procedures which allow the section 5 DVCV offence to be charged with murder or manslaughter, and if a case for section 5 DVCV is made, a defence team cannot apply for murder/manslaughter to be withdrawn until after the defence case during which parents are expected to give evidence or the jury is able to draw an adverse inference from their silence.

— the person died from the unlawful act of a household member in circumstances that the defendant foresaw or ought to have foreseen.

The offence only applies to members of the same household who had frequent contact with the victim, and could therefore be reasonably expected to be aware of any risk to the victim and to have a duty to protect them from harm. The household member must have failed to take 'reasonable steps' to protect the child. The offence only applies to those aged sixteen years and over unless they are the mother or father of the child.

15.11 Operation Marshall

Operation Marshall is a national UK database designed to inform future prevention and detection initiatives in relation to intrafamilial (carer not stranger) child homicide or suspicious death investigations. The NCA National Injuries Database (NID) hold the responsibility for collating this data which is used to:

• Source reference cases.
• Source appropriate forensic experts including medical.
• Identify national patterns in child death investigations and provide data for national strategic assessments.
• Provide a dataset for research including risk factors associated with child death investigations.
• Identify learning and good practice to be shared in national guidance and training.

Data is collated via the submission of forms that can be submitted electronically via email to childdeathinfo@nca.gov.uk. This data can be useful for assisting in providing research material for child death investigations.

15.12 Child Death Reviews

When a child dies under any circumstances, it is important for parents and families to understand what happened and whether there are any lessons to be learned. Child death reviews (CDR) are aimed at identifying any matters relating to the death that are relevant to the welfare of other children and consider what action needs to be taken regarding any learning identified.

All local organisations (including the police) that have had involvement in a SUDI/C case are expected to cooperate in the process that is conducted by child death review partners (see Figure 15.1). The coroner has a duty to notify the review partners for the area in which the child died or where the body was found within three working days of deciding to investigate a death or commission a post-mortem (Coroners Investigations Regulations 2013). If a criminal

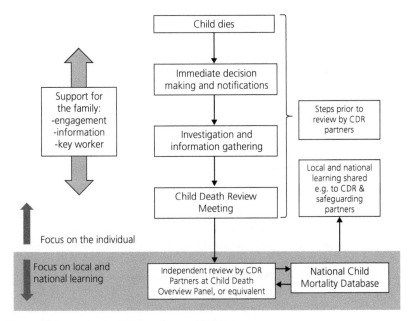

Figure 15.1 Process to follow when a child dies
Source: HM Government: 'Working Together to Safeguard Children' (2018, p 99)

investigation is ongoing, the CRT process should not interfere with the process and the SIO and CPS must be consulted.

Bibliography

ACPO, *Guidance on Investigating Child Abuse and Safeguarding Children*, 2nd edn (NPIA, 2009)

ACPO, *Guidelines: Infant Deaths—Murder Investigation Manual* (Supplement) (NCPE, 2006)

ACPO, *A Guide to Investigating Child Deaths* (ACPO HWG, 2014)

ACPO/CPS, 'Liaison and information exchange when criminal proceedings co-incide with Chapter 4 Serious Case Reviews or Welsh Child Practice Reviews: A guide for the Police, CPS and LSCB' (May 2014), HWG (child death sub-group)

Department for Children, Schools and Families, *Working Together to Safeguard Children* (The Stationery Office, 2010)

Foundation for the Study of Infant Death, *A Suggested Approach for Police and Coroner's Officers* (FSID, 2005)

Foundation for the Study of Infant Death, *Cot Death Facts and Figures* (FSID, 2008)

Foundation for the Study of Infant Death, *When a Baby Dies Suddenly and Unexpectedly* (FSID, 2007)

Fox, J, 'A Contribution to the Evaluation of Recent Developments in the Investigation of Sudden Unexpected Death in Infancy', Briefing Paper

(Department of Sociology, University of Surrey in association with the NPIA, 2008)

Fox, J, 'The police response to infant deaths' (2005) 1(1) *Journal of Homicide and Major Incident Investigation*

HM Government, *Information Sharing: Further Guidance on Legal Issues* (The Stationery Office, 2009)

HM Government, *Information Sharing: Guidance for Practitioners and Managers* (The Stationery Office, 2008)

(HM Government: 'Working Together to Safeguard Children: A guide to inter-agency working to safeguard and promote the welfare of children (The Stationery Office, July 2018).

Baroness H Kennedy QC, 'Sudden Unexpected Death in Infancy and childhood: Multi-agency guidelines for care and investigation', Royal College of Pathologists, 2nd edn. 2016. Available at: <http://www.rcpath.org>

Marshall, D, *Effective Investigation of Child Homicide and Suspicious Deaths* (Oxford University Press, 2012)

Marshall, D, 'Child homicides: A suspect in the family—issues for the family liaison strategy' (2008) 4(1) *Journal of Homicide and Major Incident Investigation*

NHS, *A Guide to the Post Mortem Examination Procedure Involving a Baby or Child* (NHS, 2003)

Police Review (18 July 2008), 'New Tricks' (the new section 5 legislation), 18 and 'Defend the Children' (investigating death of a child)

Sidebotham, P and Fleming, P, *Unexpected Death in Childhood: A Handbook for Practitioners* (Wiley, 2007)

Vaughan, JR and Kautt, PM, 'Infant death investigations following high-profile unsafe rulings: Throwing out the baby with the bath water?' (2009) 3(1) *Policing*, 89–99

Wate, R, and Marshall, D, 'Effective investigation of intra-familial child homicide and suspicious death' (2009) 5(2) *Journal of Homicide and Major Incident Investigation*

Child Sexual Exploitation and Abuse

16.1 **Introduction**

The protection of children is one of the most important roles in law enforcement. The United Kingdom has learned the hard way from a legacy of endemic historical (aka non-recent) child sexual abuse and exploitation (CSAE)[1] some of which was committed by persons with prominent public profiles (PPP). One famous example is Operation Yewtree (renamed Operation Winterkey), the investigation by the Metropolitan Police into allegations following offences committed by the late British TV personality Jimmy Savile (and others). Other well-known reported cases have occurred in places such as Rochdale, Oxford, and Rotherham (Operation Stovewood).

Consequently, the public's attitude to children (eg young people in care) who are exploited has changed. There has been a realisation these are not individuals willing to sell their bodies at any price, but instead are victims groomed and exploited by cruel and manipulative sexual predators. Violence, coercion, intimidation, rewards, alienation, entrapment, and blackmail are commonplace in sexual exploitation, with victims, being in a weaker position due to their vulnerability, having little choice but to comply. Many are incapable of recognising themselves as victims and consent as a coping mechanism, to feed drug or alcohol dependencies, or simply out of fear and hopelessness. Others fall under the spell of those in positions of power and trust who take the opportunity to exert undue power and influence through their roles or seniority. This has occurred in institutions once considered safe places, with some victims disclosing, reporting, and seeking support many years later.

Strong links have been found between child exploitation and running away from home/care or being in foster care. Other victims (including vulnerable adults) are trafficked into or within the United Kingdom for the purpose of sexual exploitation or modern slavery and become involuntarily linked to criminality and criminal gang networks.

Child exploitation investigations can be complicated as these crimes are usually hidden and involve victims who don't file reports or support prosecutions out of misguided trust, loyalty, or fear. With online exploitation the aim is to not only to identify dangerous offenders who deploy sophisticated encryption tools and use the dark web[2] to conceal their true identities but also the identification of victims in first-generation digital images in order to protect and safeguard them.

---

[1] CSEA is now referred to as CSAE. The change was agreed by national policy National Police Chiefs' Council (NPCC lead) (Chief Constable Simon Bailey) and National Crime Agency (NCA) Director Vulnerabilities Command. It was to emphasise the fact that exploitation is a form of child sexual abuse. Together with modern slavery and human trafficking, tackling the criminal exploitation of children is a clear priority by the UK Government.

[2] The dark web is inaccessible via traditional search engines and stays in the shadows of the open web providing anonymous access to a wide variety of illegal activities, goods, and services.

The threat landscape has changed. SIOs must be also change by being adaptable, flexible, and prepared to face new case types and investigations ('Prepare' being one of the 4×Ps strategy). This chapter aims to provide essential information and guidance relating to child sexual exploitation in order to recognise the signs as a starting point for investigations. SIOs and their teams must be ready to tackle these crimes to discharge one of their most important roles and mandatory legal requirements: protecting and safeguarding vulnerable, exploitable people, particularly children.

> Over the main entrance to the building housing London's Central Criminal Court (aka 'The Old Bailey'), figures are placed representing fortitude, the recording angel and truth, along with the carved inscription: 'Defend the children of the poor and punish the wrongdoer.'

16.2 Human Rights

Article 3 of the ECHR (European Convention for the protection of Human Rights) reinforces a positive duty on Law Enforcements Agencies (LEAs) to investigate torture, inhuman, or degrading treatment or punishment. According to case law,[3] this puts an onus on the authorities to conduct an adequate criminal investigation into offences that are physical or sexual in nature. It is likely that most if not all credible allegations of child abuse will engage Article 3 and failure to investigate reasonably and efficiently would amount to a breach.

Any possibility of breaching human rights adds further incentive to avoid errors and eliminate mistakes in CSAE cases. These human rights trigger a duty to investigate properly, ensuring there are adequate processes in place and not succumbing to systemic or operational failings. Applying processes contained within this chapter and elsewhere in the handbook will assist in meeting these requirements.

This means the selection of staff for these sorts of investigations must be considered carefully to try to eliminate investigative errors. Ideally, the SIO should be PIP3 accredited and staff should be specially trained such as the Specialist Child Abuse Investigator Development Programme (SCAIDP) and Ministry of Justice (2015) ABE in criminal proceedings (guidance on interviewing victims and witnesses). Welfare and well-being audits must be produced for staff engaged on CSAE cases together with appropriate support and psychological

---

[3] See *Commissioner of the Metropolis v DSD and NBV* (2015), the case of the 'black cab rapist'. Between 2002 and 2008, John Worboys committed over 105 rapes and sexual assaults on women in his cab by using sedatives. The Judge commented that systemic failings such as not providing proper training, using available intelligence sources, supervising and allocating adequate resources, failing to record a name or vehicle registration number, or checking CCTV were breaches of the victims' Article 3 rights.

assessments for suitability. Complex child sex cases can differ considerably from other investigations. In some cases, legal scrutineers might request details of any specific and focused training of key investigators. SIOs may wish to consider this when they select their team.

16.3 Revised Definition of CSE

A new government definition of CSE was released in February 2017 along with advice on working together:

> Child sexual exploitation is a form of child sexual abuse. It occurs where an individual or group take advantage of an imbalance of power to coerce, manipulate or deceive a child or young person into sexual activity: (a) in exchange for something the victim wants or needs, and/or (b) for the financial advantage or increased status of the perpetrator or facilitator. The victim may have been sexually exploited even if the sexual activity appears consensual. CSE does not always involve physical contact; it can also occur through the use of technology.[4]

16.4 Child Protection—aka 'Safeguarding'

The job of an LEA is to keep the public safe. This links into a recurring theme throughout this chapter, one of 'safeguarding' or 'child protection'. Child protection is a complex, multi-agency process with different organisations and individuals playing their part. In UK law enforcement, it features as a strong element of a national 4 × Ps strategy (Pursue, Prevent, Protect, and Prepare) represented by 'Protect' and 'Prevent'. Most importantly, Section 11 of the Children Act 2004 places a legal responsibility on a range of organisations and agencies, including the police, to ensure their functions are discharged, having regard to the need to safeguard and promote the welfare of children

Whilst it is parents and carers who have primary care for their children, local authorities and partner agencies such as the police have specific duties for safeguarding. Section 17 of the Children Act 1989, for example, places a duty on a local authority to provide services to children in need in their area, regardless of where they are found. Section 47 of the same legislation requires local authorities to undertake enquiries if they believe a child has suffered or is likely to suffer significant harm. These duties can only be discharged when there is full

---

[4] The new working together advice on CSE and definition can be found in 'Child Sexual Exploitation: Definition and a guide for practitioners, local leaders and decision makers working to protect children from CSE' (February 2017, Department for Education). See: <https://www.gov.uk/government/publications/child-sexual-exploitation-definition-and-guide-for-practitioners>.

support from others who also have specific legal duties under section 11 of the Children Act 2004.

Key guidance is contained within the publication: 'Working Together to Safeguard Children' (July 2018)[5] which applies to all practitioners and professionals who come into contact with children and their families.[6] The Children and Social Work Act 2017,[7] however, recommended several significant changes for safeguarding at both local and national levels by amending the Children Act 2004. It created a different structure that allows for much greater diversity of practice. This legislation effectively abolished Local Safeguarding Children Boards (LSCB) by removing their Children Act 2004 duties. In their place, it puts the onus on three 'safeguarding (corporate) partners': (i) the local authority; (ii) Clinical Commissioning Groups operating in the area; and (iii) Chief Officer of Police. All must make safeguarding arrangements that respond to the needs of children in their own area.

Local social services are often involved in safeguarding prior to LEA involvement. Once a referral has been received, they are required to act within one working day to make a decision about next steps and type of response required. This is to determine whether:

- The child requires immediate protection and urgent action is required.
- The child is 'in need' and should be assessed under section 17 of the Children Act (CA) 1989.
- There is reasonable cause to suspect the child is suffering or likely to suffer significant harm and whether enquiries must be made and the child assessed under section 47 of the CA 1989.
- Any services are required by the child and family and what type.
- Further specialist assessments are required to help the local authority to decide what further action to take.
- To see the child as soon as possible if the decision is taken that the referral requires further assessment.[8]

Information sharing between agencies is essential for the early identification of needs assessment in order to keep children safe. Serious Case Reviews (SCRs) have frequently highlighted missed opportunities to share information in a timely manner; particularly where children have gone missing or appear linked to a pattern of behaviour that should have highlighted an added risk or vulnerability. An SIO should not fear the sharing of information with other agencies as they have a legal and morale requirement to protect vulnerable children. The Data Protection Act and General Data Protection Regulations (GDPR) do

---

[5] This section applies to other named agencies too.

[6] See 'Working Together to Safeguard children: A guide to inter-agency working to safeguard and promote the welfare of children', July 2018, HM Government.

[7] See <https://www.childrenengland.org.uk/children-and-social-work-act-2017>.

[8] See 'Working Together' 2018, para 71, p 31.

not prohibit but rather provide a framework to enable sharing to occur. For example, in some circumstances it may not be possible to gain consent of the child or parent to share personal information because it would place them in more danger.

KEY POINTS

1. Child safeguarding and protection must be placed front, rear, and centre in all investigations, not just CSAE.
2. An approach should be child centred and properly coordinated with relevant agencies working together to share information and resources.
3. SIOs and their teams must be aware they have a *legal duty* to safeguard and promote the welfare of children under section 11 of the Children Act 2004.

16.4.1 Contextual safeguarding

Highlighted in 'Working Together' are guidelines that cover circumstances for threats to children that do not come from within families. Extra-familial threats can originate from schools, peer groups, criminal gangs, within communities, or, more relevant these days, from being online. Organised crimes such as county lines, human trafficking, online abuse, or even the influences of extremism and radicalisation[9] can be included.

16.4.2 Legal frameworks

These broadly fall under any of the following:

1. Section 17 Children Act 1989 (child in need).
2. Section 20 Children Act 1989 (provision of accommodation).
3. Section 46 Children Act 1989 (removal and accommodation of children by police in cases of emergency) and section 44 (court orders for emergency protection).
4. Section 47 Children Act 1989 (child in need of protection).

Section 17 states local authorities have a duty of care to safeguard and promote children's welfare in their area. 'In need' relates to their health needs, including mental health as well as physical, and the promotion of the upbringing of such children by their families. This involves providing a range of services appropriate to those children's needs. This section also requires police to refer these cases to the local authority.

---

[9] The Counter Terrorism and Security Act 2015 contains a duty on specified authorities in England, Wales, and Scotland to have due regard to the need to prevent people from being drawn into terrorism.

Section 20 is a voluntary agreement between all interested parties where the need to safeguard a child is recognised. It avoids the necessity to go through a court process and can mean that the child is placed outside the area to cut all ties and association with offenders; in practice most section 20 accommodation is usually in foster care not with social workers.

Section 46 provides a police power to remove a child to suitable accommodation where there is reasonable cause to believe they would otherwise be likely to suffer significant harm (aka police protection). However, police protection cannot last any longer than seventy-two hours, but an emergency protection order (EPO) under section 44 can be applied for to a court which lasts up to eight days.

Section 47 if there is a suspicion that a child is suffering, or is likely to suffer significant harm, the local authority and police must make enquiries so they can decide whether they should take any action to protect and promote the welfare of the child. There is usually a locally agreed procedure between the police and the local authority to guide both organisations in deciding how section 47 enquiries should be conducted.

Checklist—Key definitions

1. Children at risk of *'significant harm'*

A child is defined as being at risk or subject of significant harm where there is ill- treatment or impairment of health or development:

- 'ill-treatment' includes sexual and emotional abuse as well as physical abuse.

- 'health' means physical and mental health.

- 'development' means physical, intellectual, emotional, social, or behavioural development.

- 'significant harm' turns on the question of the harm suffered by a child in respect of their health and development compared with that reasonably expected of a similar child.

2. Children *'in need'*

Defined as:

- unlikely to achieve or maintain, or have the opportunity of achieving or maintaining a reasonable standard of health or development without the provision for him/her of services by a local authority; or

- their health or development is likely to be significantly impaired, or further impaired, without the provision of such services; or

- they are disabled.

(Section 17(10) Children Act 1989)

KEY POINT

When there is a risk to the life of a child or likelihood of serious immediate harm, the powers provided under section 46 CA 1989 can be used to act quickly to secure their safety. The needs of other children in the same locality of an alleged suspect should also be considered.

16.4.3 Safeguarding

Safeguarding is a term used to denote measures to protect the health and wellbeing of children, young people, and vulnerable adults to prevent abuse, harm, and neglect.

Safeguarding means:

- Protection from abuse and maltreatment.
- Preventing harm to their health or development.
- Ensuring children grow up with the provision of safe and effective care.
- Taking action to enable all children and young people to have the best outcomes.

Safeguarding can vary from being broadly based on welfare and wellbeing (wider safeguarding) to being very specific and individual focused. For example, making an early intervention such as the direct removal of a child from danger. Safeguarding can be a complex area for LEAs dealing with a wide spectrum of crime types where it can be useful to access specialist professional assistance when undertaking operational activity in order to have a positive impact on a person's welfare and/or safety. There are a number of ways advice can be taken, eg from trained internal organisational experts or from the National Crime Agency's (NCA) Child Protection Advisors (CPA). Wherever possible, advice should be sought prior to any pre-emptive operational activity or in emergency situations.

Where a case involves the digital use of indecent images of children (IIOC), safeguarding could include a duty of care to protect the child/children from further harm and further sharing of the images. This refers to any subsequent distribution or handling of the material to avoid the child victim(s) having their indecent images viewed unnecessarily (in essence, further 'abused').

Safeguarding can become operationally complex if there is a wide geographic spread of where victims reside. Primacy would have to be negotiated and agreed if other police areas and organisations need to become involved.

KEY POINT

When balancing operational objectives with safeguarding, SIOs are wise to remember their section 11 (CA 2004) responsibilities. It might be too risky to opt for the 'do nothing' or 'defer' options (see section 3.5.2) when a child's safety is at risk.[10]

Checklist

5WH safeguarding queries:

- What are the concerns for children in the operational activity?

- What are the particular risks, vulnerabilities, and issues to be aware of?

- Who are the children on the premises or in targeted premises/household (names, ages, gender, specific vulnerabilities)?

- Who is/are the suspect(s) and have they got current access to children (or other vulnerable persons)?

- What other agencies have been consulted/informed under WT guidelines?

- What is the suspect's relationship with the child and are they in a position of trust (PoT)?

- Do they have access to any other children who could be at risk?

- What sort of safeguarding or protection is required, when, and who by?

- How urgent is the requirement to intervene?

- What is the suspect management strategy after intervention (eg while on bail or released under investigation (RUI) to prevent further risk to children or themselves)?

- What are the wider safeguarding issues (eg other victims/PoT/prevent activity)?

While gathering information to assess the risk of harm (and applying the NDM; see Chapter 3 and Appendix A), it should be noted that there are useful sources of information other than the usual LEA databases, eg from agencies such as the local authority, education/schools (from where some of the most useful

---

[10] During a covert operation, officers outside a suspect's home saw a thirteen-year-old boy and a man (Dominic Noonan) enter a house. They saw the windows being closed and curtains drawn. Worried the boy might be in danger, surveillance teams sought advice about expediting safeguarding immediately, something that was not acted upon. A whistle-blower raised concerns with the IPCC (now IOPC), who found the SIO had a case to answer for misconduct. Operation Nixon (GMP) as reported by F Hamilton, 'Police Scandal over child left in paedophile's home' *The Times* 23 June 2018.

information can be gained), health services, and from government agencies such as Her Majesty's Revenue and Customs (for employment checks), and other third-party material. If the operational activity is to take place in another area or region, it is strongly advised that checks be made in the locality of where the child or suspect resides and the SIO not to become over dependent on nationally shared intelligence databases (to avoid mistakes being made and to ensure there is the most current information available).

Where applicable, the SIO should produce and record a strategy to address all safeguarding issues related to the investigation to ensure compliance with the statutory duty under section 11 Children Act 2004. An effective safeguarding response also increases the likelihood of achieving best evidence and supporting judicial processes. The aims and objectives of a child protection/safeguarding strategy (in conjunction with an operational plan/order containing a victim/child/vulnerable person risk assessment) are to ensure:

- Children and vulnerable persons at risk are identified early and protected.
- Wider safeguarding risks are fully assessed and appropriate actions taken to manage them.
- Safeguarding and protection of vulnerable persons remains a <u>golden thread</u> running through all operational decision making.

KEY POINT

The National Decision Model (NDM) is the best tool for structuring decision making when faced with potential child safeguarding requirements (refer to the Appendix).

16.4.4 **Positions of Trust (PoT)**

A wider safeguarding risk may emerge if a suspect or offender happens to be in a position of power and trust (PoT). Such status may grant them direct access to or a controlling influence over vulnerable people such as children. This includes anyone who might work with or have access to children such as in schools, sports and youth justice settings, residential care, youth clubs, nurseries, religious institutions, voluntary and charity work, etc, in fact any role providing enhanced access to children.[11] This can either be working directly with children or in an ancillary role.[12] Unmanaged risks can and do occur despite the best efforts of the Disclosure and Barring Service (DBS).

---

[11] Following the Jimmy Saville disclosures, there has been a vast increase in public and policy concern about the role of institutions in relation to CSAE.

[12] B Gallagher, The extent and nature of known cases of institutional child sexual abuse. *The British Journal of Social Work* (2000) 30(6) 795–7.

Those who commit CSAE in institutional settings frequently target multiple victims. It is an aggravating factor in such investigations that offenders might have had access potentially to a larger number of victims (eg at a school or sports club). Once an intervention is made by, say, an arrest, the wider consequences must be considered of further victims coming forward, together with a perception created by media attention that there may be more victims still. Any parents with children who might have come into contact with an offender in a PoT will be concerned as to whether their child may too have been a victim.

Research may indicate a suspect has had access to or contact with children within their own familial network, and that they may have abused some of them. In these circumstances, an agreed plan as to how these children are approached and how information might be disclosed to the parents is required. From an investigative perspective, this might provide evidence gathering opportunities. However, these are situations that have to be handled with enormous tact.

Identification and management of wider safeguarding concerns means engagement with any relevant agencies or institutions that have been identified (eg a school or place of employment). The parents of children connected to the organisations may need to be briefed and kept updated to alleviate concerns. They may also need to be allowed to voice their concerns with the investigation team and key stakeholders (eg a local school) and provided with information. They may also require some level of support. The timing of any communication with them will need careful consideration so it doesn't interfere with the investigation, cause unnecessary risk of alarm, or unduly impact on those suspected (see suicide risk management in section 12.7.1).

Consequence management may be required once knowledge of a suspect or local offender who is in a PoT is publicly revealed. Information release may create community tension or impact with the potential for uncovering further victims of non-recent (historical) child abuse who could feasibly be adults and who subsequently report as previously unknown victims (ie by reporting to the police, support agencies, or the media).

KEY POINT

When a suspect or offender is in a PoT, there are wider risk implications to consider for safeguarding as they may have had access to and consequently have abused further victims.

16.4.5 Multi-Agency Public Protection Arrangements (MAPPA)

Many agencies who have a section 11 CA 2004 duty are also members a MAPPA-type body (colloquially known as MAPPA) which might include the police, local authority, prison, and probation service. Joint membership enables these and other agencies to work closely together to manage the risk to safeguarding posed by violent and sexual offenders living in their communities. Safeguarding partners are usually included in these arrangements and they are important means of managing any risks.

16.4.6 Modern slavery

Section 52 of the Modern Slavery Act 2015 stipulates that the police, local authorities, the NCA, and other agencies such as the Gangmasters and Labour Abuse Authority (see <http://www.gla.gov.uk>) have a duty to notify the Home Office if they encounter a potential victim of modern slavery in England and Wales. This includes children, who can be criminally exploited by modern slavery (ie not always just for sexual reasons), in which case immediate and effective steps would need to be taken to safeguard the child. Such a victim is most likely to be severely traumatised and extremely vulnerable.

Child victims of modern slavery are amongst the most vulnerable because they are the easiest to control and the least likely to admit to their situation. They may not show obvious signs of distress as they may not realise that they have been enslaved or view themselves as being at risk of harm and in danger. Parents and relatives may also be involved in their exploitation. Children are likely to be extremely loyal to their parents or carers so it is not likely that they will, of their own initiative, seek protection from them. It is also possible that a child's experiences of modern slavery by adults, plus experience of corruption and abuse by police, officials and/or authorities in their home countries, may make them wary of all adults, including police officers. They may, therefore, be reluctant to engage with authorities or disclose any information until they have built a trusting relationship with those safeguarding them. This needs to be borne in mind when preparing for any interviews at any stage in the investigation. Note: potential child victims of modern slavery must be referred into the National Referral Mechanism (NRM)[13] automatically (whereas adults provide their consent before being referred).

16.4.7 Cross-border and international safeguarding

Some victims reside outside the geographical boundary in which the investigating force or agency is located. Some are even located in a foreign country. Usually, safeguarding responsibility rests with the agency located in the locus in which the offences have occurred. This becomes more complex if there are multiple victims in multiple locations, for which liaison and agreement is

---

[13] The NRM was introduced in 2009 to meet the UK's obligations under the Council of Europe Convention on Action against Trafficking in Human Beings. Following initial referral, there is a two-stage process to decide whether a person is a victim of modern slavery based on a reasonable grounds (RG) test.

required to agree primacy. A Gold Group may be required (or at least very senior collaboration) to agree roles and responsibilities and provide deconfliction. Safeguarding has to be coordinated to provide consistency of approach. In the United Kingdom, the NCA might become involved under pre-existing protocols for conducting complex investigations like these, and also Operation Hydrant (see section 11.5.2).

The NCA can also advise on international investigations, particularly those involving Transnational Child Sex Offenders (TCSOs). This is where there might be an option to consider offences under section 72 of the SOA 2003 enabling a prosecution to be brought in the United Kingdom for certain types of sexual offences committed by a UK national overseas. However, in these types of investigations, any child safeguarding requirements (of overseas victims) involving foreign LEAs usually becomes extremely challenging and seeking specialist advice is always advisable.

16.5 **Warning and Assessment Tools**

Early intervention in child exploitation cases not only helps protect and safeguard victims from further harm but also allows more opportunity for effective investigation, disruption, and prevention strategies. Links to other related activities, incidents, and acts are frequently involved and the following checklist may be useful in helping identify children being exploited.

Checklist—Warning and vulnerability indicators

- Adults or youths loitering outside or visiting a child's usual place of residence.

- Children and young people who persistently run away, go missing, stay out late, overnight, or don't return home on time, or are homeless.

- Appearance unusual for the individual (ie inappropriate for age or occasion).

- Unexplainable acquisition of money, gifts, expensive clothes, cosmetics, money, mobile phones, digital devices, or other accessories, and overnight bags/suitcases.

- Possession of contraceptives, lubricating gel, sex toys, pornography, provocative clothing.

- Rapid change in appearance without explanation.

- Drug, alcohol, or substance misuse.

- Truancy/disengagement with/exclusion from mainstream education or considerable change in performance at school.

- Volatile behaviour exhibiting expressions of despair, extreme array of mood swings, or use of abusive language.

- Disclosure of sexual/physical assault followed by withdrawal of allegation.

- Involvement in petty crime, eg shoplifting and other minor thefts.

- Hanging around late-night-opening shops and premises, eg fast-food outlets.

- Entering or leaving vehicles driven by unknown male adults.

- Hostility in relationships with parents/carers and other family members.

- Returning home after having been missing, appearing well fed and cared for despite having no proper home base.

- Personality disorders such as psychosis, depression, self-harming, suicidal tendencies, eating disorder, severe low self-esteem, and self-neglect.

- Unsupervised/regular/secretive use of Internet, social networking, phone apps/chat rooms/sites/sexting.

- Sexually transmitted infections (STIs), numerous sexual partners, pregnancy, and terminations.

- Physical injuries, illnesses, frequent visits to medical care.

- Evidence of bullying and/or increased vulnerability.

- Gang affiliation or residing in a gang-affected neighbourhood.

- Residing in a household where there has been domestic violence or familial child sexual abuse, and/or is chaotic or dysfunctional, there is disrupted upbringing and/or family conflict.

- Living in a household where there are parental mental health issues or criminality.

- Children and young people who have been trafficked.

- Children and young people at risk of forced marriage or 'honour' -based violence.

- Friends or associates who are victims of exploitation.

- Evidence of grooming others or leading them astray.

- Recent bereavement or loss.

16.6 **Locations of Offending**

There are a range of places where exploitation is known to occur, often linked to the type of 'relationship' developed and the context in which the abuse takes place. Some of these may also be potential crime scenes.

Checklist—Examples of exploitation locations

- Organised parties in a variety of locations, eg warehouses/private premises, schools, or public places in the neighbourhood such as parks and stairwells.

- Vehicles while being transported to meetings/parties, being groomed, trafficked, or abducted (the offer of transport may also be the means by which the abuse takes place, eg taxi drivers who exchange lifts for sexual favours).

- Hotels, guesthouses, budget bed-and-breakfasts and hostels (especially when the abuse activity involves several offenders or so-called sex parties).

- Private residences, eg if children have ongoing contact with a group or gang member.

- Public places such as shopping centres, social networks, and online gaming sites, arcades, cafes, fast-food outlets, cinemas, alcohol outlets, taxi/bus ranks, and any other places where there is little or no adult or parental supervision.

- Over the Internet (online) and through mobile phones/digital devices, eg via social media.

Opportunities may present themselves for identifying victims, offences, offenders, and evidence at locations such as those listed above (including online through virtual crime scenes). For example, if victims are transported to venues, this may provide opportunities for evidence recovery through searching and examining the means of transport or along the route. Stop-checks are a way of identifying offending taking place if children are passengers in vehicles as a consequence of being groomed, trafficked, abducted, or being used to transport illegal items such as drugs, stolen goods, or weapons eg so called county lines offending.

KEY POINT

Identifying offence locations provides opportunities for evidence gathering and disruption/prevent tactics. Proactive targeted, intelligence led stop-checks may, for example, reveal passengers in vehicles who are being transported, groomed, or trafficked for exploitation.

16.7 **Exploitation by Criminals and Gangs**

Exploitation can be used by criminals and gangs to:

- Target young people to commit criminal acts (eg selling, concealing, or transporting drugs/firearms/stolen goods/cash—eg county lines; see section 16.7.1).
- Exert power and control.
- Initiate young people into the gang.

- Exchange sexual activity for status or protection.
- Entrap rival gang members by exploiting girls and young women.
- Inflict sexual assault as a weapon in conflict.
- Hold children against their will in so-called cuckoo houses (homes taken over by gangs to use as drug bases).[14]

Physical abuse and the use of violence is not uncommon by gangs, with assaults and threats of violence aimed at making their victims conform. This may include the use of weapons including firearms and knives to intimidate or coerce, including videoing and photographing sexual abuse and threatening to post the images online. Mobile phones, social networking sites, and other forms of digital technology are used as a means of grooming, bullying, threatening, blackmailing, and pursuing victims.

When targeting gang exploitation and criminality, it is advisable to set a focused intelligence requirement (IR) through various feeds including making best use of proactive covert opportunities. Use of collective evidence gathering to cover a wide range of gang-/group-related activities and behaviour helps build a strong case which, when presented collectively, more accurately portrays the true extent of their networks and criminal enterprise. Seeking evidence of gang affiliation through social networks, lifestyle, and items seized (eg photographs and online posts) is useful. Evidence can be obtained of the impact of this type of criminality through victim and community impact statements, eg witness testimonies from a local politician, community representative, or neighbourhood police officer.

16.7.1 County lines

The term 'county lines' relates to the supply of controlled drugs (usually class A, primarily crack cocaine and heroin) from an urban hub into rural towns or county locations. This is facilitated by groups who may or may not be gang affiliated, but who have developed networks across geographical boundaries to access and exploit existing drugs markets in certain areas. Branded phones are often used to communicate with customers and controlled by senior gang members.[15]

The exploitation of young and vulnerable persons is a common feature in the facilitation of county lines drug supply, whether for the storage or supply of drugs, the movement of cash, or to secure the use of dwellings held by vulnerable people in the rural marketplace (commonly known as 'cuckooing'). Once again, levels of violence and threats are used against child (and vulnerable adult) victims including sexual violence and sexual exploitation and frequent use of firearms, knives, and harmful substances such as boiling water or

---

[14] Some of this list was taken from: 'If only someone had listened', Final Report from the inquiry into CSE in gangs and groups 2014. Available at: <http://www.childrenscommissioner.gov.uk/content/publications/content_743>.

[15] As reported in 'County Lines Violence, Exploitation & Drug Supply', National Briefing Report, Drug Threat Team, Commodities Branch, National Crime Agency, (November 2017).

corrosive acid (eg ammonia). Young victims may be used to transport drugs, including by means of 'plugging' (internal concealments).

The Policing and Crime Act 2009 contains provisions for seeking injunctions against individuals to prevent gang-related violence and drug dealing activity. These injunctions offer a useful tool to prevent and disrupt the sorts of activities outlined in this section. This may be alongside other more traditional offences such as those under Misuse of Drugs Act 1971 and Firearms Act 1968 (unlawful possession of illegal substances and firearms), plus the Sexual Offences Act 2003 (for sexual assaults, etc). There may be cases where, properly directed and evidenced, an offence under the Modern Slavery Act (MSA) 2015 can be considered (eg section 1 offence: holding someone in slavery, servitude, or forced compulsory labour).

Checklist—Gang and county lines investigations

- Check for links to vulnerable children who are regular mispers or 'runaways'.

- Identify transport routes and methods (eg hire vehicles, taxis, public transport including railways).

- Cater for use of mobile phones, changing handsets, SIM cards, and numbers.

- Check places of accommodation such as hotels, holiday lets, caravans, etc.

- Gangs like to exploit children who are 'cleanskins' (previously not known to the authorities).

- Money laundering may be involved including movements of cash and using multiple ghost accounts (financial investigation plan).

- Cross-agency collaboration and information sharing are required to build intelligence and evidence, protect the vulnerable, and carry out disruption activity.

- Standard charges such as drug trafficking or sexual assault are effective; also consider offences under Modern Slavery Act 2015.[16]

- Exploited victims are likely to be hostile initially to police intervention and need careful protection foremost with evidence gathering secondary (although they may be a crime scene).

- If potential victims of trafficking and exploitation, consider referral through the NRM mechanism (see also section 16.4.4).

- Set the intelligence requirement and use pro-active covert intelligence gathering.

- SOCPA legislation can be considered for assisting offenders (see section 12.6) and the applicability of conspiracy charges.

---

[16] Section 45 of the MSA 2015 provides a defence for certain offences including but not limited to drug trafficking and money laundering for those who are considered to be exploited victims not offenders. Early and close link up with the CPS is advisable.

16.8 **Missing Children Reports**

Missing children reports merit close scrutiny and supervision, particularly when they might involve CSAE, other forms of criminal exploitation or serious offences such as abduction, modern day slavery or human trafficking, or at worst homicide. Some children are coerced and groomed by those who later exploit and harm them (such as in the Rochdale and Rotherham cases) and go missing for all the wrong reasons. Others become so desperate they run away and take huge risks on the streets, begging or stealing to survive or resorting to using drugs and alcohol. Some may be subject to the forms of exploitation outlined in the preceding sections (eg targeted by criminal gangs and forced to become involved in activities such as county lines).

Response officers and investigators who deal with these types of reports must remain vigilant to recognise the signs and symptoms of CSAE offending. In the initial stages there is a golden opportunity to arrange early safeguarding and gather valuable evidence. Physical searches not only have the objective for locating and protecting the missing person but also identifying and securing evidential and investigative material. The latter might assist in understanding why a person went missing in the first place and help prevent others from suffering the same fate.

After a report is received, the primary consideration for investigators should be the safety and welfare of the child (ie safeguarding). Few missing child reports result in a serious or major crime investigation, but when they do early identification and correct categorisation and response are vital.

Missing person reports are usually graded as low, medium, or high, with the level of risk determining the level of investigation. If there is a high risk, then an SIO is usually appointed to lead the investigation in the event of serious criminality. Gradings *must* be subject of regular reviews to cater for circumstance and information changes, and to ensure the correct level of response is being applied. Early notification to and engagement with the NCA's Missing Person's Unit (MPU) is not only mandatory in the United Kingdom but also extremely helpful for providing advice and tactical support (see also section 10.9). Providing support to the families of missing children is key as they can experience enormous trauma and stress, particularly if there is public and media interest which can occur in extreme and noteworthy cases. If it is not deemed appropriate to provide support through an FLO (not usually routine except in exceptional cases), then a single point of contact (SPoC) should be appointed with whom they can make contact and obtain regular updates. Other support services such as missing people charities may also prove helpful.

Checklist: 5WH missing children

- Who is the child, what are their full descriptive details and personal history?

- Who are there associates and what are their lifestyle details, including online and social media presence (see also section 11.5 on victimology)?

- What risk has the misper report been graded as and why?[17]

- Why have they gone missing?

- When and where last seen, by whom, and what where they doing?

- What related background information is available and what is it indicating?

- What do any previous missing reports indicate, including 'return interviews'?

- What information gaps are there and what is the intelligence requirement (IR) (consider timeline of last known movements)?

- What lines of enquiry/HP actions have been raised, allocated, and completed?

- What searches/circulations have been done/made, by whom, and to what standard?

- Who has informed and is supporting the missing child's family?

- Who has reviewed the wider safeguarding issues (eg further victims)?

- Who has been involved so far and have they been debriefed?

- What review mechanisms are in place?

- Where and how is all the activity and response phase being logged and by whom?

- What media interest is there?

- What is being reported online and over social media platforms?

- What specialist resources have been considered and have NCA MPU been notified?

Note: Fast-track (Golden Hour(s): high priority) actions are a requirement to help rule in or out evidence of sexual/criminal exploitation. These might include tasks such as: checking CCTV, searching possessions and bedrooms for unusual, provocative, or soiled clothing, tattoos, jewellery, perfume, cash, expensive items and gifts, contraceptives, lubricating cream, notes about menstrual periods, medical appointment cards, eg for STIs, travel tickets, items with hotel branding, receipts, drug/alcohol abuse, diaries, letters, doodles and drawings, multiple communication devices, SIM cards, sex toys, inappropriate DVDs and pornography; and also physical clues on the missing person themselves once returned, such as bruises and abrasions (eg on their knees). Early evidence kits (EEKs) might also be required.

---

[17] Any suggestion a reported missing child is a victim of CSAE means the report should be given a higher priority and response grading, having made good use of the investigative mindset and ABC models (see Chapter 3). Frequent missing children reports should not provide any excuse for a reduced investigative response, such as waiting to see if they return before enquiries are instigated. The level of risk of a child being the victim of exploitation increases (not decreases) the more times they go missing.

> **KEY POINT**
>
> Physical searches for missing children play a crucial part in an investigation and they must be conducted meticulously. Sometimes they have to be intrusive, eg if in the family home, and are hugely challenging if large outdoor areas are involved. The best tactic is to seek early advice and expertise from an accredited Police Search Adviser (see also Chapter 6).

16.9 Online CSAE

Information technology and the Internet have provided a multitude of ways and means (such as peer-to-peer sharing, aka P2P) by which offenders can not only up/download indecent images of children (IIOC) but also identify, contact, groom, abuse, blackmail and sexually exploit them (across the globe). The world of digital media and the Internet is rapidly and continually evolving and offers not just offenders but children themselves the opportunity to create separate identities, often in secret, in which they can be whoever they wish and take huge risks they would never countenance taking in real life (ie offline). It is when these two factors meet that children suffer most from people wishing to cause them harm.

Online CSAE (OCSAE) has a massive impact on victims. Those who are unfortunate enough to be depicted in online sexual abuse (ie IIOC) are re-victimised every time their images are viewed or shared. There is also a high likelihood that an offender targeting a child online will want to move them onto the next stage, ie offline, for physical (or contact) abuse. Those who do so are commonly known as 'dual offenders'.

As a child's Internet presence becomes inextricably linked to their true identity, the risk of exploitation increases. Social media chatrooms, phone apps, sites, and online gaming platforms are used as common access points for online offenders who trawl the Internet looking for victims and then hide behind sophisticated encryption and anonymisation tools, or even overseas-based cloud and service (eg chatroom or live streaming) facilities whom they assume will not cooperate with LEAs, in order to mask their true identities. They do so by clever use of the hidden web or using public Wi-Fi hotspots, Tor,[18] proxy servers, Virtual Private Networks (VPN), and Virtual Private Servers, all of which obfuscate the true IP address of the offenders. This is so they can abuse victims whom they spend considerable time finding, researching, manipulating, extorting, or blackmailing. Applications

---

[18] TOR (The Onion Router) is an example of free software enabling anonymous communication by concealing a user's identity, location, and usage from any LEA conducting network surveillance or traffic analysis.

that provide end-to-end encryption provide offenders with a perfect means of masking their identities, and anonymously grooming and abusing their victims.

Some offenders are clever enough to find and entrap their victims by offering to expose images they have tricked them into providing, on social media. Some, such as Dr Matthew Falder,[19] find their victims through genuine sites and manage to manipulate and entrap them into compromising themselves and uploading explicit images. The offender then introduces threats and coercion tactics to torment their victims into providing more material, controlling them through threats of exposure into doing harmful, degrading, and often lewd sexual acts to themselves and recording it for others to use for sexual gratification.

Some produce and share IIOC through various means and forums, even uploading them onto popular social media sites such as Facebook. Live streaming of CSAE can also be facilitated for distance viewing (often from poorer communities in countries such as those in South East Asia) by paedophiles, some of whom might either share the live images (some also may be pre-recorded) or pay a fee to watch as a 'live show'. Fuelled by extreme poverty and corruption, high-speed Internet connection, and wealthy overseas customers, organised crime gangs/groups (OCGs) have been able to exploit the very vulnerable and poor for financial gain. The financial element is one that can be used as part of an investigative strategy provided the right support and advice is sought from an experienced FI or the NCA.

KEY POINT

Online CSAE offenders are often well educated, highly skilled, and knowledgeable individuals who know exactly how to manipulate information technology. The required know-how is also freely available over the dark web. Some overtly present as being perfectly normal and respectable individuals while masking highly secretive, devious, and dangerous online behaviour using false identities and suggestive pseudonyms. Even the most seasoned investigators must prepare themselves for the extreme levels of depravity and appalling disregard for their vulnerable victims by those engaged in these atrocious activities.

---

[19] Dr Matthew Falder is a convicted English paedophile and blackmailer who, over a period of time, coerced over 200 victims online into sending him degrading images of themselves and of carrying out depraved sexual and physical acts on themselves. He was a Cambridge University graduate who, in 2018, eventually admitted 137 offences, but only after it had taken several years to track him down and a massive enquiry led by the UK National Crime Agency (CEOP). Falder managed to remain untraceable by using sophisticated encryption software including sixty-four-digit passwords and TOR to conceal his true identity. He was jailed for twenty-five years.

16.9.1 **Investigative considerations**

Online child exploitation provides investigative opportunities when a digital device connects via the Internet to any site, forum, or other user as it complies with Locard's principle (mentioned in section 6.1) by leaving a trace. That trace is the Internet Protocol (IP) address of the device the person is using, which allows it to communicate. It is used like an address to respond to and comprises of a string of numbers separated by full stops. Static IP addresses can reveal sufficient information as to whereabouts (country, city, etc) in which the device is located. This is convenient for investigators as they can, with the necessary authority through an application to the service provider, establish to whom the IP address belongs (as they assign IP addresses to subscribers' computers). However, there are various ways to hide an IP address by using, for example:

- VPN service (Virtual Private Networks)
- Using the dark web, eg Tor (The Onion Router)
- Proxy servers
- Free/public Wi-Fi

Individuals whose true identities are the most difficult to trace are those who have usually perfected their tradecraft and use sophisticated encryption. They introduce their own security and are meticulous enough so as not to reveal their true identities. Information on how to do this is freely available on the Internet if you know where to look, but, like every other criminal at some point they get sloppy and make mistakes and these are there to be found. Every small mistake can be pieced together like a jigsaw puzzle to reveal the true identity of even the most clever online offender.

Conducting research before acting on information regarding subscriber details of an IP address is vitally important to avoid targeting innocent people (which can have devastating effect). Care must always be taken to ensure that the IP number and data received is accurately recorded before applications are made; one small digit in the wrong place can ruin the chances of accurate detection. A visit to a wrong address of a completely innocent person or family can have a devastating effect. It must be remembered that data from service providers, however, is only kept for a certain length of time (usually twelve months) and this varies outside of the UK.

Researching the known occupants of the IP address is a good starting point, finding out what is known about them with comprehensive subject profiles. Research needs to indicate if there are added risks to children from those suspected, ie if these individuals pose an increased risk by having access to children or who are in a position of trust. Planning and preparation needs to include checks with local authorities to see if there are any vulnerable persons at the address and if so, a plan needs to be in place to ensure they are adequately safeguarded (see section 16.4).

There may be a number of persons listed at some multi-occupancy premises, but only one of them might be using the IP address for uploading, sharing, producing, live streaming, or distributing IIOC child abuse material (CAM). The key is establishing which one is the likely guilty party.

The entire approach to any proactive phase needs to be meticulously planned down to the last detail, and include such aspects as methods of approach to the suspects and premises (often low key to comply with a suicide prevention strategy; see section 12.7.1). The planning needs to include comprehensive digital forensics search, triaging of devices, and a seize and recovery strategy. The latter should be undertaken by accredited Digital Forensics (DF) experts who, armed with the right equipment, can quickly scan premises for devices and connections to the Internet and triage them once located to see if they contain CAM (particularly helpful if there are multiple devices). Offenders, who are more often than not taken by surprise by an unexpected LEA visit, can be asked for important information while at the scene of a search/arrest. The investigation team might get lucky by catching the suspect online at the time of the strike, or they might voluntarily offer up important access details and passwords to their encrypted devices or hidden files.

Finding digital evidence from digital devices is vitally important in these investigations. Often, the evidence is present and irrefutable, and most online offenders have no option but to accept their guilt. Care must be taken, though, to have robust processes and an adequate DF strategy that will ensure every opportunity is taken to identify victims and evidential material. All DF services in the United Kingdom have had to achieve the ISO17025/20 quality standard accreditation for their methods and processes, as required by the Forensic Science Regulator (FSR).

Checklist—Online investigative considerations

- Victim identification and safeguarding plan: always the most important consideration and sits at the top of any list of priorities in CSAE.

- Passive and covert data: to collect evidence of important movements of persons to premises where IP addresses and devices have been used, and for comparison with timings of online usage.

- H2H enquiries: eg to evidence frequent movement or occupancy at relevant premises and times.

- Communications data: phone records can provide evidence of contact between offenders, not just to and from victims but also between and amongst themselves at relevant times and dates. Cell site analysis can also be used for tracking any offender and victim locations and movements (eg if they arrange to meet their victims after grooming them online).

453

- Open source analysis: social media and networking usage and sites may contain useful information readily available on the Internet. Offenders might leave information about themselves on open source sites and forums that can be used as an evidential link to their presence on other more significant sites of interest.

- Financial information: evidence of devices and phones purchased and topped up, travel tickets, payments into forums or sites, global money transfers made, hotels, accommodation, and ATMs used for withdrawals at significant times. Frequent transfers of cash to noteworthy overseas locations and usage of cryptocurrency. Some online offenders also exchange money to access sites and services, and to access live streaming services (eg from overseas). Some opt to use cryptocurrencies to conceal their true identities that can make enquiries more challenging. Some third-party providers facilitate financial exchange between countries that might provide fruitful lines of enquiry or through SARs (Suspicious Activity Reports).

- Physical searching: best incorporated into a DF strategy, can be used for locating evidence of social media usage and data access/storage/transfer devices including memory storage and cloud computing and 'digital crime scenes'. Password and encryption solving is included and triage of devices on site to scan for IIOC and any CAM including 'chat'. Confirmation of fixtures, fittings, interior decoration, etc and confirming identities in images that help identify/confirm the place where offences took place or to assist in victim identification. Traditional (wet) forensic and physical evidence (including DNA from or physical trace evidence of victims if offender has progressed to contact offending) can also be included.

- Covert tactics: proactive use of intelligence and innovative covert evidence -gathering methods (eg CHIS, Undercover online or Covert Internet Investigators (CIIs) and surveillance online (as well as offline) can provide investigative opportunities for finding offenders and corroborating victim and witness accounts, plus proving when offenders are online/offline. Offenders and significant locations (eg business premises or hotels) can also be targeted as the investigation progresses (note: there are far more secret and confidential methods that can be considered, and cannot be mentioned here. It is highly advisable to seek advice from experts as this area is constantly evolving).

- Overt options: disruption, protection, and prevention can be a considered option under a 4 × P strategy (eg high-profile activities, use of the media, removal of IIOC material or particular forums from Internet platforms. partnership engagement with industry, etc).

- Planning of victim/witness approaches and interviews (victim/witness care and management).

- Planning of arrests and interviews (suspect management)—this must incorporate an assessment of whether the suspect has access to children and/or are in a POT) carefully balancing the needs of safeguarding children and other potential victims, and the human rights of suspects and their close families). A suicide risk-management plan is very important for online offenders.

- Community impact and consequence management. Where offenders and/or victims originate from a particular ethnicity or community group, consideration should be given to managing any adverse reaction within the community and from other sources such as the media who may seek to report negatively.

- Communications (media) strategy. Care must be taken not to cause any further harm to victims by identifying them (and might be legally prohibited).

- DF strategy. This will include device examinations and image grading. Once digital devices have been seized, a lot of time and effort may need to go into searching for IIOC material and relevant 'chat' logs and files (devices might contain details of conversations and discussions with victims or other paedophiles, the content of which will need to be found and examined). Some of the search and grading for images can be automated, remembering the quest must include a check for 'first-generation' images (ones that haven't been seen previously by law enforcement and may provide details of previously unknown victims). Devices can be searched using software and checked against CAID (Child Abuse Image Database), then graded, ie Category A, B, or C (this can be done through machine learning methods). Some devices may contain large volumes of 'big' data and this will have to be managed carefully, as there may be victims contained within all the bulk data that need safeguarding.

- Disclosure and exhibits management. The use of DF within law enforcement comes under great scrutiny. There has been some criticism about lack of thoroughness in digital devices and criminal investigations. The DF evidence and disclosure process must be deemed as being sound and reliable with proper scrutiny of processes around material recovered and how it is subsequently referenced and exhibited.

- Staff welfare. Investigating child sexual offences can be a very distressing and harrowing experience, particularly where the viewing or handling of child sexual abuse material (CSAM) such as IIOC is concerned. This can also include other forms of media such as chat logs and audio material. SIOs should risk assess and monitor all CSAE-related tasks to assess likelihood and level of potential impact on their staff and provide ease of access to desensitisation processes, psychological assessments, and plenty of welfare and wellbeing support.

16.9.2 Victim identification in IIOC

Victim identification is the term given to the analysis of digital images depicting the sexual abuse of children. When CAM is found, there is a responsibility to try to identify locations, offenders, and victims. Identifying victims from IIOC recovered from online systems in order to protect and safeguard them should be one of the primary objectives of any OCSAE investigation.

The UK Child Abuse Image Database (CAID) has fast developed and is available to LEAs in helping identify victims and providing deconfliction when searching through and cataloguing identical copied images. Often when digital equipment such as computers are seized, there may be thousands or even millions of images stored on them (sometimes amongst terabytes of data).

To help compare images, CAID makes use of a unique digital signature assigned to each image known as a *'hash value'*—the equivalent of a digital fingerprint. Seized storage systems, such as computer hard drives, can be automatically searched on CAID to see if the resulting signatures match. Other techniques, such as object matching and visual similarity analysis, can also be employed. CAID can then identify known images, classify the content, and flag those never seen before more quickly (aka 'first-generation' images), allowing more time to be spent on victim-centred enquiries, ie safeguarding.

On a much wider global scale and managed by Interpol is the International Child Sexual Exploitation (ICSE) Image database that allows investigators to share images internationally. Like CAID, it uses sophisticated image-comparison software to make connections between victims, abusers, and places. The NCA victim identification (VID) team in CEOP Investigations provides the UK link for coordinating searches and uploading onto the ICSE platform.

16.9.3 NCA VID team

Victim identification by image analysis is a specialist investigative function carried out by trained investigators. Their primary role is the identification of victims, offenders, and locations of child abuse.

The NCA VID team has specialists who are very experienced and can provide image analysis advice to LEAs. They coordinate the UK's 'identified victim', 'unidentified victim', and 'offender only identified' library and feed data into Interpol's ICSE Database. This is to avoid duplication of effort in finding victims already identified.

Innovation has seen the introduction of auto-categorisation software that enables investigators to stop working on categorisation and concentrate on identifying more victims through the use of advanced technology. The team are available to provide expert guidance and help find solutions to operational CSAE problems and can be consulted when and where necessary. They are dedicated to safeguarding children depicted within imagery and can help with intelligence development and proving cases at court.

There are also specifically trained victim identification SPoCS located around the United Kingdom who are trained and supported by the NCA VID team.

16.9.4 Liaison with the CPS

Early liaison with the CPS is of paramount importance for initial discussions over the investigative strategy. These types of cases are not the usual ones that most prosecutors are used to dealing with. They require an extra degree of specialism and knowledge. The CPS has developed a network of solicitors who specialise in online CSAE and child abuse, with a responsibility for establishing general good practice and procedure. The CPS have published guidelines on prosecuting cases of child abuse.[20]

16.10 **Exploited Victims and Witnesses**

Persuading exploited and abused teenage victims to engage with and trust the police/other agencies and investigation/criminal justice processes is not always a straightforward task. Any approach to try and interview a victim (or 'complainant'; see section 11.2) requires careful planning and preparation. Building trust is a key element because levels of trauma and misguided loyalties can be significant barriers to overcome. There may also be problems in obtaining accurate accounts from the abused due to their disorientation and their confused lifestyles.

No two victims are the same; the impact of the exploitation upon each individual varies and each individual must be treated on their own needs and experiences. Some may have developed coping mechanisms to survive (and used to displaying hostility or aggression openly) and will respond and behave the same way they do with their abusers. Others may just be too embarrassed or frightened to engage.

Victims and witnesses will have not only their evidential testimonies to offer but are likely to possess evidential material such as mobile phones and other items like gifts and clothing given to them over the course of the grooming process. They may also be 'crime scenes' themselves, and able to provide forensic evidential-gathering opportunities, dependent on the nature and circumstances of their exploitation, sexual contact, and abuse.

A range of resources are available that can provide support to exploited victims. In addition to the general measures outlined within Chapter 13, the use of Registered Witness Intermediaries[21] can be extremely valuable. Of note is that this option needs to be given early consideration at the planning and preparation stage.

In most cases, the plan to support and win the trust and willing cooperation of victims and witnesses is the biggest challenge. Tactics such as using highly experienced and trained staff to make the first contact or an 'exploratory approach' accompanied by a person from an agency whom the victim already trusts as a conduit can make all the difference. Making victims aware they are not on their own and that others have made similar complaints and provided

---

[20] See CPS, *Guidelines on Prosecuting Cases of Child Sexual Abuse* (CPS, 2013).
[21] The Witness Intermediary Service is available through MCIS at the NCA.

evidence against their abusers is also key to success, and that their stories and allegations will be taken seriously.[22]

Child victims will require a very high level of support and the LEA is usually responsible for facilitating this, although they cannot be expected to deliver emotional or psychological support which is provided by other agencies and professionals. A document entitled 'Achieving Best Evidence (ABE) in Criminal Proceedings—Guidance on interviewing victims and witnesses and guidance on using special measures'[23] provides guidelines for conducting interviews with young victims and witnesses and should be followed closely. It provides assistance for those responsible for conducting video-recorded interviews with vulnerable and intimidated witnesses as well as those tasked with preparing and supporting witnesses during the criminal justice process. There is also a relevant National Policing Position Statement, 'Advice on the Structure of Visually Recorded Interviews with Witnesses'.[24] In any event, it is recommended good practice that a suitably qualified and experienced specialist interview advisor be brought in to assist with the interview planning and conducting process.

Victims may not always give their best and fullest account during an initial interview (ie ABE interview or statement). This may be for a variety of reasons, eg they may have been threatened or be fearful of reprisals for themselves or their families. They may not have identified themselves as a victim or they could be fearful they will not be believed. They may well use the first interview to test the credibility of the supporting authorities. The key is to be patient, with a carefully considered strategy that will ultimately build up trust and break any link or loyalty to the offender(s). A seemingly contradictory account is not a reason in itself to disbelieve subsequent accounts by the victim, and contradictory accounts should instead be seen as at least potentially symptomatic of the abuse.

Some victims may have previous convictions, which could be seen to cast doubt upon their reliability as a witness of truth. Thorough enquiries need to be made into the circumstances of any offending before coming to any conclusion regarding credibility. The drivers and circumstances of the offending behaviour must be examined carefully as victims sometimes commit 'survival crimes' to look after themselves or to find safety, and these may well have been committed as a consequence of being under the influence of the offender. The rule is to focus on the credibility of the allegation not the person reporting it.

It is worth assessing factors that may work against the credibility of victims of sexual abuse. Such matters may include the offence not being reported, inconsistent accounts, the victim returning to the offender(s), perceived consent,

---

[22] See HMIC, *'Mistakes were made': HMIC's review into allegations and intelligence material concerning Jimmy Saville between 1964 and 2012* (HMIC, 2013).

[23] Ministry of Justice, March 2011.

[24] National Strategic Steering Group on Investigative Interviewing, 2013.

previous untruths from the same victim, or the abuse of drugs/alcohol. However, these are factors that are also *indicative* of sexual exploitation and it may be possible to build a case that focuses more on the credibility of the overall allegation rather than focusing primarily on the credibility and/or reliability of the victim.

Specialised support can be provided by a range of national organisations and is likely to be essential in ensuring the child or young person (and where appropriate their parents or guardian) maintains engagement with the criminal justice system. In some areas the local Witness Service/Victim Support Scheme will provide a specialist Young Witness Service and there are others that can be considered as a vital source of support (eg Independent Sexual Violence Advisers (ISVAs)). Support for parents, who often feel powerless when confronted with the problem, can also be provided through organisations such as PACE (Parents against Child Sexual Exploitation).

There is plenty of experience now in the United Kingdom of managing the delicate processes involved when dealing with victims (current and historical) of sexual exploitation. Operation Stovewood[25] is one of the biggest enquiries ever mounted (dealing with well over 1,500 victims), operating in the South Yorkshire Police (SYP) area around Rotherham. This is an investigation being run on behalf of SYP by the NCA. It might prove extremely beneficial for an SIO who is looking to gain advice and useful learning points to make contact with the SIO from this operation.

16.10.1 Third-party material

Many CSAE cases will involve and require access to third-party material when building an evidential case. This might include material such as medical notes, social services information, Children's Services material, educational notes, counselling/therapy notes, information or evidence arising in parallel family/civil proceedings, or information kept by voluntary sector organisations.

Partner agencies may have to provide evidence and material for a CSAE investigation and prosecution. Corroborative evidence to support a case may have to come from a range of sources such as third parties who can provide evidence about changes of behaviour or victim and offender movements. This may be particularly relevant if a victim is unwilling or reluctant to assist.

Investigators (under CPIA rules) are under a duty to pursue all reasonable lines of enquiry, whether they point towards or away from a suspect. (see section 2.9). Reasonable lines of enquiry may include queries about the existence of relevant material in the possession of a third party, eg the local authority. This material must be gathered as early as possible as it may contain information that could enhance and strengthen the prosecution case.

---

[25] Operation Stovewood is also mentioned in section 1.2.

If such information is obtained and proves to be relevant to the prosecution case, it is worth considering creating a written agreement between the third party, enquiry team, and CPS/Counsel to cover how the information is to be disclosed, when, how, and by whom. This can be arranged prior to trial to prevent any undue delays to proceedings, whether it be through PII (public interest immunity) applications or objections to disclosure.

KEY POINTS

1. 'All services should recognise that once a child is affected by CSAE, he or she is likely to require support and therapeutic intervention for an extended period of time. Children should not be offered short term intervention only, and cases should not be closed prematurely.'[26]
2. DPP guidelines on prosecuting cases of CSAE issued on 17 October 2013 draws attention to the presentation of CSAE victims, with paras 48/49 making the following point: 'The Prosecutor should focus on the credibility of the allegation rather than the credibility of the victim.'
3. There is a Code of Practice for victims of crime (see ch.11.3).[27]

Checklist—Considerations for victims/witnesses

• Child victim/witness interviews are conducted in line with ABE guidelines.

• Gathering useful background detail with an initial assessment is good practice.

• Consider a welfare plan (including referral and support planning). Anticipate a wide range of barriers and difficulties, eg some victims may have a range of psychological and physical problems, including STIs (sexually transmitted infections), have been deprived of food or sleep, have been given drugs/alcohol, or be in general need of emergency medical treatment.

• Consider a victim and witness needs assessment (see also Chapter 11 as victims needs assessments are mentioned under the Code of Practice for Victims of Crime).

• Plan for any language and communication barriers, including literacy or learning disabilities as well as cultural considerations (check if an interpreter is required).

• Consider exploratory interview by person they trust (eg social worker/CPA).

---

[26] A Jay, *Independent Inquiry into Child Sexual Exploitation in Rotherham 1997–2013* (2014), Recommendation 9.

[27] Code of Practice for Victims of Crime: Presented to Parliament pursuant to section 33 of the Domestic Violence, Crime and Victims Act 2004, HM Stationery Office, October 2015) in England and Wales was published in October 2015. Chapter 3, Parts A and B refer to entitlements of victims who are children and young persons. See also section 11.3.

- Determine categorisation and prioritisation (ie vulnerable, intimidated, significant).[28]

- If multiple numbers, consider order in which they are to be approached/interviewed.

- Focus on credibility of allegation not credibility of victim.

- Decide on location for contact (eg home address, foster carers, school, or en route to/from).

- Plan for resources required (eg PIP level 2/specialist interviewers/advisers, registered witness intermediary, NCA CPA specialists and the National Vulnerable Witnesses Adviser[29]).

- Facilities and equipment (eg video interview suite or portable equipment).

- What to mention/not mention about the investigation (to victim/witness and parent/carer).

- Contingencies required (eg prevention of intimidation of self or others, tactics to deal with reluctance/refusal).

- Identification of fast-track actions resulting from interview.

- Post-interview safeguarding plan (see section 16.4).

16.11 **Managing CSAE Suspects and Offenders**

A strategy for the management of suspects under investigation for CSAE-type offences must take cognisance of the risk these individuals may pose to victims, other children, communities, and themselves. They are also likely to be people who are in the habit of frustrating law enforcement by using nicknames or pseudonyms online, or swapping their phones and SIM cards around. They will use (IP) addresses and premises that are not easily linked to them and their identification and attribution to victims, and evidence is likely to be challenging. They will also probably those who are better educated than the average criminal and used to manipulating and controlling others.

The timing of any executive action (ie arrests) can be crucial. Revealing details of the operation may significantly increase the risk of harm to victims and possibly others. This must be carefully balanced against the risks posed by not acting expeditiously (risk management and linking in with a 'Prevent' strategy). This is a decision that is to be recorded in a policy log (ie to act *or*

---

[28] See also Chapter 13.
[29] Witness intermediaries and the National Vulnerable Witnesses Adviser are available through the NCA MCIS via telephone: 0345 000 5463.

not to act: both need recording whichever is applicable with reasons) together with the plan to mitigate risks. Periods of custody for suspects may need to be planned carefully as part of a plan to mitigate risk with custody extension, warrants of further detention, and subsequent bail conditions being used to good effect.

A decision whether or not to release the details of a suspect once arrested may be a difficult one if they are well known to victims or their parents. Usually suspects are not named until they are formally charged (see section 9.6.11), but the arrest or even declaration of suspect status and investigation might be something that could quite easily leak out. There may then follow a demand from parents of other children who might have come into contact with the suspect with a demand for further information on how their own children might have been affected. This might happen with online offenders, for example if the suspect is in a POT such as sports coach or school teacher, or well-known individual (or PPP) who could feasibly have committed offences against or had access to a much wider range of potential victims. This situation can and should be anticipated in advance.

Some suspects and offenders may already be registered sex offenders (RSOs), in which case they are likely to have conditions as to what they can and cannot do aimed at managing any risk they pose. They may also be under restriction from orders such as SHPO (Sexual Harm Prevention Order) or SRO (Sexual Risk Order). They are therefore likely to have an appointed MOSOVO (Management of Sex Offenders and Violent Offenders) officer who needs to be alerted once a person appears on the radar for similar offending. Some of these offenders pose a very real threat of harm to children and must be closely monitored. If they are RUId then, as conditions cannot be placed on them (as with bail), any risks they pose while awaiting the outcome of an investigation must be carefully assessed and managed (eg by regular checks or visits).

Finally, offenders who commit offences against children may be/or perceive themselves to be demonised not just by their close friends and family but the wider general public and media. This may prompt vigilantism and/or an increased risk of them committing suicide or self-harming and is where a risk assessment becomes important. Care should be taken to reduce the impact of the arrest/investigation on the suspect's close family and the officer's themselves who may suffer as a result of any subsequent suicide. This issue, one of duty of care, is discussed in more detail in section 12.7.1 A really useful guidance document is available from the NPCC and NCA CEOP containing guidance and a detachable checklist/action plan.[30]

---

[30] There is published guidance with a detachable checklist/action plan that was published in 2018 by the NPCC and NCA on how to manage the risk of suicidal ideation from online offenders and is available on the CoP APP website.

KEY POINT

CSOs who are under investigation for online CSAE offending are more likely to be at risk of committing suicide. An appropriate suicide risk assessment and management plan should be included in a suspect arrest strategy, particularly to cater for the first forty-eight hours after police contact when they are known to be at their most vulnerable.

Bibliography

ACPO, *Child Sexual Exploitation Action Plan* (ACPO, 2012)

ACPO/CPS, 'Liaison and information exchange when criminal proceedings co-incide with Chapter 4 Serious Case Reviews or Welsh Child Practice Reviews: A Guide for the Police, Crown Prosecution Service and Local Safeguarding Children Boards', National HWG child death sub-group (May 2014)

Barnardos, *Puppet on a String: The Urgent Need to Cut Children Free from Sexual Exploitation* (Barnardos, 2011)

Berelowitz, S et al, 'I thought I was the only one. The only one in the world.' The Office of the Children's Commissioner's inquiry into CSAE in gangs and groups: Interim report (Office of the Children's Commissioner, 2012)

Chase, E and Statham, J, 'Commercial and sexual exploitation of children and young people in the UK—a review' (2005) 14(1) *Child Abuse Review*, 4–25

College of Policing, *Responding to Child Sexual Exploitation*, APP online (2015) <http//www. app.college.police.uk>

College of Policing, *Operational Hydrant SIO Advice*, Operation Hydrant, November 2016 (<http://www.college.police.uk/legal/Documents/Non_Commercial_College_Licence.pdf>)

Child Exploitation and Online Protection Centre (CEOP), *Out of Mind, Out of Sight: Breaking Down the Barriers to Understanding Child Sexual Exploitation* (CEOP, 2011)

Children's Commissioner, 'If only someone had listened': Final Report from the inquiry into CSAE in gangs and groups 2014 (OCC, 2013) <http://www.childrenscommissioner.gov.uk/content/publications/content_743>

CPS, Guidelines on Prosecuting Cases of Child Sexual Abuse (CPS, 2013) http://www.cps.gov.uk/legal/a_to_c/child_sexual_abuse

County Lines Violence, Exploitation & Drug Supply' (November 2017), National Briefing Report, Drug Threat Team, Commodities Branch, National Crime Agency.

Department for Children, Schools and Families and Home Office, *Safeguarding Children and Young People from Sexual Exploitation: Supplementary Guidance to Working Together to Safeguard Children* (DCSF, 2009)

Department for Education, *Tackling Child Sexual Exploitation: Action Plan* (Department for Education, 2011)

Gallagher, B. (2000) 'The extent and nature of known cases of institutional child sexual abuse.' *The British Journal of Social Work*, 30(6):795–817

HMIC, *'Hotel Watch': South Yorkshire Police's Response to Child Sexual Exploitation* (HMIC, 2013)

HMIC, *'Mistakes were Made': HMIC's Review into Allegations and Intelligence Material concerning Jimmy Saville between 1964 and 2012* (HMIC, 2013)

HM Government: 'Working Together to Safeguard Children: A guide to inter-agency working to safeguard and promote the welfare of children (The Stationery Office, July 2018)

Jay, A, *Independent Inquiry into Child Sexual Exploitation in Rotherham 1997–2013* (2014)

Ministry of Justice, *Achieving Best Evidence in Criminal Proceedings: Guidance on Interviewing Victims and Witnesses, and using Special Measures* (Ministry of Justice, 2013)

Code of Practice for Victims of Crime: Presented to Parliament pursuant to section 33 of the Domestic Violence, Crime and Victims Act 2004 (HM Stationery Office, October 2015) available at: <http://www.gov.uk/moj>

Ministry of Justice, *Witness Charter* (Ministry of Justice, 2013)

National Policing Position Statement, *Advice on the Structure of Visually Recorded Interviews with Witnesses* (National Strategic Steering Group on Investigative Interviewing, 2013)

Oxfordshire Safeguarding Children Board, *Serious Case Review into Child Sexual Exploitation in Oxfordshire: from the experiences of Children A, B, C, D, E, and F* (Operation Bullfinch) (OSCB, 26 February 2015)

WAG, *Safeguarding Children and Young People from Sexual Exploitation* cited in Dr S Hallett, 'Cascade Research Briefing: Problems and Solution from the perspectives of young people and professionals' (2015) 3. Available at: <http://www.nwgnetwork.org/resources>

Appendix A

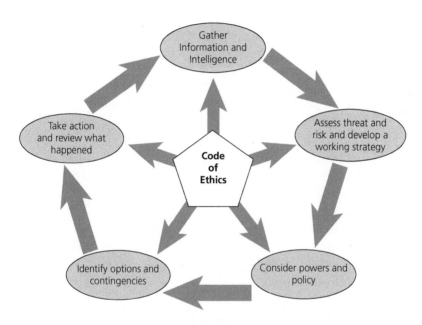

National Decision Model

© College of Policing 2019 https://www.app.college.police.uk/app-content/national-decision-model/
the-national-decision-model/

Appendix B

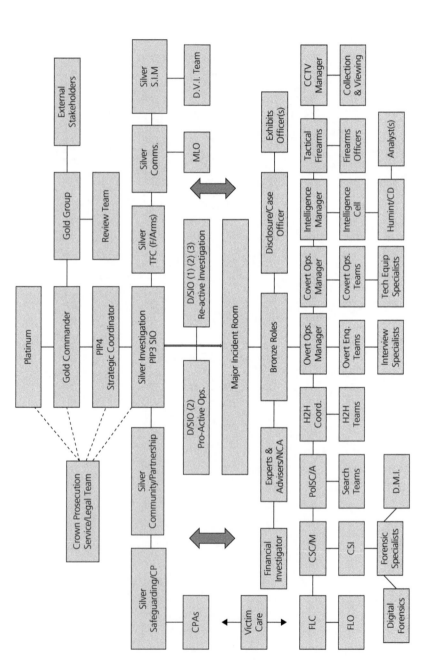

Enquiry Team Structure

Index

Note: For the benefit of digital users, indexed terms that span two pages (e.g., 52–53) may, on occasion, appear on only one of those pages.